CLIMATIC
Atlas of the

1 Relief map of the United States (U. S. Geological Su

United States

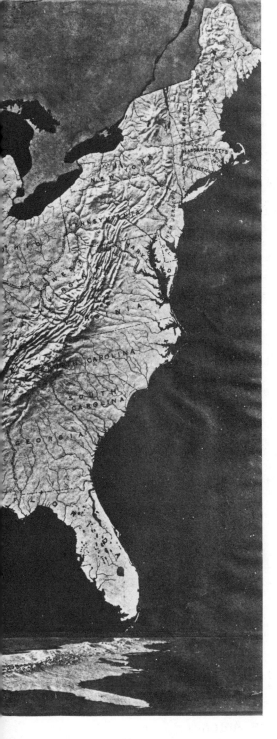

STEPHEN SARGENT VISHER

Professor of Geography

Indiana University

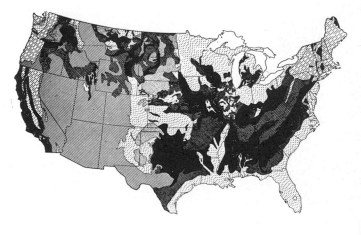

HARVARD UNIVERSITY PRESS

Cambridge, 1966

THIS VOLUME IS DEDICATED TO THE UNITED STATES WEATHER BUREAU
OFFICIALS WHO, THROUGHOUT MANY DECADES, HAVE ASSEMBLED THE DAILY
OBSERVATIONS OF THE NUMEROUS COÖPERATIVE AND OTHER OBSERVERS,
AND HAVE ANALYZED THE RESULTING CLIMATOLOGICAL DATA. OF THE SUC-
CESSIVE CHIEFS OF THE CLIMATE DIVISION OF THE BUREAU, JOSEPH BURTON
KINCER MERITS SPECIAL MENTION; EXTENDING THE WORK OF OTHERS, HE
DEVOTED FOUR DECADES OF FAITHFUL EFFORT TO DISCOVERING AND MAKING
KNOWN THE CLIMATE OF THE UNITED STATES.

PREFACE

The weather affects everyone in numerous subtle ways, and occasionally with profound economic consequences. A needed rain, by increasing the yield of a crop, may be worth many thousands of dollars to the farmers of even a small region. The same rain, however, may spoil picnics and damage other crops, roads, or equipment, and locally the incidental lightning, hail, or violent wind may be destructive. The weather continually illustrates the fact that there is nothing wholly good or wholly bad.

Climate — the aggregate of the weather as revealed by past experience — includes the temperature, winds, atmospheric moisture, cloudiness, precipitation, and air pressures that have prevailed during any considerable period. It comprises such topics as the average annual temperature, the temperatures of each season, the usual temperature during the hottest time of the day, and the normal frequency of temperatures above or below certain limits, for example 100° and 0°F.

The climate at no two places is quite the same, because invariably at least one of the several influences determining climate differs. These influences are distance from the equator, elevation, relation to the ocean and to ocean currents, relation to lakes and other bodies of water, relation to mountain ranges and to hills and valleys, the color and wetness of the soil, and the character of the vegetation. Very local climatic differences are likewise produced by buildings, roads, and fields.

Many people in any region are interested in studies of climate, partly because knowledge of what has happened is perhaps the best basis for prediction. Moreover, in order to use the soil and numerous other resources efficiently, adequate knowledge of the climate is essential. A better selection and distribution of crops is facilitated by such knowledge. In order to construct efficient roads, sewers, bridges, and buildings, it is necessary to know what may reasonably be expected in the matter of rainfall, ice, snowfall, winds, and drought. It is not enough that a few specialists have this knowledge; specialists are seldom consulted except by those who are already well informed. Those who know least are least likely to seek expert advice; those who already know most are especially alert to add to what they know.

The climate of the United States affects not only all of our people, but, indirectly, the many people in foreign lands who obtain products or other assistance from this country, or who find a market here for part of their exports. A fuller knowledge of climate facilitates a more efficient adjustment to it and increases understanding not only of one's own region but of other regions, and some of the problems that confront their people.

The United States has sufficient climatic diversity, related in part to elevation (see the frontispiece), to enable it to produce somewhere within its borders most of the world's wide variety of plant and animal products. Indeed, little of the rest of the world, except the equatorial and polar regions, has a climate that is not simulated somewhere in the continental United States. Hence those who come to understand our climate are prepared to understand the climate of much of the rest of the world.

The first chapter of this book, as an introduction, calls attention to a few of the many reasonable deductions obtainable from study of the maps of the following chapters. The body of the book considers in turn various aspects of temperature, winds, storms, sunshine, humidity, evaporation, precipitation, some consequences of the climate, and, finally, climatic regions and changes of climate. Some of the maps are supplemented by data of interest. Various graphs are also presented, especially in the chapter on changes of climate.

Here are given adaptations of almost all the latest maps of the climate of the United States that are based on adequate data. Instead of reproducing the original maps, nearly all have been redrawn in a form better adapted to the present use. The large number of maps (1031), while at first perhaps bewildering, presents a mass of detailed information in a form that is relatively comprehensible. Of course no reader will be interested in nearly all of these maps, but various maps of no value to one user will be helpful to another. The diagrams are mostly reproduced in their original form, or with only slight modification.

In order to provide within practicable compass a rather complete coverage of many aspects of the climate of the United States, it has been necessary to use a relatively small scale and related generalization of the isopleths. Larger-scale, more detailed maps of some aspects of the climate may be found in the *Atlas of American agriculture*, *Climate and man*, and various climatological summaries by states listed among the references at the end of this volume.

Figure 2 shows the locations of the climatic stations. The subsequent maps indicate the distribution of the climatic element dealt with, as shown by observations made at numerous stations over a long period of years. For example, Fig. 3 indicates the "normal annual temperature," which means the average of the temperatures of all days of the years for many years. The curved lines (isotherms), numbered from 40° in the north to 75° in the extreme southeast, indicate that within the United States the normal annual temperature ranges from below 40° to above 75°. Chicago is between the 45° and the 50° isotherms, close to the latter. The normal annual temperature of Chicago is about 49°. New York, between the 50° and 55° isotherms, much nearer the former, has a normal annual temperature of about 51°. Since an isotherm passes through places with the same temperature, by following the 50° isotherm across the country, one can see which places have an annual temperature close to that of New York or of Chicago.

Many thousands of patient volunteer observers have daily recorded the temperature, rainfall, and certain other climatic data for their localities. Fuller records are taken several times daily at each of about

600 (at present) regular Weather Bureau stations. Figure 2 shows the location of the stations where the data upon which most of the following maps are based were accumulated. The abbreviations of the names of the states have been added to this official map as an aid to some who will examine the later maps, which lack place names.

The present volume is dedicated to those who assembled, analyzed, and studied the data gathered by the coöperative and employed observers. Without the efforts of these men, the crude data gathered by the observers would have comparatively much less value. Indeed, as the late Isaiah Bowman, President of the American Association for the Advancement of Science in 1943, put it: "Facts more valuable than all the gold of the Klondike lie buried in the Weather Bureau's climatological records." The following maps and summaries are attempts to make more readily available some of these "frozen assets."

The author is under obligation to many people — to the observers, to the climatologists who have presented and analyzed the crude data, to the succession of scientists who for nearly a century have earnestly endeavored to make more widely useful the results of previous studies. Fine coöperation has been received from the Weather Bureau, especially from J. B. Kincer. The preparation of this atlas was greatly facilitated by the nearly 200 maps that Kincer prepared for the climatic part of the official *Atlas of American agriculture*, which was conceived and edited by O. E. Baker, an outstanding leader in American agriculture. Kincer's many maps in *Climate and man* have nearly all been useful here, as have most of his other maps, many of which have appeared in the *Weekly Weather and Crop Bulletin*, of which he was the editor for twenty years. Indeed, about a fifth of the maps in this atlas are adaptations of Kincer's maps, and many of the remainder were made possible by his work.

Other publications that have been of great value are *The climates of the United States* by R. DeC. Ward; *Rainfall intensity-frequency data*, by D. L. Yarnell; *Atlas of climatic types*, by C. W. Thornthwaite; *Crop yields and weather*, by L. H. Bean; *Seasonal precipitation, 1886–1938*, a Weather Bureau publication; and the mimeographed atlas of average weekly temperatures and precipitations, by W. F. McDonald.

Professor J. Paul Goode, eminent cartographer, merits special mention. As my teacher in 1913–14, and as a good friend until his death in 1932, he effectively urged that in the making of maps those who use them should always be carefully considered. Although he made no similar maps, these all strongly reflect his helpful influence, which is gratefully acknowledged. Moreover, the base map upon which most of these maps are drawn is modified from one that he prepared (Goode's Outline Map No. 10, University of Chicago Press, used by special permission). In accordance with his admonitions to stress legibility, only a part of this copyrighted outline map is here used. As a result, the essential part is reduced less; moreover, the scale is deleted, because at the reduction here used it is not readily legible. The blackening of the national boundary also increases legibility for the present use.

Acknowledgment is also due to the editors and some readers of several journals which have published articles containing many of these maps. The reception that these articles received encouraged the completion of this *Atlas*, and suggestions made by editors and readers led to the improvement of some of the maps. Journals, with the number of articles on aspects of the climate of the United States which they have published, are: *Monthly Weather Review* (4), *Quarterly Journal of the Royal Meteorological Society* (4), *Bulletin of the American Meteorological Society* (5), *Geographical Review* (4), *Annals of the Association of American Geographers* (5), *Journal of Geography* (7), *Economic Geography* (4), *Scientific Monthly* (12), *Transactions of the American Geophysical Union* (2), *Bulletin of the Geological Society of America* (2), *Ecology* (4), *Weatherwise* (4), *Weather* (1).

The comments and suggestions received from various readers of my previous volumes on aspects of climate have afforded encouragement and aid which also merits acknowledgment. Among these books are *Climatic laws*, *Climate of Kentucky*, and *Climate of Indiana*.

Indiana University facilitated the preparation of this book by releasing me from teaching for one semester and permitting a reduced teaching load for another semester. Grants from the Graduate School Research Fund were helpful in the drafting of the maps, in typing, and for a few of the calculations.

S. S. V.

Bloomington, Indiana

CONTENTS

FOREWORD

This is the first book on the climates of the United States since *Climate and man*, published as the Yearbook of Agriculture 1941. It is the first attempt since *The Climates of the United States* by Robert DeCourcy Ward (1925) to assemble under one cover the (now many more) available maps on the climates of this country. Our climates are very diverse and have many facets. The diversity can best be shown by maps. The facets can also be shown if there are enough maps.

Professor Visher has done a notable service to climatology and to all who use climatic maps of the United States. He has not only assembled, and in many instances simplified, some 600 maps from many different sources but also prepared more than 400 himself to round out the picture. Furthermore, he has arranged, annotated, and presented them in a readily usable form.

The 1031 maps and diagrams are presented in 34 chapters grouped into seven parts. Five parts embrace the major elements of climate: temperature, wind, sunshine, humidity, and precipitation, and the other two, some consequences of climate and weather, and climatic regions and climatic changes. The consequences include those to agriculture, health, soil erosion, soil moisture, soil freezing, lakes, streams, and topography. The part on climatic regions is a notable collection of 48 maps of climatic regions or zones, based on a great variety of criteria. The presentation of climatic change includes a number of diagrams showing annual sequences, in some cases for 100 years or more.

There are, of course, the ordinary runs of monthly and annual maps of mean temperatures, frost dates, degree days, ranges, precipitation, and so on; less familiar, though no less useful, are those of the annual courses of mean, maximum, and minimum temperature and precipitation by weeks or alternate weeks, variabilities, and expectancies (especially frequencies of extremes). Some particularly important ones are those of: duration of hot weather (Nos. 251–272); depth of soil freezing (Nos. 322–327); average July wet-bulb temperature, a good index to comfort (No. 468); normal July difference between wet-bulb and air temperatures, a measure of potential evaporation (No. 337), and average depression of wet-bulb temperature at time of minimum humidity, which indicates the daytime maximum rate of potential evaporation (Nos. 469–471). The coverage of precipitation is very impressive, with 428 maps and diagrams (Nos. 487–908, 1024–1029). Droughts, wet spells, excessive precipitation, *inter alia*, are presented in especial detail.

Numerous though the maps in this atlas are, there are many obsolete ones that have been omitted. It is one of the satisfactions of the climatologist that, by virtue of new data, from more stations, and longer records from old ones, he can always prepare climatic maps that are better than those previously made. Anyway, in the present period of ameliorated climate we are more interested in maps based considerably on observations of recent decades than in maps too heavily weighted by the colder past. Nevertheless, for some of the interesting items the latest maps available were made 20 or 30 or more years ago. Fortunately (for many reasons), our climate has not changed so much or so rapidly as to make more than a degree or two difference anywhere between what the temperature maps in this atlas show and what maps of even the last 30 years would indicate. Moreover, the present relatively high level of temperature will not necessarily be maintained. If it should trend downward, the atlas would improve slightly in applicability. Indeed, for any long-term planning, such as is involved in the choice of the architecture and heating and cooling facilities for a house or other building, it is probably more conservative to plan on the basis of what our climate has been in our period of record than on an assumption that the coming decades will be the same as, or warmer or colder than, now.

Many of the maps that the author chose to reproduce contained much greater detail than he has presented here. While it may seem undesirable to lose detail, there are distinct gains in having maps sufficiently generalized to be read easily and in keeping the atlas to a size convenient to handle and to a cost low enough to assure wide distribution. In every case, however, the source of the more detailed map is given, so that anyone wanting the details can readily obtain them.

A great many of the maps are based on data from only the first-order stations of the Weather Bureau, which alone can supply the type of data required for these maps. Since these stations are mostly in the larger cities, and in valleys rather than on mountains, their data and the maps based on them represent conditions where most of the people live rather than those of the general countryside.

The atlas aims primarily to present the facts. There are general interpretations, based on the physical controls of climate, in the first chapter, and here and there through the book. There are many places where more interpretation could have been inserted, but to have done so would have lengthened the book materially. Ward's *Climates of the United States* may be used by anyone seeking further interpretations. The Köppen-Geiger *Handbuch der Klimatologie* (of which the section on North America is in English) is later (1936) than Ward but more general, and many articles are to be found in periodical literature of the last two decades. Nevertheless, Professor Visher's atlas, as it stands, would form an excellent basis for teaching climatology, in addition to the climatography shown by the maps.

CHARLES F. BROOKS

Blue Hill Meteorological Observatory,
Harvard University

CLIMATIC ATLAS OF THE UNITED STATES

CHIEF CLIMATIC REGIONS

Although the climatic diversity of the United States is great, the climate of most of the country consists of one or another of the several subtypes of one major climatic type, the Continental. This type is characterized by well-marked temperature seasons, which are responses to the fact that most of the country is situated in middle latitudes, 30° to 49° from the equator, in the interior of a large continent, with mountain ranges near the western and eastern coasts, which mountains reduce the penetration of oceanic influences. The well-marked seasons result from the sharp change in the height of the noonday sun (47° between the solstices) and in the length of the day (4 hours and 42 minutes between the solstices at latitude 40°N and about 8 hours at the 49th parallel).

The approximately three-fourths of the United States which has Continental Climate displays gradual variation with latitude, and often is subdivided into a warmer, a cooler, and an intermediate zone. It also varies in precipitation. Subdivisions based on contrasts in precipitation which are often recognized are humid, arid, and the intermediate semiarid. Sometimes a fourth type is recognized, the subhumid, transitional between the humid and semiarid.

Although the precipitation zones commonly recognized are based chiefly upon the annual average totals received, various other precipitation conditions are highly significant, including form (rain, sleet, snow, hail, freezing rain), seasonal distribution, type (gentle, torrential, and mixed), and dependability or variability.

In addition to the subdivisions of the Continental Climate due to contrasts in temperature and in precipitation, there are zones of sunshine, which differ appreciably from those of temperature, and zones of atmospheric humidity and fog, which are not nearly identical with the precipitation zones. Zones based on winds are also significant, although less clearly evident than are the zones, on the oceans, of the planetary winds known as the trades and westerlies and the belts of "calm" between. In the Continental Climate part of the United States, wind zones, despite their vagueness, introduce notable complications. Of particular importance are the zones of different frequencies of various types of wind storms, including the cyclonic lows, thunderstorms, tornadoes, and tropical cyclones.

With the superimposition within the Continental Climate of these several types of zones, it follows that a considerable number of climatic subdivisions are logical, and have been made by various persons delimiting the climatic subdivisions. Many of these are mapped in Chapter 34, "Climatic Regions."

Nevertheless, the changes within the Continental Climatic Regions are almost all so gradual that comparative uniformity of conditions, rather than diversity, often prevails. For example, it repeatedly happens that much of the vast continental interior is comparatively warm for the season or cold, or wet or dry. Likewise, the entire region is subject to frequent changes of weather, and to the same types of storms, although not to the same degree. This comparative uniformity is, however, far less real than most people believe, as a study of the maps will reveal.

Within the Continental region, the mountains introduce a conspicuous complication. Three types of mountain climates are easily recognized, although intergradation occurs. These are the wet mountains, the dry mountains, and the high mountains. The Appalachians are wet mountains and are forested; the ranges in the Great Basin and the dry sides of the Sierras and Cascades, and most of the Rockies, are dry mountains. The Rockies seemed bare to those who named them. The high mountains are those parts which are snow-covered all or most of the year. These three mountain types notably increase the country's diversity, perhaps especially its recreational riches.

Bordering the various Continental Climates, four coastal climatic type extends north nearly to the 40th parallel, and east to the Pacific Coast. The dry subtropical, California, or Mediterranean type extends north nearly to the 40th parallel, and east to the Coast Ranges, and in a modified form it extends eastward to the foothills of the Sierra Nevadas.

The California type of climate is characterized by mild, rainy, but rather sunny winters and hot, dry, almost cloudless summers. Adjacent to the ocean, the summer heat is tempered by sea breezes, and often by fog. At high elevations — and much of California is elevated — the daytime heat is tempered by nocturnal cooling, and occasionally the summer drought is broken by showers. It should be emphasized that less than one-fourth of California has the California type of climate; about half of California has a climate transitional between the California type and the Arid Continental or the Marine, which cover the rest of the state.

The Marine or Oregon type of climate is found in Oregon and Washington west of the Cascades, and most typically west of the Coast Ranges. It is characterized by mild winters and moderate summers. Rainfall is heavy in winter, and rather abundant in spring and autumn, but is inadequate or even lacking in midsummer. This type of climate is the most temperate in the United States, sharply contrasting with the Continental type. The winters are cloudy, often dreary despite their mildness. The Oregon type of climate closely resembles that of the British Isles, and is exceptionally healthful, as revealed by the comparatively abundant energy of the people and their generally rather ruddy complexions. Because of the mountains, only a small part of the states of Washington and Oregon have this climatic type. Just east of the Coast Ranges, notably of the northern, snow-capped Olympics part, there is relatively little rainfall (less than 25 inches per year in some places), and warmer spells often occur in the dry summer. East of the Cascade Mountains, the climate is Continental, except that some marine influence penetrates the Columbia River Gap.

On the east coast north of the 40th parallel, the continental influences are commonly borne even out to sea by the prevailing westerly winds. Hence some experts do not recognize a coastal type of climate in that region. However, close to the sea, winter temperatures average notably milder and summer temperatures less hot than those even a short distance inland. Various other departures from the characteristic of the cooler humid Continental type also occur; for example, on the coast there is much less snowfall, and snow covers the ground less continuously. Whittier's *Snowbound* describes the interior of New England, not the littoral.

On the southern Atlantic Coast, and extending westward near the Gulf of Mexico to southeastern Texas, is another climatic type which differs significantly from the Continental. This is sometimes known as the Humid Subtropical, the Mild East Coast, or the modified Monsoonal type. Here it is sometimes called the Carolina type, because the eastern parts of North and South Carolina have it. It is characterized by rainfall throughout the year, by hot summers which are made relatively enervating by high humidity, and by generally mild winters, during which, however, really cold spells occur occasionally. The masses of cold air from the continental interior, including Canada, often sweep to the coast; and even northern Florida experiences subzero temperatures, while other southern states have had more than 10° below zero not far from the coast. These "cold waves," while distressingly frequent from the standpoint of agriculture, notably the growing of early crops for the northern market, are not sufficiently frequent to make this a stimulating climate. Indeed, much evidence indicates that it is less well adapted to the development of civilization than any other American climate. Two other unfavorable aspects, in addition to the humid heat of summer and the general lack of stimulating changes of temperature, are the abundance of torrential rains, which have caused much leaching of the soil, and serious soil erosion on sloping land. The presence of more severe storms than is characteristic of any other American climate is another unfavorable aspect. The most numerous of these storms is the thunderstorm, which here surpasses in average intensity and frequency those of the other American climates; tornadoes are more numerous than in three-fourths of the country, and tropical cyclones cause more frequent damage in this climate than elsewhere in the United States.

The foregoing summary of a few of the characteristics of the major climatic types of the United States affords an introduction to the mass of detail in following chapters. (A summary table as to precipitation regions, following Fig. 908, supplements the foregoing.)

SOME CLIMATIC EXTREMES

Another sort of summary presents extremes. For example, an official shade temperature of 134°F [1] has been recorded in California and 120° to 127° in nine other states, and 109° or higher in all other states except New York and in New England. Conversely, at fairly moderate elevations, –68° has been recorded in Montana, –66° in Wyoming, –60° in three other nearby states, and –50° in 12 additional states. Considerable northern areas, in addition to mountain tops, have had killing frosts every month in the year, while some southern areas seldom have a frost. Likewise, while much of the country is hotter during the summer than are most equatorial regions (where 100° is almost unknown), in winter even

[1] All temperatures in this atlas are in degrees Fahrenheit.

the South repeatedly has more severe cold than southern Iceland ever experiences. Indeed, of the 48 states, only South Carolina (−13°) and Florida (−2°) lack records of −16° or colder.

Although the average annual precipitation in the United States is about 29 inches, more than half of the country receives less than 15 inches. The driest state (Nevada) has an average of less than 9 inches, and several stations in the Southwest have averages of less than 5 inches. One California station has an annual average of only 1.35 inches. At the other extreme, scores of widely scattered stations have received more than 100 inches of rainfall in a year, and several have received more than 150 inches. One Washington station has an annual average of 150.7 inches, and received 184.5 inches in one year. In a single month, several stations have received more than 60 inches, one of them 71.5, and 16 others over 50 inches. In a single 24 hours, more than 30 widely distributed stations have received more than 15 inches of rainfall, and 12, in six states, have received more than 20 inches. The official record of 23.2 inches in 24 hours, long held by Florida, was broken in 1943 by a California record of 25.8 inches, with two nearby stations receiving 24.1 inches.

As to snowfall, while it generally is light or almost lacking in the South and in southwestern California, 884 and 814 inches have been officially measured as having fallen in a season in the mountains of California and Oregon and 789 inches in Washington. In a month, more than 200 inches has been received repeatedly at several western mountain stations. In shorter periods, some records are: 60 inches in one day in California, 42 inches in 2 days in New York, and 54 inches in 3 days in Oregon.

SOME CLIMATIC EFFECTS OF VARIOUS PHYSICAL CONDITIONS

A third sort of summary, less spectacular and more detailed, is the following discussion of some climatic effects of latitude, the oceans, the Gulf of Mexico, and mountains. The maps in this volume reveal that there are sharp climatic contrasts within the United States. Each map reflects the effects of a number of influences. Here, in summary, the more significant influences are mentioned, and some of their effects are sketched.

Latitude and Longitude

Latitudinal (north-south) gradients are conspicuous on most maps of low temperatures and associated conditions, such as penetration of frost, duration of snow cover, and length of the growing season. On such maps, the isotherms or corresponding lines often follow approximately the parallels of latitude. The chief exceptions to this rule are near the coasts and the Great Lakes and in mountainous areas. The low-temperature map which shows least latitudinal influence is that of the lowest temperatures ever recorded (absolute minima). Upon it, the lines of equal temperature (isotherms) are distinctly irregular as a result of local conditions which permitted appreciably lower temperatures in the coldest few minutes of some areas than occurred nearby.

The influences of latitude are evident on the maps of average July temperatures, especially those of the wet-bulb thermometer, but the contrasts are less than half as great in July as in January. Average highest temperatures show little correlation with latitude. The highest temperatures ever recorded (absolute maxima) in the southern third of the country average less than in the central third, and are only slightly higher than in the northern third. Indeed, along the Gulf Coast, they are distinctly lower than along most of the Canadian border.

Except on the coasts, near the Great Lakes, and in the mountains, north-south influences are apparently the most significant ones affecting the variation in the occurrence of average first and last killing frost, and the length of the growing season.

North-south contrasts are large in average snowfall, and in average rainfall in the eastern third of the United States. On the Pacific Coast also precipitation varies with latitude, but there it increases northward. North-south contrasts in precipitation are least in summer and greatest in winter. They are notably greater in relatively wet years and summers than in dry ones. North-south contrasts in maximum monthly rainfall are irregular and rather small. (On the average, the Southeast has had during the period from 1899 to 1938 at least one month with 20 inches of precipitation; the Northeast, one with 10 inches; southern California had one month with 10 to 20 inches; northern California, one with 20 to 40; Washington, one with 30 to 40.) With respect to maximum precipitation in 24 hours, the zonal contrast is considerable in the

East, each sizable area in the Deep South having received more than 12 inches, the Upper North less than half that much. On the Pacific Coast there is less zonal range, but the heaviest rainfalls in California are nearly twice as great as the heaviest in Washington.

The total maximum rainfalls in an hour average about 50 percent more in the southern half of the country than in the northern half. Exceptionally heavy downpours are, however, many times more frequent in the South than in the North (Visher, "Torrential Rains as a Serious Handicap in the South," *Geographical Review,* October 1941).

In the eastern half of the country, the average number of thunderstorms increases southward. The frequency of hail increases northward, however, except near the coasts, to about the 40th parallel on the average, and then decreases.

The influence of latitude upon relative humidity is slight as compared with the influence of water bodies and elevation. The same is true for fog and summer sunshine. The duration of winter sunshine shows, however, some effects of latitude, as does the number of clear days.

Longitudinal or east-west influences are often said to dominate precipitation distribution in the United States. It is true that the lines of equal rainfall (isohyets) run nearly north and south in the west-central part of the country, and also locally near the north Pacific Coast. This is, however, associated with mountains and is largely a result of the accessibility of moisture. Other maps upon which the isolines of temperatures or of precipitation approximately follow meridians for some distance are: the several temperature maps (near the Pacific, and to a lesser degree near the Atlantic north of Chesapeake Bay); frequency of hailstorms (especially near the coasts but also in the western half of the country); noon humidity (in the western half of the country); evening humidity in July (in the western two-thirds of the country); frequency of fog (near the Pacific Coast and the North Atlantic); summer sunshine duration, and to a lesser degree, winter sunshine; and number of cloudy days (in the northern half of the country).

In conclusion, latitudinal influences are conspicuous in the distribution of temperatures and associated phenomena, such as snowfall and length of growing season. They are of only secondary importance, however, in the distribution of highest temperatures; they are significant in the distribution of thunderstorms, hail, and torrential rains; and they clearly affect the distribution of clear days and winter sunshine. Longitudinal influences, except those due to the coasts and mountain ranges, are slight. The isohyets on many precipitation maps roughly follow meridians along parts of their course, as do some of the lines of humidity, summer sunshine, and the frequency of fog and cloudy days.

The Pacific Ocean

Conditions on the Pacific Coast are, according to almost all climatic maps of the United States, significantly different from those which prevail a short distance inland. The chief exception is in the map of summer rainfall, which shows no more rain near the coast than inland. The maps that indicate the sharpest contrasts between coast and inland are those of extreme temperatures. A hundred miles or less inland, the normal annual highest temperatures are 15° higher in the lowlands than on the coast, where they are only 85° north of San Francisco, and 90° to 100° in southern California. As to the highest temperatures ever recorded, the differences between the immediate coast and the nearest inland valleys, those between the Coast Ranges and the Cascades or Sierras, are somewhat less than between normal maxima. The spread is about 8° in Washington and 10° in Oregon, but both ends of the Great Valley of California have been about 15° hotter than on the coast. East of the gap through the Coast Ranges at San Francisco Bay, however, the difference is less than 10°.

The difference in temperature between the Pacific Coast and the lowland just east of the Coast Ranges is greater in cold weather than in hot. The average annual lowest temperatures (minima) are about 15° lower 100 miles from the coast than on the coast of Washington, 20° lower in Oregon, and 25° lower in northern California. Near San Francisco Bay and in southern California, however, the difference is only about 10°. The extreme minima display similar differences, about 10° at the north (10° on the coast to 0° inland); and about 20° at both the northern and southern ends of the Great Valley of Southern California (20° to 0°). The Bay gap in the Coast Ranges has, however, no appreciable effect in raising the extreme minima just to the east, where 0° has occurred. This reflects the well-known fact that in the coldest weather the wind there is from the northeast, not from the northwest, as it is in most of the country.

The difference between the average July temperature by a wet-bulb thermometer near the coast and in nearby lowlands is 5° to 10°, which is a smaller contrast than might be expected.

The contrast in annual precipitation between the Pacific Coast and nearby inland valleys is 10 to 15 inches in southern California; it is 40 inches at the latitude of the northern end of the Valley of California, in Oregon, and at the southern end of the Puget Sound Valley. Just east of the Olympic Mountains, however, part of the mainland and some Puget Sound islands receive less than 25 inches of rain, in contrast with more than 130 inches on the west coast.

In summer, as already remarked, the Pacific Coast receives little or no more rain than the nearby inland valleys. The large contrast for the year as a whole results from sharp contrasts in winter and, at the north, also in autumn and spring. In southern California, however, the coast receives in spring and fall only an inch or two more than the nearby interior.

Distance from the Pacific is of less significance in relatively wet or dry years than in average years. In such relatively wet years that only one-eighth of the years are wetter, the nearby inland valleys receive as much or almost as much as the coast. Likewise, in such relatively dry years that only one-eighth of the years are drier, the coast receives little or no more than the inland valleys.

Nearness to the Pacific Ocean has only a moderate influence on the number of days with some precipitation (0.01 inch or more). On the average the north coast has about 20 more such days per year than the intermontane valleys; in California the difference is about 10 days.

With respect to the maximum precipitation in a month and in a day, the difference between the coast and the inland lowlands is slight. The inland valleys have received in their hardest hour of rain somewhat more than the coast.

Proximity to the Pacific has a notable influence upon the amount of snowfall, and especially upon the duration of snow cover. Less than an inch of snow falls along the California coast; 1 to 10 inches, along the Oregon coast; and 10 to 20 inches, along the Washington coast. In the inland valleys, except the San Joaquin Valley and

Puget Sound itself, there is from two to ten times as much. Snow covers the ground less than 1 day per year in most of California, less than 10 days on the north coast, but about 20 days in the nearest northern inland valleys.

Thunderstorms are rare on the Pacific Coast, occur on an average of 5 days a year some 100 miles inland, and about twice that often at about twice that distance from the coast. Hail increases similarly; it occurs less than once a year near the coast, twice a year some 300 miles inland.

The July noon humidity of the coastal zone is much greater than that of the inland lowlands (about 80 percent vs. 50 percent in Washington, Oregon and northern California; about 65 percent vs. 30 percent in southern California). In January, however, the difference in noon humidity is much less, about 15 percent in southern California and 5–10 percent in Washington and Oregon. Near San Francisco and for some distance south, the relative humidity in January is actually less on the coast than in the Great Valley.

The number of days with dense fog is appreciably greater west of the Coast Ranges than east of them. The difference is greatest in southern California, 20–30 vs. about 5–10; in Washington and Oregon the contrast is between about 45 days per year and about 30.

The local influence of the Pacific Ocean upon the amount of winter sunshine is small, but in summer the coast has about an hour a day less sunshine at the north and about two hours a day less at the south than do the inland valleys. The north coast has sunshine about half of the possible time in summer; the inland valleys have it about two-thirds of the possible time. In most of California the coast has sunshine about two-thirds of the possible time in summer; the inland valleys, about 90 percent. In winter the contrast between the coast and the interior is appreciably less than in summer; the interior is sunny about one-third more of the time than the coast at the north, one-sixth more at the south.

The influence of the Pacific Ocean upon the dates of killing frosts is conspicuous; they come a month or two later on the coast in autumn and a month or two earlier in spring than a short distance inland. On the coast of Washington the average length of the frost-free period (240 days) is about twice that in the Puget Lowland. In the Willamette Valley of Oregon, the season is about 200 days,

in contrast with 240 on the coast. In the Sacramento Valley, however, it is as long as it is on the coast, and in the Imperial Valley it
is about as long as near San Diego. In the southern San Joaquin
Valley, however, it is 20 days shorter than on the coast directly
west.

In conclusion, as to the significance of the Pacific: the coastal
zone differs from the nearby inland valleys most conspicuously in
the cold season — the coast has much less severe cold. In summer,
the difference is notably less. As to precipitation, the coast normally
gets much more rainfall than the inland valleys in winter but little
if any more in the summer. In exceptionally wet and exceptionally
dry years, the regional contrast is less than in the average year.
Proximity to the coast is conspicuous in reducing snowfall and duration of snow cover. Thunderstorms and hail are distinctly rarer on
the coast than inland. The relative humidity at noon in July is
notably greater on the coast than inland; the contrast inland in
January is much less. Fog is relatively more frequent on the coast
and sunshine less plentiful than inland. The frost-free season lasts
much longer on the northern coast than inland, but in California
the contrast is small. Thus the influence of the Pacific Ocean varies
widely among the various climatic elements and seasons, and also
with latitude.

The Atlantic Ocean

The Atlantic Ocean has much less influence than the Pacific upon
American temperatures. Except in New England, the mean annual
lines of equal temperature (isotherms) and those for July and
January reach most of the coast almost at right angles. The ocean,
however, notably raises low temperatures: as to the annual minima,
the coast of New England is 10° to 15° warmer than are areas a
few miles inland; in Virginia and Carolina, the coast rise is 5° to
10°. In the coldest weather, the immediate coast is about 10°
warmer from Georgia to Maine than areas a few miles inland. In
lowering high temperatures, the coastal influence is somewhat less
than 5°, except in two exposed areas near Cape Cod and Cape
Hatteras, where it is 5° to 10°. The coastal influence on average
July temperatures by the wet-bulb thermometer is slight. In southern
New England and South Carolina, such temperatures are higher
on the coast than a short distance inland.

The Atlantic coastal influence upon temperature is greatest on the date of the first killing frost in autumn, much delaying it. As a result, the average length of the frost-free period is from 20 to 40 days longer on the coast than a short distance inland. The relative importance of this gap decreases southward, with the lengthening of the season. Nevertheless, the season is 180 days on the coast of Maine, as long as it is in inland northern Alabama; and it is 200 days on part of Long Island — 40 days longer than that 40 miles inland. However, on the ocean side of Long Island the frost-free season is 10 to 20 days shorter than on the northern, Sound, side, which is the windward shore under frosty conditions.

As to annual precipitation, the Atlantic Coastal strip receives an average of 3 or 4 inches more precipitation than do nearby inland areas. Most of this difference results from heavier autumn precipitation, as in spring and winter most of the coast receives less than nearby inland areas. In summer, the Carolina, Georgia, and Maine coasts receive more than the area immediately inland, but the opposite is true in Florida and in southern New England.

The contrast between the Atlantic coast and the adjacent inland in the amount of precipitation in relatively wet or in relatively dry years and summers, as compared with the average, is small and irregular. For some reason, the middle section of the coast differs from the northern and southern parts. In a wet year (the entire year) this middle section is relatively dry, but in a wet summer it is comparatively wet. The converse holds in New England and Florida.

To the south of Virginia, the map of maximum precipitation in one month shows greater totals by about 5 inches on the coast than nearby inland. North of New Jersey the reverse is true. The maximum precipitation in 24 hours averages an inch or two greater on or close to the New England and Middle Atlantic coasts than in the interior. South of South Carolina, the average difference is about 4 inches. The maximum precipitation in an hour is relatively heavy on the middle coast, near Cape Hatteras, but is appreciably less than the average for that latitude both to the south and to the north of that section.

Snowfall is appreciably less near the Atlantic Coast than inland, less than half as much in North Carolina and Virginia, three-fourths as much in New England. The zonal difference in duration of snow cover is slight south of New Jersey but is larger in New England.

As to the frequency of thunderstorms, the Atlantic and Pacific coasts contrast sharply. Thunderstorms are rare on the Pacific Coast, relatively common on the Atlantic. In South Carolina and Georgia such storms are more frequent on the Atlantic Coast than a short distance inland. The reverse is true, however, in Florida and to the north of Carolina. Hail is appreciably less frequent on the immediate coast than inland, but throughout a rather wide coastal zone only one or two storms occur in an average season.

Relative humidity at noon is greater on the coast than a short distance inland in both January and July. The average difference is about 5 percent in January but is about 10 percent in July. The July zonal contrast increases from about 5 percent in South Carolina and 10 percent in North Carolina to nearly 15 percent in Massachusetts.

Dense fog occurs on an average of about 10 more days a year on the littoral than a short distance inland north of the Chesapeake Bay; south thereof, the difference is less than 5 days and the annual frequency is only a quarter that of the southern Appalachian Mountains. Valley stations in the northern mountains (Catskills, Adirondacks, and White Mountains) have reported fog less often than have coastal stations. Despite the greater fog on the coast, the number of hours of sunshine is greater in winter on the coast than inland, and also in summer, except in southern New England and the Carolinas.

In conclusion: Because the prevailing winds are offshore, the Atlantic has relatively little evident local effect upon the climate of the United States. Its effect is greatest upon the duration of the frostless season, and is next greatest upon lowest temperatures. On annual seasonal and monthly average temperatures it has slight effect; upon high temperatures, surprisingly little. Relative humidity is somewhat greater upon the coast than a short distance inland, as is fog. Sunshine, however, occurs in more hours on the coast than inland in winter and also in summer for most of the coast. Precipitation averages slightly greater on the coast than a short distance inland, chiefly because of larger autumn totals; in winter and spring, the coast receives less, as does much of it also in summer. Except in South Carolina and Georgia, thunderstorms are less numerous on the coast than nearby inland, as is hail. Snowfall is less than half as heavy near the coast as a short distance inland in North Carolina and Virginia; in

New England, it is about three-fourths as heavy. The duration of snow cover is notably reduced in New England by proximity to the sea, but not so south of New Jersey. As to exceptionally large amounts of precipitation, the coastal-inland difference varies with latitude. It is great at the south, moderate at the north. In exceptionally dry summers, the coast is less dry than the nearby inland.

The Gulf of Mexico

Although the Gulf is the source of the precipitation of most of the eastern half of the United States, it has relatively little effect upon temperatures. When allowance is made for latitude effects, it appears that the Gulf depresses mean maximum temperatures and elevates mean minimum temperatures each only about 5°. It affects annual, seasonal, and monthly averages considerably less than 5°. It lengthens the frost-free season, however, an average of about 30 days, except near the tip of the Mississippi Delta, where the growing season is prolonged about 60 days, to more than 340 days. About two-thirds of the prolongation of the growing season apparently due to the Gulf is caused by a delay in the coming of the first killing frost in December.

The local effects on precipitation vary with the seasons; in both summer and autumn, coastal zones receive an average of about 2 inches more rain per season than do areas 100 miles inland; but in spring the coast receives about 2 inches less than the inland area, and in winter about an inch less. In exceptionally dry years, the local effects of the Gulf are less than in exceptionally wet years and are largely limited to the region east of Texas. In exceptionally wet summers — so wet that only one-eighth are wetter — the littoral receives, however, an average of 4 to 6 inches more rain than the inland; in exceptionally dry summers, the increase is about 4 inches. Hence the percentage difference is greater for dry than for wet summers, which receive about twice as much rain. This sharp zonal contrast in rainfall is largely due to an average of about 10 more thunderstorms a year near the coast, and to the greater rainfall yielded by tropical cyclones when they first reach the land. A study of the torrential rainfalls revealed that exceptionally heavy rains are much more frequent, and their magnitude notably greater near the coast than 200 miles inland (Visher, *Monthly Weather Review*, December 1941). The Gulf produces an increase of about 5 percent in average noon relative humidity in January and a 5- to 10-percent increase in July. At 7 p.m. in both January and July the increase is 5 to 10 percent. Fog occurs on 5 to 10 more days a year near the Gulf than inland, but winter sunshine is somewhat greater near the coast than inland; in summer, however, the reverse is true.

In conclusion: The Gulf of Mexico affects temperatures only slightly, except by a prolongation of the frost-free season. Precipitation is appreciably less near the coast than inland in winter and spring, but during autumn and summer (largely because more thunderstorms and heavier torrential rains are associated with tropical cyclonic disturbances) rain is heavier on the coast than inland. The zonal contrast is greatest in exceptionally dry years. The Gulf produces a greater increase of relative humidity in summer than in winter. Sunshine is greater in winter on the coast than inland, but the reverse is true in summer.

The Great Lakes

The influence of the Great Lakes is discernible on most of the climatic maps here being studied. Although the effect of a lake is chiefly to the leeward, in the Great Lakes region winds are so varied in direction that effects are evident on all sides. On the average, the Lakes raise the January average temperature of their surroundings about 5°, the absolute minimum temperatures about 10°, and the annual minima about 15°. They depress the average July air temperatures and wet-bulb temperatures each an average of about 3°, and the annual absolute maxima are decreased about 5°. They increase the average length of the frost-free season about 30 to 40 days on their eastern and southern sides. They have a slight negative total influence upon precipitation, decreasing it appreciably in summer, largely by reducing convectional thunderstorms, but increasing it slightly in late autumn and winter. Their effect upon snowfall is appreciable; on the average, they increase it about 20 inches, but in Upper Michigan and just east of Lake Ontario, the increase is more than 40 inches. The depressing effect of the Lakes upon summer rainfall is relatively as great in exceptionally dry as in exceptionally wet summers, in both of which the amount of precipitation received near the Lakes is no greater than in such summers in central North Dakota and South Dakota. Precipitation falls on about 20 more days a year near the Lakes than in areas not far away; hence the average fall per day is decreased. The maximum fall in 24 hours averages less than 4 inches near the Lakes, which is about 2 inches or 50 percent less than occurs not far away. The maximum in an hour averages about 1.5 inches near the Lakes; a third more (2 inches) falls per hour somewhat farther from the Lakes. The Lakes produce an average decrease of about five thunderstorms per year, and decrease the violence of many of those which do occur. They increase the average July noon relative humidity about 5 percent, but have less effect on winter humidity. They do increase the number of days with fog, however, having an average of almost twice as much fog as areas not far away. Much of Lake Superior has five times as much fog as nearby areas. Nevertheless, the south shore of Lake Erie, with only five dense-fog days a year, has less fog than any other coastal area except southern Florida. The foggiest part of the Great Lakes, the southern shore of Lake Superior, has 30 days of dense fog per year, which is, however, less than that of the Appalachian Mountains or the coasts of New England and the North Pacific. The Lakes region has about an hour a day less winter sunshine than normal for the latitude. In summer, the deficiency is about half an hour, which is a smaller deficiency than that prevailing in New England or on the North Pacific Coast. The Lakes region also has more summer sunshine than Florida or the New Orleans area.

In conclusion: The Great Lakes on the average depress exceptionally high temperatures about 3° to 5° and elevate exceptionally low ones 10° to 15°; they prolong the frost-free period conspicuously, by 40 to 50 percent; they slightly decrease precipitation except snowfall, which they increase fully 50 percent; they decrease summer rainfall partly by reducing thunderstorm frequency and intensity, torrential rains being notably less frequent and less heavy than at some distance inland. The Lakes increase the number of days receiving some precipitation and the number of cloudy and foggy days. In summer, however, they have more sunshine than most of the South, or the North Pacific or Atlantic coasts.

Mountains

Mountains influence all aspects of the climate of the United States. Their influence upon precipitation and temperatures is profound. Some of the effects are illustrated by the maps of the United States as a whole, and even more by those of individual states. Additional facts are disclosed by more detailed studies.

The map of average January temperatures shows that in the mountains of northern New Mexico average temperatures are as low as in the lowland interior of Washington or New York, more than a thousand miles farther north. The great effect of the mountains upon temperature is shown indirectly by the conspicuous consequence of the opening across the Cascade Mountains made by the Columbia River, east of which, even as far as the edge of Idaho, the January average is above 30°, almost 10° higher than in nearby areas. The Appalachians deflect the January isotherms only moderately, depressing the average temperature about 5°. The eastern mountains and the Rockies depress the annual minima an average of about 10°; the Sierras and Cascades depress it about 15°. The Columbia Gorge gives to a narrow belt along the river east of the Cascades minimum temperatures 20° higher than prevail in nearby areas to the south and north. The effect of mountains is much less upon the absolute minimum temperatures than upon the annual minima. There is a marked effect upon the duration of the frost-free period, however. Every mountain range, even the Ozarks, is evident on detailed frost maps. The Appalachians shorten the season (at the Weather Bureau stations, most of which are situated in the valleys) an average of 20 days at the south, 40 days in the Adirondacks; the Rockies shorten the season an average of about 40 days, except at rather high (Weather Bureau station) elevations, where the shortening is about twice as great.

The maps showing high temperatures afford many illustrations of mountain influence. The Appalachians depress average Weather Bureau July temperatures 5° to 10°; the Rockies and Cascades depress them 10° to 15°; the Sierras 5° to 10°. As a result, northwestern North Carolina is cooler in hot weather than is eastern North Dakota, and northern New Mexico is cooler than any large part of the East and is 30° cooler than some lowland areas in southern California in similar latitudes. Annual maxima are depressed at Weather Bureau stations in mountainous areas an average of about 10° in the Appalachians, 15° in the Rockies, and 20° in the Sierras. The highest temperatures ever recorded, as reported in these maps, are less affected by mountains than are the annual extremes. The

Appalachians lower, at the Weather Bureau stations, absolute maxima an average of only about 5°, the Rockies 5° to 10°, and the Sierras 10° to 15°. Average July wet-bulb temperatures are apparently depressed less than 5° by the eastern mountain ranges and 5° to 10° by the western ones.

The great effect of the Coast Ranges and the Cascades and Sierras upon precipitation is well known. On the western slopes of the coastal Olympics, the annual average is more than 120 inches. (The 13-year record at Wynooche Oxbow shows an average of 150.7 inches.) By contrast, in the Puget Sound region just to the east of the Olympics, the average is less than 30 inches; part of it, less than 20. On the western slopes of the Cascades, the precipitation, about 100 inches, is about 6 times as great as on the eastern slopes; on the western slopes of the Sierras, fully 10 times as much precipitation is received as just to the east (40–60 inches vs. 4–6). The southern Appalachians, also, strongly affect the annual total; two stations in western North Carolina have an annual average of 84 inches, which is about 35 inches more than in the nearby lowlands beyond the mountains and 45 inches more than in some nearby valleys surrounded by mountains. Indeed, two North Carolina areas separated by less than 50 miles have respectively 84 and 39 inches of annual precipitation. (Each of these areas has two Weather Bureau stations with long records.) In West Virginia, two areas only about 30 miles apart have 56 and 32 inches of average precipitation. In Wyoming, just west of the Big Horn Mountains, the average precipitation is only a third as great as in the mountains (8 vs. 25 inches). In Arizona, several mountain stations receive three times as much precipitation as nearby lowland stations; two of them have four times as much (24 vs. 6 inches, 28 vs. 7 inches).

The effect of mountains upon annual precipitation apparently is greater in average years than in either wet or dry years. The map for the total precipitation received in the driest one-eighth of the years shows that mountains increase the precipitation only a little, except in the rainiest part of the southern Appalachians. In wet years, American mountains appear to receive little more rain than nearby lowlands.

Among the seasons, mountain influences upon precipitation are greatest absolutely in winter in the western mountains; but relatively, they appear to be greatest in summer, except in the Sierras. This is because thunderstorms bring rain to various western mountains in summer, when the nearby lowlands are almost rainless. The Appalachians are least evident on the map of autumn rainfall, next least on the one for spring; they are somewhat more evident in summer than in winter. The eastern mountains have relatively greater effect in dry than in wet summers, but in the West, dry summers receive so little rainfall that the mountain influences are not conspicuous. In exceptionally wet summers, also, western mountains do not appear to receive much more rainfall than the lowlands.

The form of precipitation most clearly influenced by mountains is snowfall, especially in regions where there is little in the lowlands. In the southern Appalachians, the mountain stations receive an average of about twice as much as nearby lowland stations (Mount Mitchell, with 70 inches, gets nearly twice as much as Boston, 450 miles farther north); the stations in the Cascades receive about twice as much snow as the lowland to the east; the Sierras receive about twice as much snow as the plateau to the east and many times as much as the lowland to the west. In regions where the surrounding lowlands receive much snowfall, the influence of the mountains is less evident; for example, stations in the Adirondacks receive little or no more snow than stations near Lake Ontario, and stations in the White Mountains no more than areas in the lowlands of northern Maine. The northern Rocky Mountain stations receive, on an average, only about twice as much snow as the nearby lowlands. Many mountain slopes receive, however, notably more snow than the regular Weather Bureau stations, most of which are in valleys.

As to duration of snow cover, the mountains retain their snow much longer than do the lowlands. Snow also falls upon them earlier in the autumn. Some snow persists throughout the summer as far south as southern Colorado and the central Sierras. Many northwestern peaks are snowcapped, but none in the East. The high ravines in the White Mountains, however, retain a little snow until July, rarely into August.

With respect to maximum precipitation in a month, one effect of the mountains is evident. The eastern (southeastern) side of the Appalachians has notably greater totals than the opposite side. In other words, the northwestern side is the lee or rain-shadow side for the rains that yield great totals, although for the year as a whole, the amount of precipitation received by both sides is substantially equal except at the south end of the range. Thus, it appears that the exceptionally heavy monthly totals are caused by winds from the southeast, the Atlantic, rather than from the Gulf of Mexico.

As the maximum precipitation in 24 hours is, for most of the eastern half of the country, about half of the maximum for the wettest month of the period from 1899 to 1938, it is evident that the exceptionally large monthly totals are chiefly due to one exceptionally heavy rain — a record-breaking 24-hour rain plus some rain shortly before or after. Along the Atlantic Coast, most record-breaking 24-hour rains occur in tropical cyclones which proceed northward not far from the coast. As the mountains interfere with penetration inland, and as the wind spirals towards the center on a counterclockwise course, the heavier rainfall on the eastern slope is easily understood. The fact that for the year as a whole the western side receives about as much precipitation as the eastern, except near the southern end of the range, is due to the normal movement of mid-latitude lows, supplemented by such tropical cyclones as have moved a considerable distance up the Mississippi Valley before turning east.

Although, excepting the Appalachians, the mountain ranges are mostly not evident on these maps of humidity, fog, or sunshine, the central section of the Appalachians has two to four times as much fog as nearby lowlands and only about seven-eighths as much summer sunshine. They have, however, little or no less winter sunshine than have adjacent lowlands.

PART I   TEMPERATURE

2. NORMAL TEMPERATURES: ANNUAL, SEASONAL, MONTHLY
CONTRASTS, EXPECTANCIES

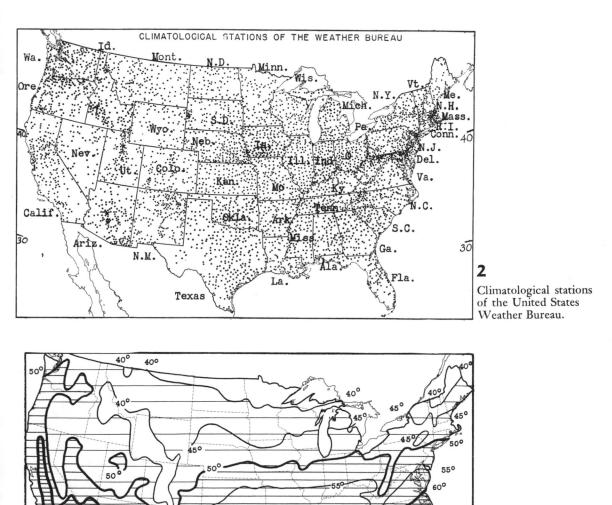

2
Climatological stations
of the United States
Weather Bureau.

3
Normal annual
temperature (°F).

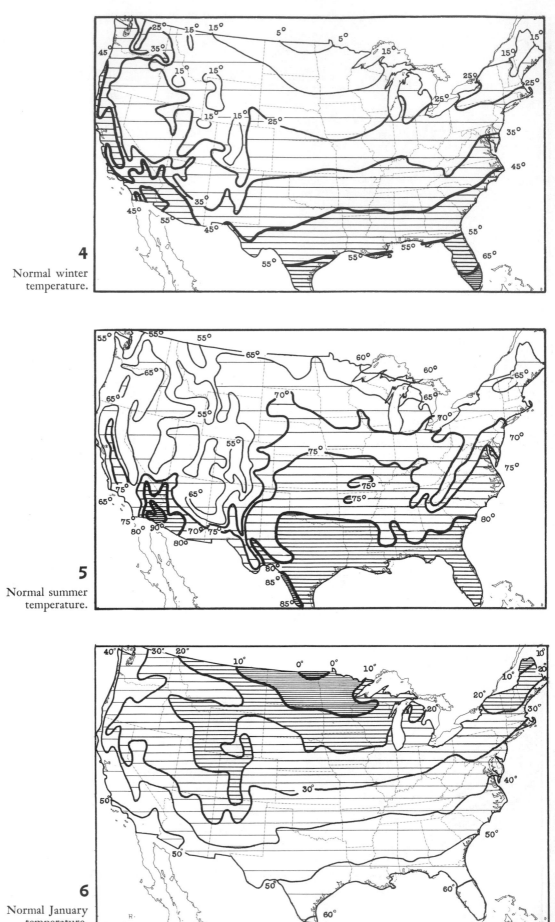

4
Normal winter
temperature.

5
Normal summer
temperature.

6
Normal January
temperature.

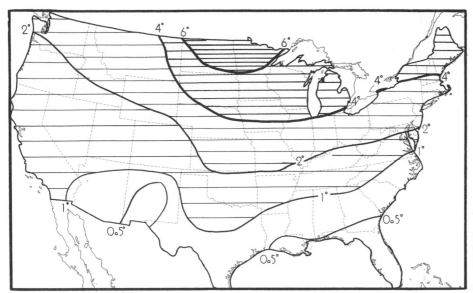

7
Decrease in normal
temperature from
December to January
(based on state
averages).

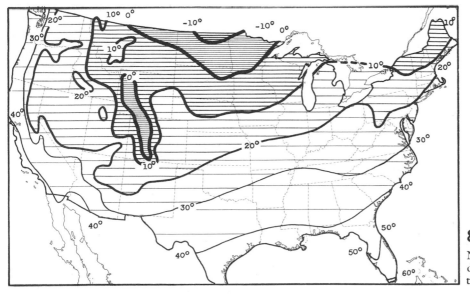

8
Normal January
daily minimum
temperature.

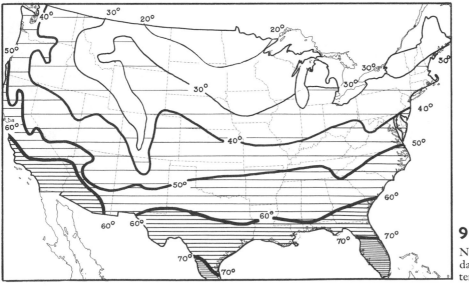

9
Normal January
daily maximum
temperature.

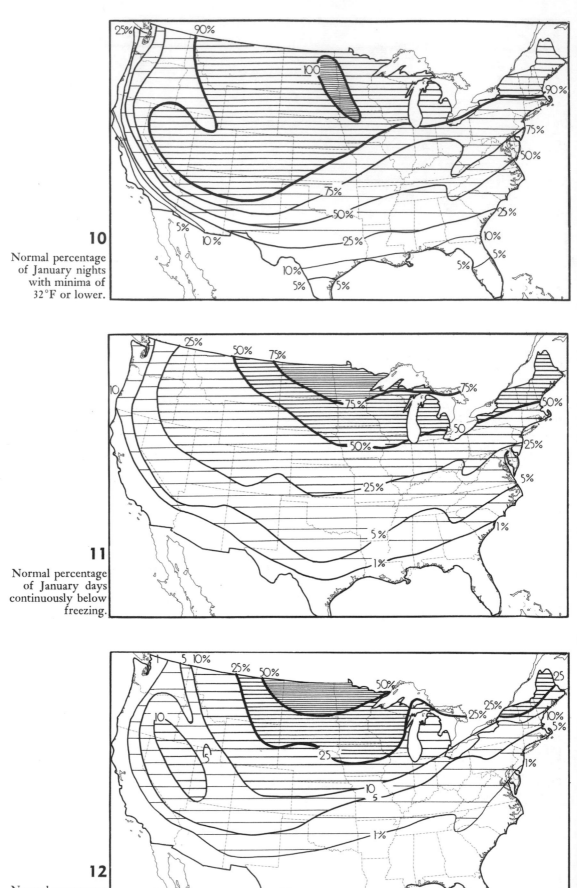

10 Normal percentage of January nights with minima of 32°F or lower.

11 Normal percentage of January days continuously below freezing.

12 Normal percentage of January nights with minima of 0°F or lower.

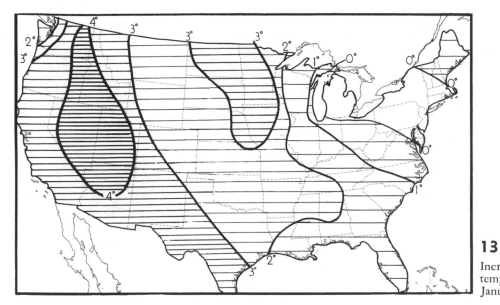

13

Increase in normal
temperature from
January to February.

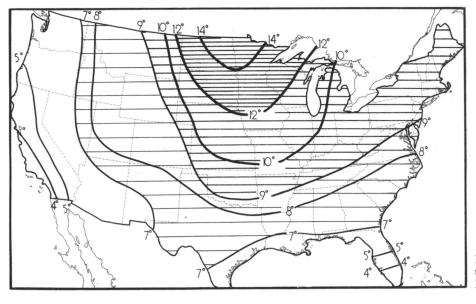

14

Increase in normal
temperature from
February to March.

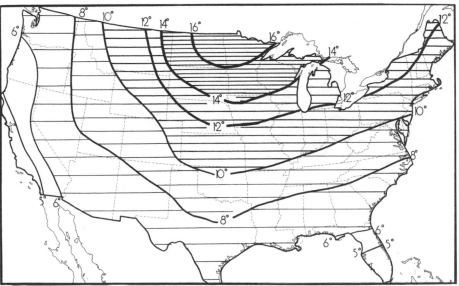

15

Increase in normal
temperature from
March to April.

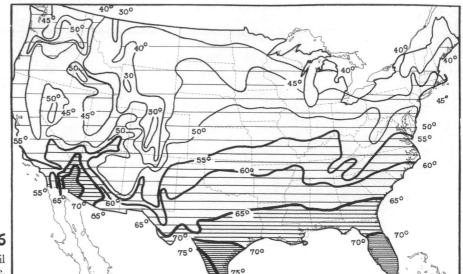

16
Normal April
temperature.

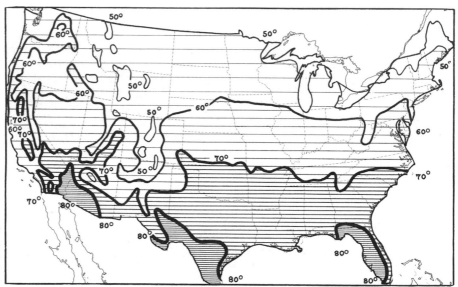

17
Normal April
daily maximum
temperature.

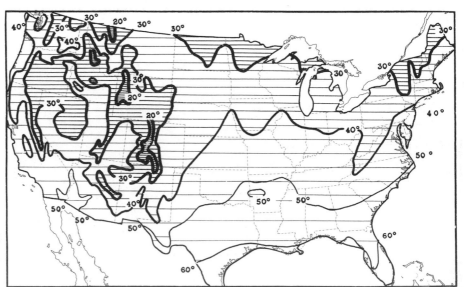

18
Normal April
daily minimum
temperature.

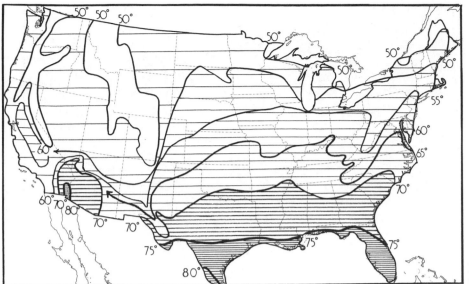

19
Normal May
temperature.

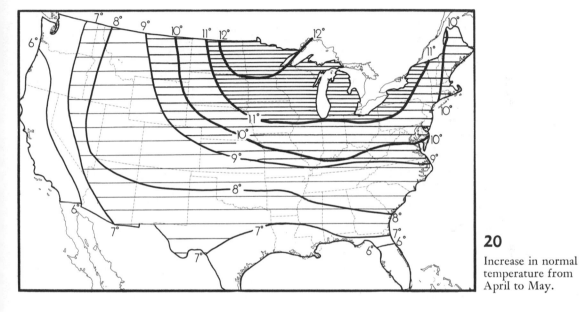

20
Increase in normal
temperature from
April to May.

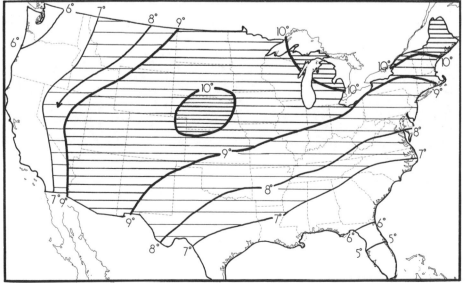

21
Increase in normal
temperature from
May to June.

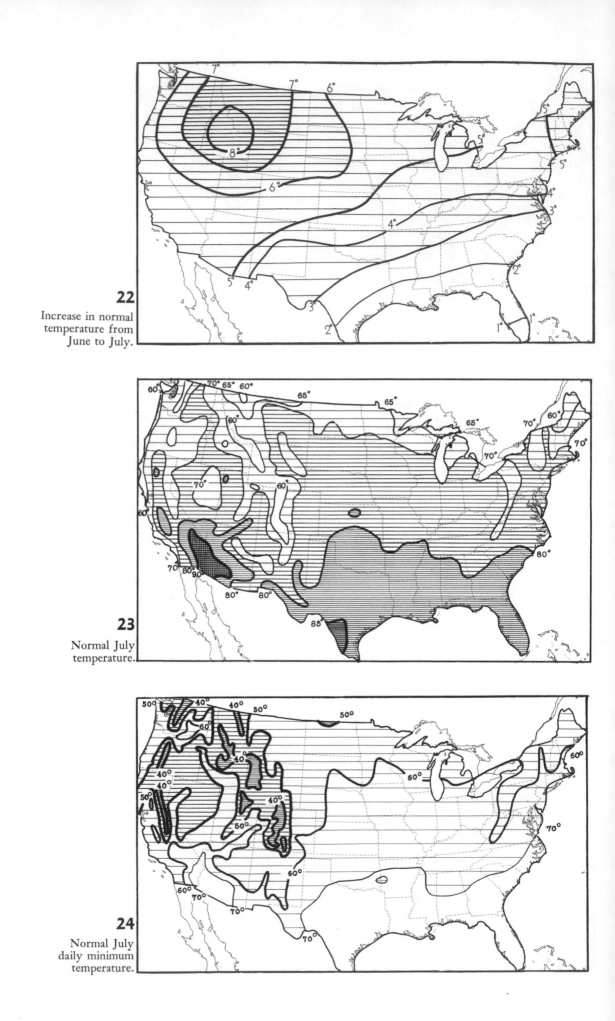

22 Increase in normal temperature from June to July.

23 Normal July temperature.

24 Normal July daily minimum temperature.

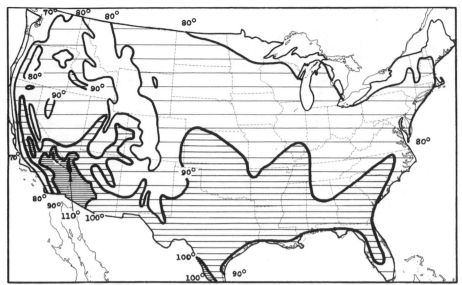

25

Normal July
daily maximum
temperature.

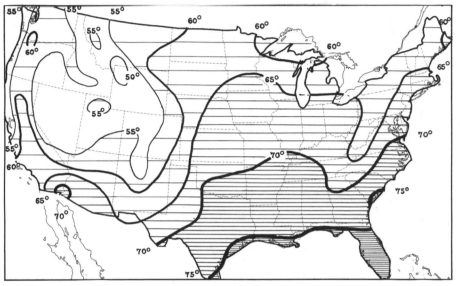

26

Normal July
wet-bulb
temperature.

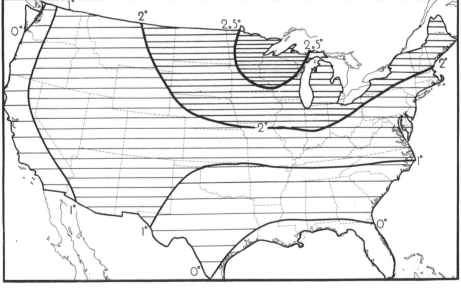

27

Decrease in normal
temperature from
July to August.

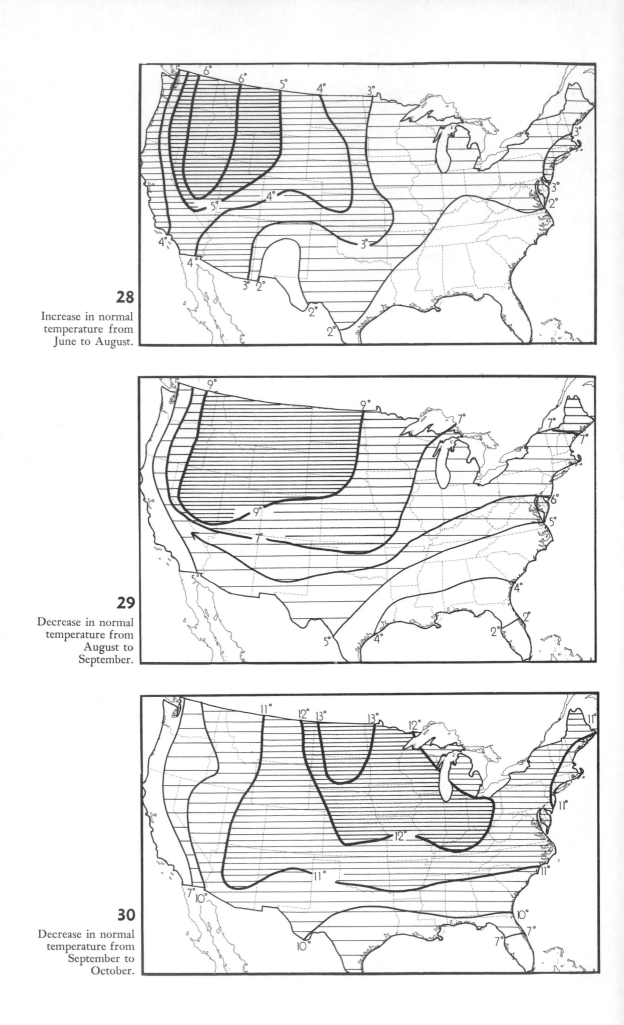

28
Increase in normal
temperature from
June to August.

29
Decrease in normal
temperature from
August to
September.

30
Decrease in normal
temperature from
September to
October.

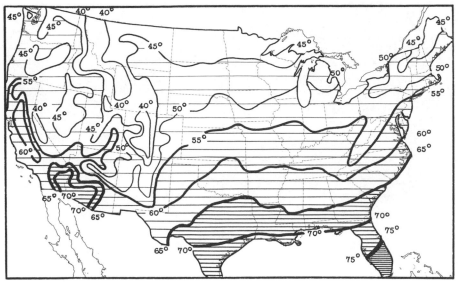

31
Normal October
temperature.

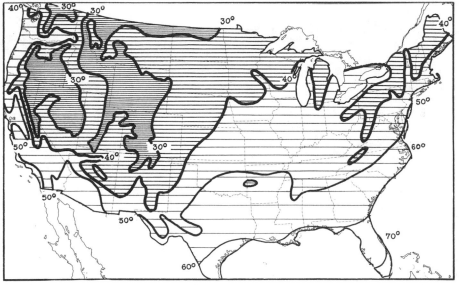

32
Normal October
daily minimum
temperature.

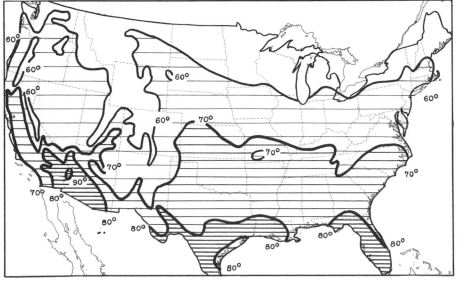

33
Normal October
daily maximum
temperature.

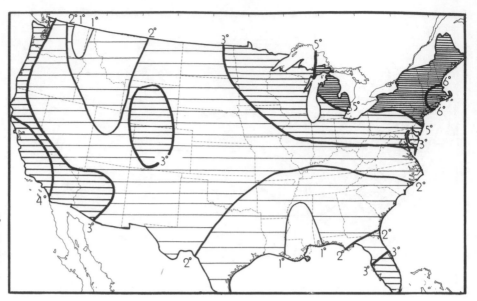

34

Increase in normal
temperature from
April to October
(mid-spring to
mid-autumn).

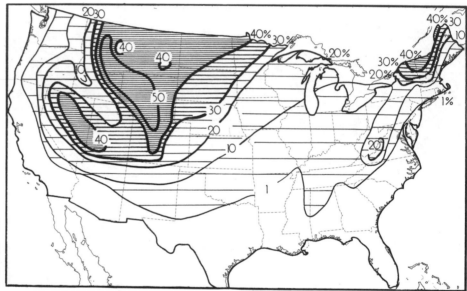

35

Normal percentage
of October nights
with freezing
temperatures.

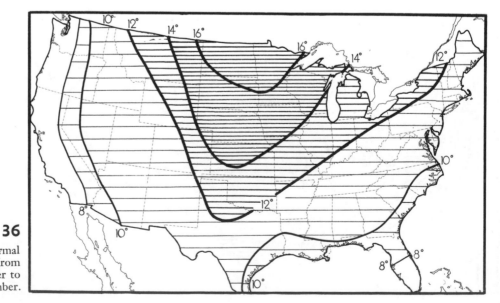

36

Decrease in normal
temperature from
October to
November.

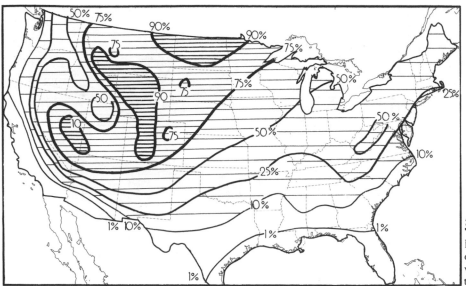

37
Normal percentage
of November nights
with freezing
temperatures.

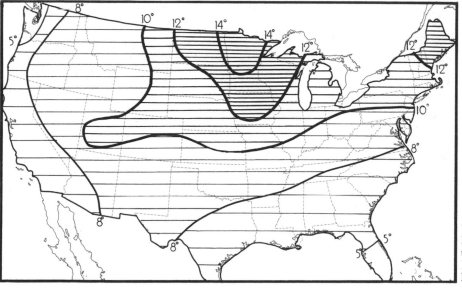

38
Decrease in normal
temperature from
November to
December.

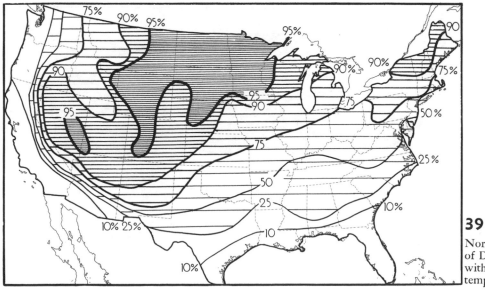

39
Normal percentage
of December nights
with freezing
temperatures.

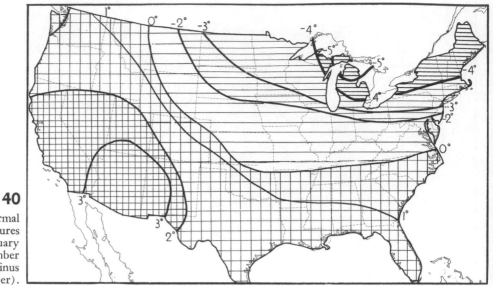

40

Differences in normal
temperatures
between February
and December
(February minus
December).

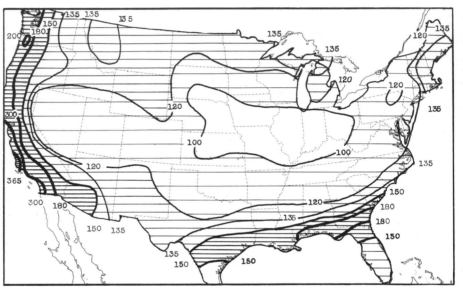

41

Normal duration
of warm weather:
annual number of
days with normal
temperatures of
50°–68°.

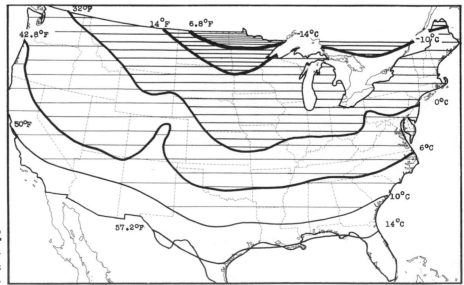

42

Normal January
sea-level isotherms
(°F and °C).

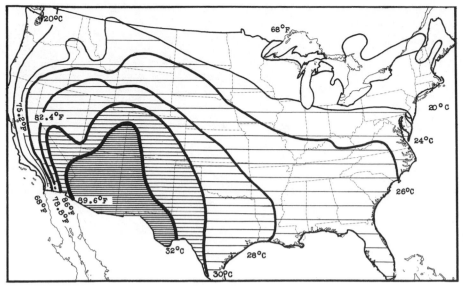

43

Normal July
sea-level isotherms
(°F and °C).

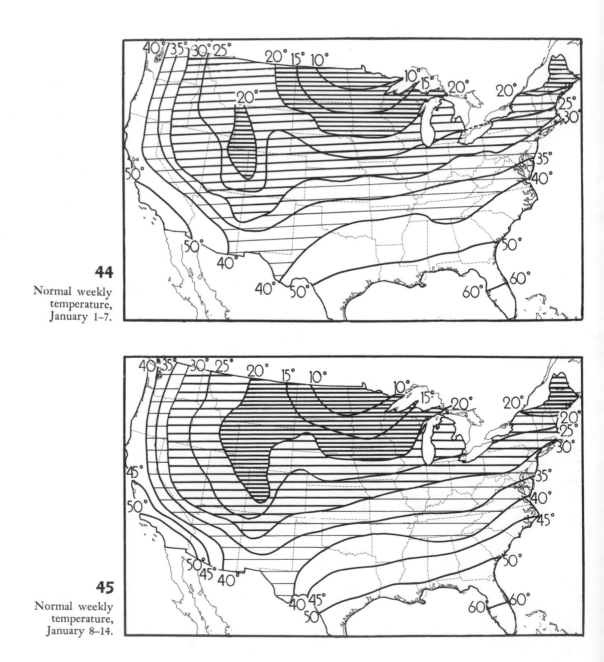

44
Normal weekly
temperature,
January 1–7.

45
Normal weekly
temperature,
January 8–14.

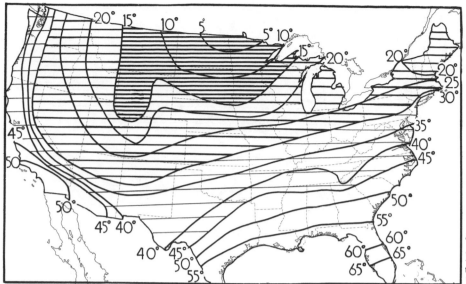

46
Normal weekly
temperature,
January 15–21.

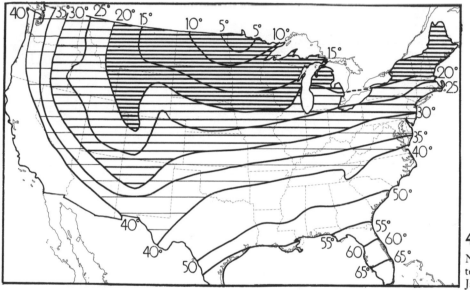

47
Normal weekly
temperature,
January 22–28.

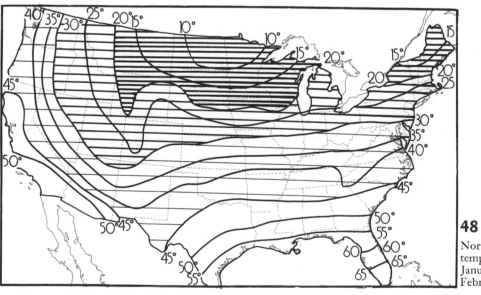

48
Normal weekly
temperature,
January 29–
February 4.

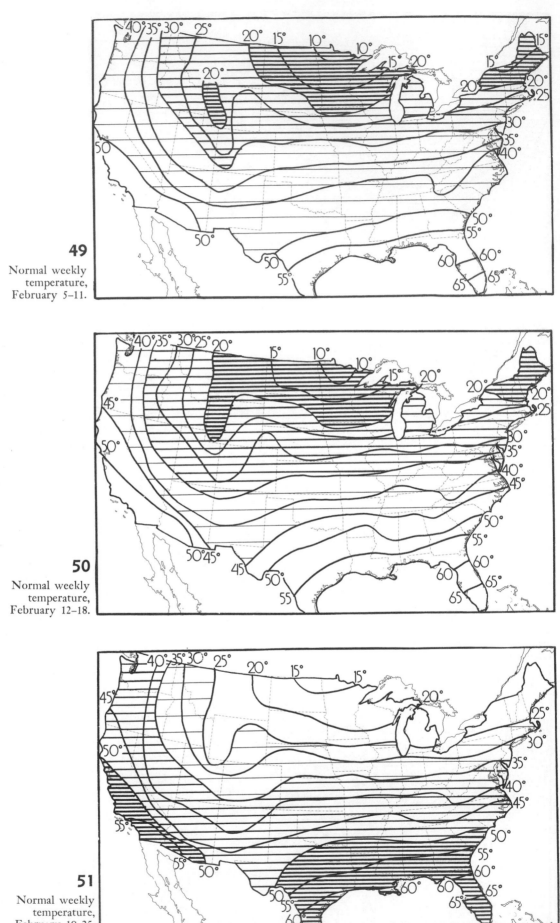

49
Normal weekly
temperature,
February 5–11.

50
Normal weekly
temperature,
February 12–18.

51
Normal weekly
temperature,
February 19–25.

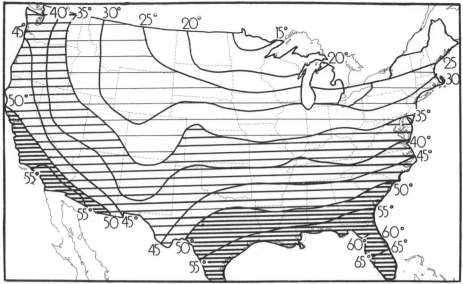

52
Normal weekly temperature, February 26–March 4.

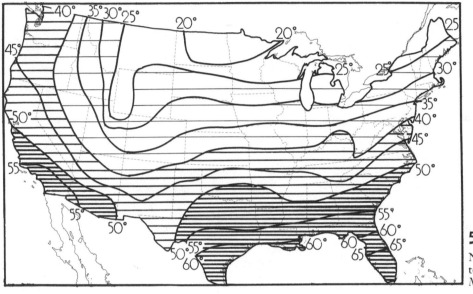

53
Normal weekly temperature, March 5–11.

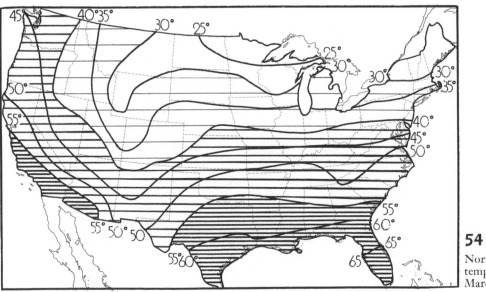

54
Normal weekly temperature, March 12–18.

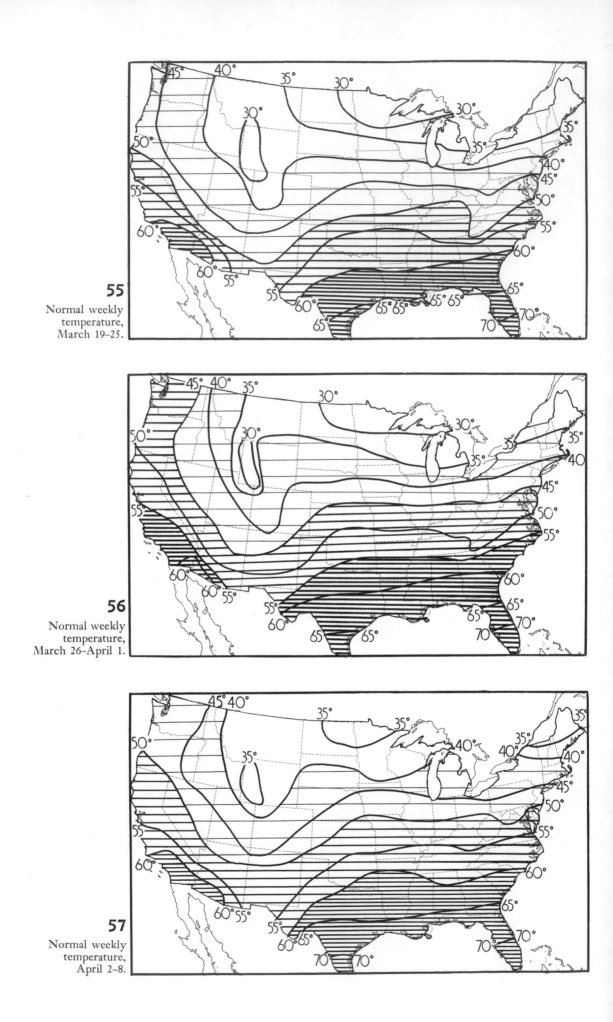

55
Normal weekly
temperature,
March 19–25.

56
Normal weekly
temperature,
March 26–April 1.

57
Normal weekly
temperature,
April 2–8.

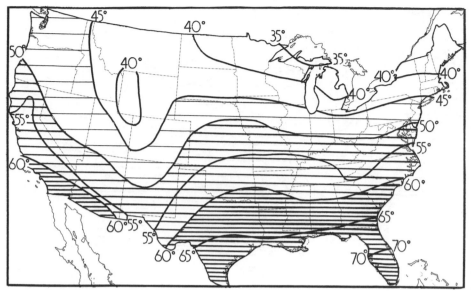

58

Normal weekly temperature, April 9–15.

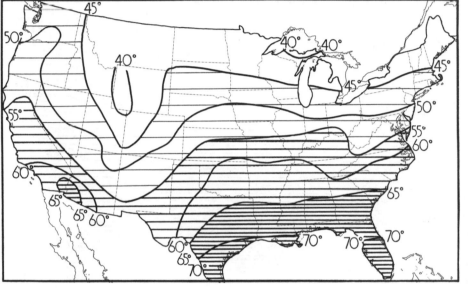

59

Normal weekly temperature, April 16–22.

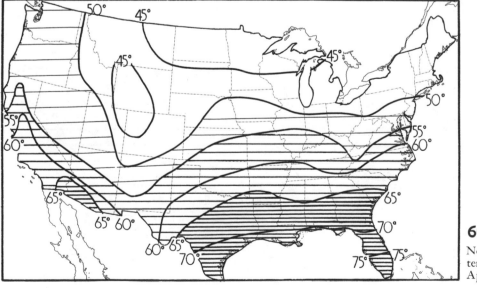

60

Normal weekly temperature, April 23–29.

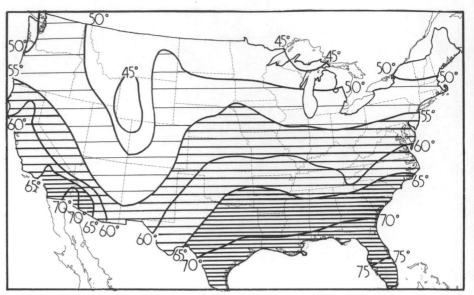

61

Normal weekly
temperature,
April 30–May 6.

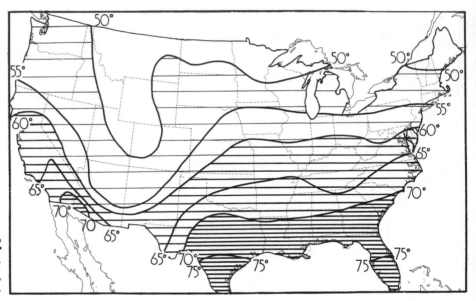

62

Normal weekly
temperature,
May 7–13.

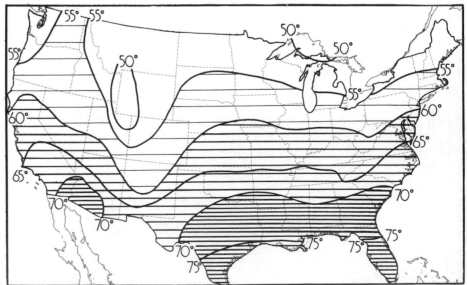

63

Normal weekly
temperature,
May 14–20.

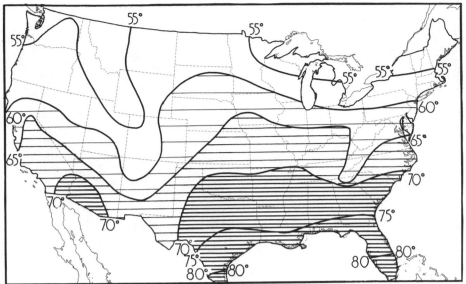

64

Normal weekly
temperature,
May 21–27.

65

Normal weekly
temperature,
May 28–June 3.

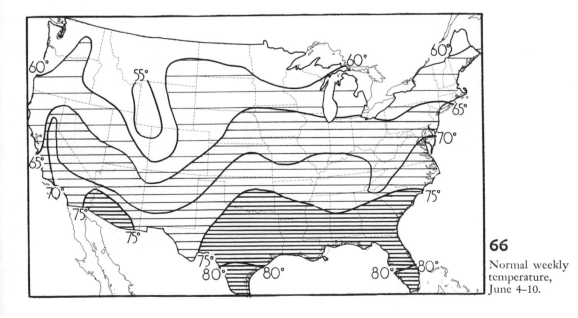

66

Normal weekly
temperature,
June 4–10.

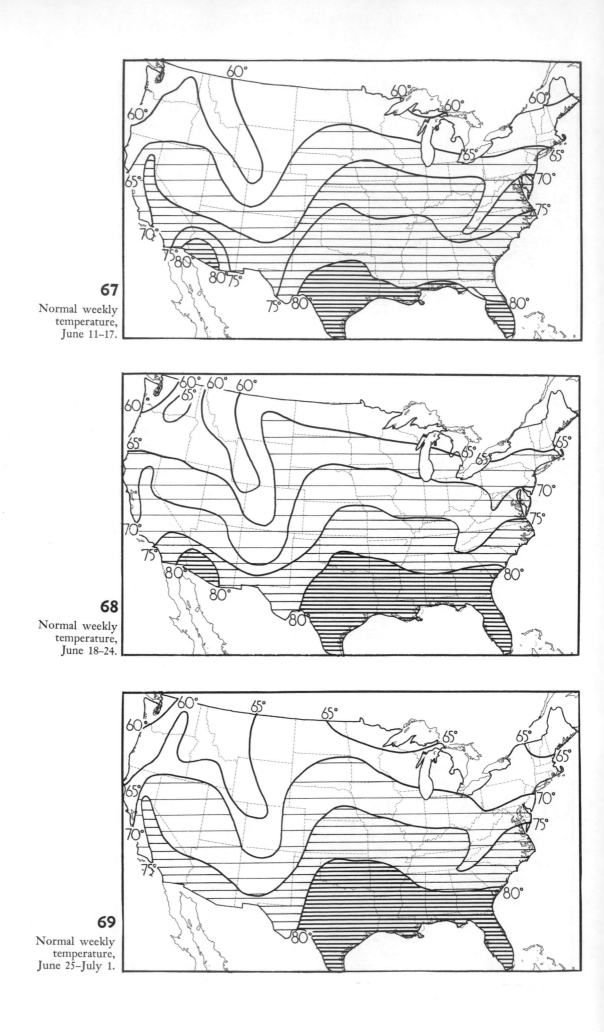

67 Normal weekly temperature, June 11–17.

68 Normal weekly temperature, June 18–24.

69 Normal weekly temperature, June 25–July 1.

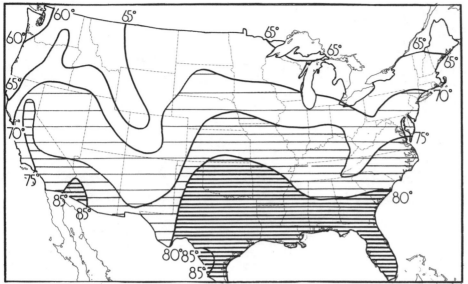

70
Normal weekly
temperature,
July 2–8.

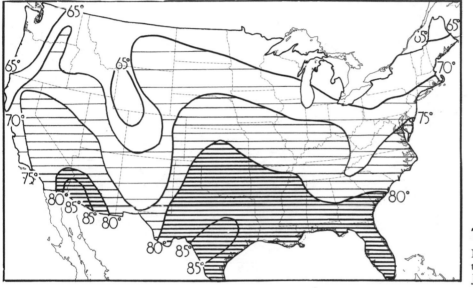

71
Normal weekly
temperature,
July 9–15.

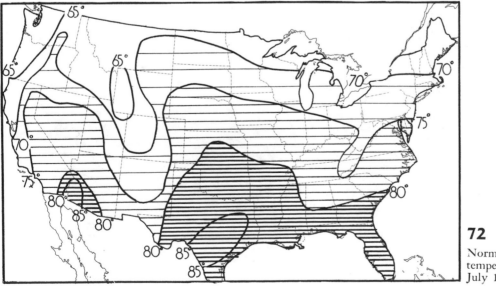

72
Normal weekly
temperature,
July 16–22.

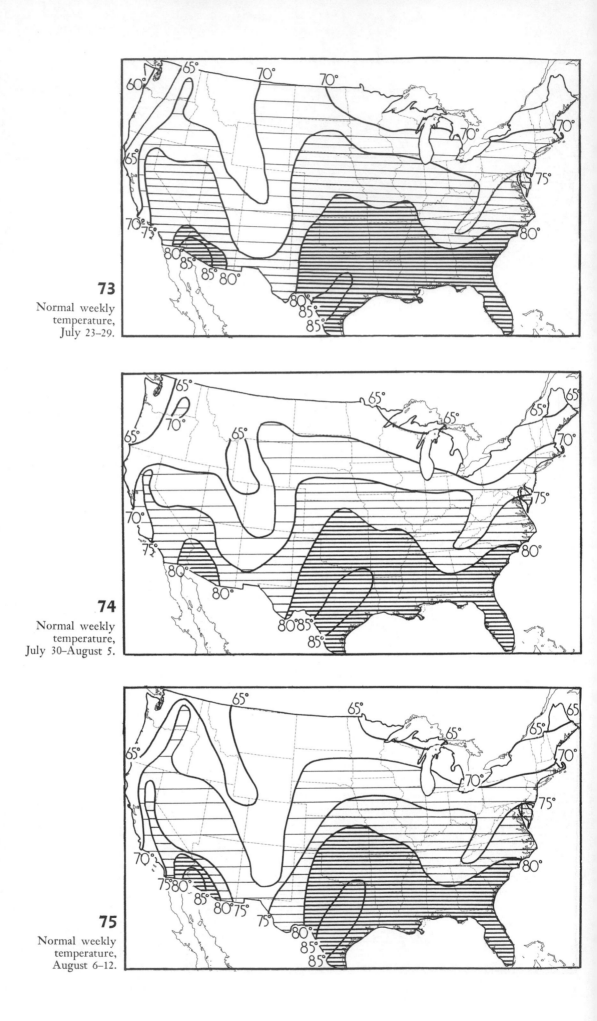

73
Normal weekly
temperature,
July 23–29.

74
Normal weekly
temperature,
July 30–August 5.

75
Normal weekly
temperature,
August 6–12.

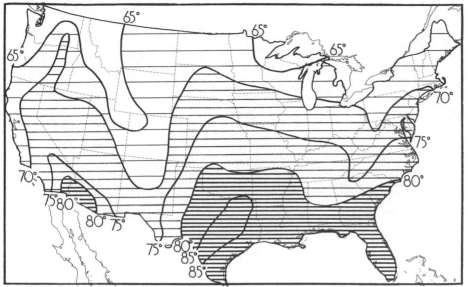

76

Normal weekly temperature, August 13–19.

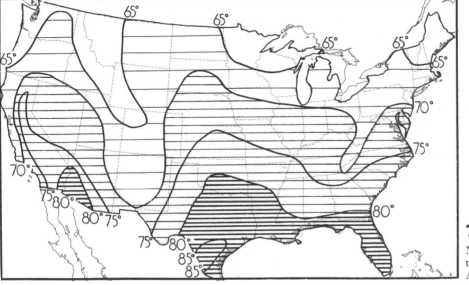

77

Normal weekly temperature, August 20–26.

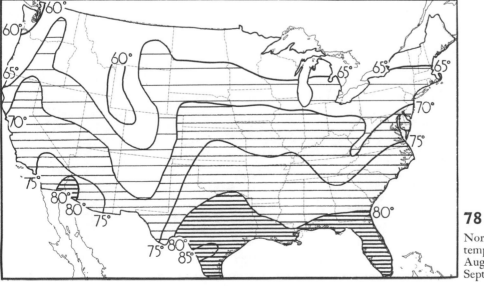

78

Normal weekly temperature, August 27– September 2.

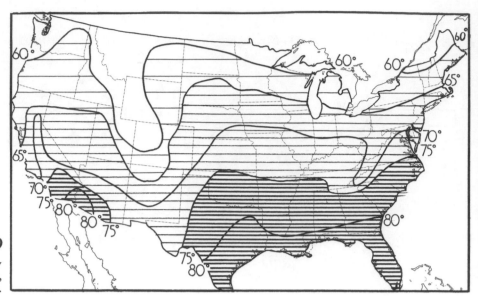

79

Normal weekly
temperature,
September 3–9.

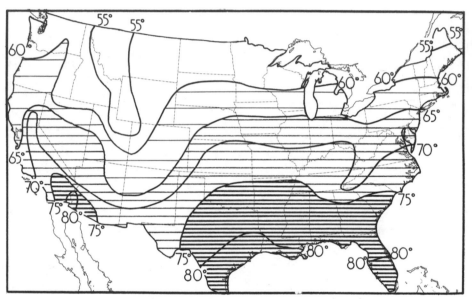

80

Normal weekly
temperature,
September 10–16.

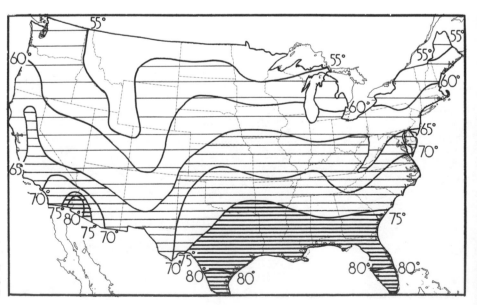

81

Normal weekly
temperature,
September 17–23.

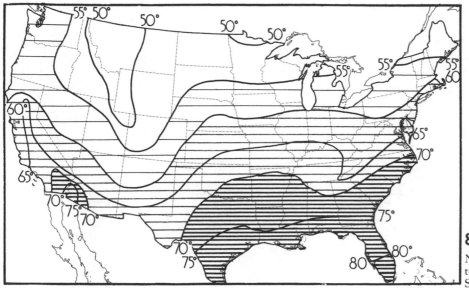

82
Normal weekly temperature, September 24–30.

83
Normal weekly temperature, October 1–7.

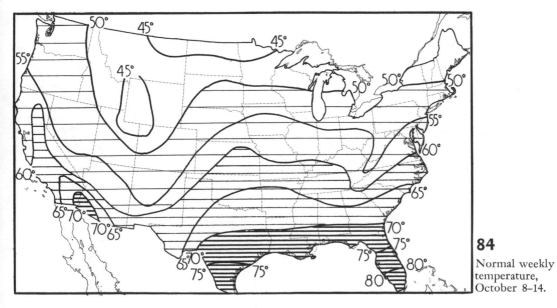

84
Normal weekly temperature, October 8–14.

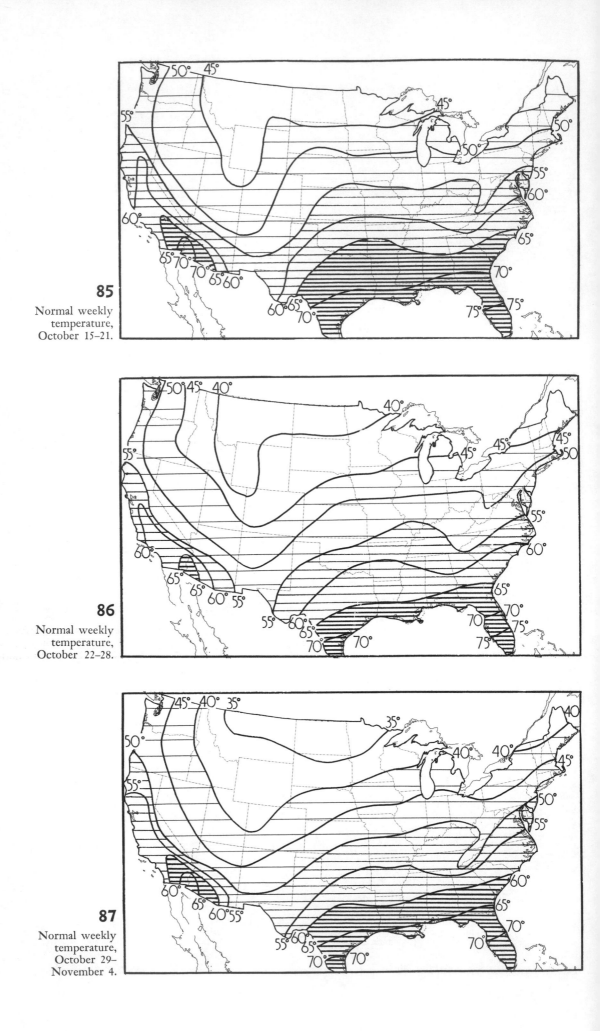

85

Normal weekly
temperature,
October 15–21.

86

Normal weekly
temperature,
October 22–28.

87

Normal weekly
temperature,
October 29–
November 4.

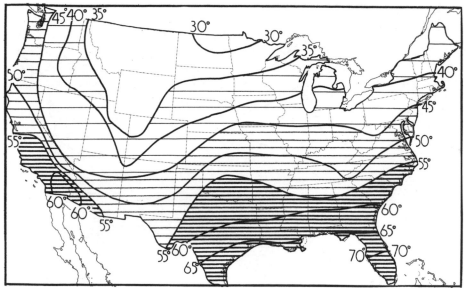

88
Normal weekly temperature, November 5-11.

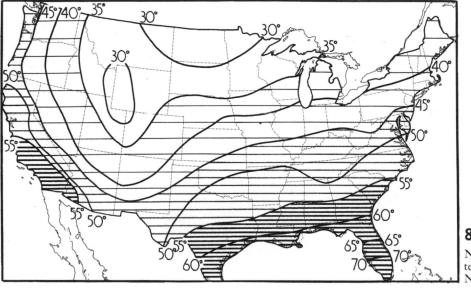

89
Normal weekly temperature, November 12-18.

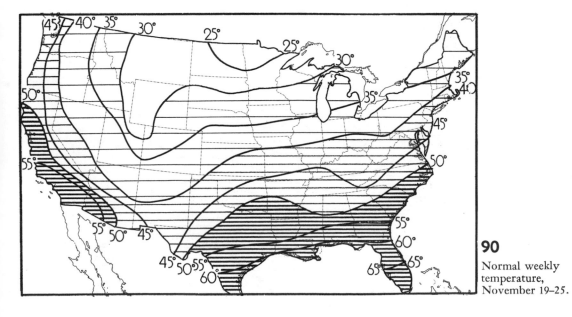

90
Normal weekly temperature, November 19-25.

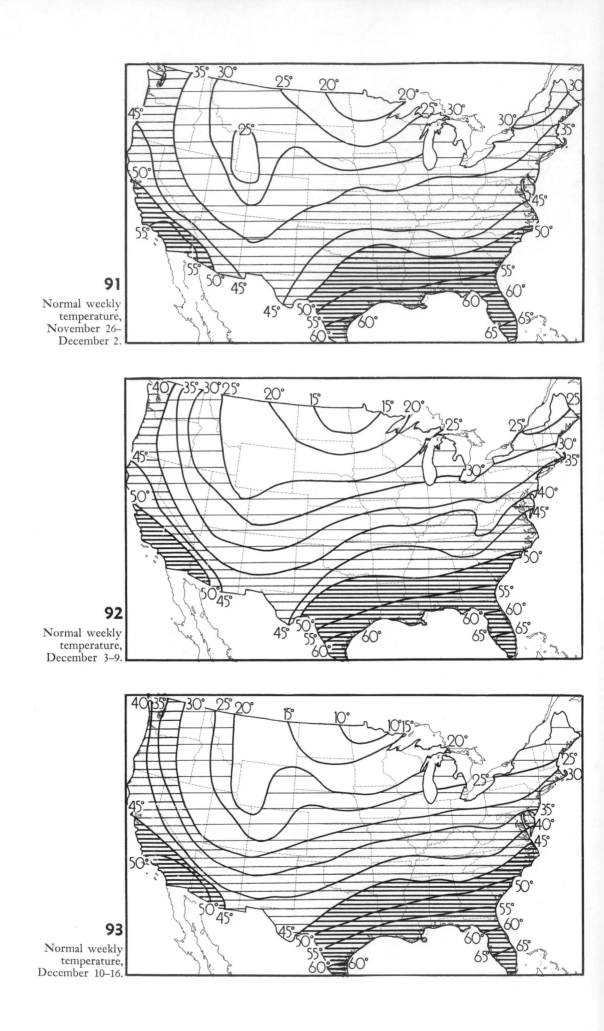

91 Normal weekly temperature, November 26–December 2.

92 Normal weekly temperature, December 3–9.

93 Normal weekly temperature, December 10–16.

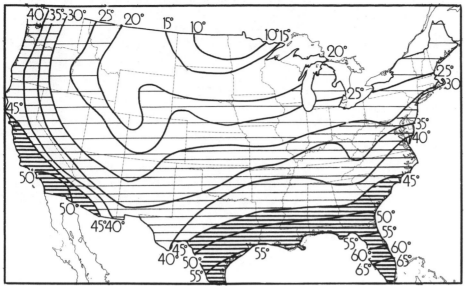

94

Normal weekly
temperature,
December 17–23.

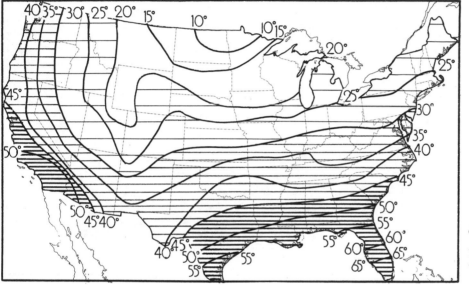

95

Normal weekly
temperature,
December 24–31.

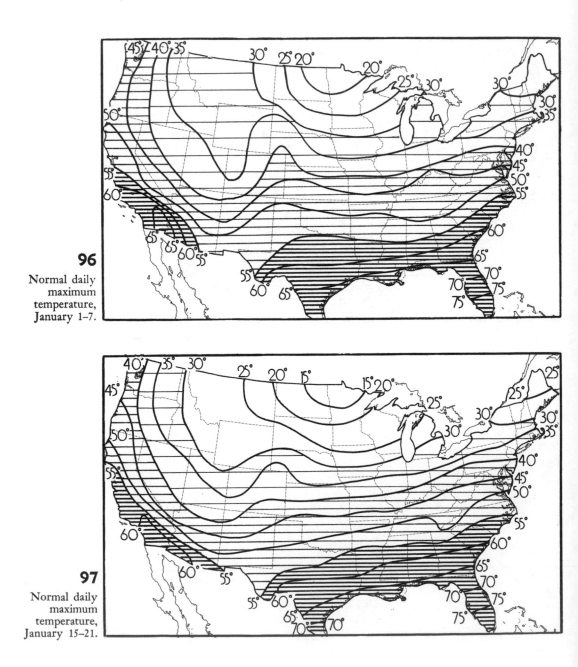

96

Normal daily
maximum
temperature,
January 1–7.

97

Normal daily
maximum
temperature,
January 15–21.

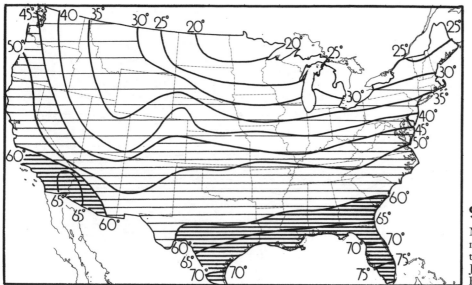

98

Normal daily
maximum
temperature,
January 29–
February 4.

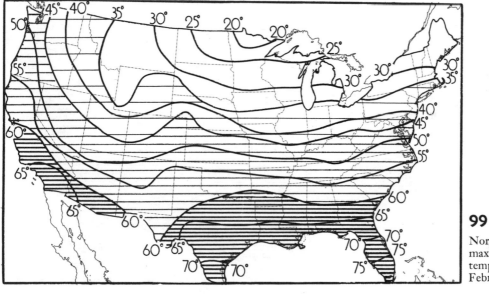

99

Normal daily
maximum
temperature,
February 12–18.

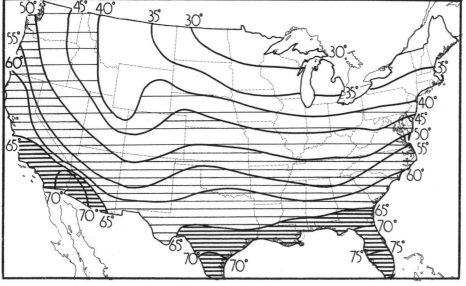

100

Normal daily
maximum
temperature,
February 26–March 4.

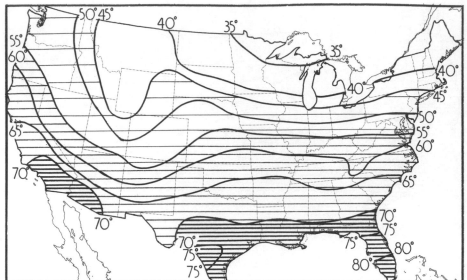

101

Normal daily
maximum
temperature,
March 12–18.

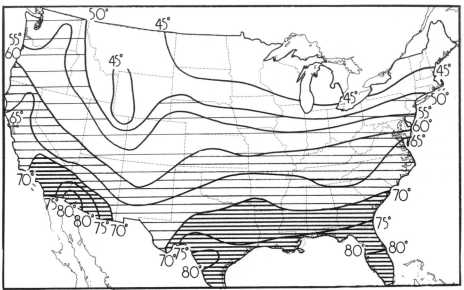

102

Normal daily
maximum
temperature,
March 26–April 1.

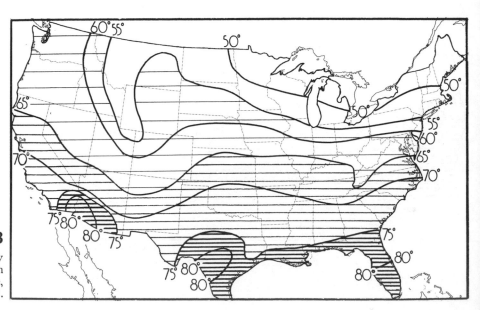

103

Normal daily
maximum
temperature,
April 9–15.

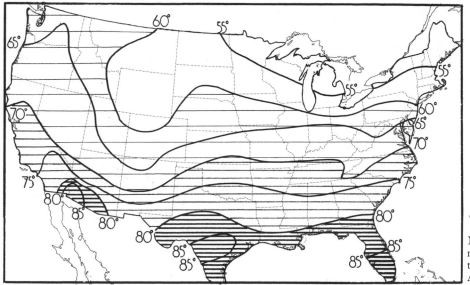

104

Normal daily maximum temperature, April 23–29.

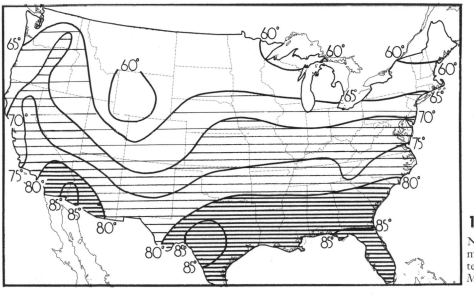

105

Normal daily maximum temperature, May 7–13.

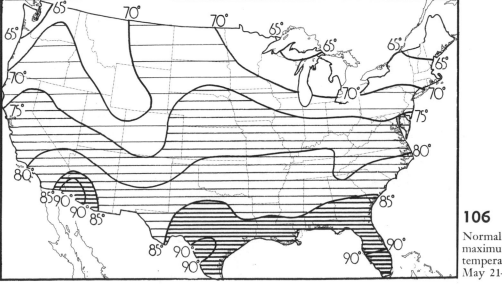

106

Normal daily maximum temperature, May 21–27.

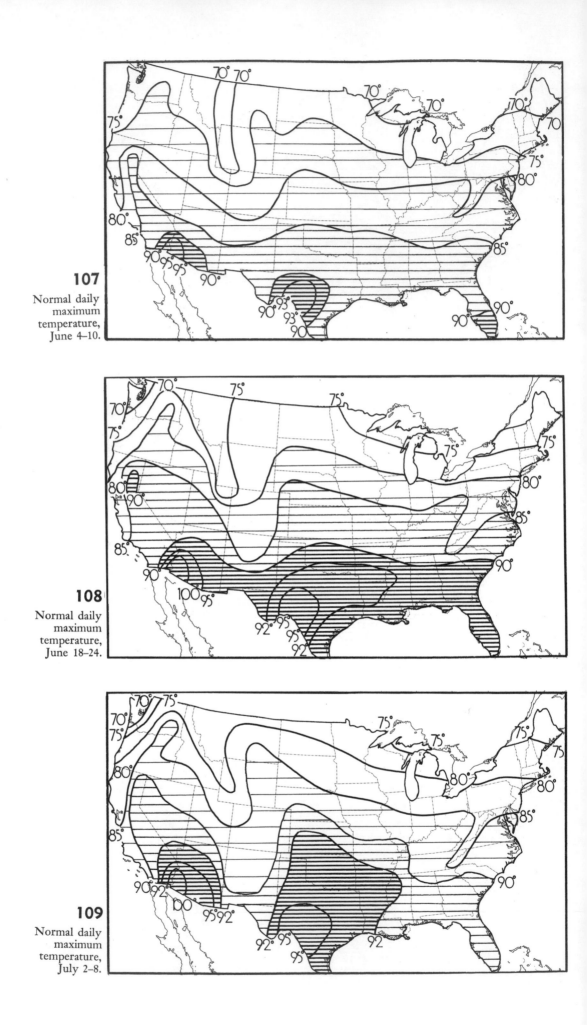

107

Normal daily maximum temperature, June 4–10.

108

Normal daily maximum temperature, June 18–24.

109

Normal daily maximum temperature, July 2–8.

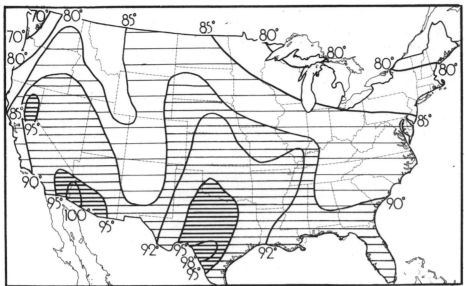

110

Normal daily
maximum
temperature,
July 16–22.

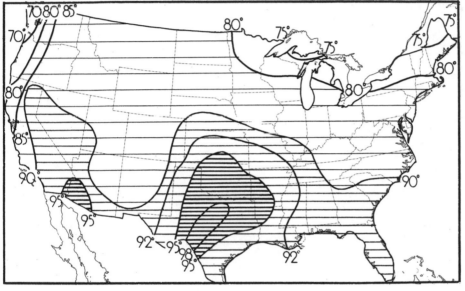

111

Normal daily
maximum
temperature,
July 30–August 5.

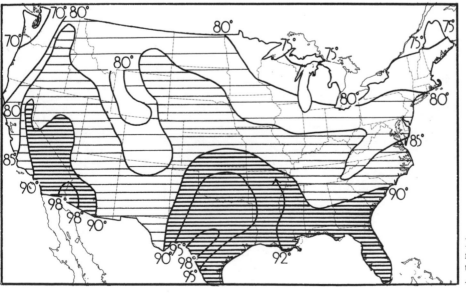

112

Normal daily
maximum
temperature,
August 13–19.

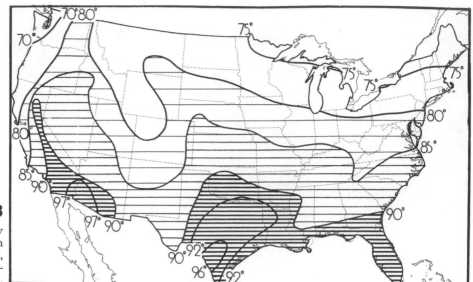

113

Normal daily
maximum
temperature,
August 27–
September 2.

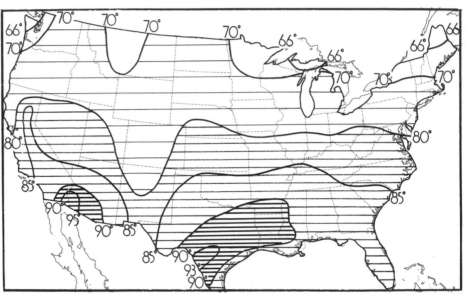

114

Normal daily
maximum
temperature,
September 10–16.

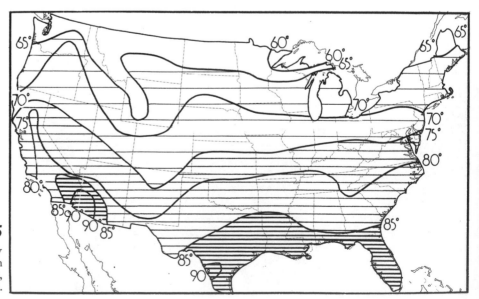

115

Normal daily
maximum
temperature,
September 24–30.

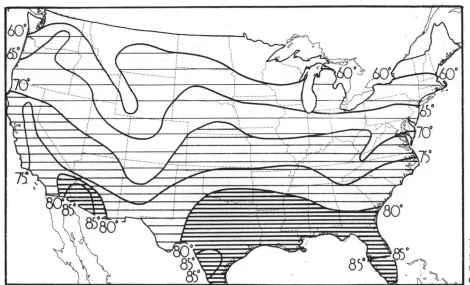

116

Normal daily
maximum
temperature,
October 8–14.

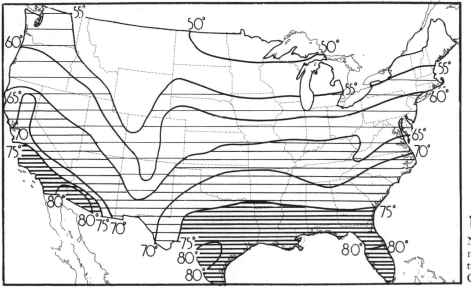

117

Normal daily
maximum
temperature,
October 22–28.

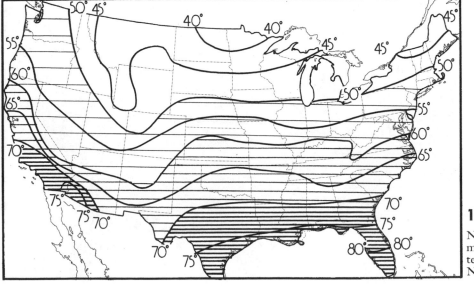

118

Normal daily
maximum
temperature,
November 5–11.

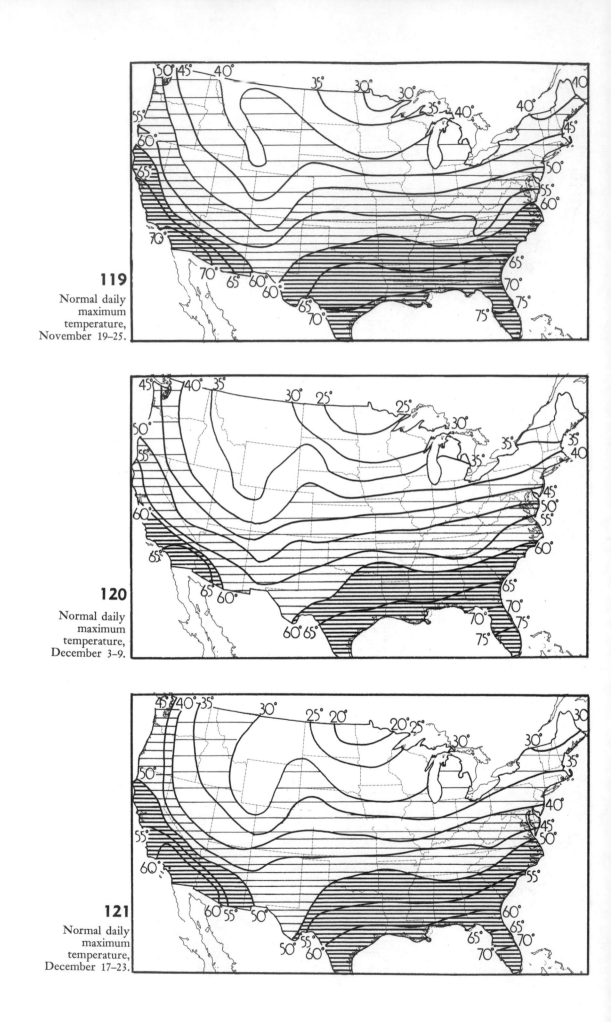

119

Normal daily
maximum
temperature,
November 19–25.

120

Normal daily
maximum
temperature,
December 3–9.

121

Normal daily
maximum
temperature,
December 17–23.

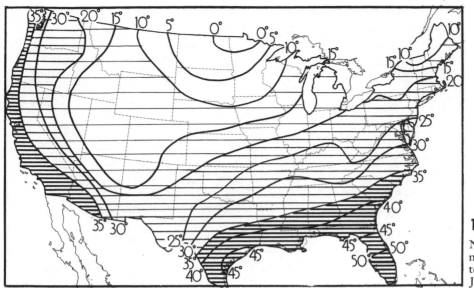

122

Normal daily
minimum
temperature,
January 1–7.

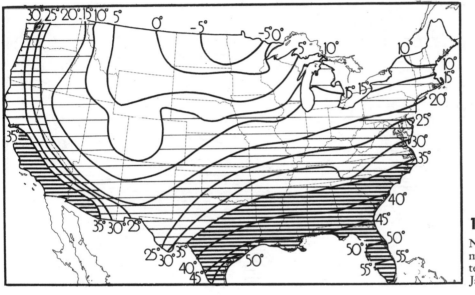

123

Normal daily
minimum
temperature,
January 15–21.

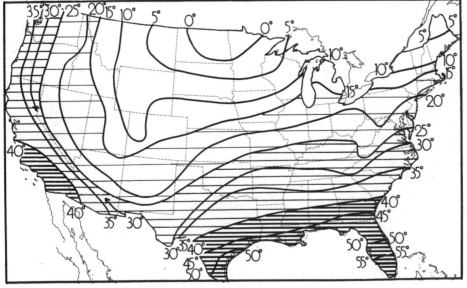

124

Normal daily
minimum
temperature,
January 28–
February 4.

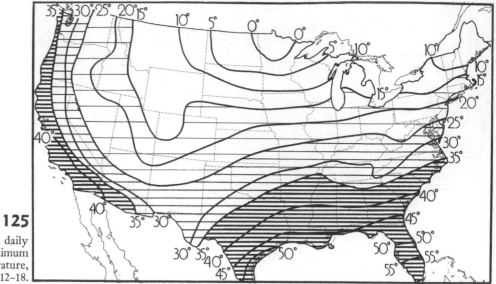

125

Normal daily
minimum
temperature,
February 12–18.

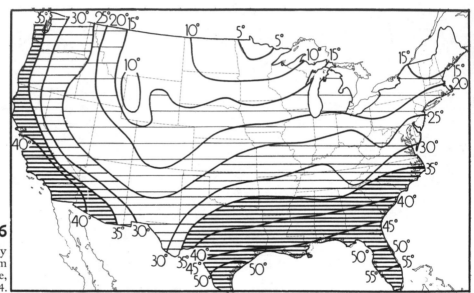

126

Normal daily
minimum
temperature,
February 26–March 4.

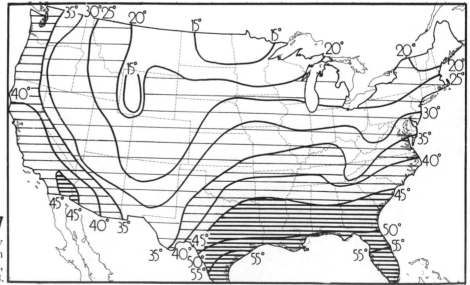

127

Normal daily
minimum
temperature,
March 12–18.

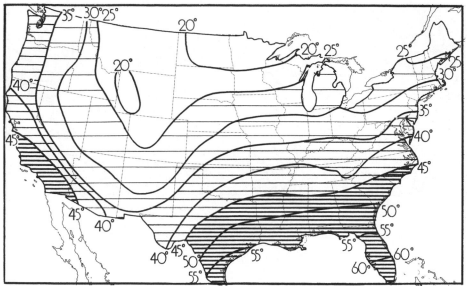

128

Normal daily
minimum
temperature,
March 26–April 1.

129

Normal daily
minimum
temperature,
April 9–15.

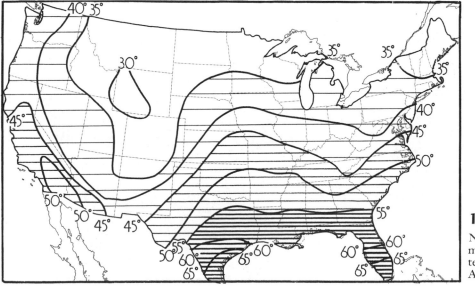

130

Normal daily
minimum
temperature,
April 23–29.

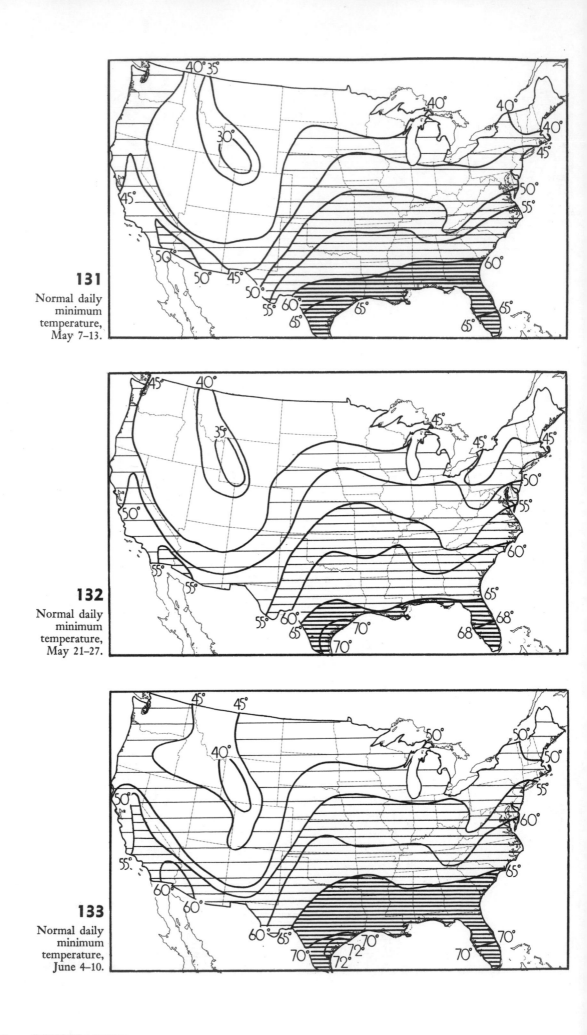

131
Normal daily
minimum
temperature,
May 7–13.

132
Normal daily
minimum
temperature,
May 21–27.

133
Normal daily
minimum
temperature,
June 4–10.

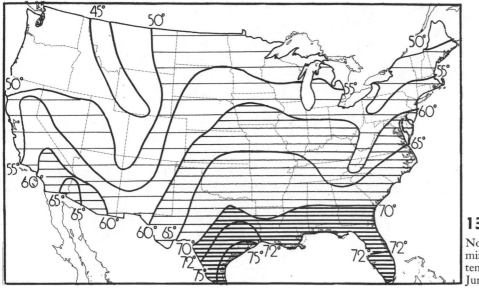

134
Normal daily
minimum
temperature,
June 18–24.

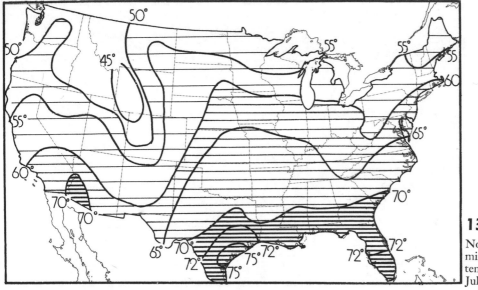

135
Normal daily
minimum
temperature,
July 2–8.

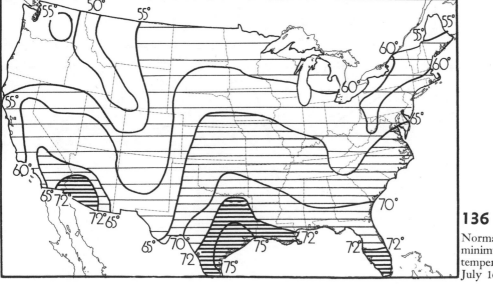

136
Normal daily
minimum
temperature,
July 16–22.

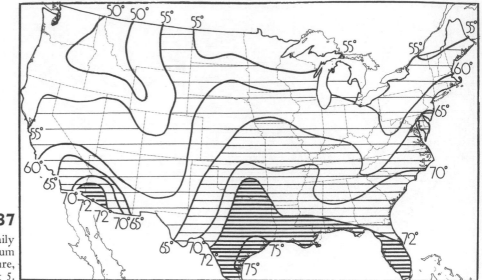

137
Normal daily
minimum
temperature,
July 30–August 5.

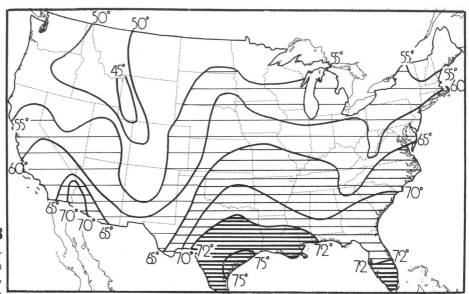

138
Normal daily
minimum
temperature,
August 13–19.

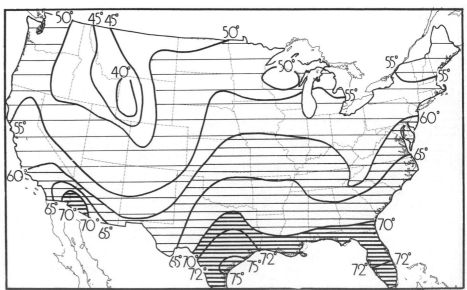

139
Normal daily
minimum
temperature,
August 27–
September 2.

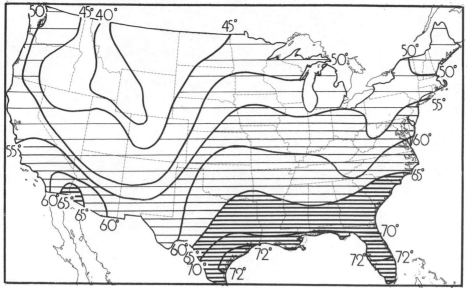

140

Normal daily
minimum
temperature,
September 10–16.

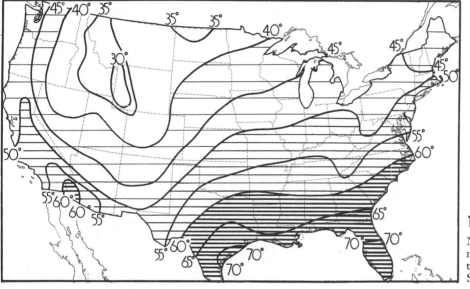

141

Normal daily
minimum
temperature,
September 24–30.

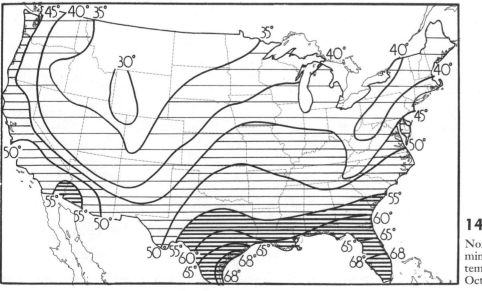

142

Normal daily
minimum
temperature,
October 8–14.

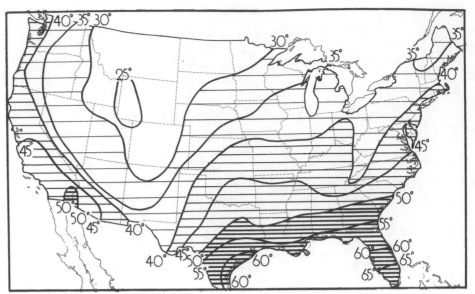

143

Normal daily
minimum
temperature,
October 22–28.

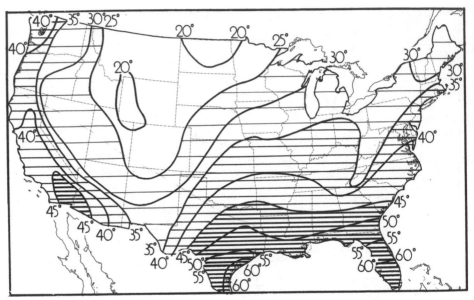

144

Normal daily
minimum
temperature,
November 5–11.

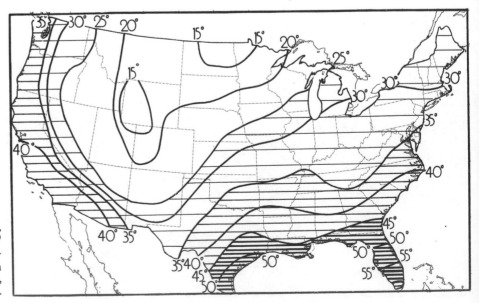

145

Normal daily
minimum
temperature,
November 19–25.

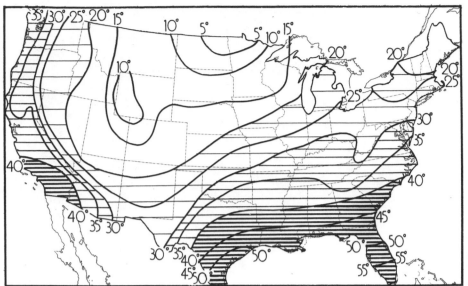

146

Normal daily
minimum
temperature,
December 3–9.

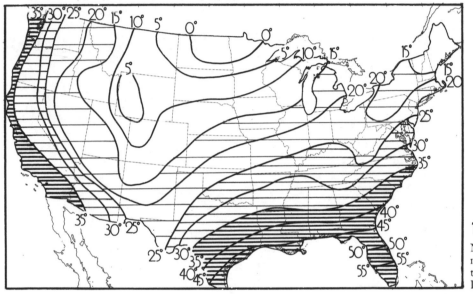

147

Normal daily
minimum
temperature,
December 17–23.

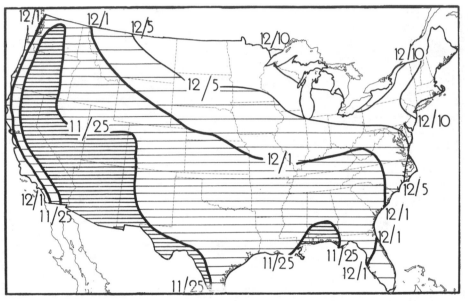

148

Date when the
coldest quarter of
the year (winter)
normally begins.

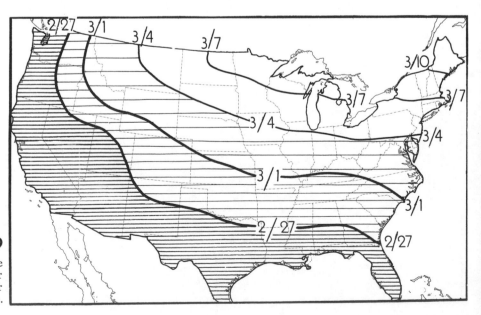

149

Date when the
spring quarter
of the year
normally begins.

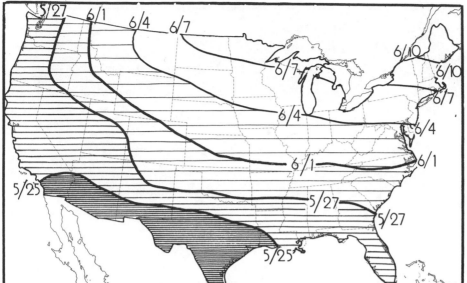

150

Date when the warmest quarter of the year (summer) normally begins.

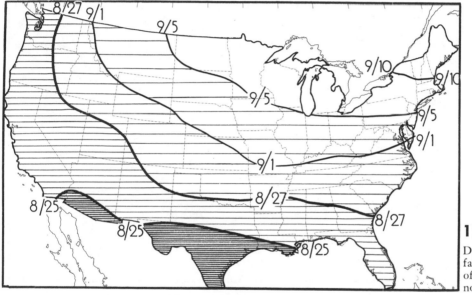

151

Date when the fall quarter of the year normally begins.

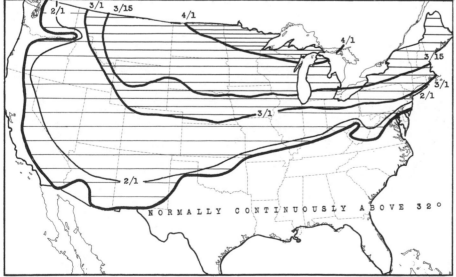

NORMALLY CONTINUOUSLY ABOVE 32°

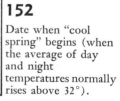

152

Date when "cool spring" begins (when the average of day and night temperatures normally rises above 32°).

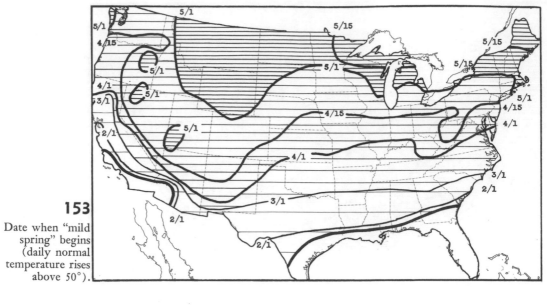

153

Date when "mild spring" begins (daily normal temperature rises above 50°).

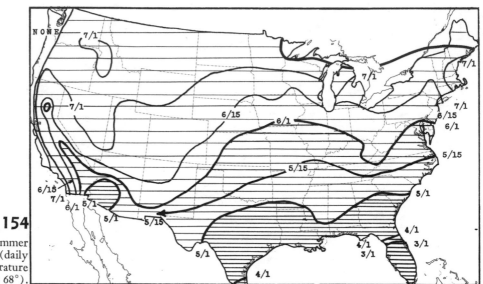

154

Date when summer begins (daily normal temperature rises to 68°).

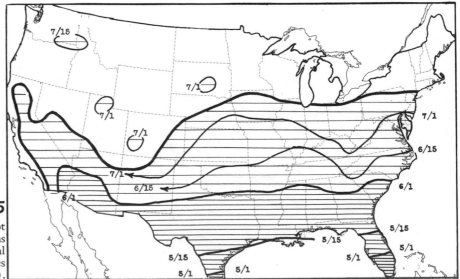

155

Date when "hot summer" begins (daily normal temperature rises to 75°).

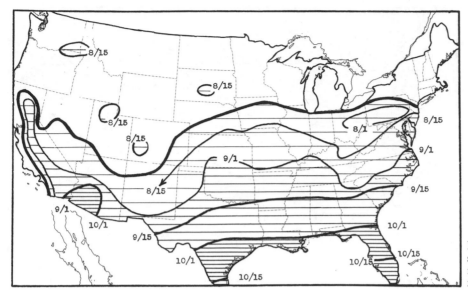

156

Date when "hot summer" ends (daily normal temperature falls to 75°).

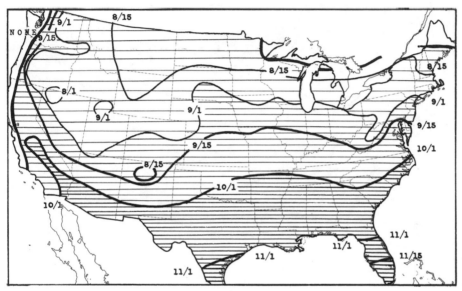

157

Date when "mild fall" begins (daily normal temperature falls to 68°).

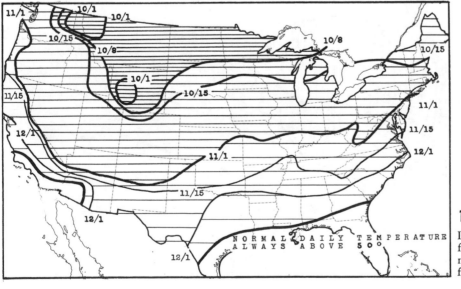

158

Date when "cool fall" begins (daily normal temperature falls to 50°).

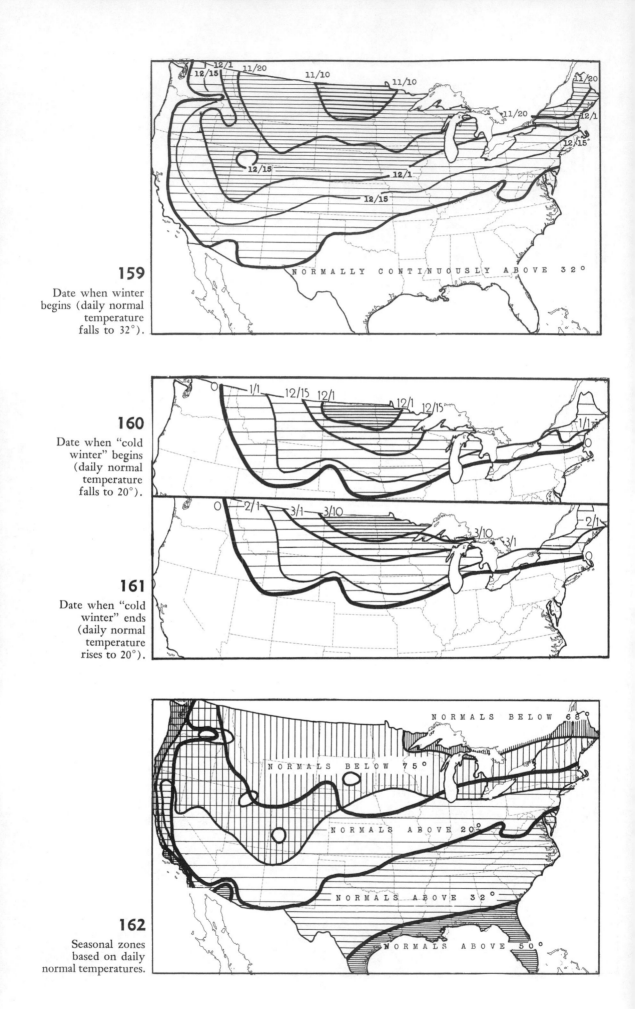

159

Date when winter begins (daily normal temperature falls to 32°).

160

Date when "cold winter" begins (daily normal temperature falls to 20°).

161

Date when "cold winter" ends (daily normal temperature rises to 20°).

162

Seasonal zones based on daily normal temperatures.

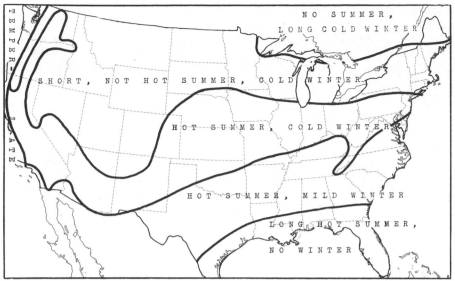

163

Seasonal zones on the basis of selected temperatures: summer, daily mean temperature above 68°; winter, daily mean temperature below 32°.

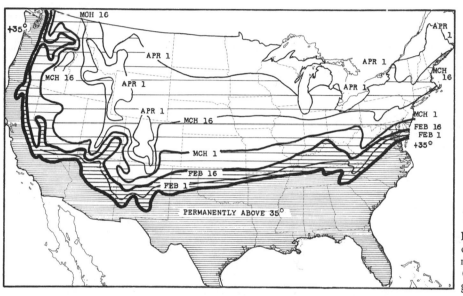

164

Date when mean daily temperature normally rises to 35° (some vegetative growth begins).

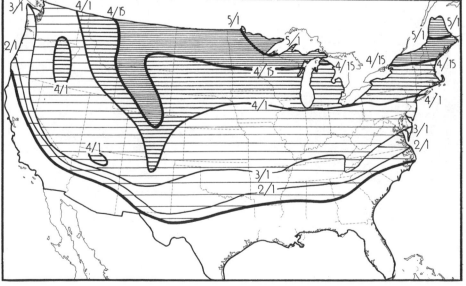

165

Date when mean daily temperature normally rises to 43° (rapid plant growth begins).

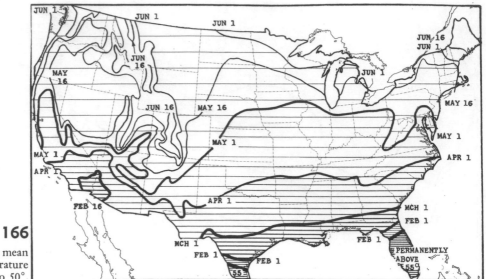

166

Date when mean daily temperature normally rises to 50°.

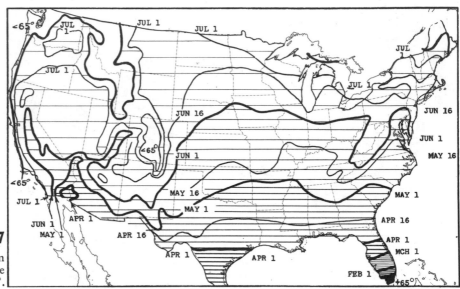

167

Date when mean daily temperature normally rises to 65°.

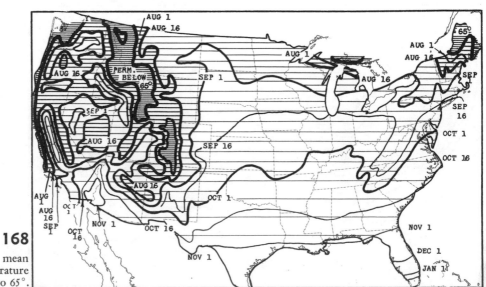

168

Date when mean daily temperature normally falls to 65°.

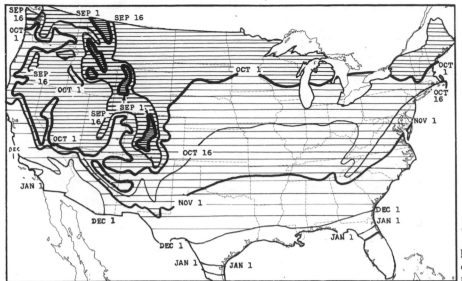

169

Date when mean daily temperature normally falls to 55°.

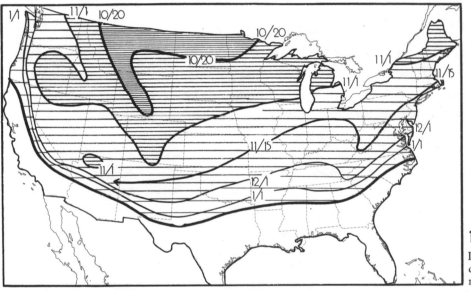
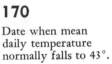

170

Date when mean daily temperature normally falls to 43°.

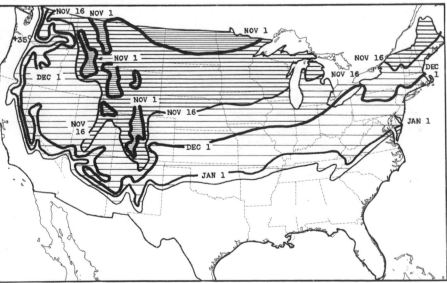

171

Date when mean daily temperature normally falls to 35° (vegetative growth largely ceases).

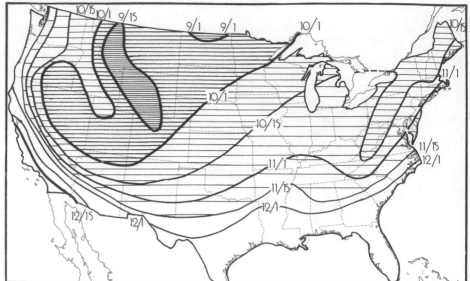

172

Date when the increasing probability of frost in fall reaches 10 percent.

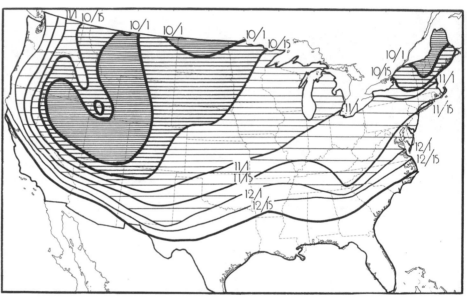

173

Date when the increasing probability of frost in fall reaches 25 percent.

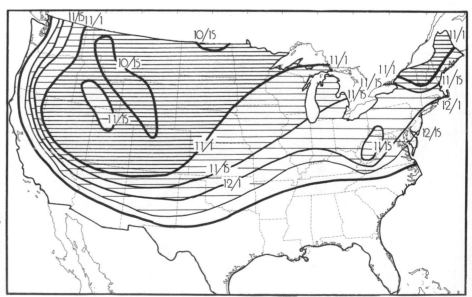

174

Date when the increasing probability of frost in fall reaches 50 percent.

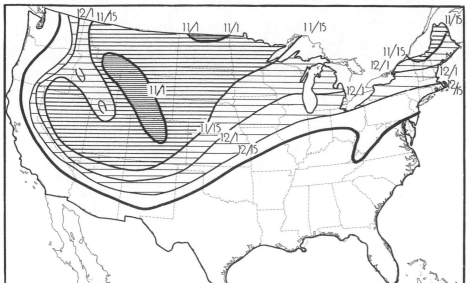

175

Date when the increasing probability of frost in fall reaches 75 percent.

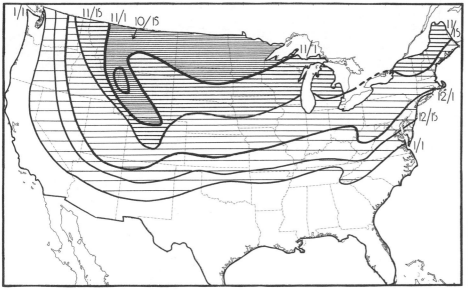

176

Date when the increasing probability of freezing temperatures throughout the day reaches 10 percent.

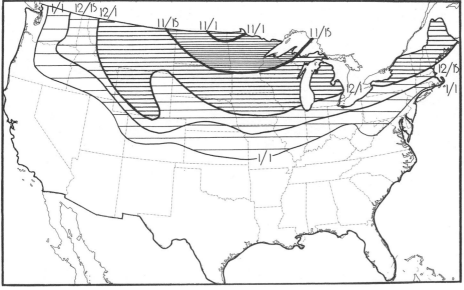

177

Date when the increasing probability of freezing temperatures throughout the day reaches 25 percent.

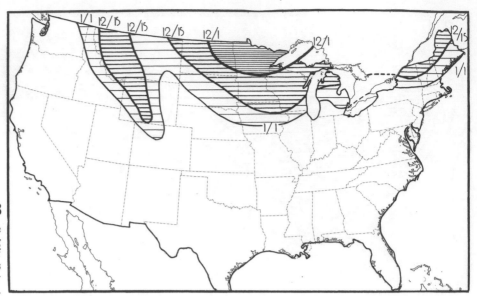

178

Date when the increasing probability of freezing temperatures throughout the day reaches 50 percent.

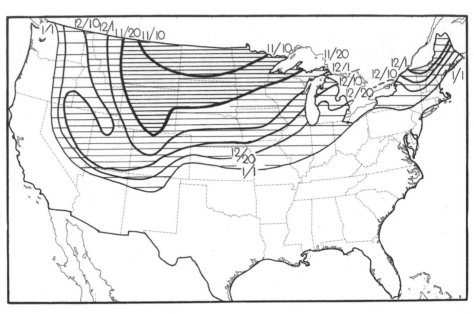

179

Date when the increasing probability of a minimum temperature of 0° or lower reaches 5 percent.

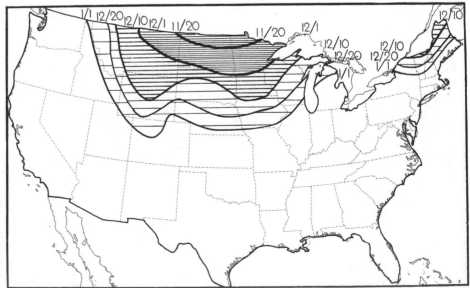

180

Date when the increasing probability of a minimum temperature of 0° or lower reaches 15 percent.

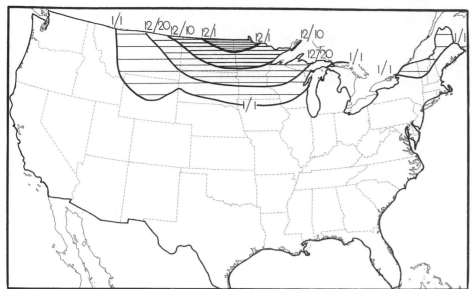

181

Date when the
increasing
probability of a
minimum temperature
of 0° or lower
reaches 25 percent.

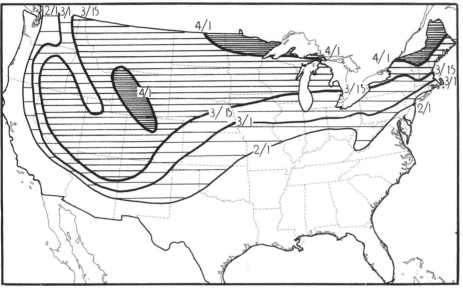

182

Date when the
decreasing
probability of frost
in spring reaches
75 percent.

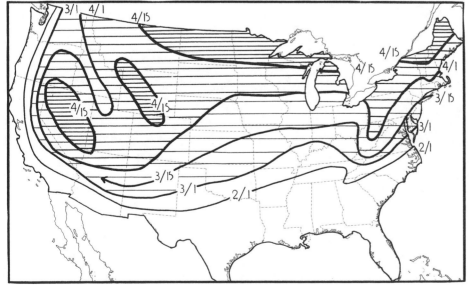

183

Date when the
decreasing
probability of frost
in spring reaches
50 percent.

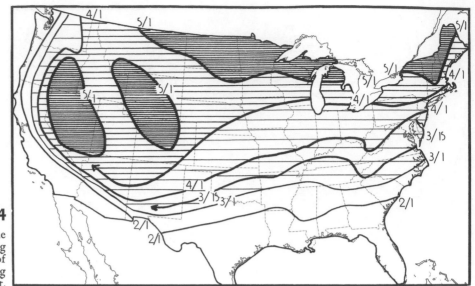

184

Date when the decreasing probability of frost in spring reaches 25 percent.

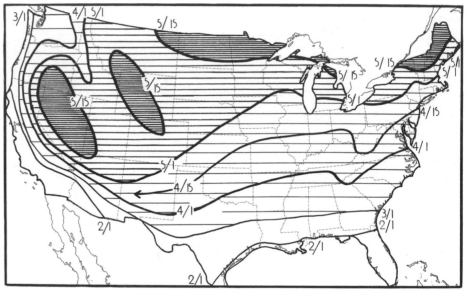

185

Date when the decreasing probability of frost in spring reaches 10 percent.

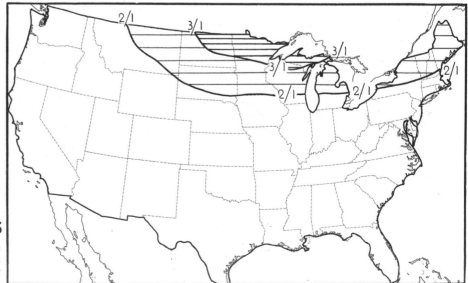

186

Date when the daily maximum temperature normally rises to 30°.

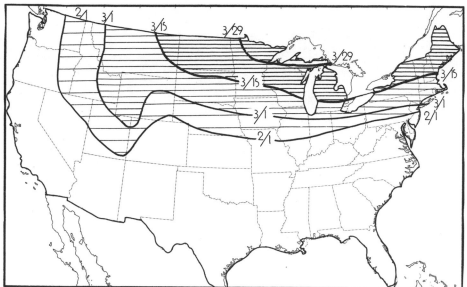

187

Date when the daily maximum temperature normally rises to 40°.

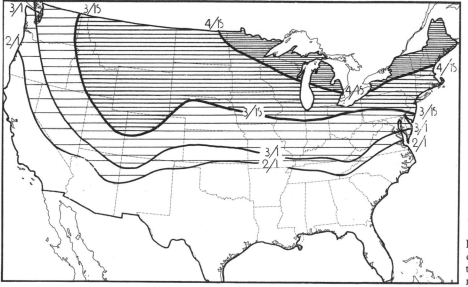

188

Date when the daily maximum temperature normally rises to 50°.

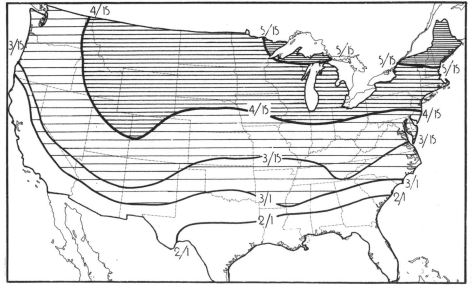

189

Date when the daily maximum temperature normally rises to 60°.

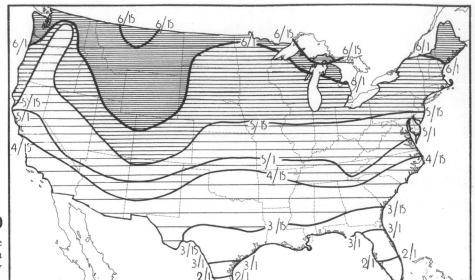

190

Date when the
daily maximum
temperature normally
rises to 70°.

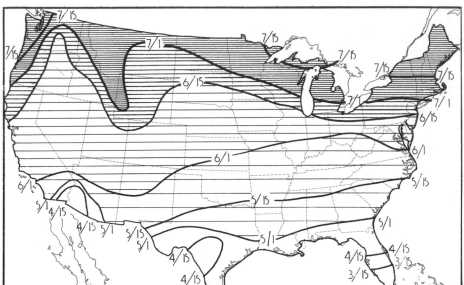

191

Date when the
daily maximum
temperature normally
rises to 80°.

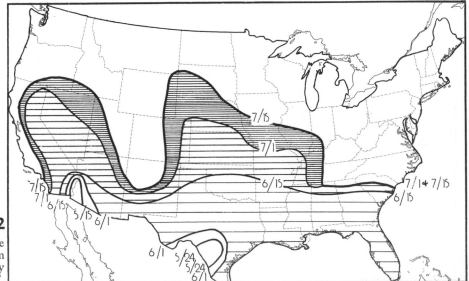

192

Date when the
daily maximum
temperature normally
rises to 90°.

Figures 172–185 present frost prospects differently. "Frost" means either that frost is observed or that the minimum temperature is 32°. "Killing frost" means that vegetation is seen to be killed, or, in the absence of a record of it, that the shelter temperature was appreciably below 32°; sometimes 30° is used, sometimes 28°.

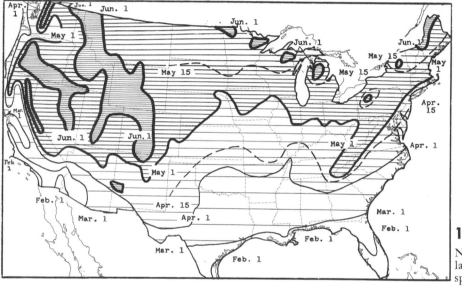

193

Normal date of the last killing frost in spring, 1899–1938.

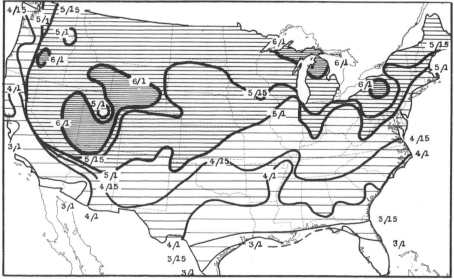

194

The last killing frost came after these dates in only one-fifth of the springs, 1899–1938.

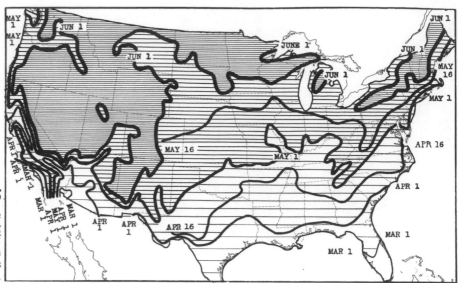

195

Date when the decreasing probability of killing frost in spring reaches 10 percent.

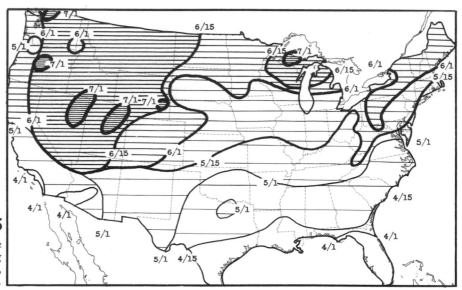

196

Date of the latest killing frost in spring, 1899–1938.

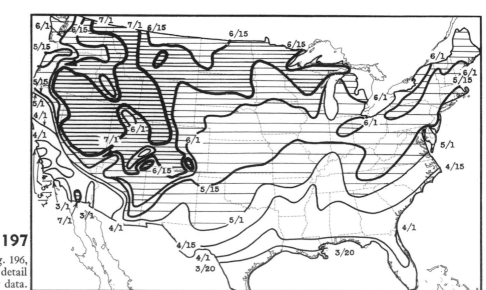

197

Same as Fig. 196, but in more detail and with older data.

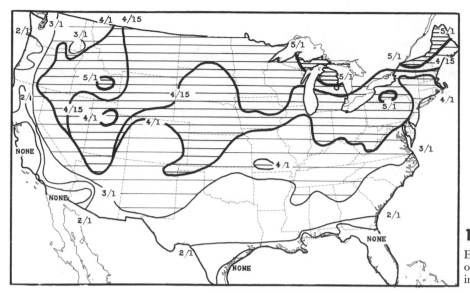

198

Earliest occurrence of last killing frost in spring, 1899–1938.

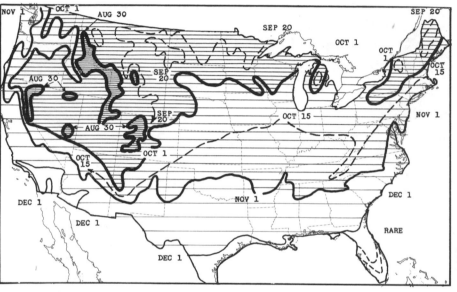

199

Normal date of first killing frost in fall, 1899–1938.

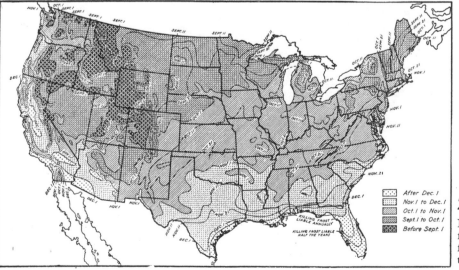

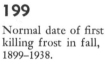

⋯	After Dec. 1
	Nov. 1 to Dec. 1
╱	Oct. 1 to Nov. 1
▨	Sept. 1 to Oct. 1
▩	Before Sept. 1

200

Normal date of first killing frost in fall, in more detail than Fig. 199.

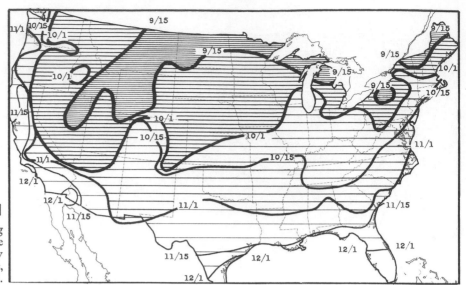

201

The first killing frost came before these dates in only one-fifth of the falls, 1899–1938.

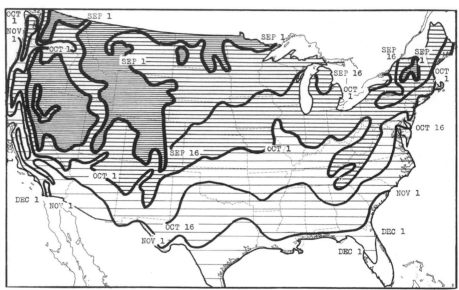

202

The first killing frost came before these dates in only one-tenth of the falls, 1899–1938.

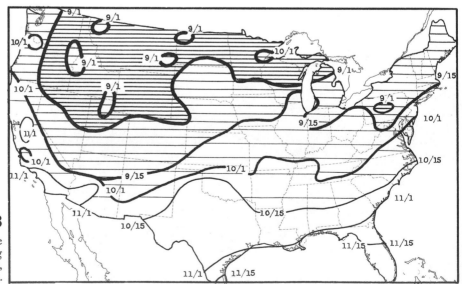

203

Date of the earliest killing frost in fall, 1899–1938.

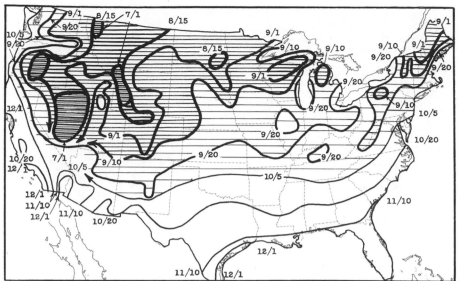

204

Same as Fig. 203, but in more detail and with older data.

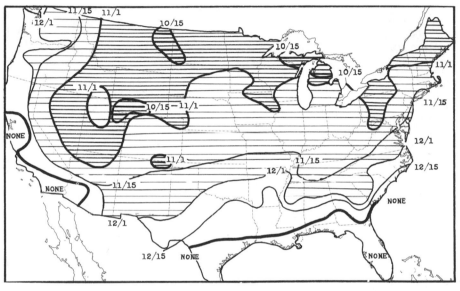

205

Latest occurrence of first killing frost in fall, 1899–1938.

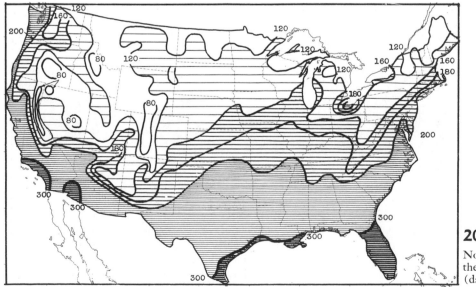

206

Normal length of the frost-free season (days).

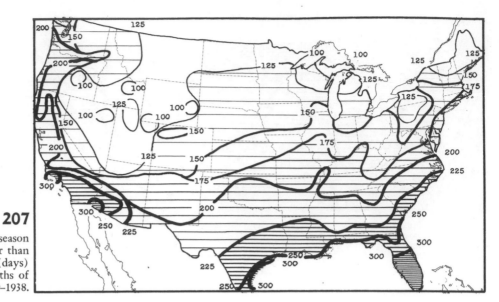

207

The frost-free season was longer than here shown (days) in four-fifths of the years, 1899–1938.

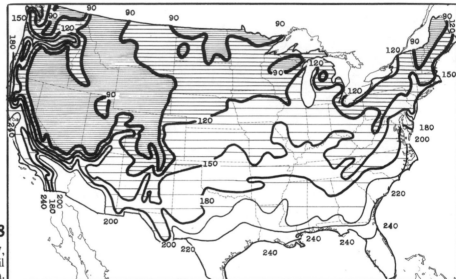

208

Same as Fig. 207, but in more detail and with older data.

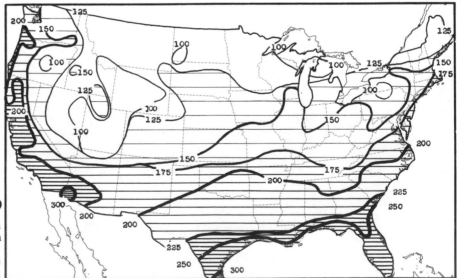

209

The frost-free season was longer than here shown (days) in nine-tenths of the years, 1899–1938.

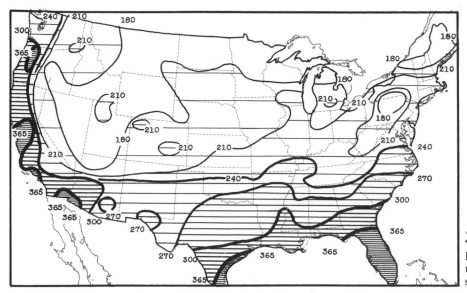

210

Duration (days) of the longest frost-free season, 1899–1938.

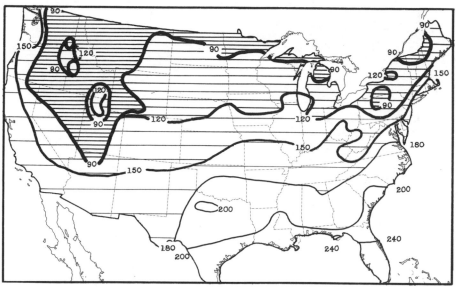

211

Duration (days) of the shortest frost-free season, 1899–1938.

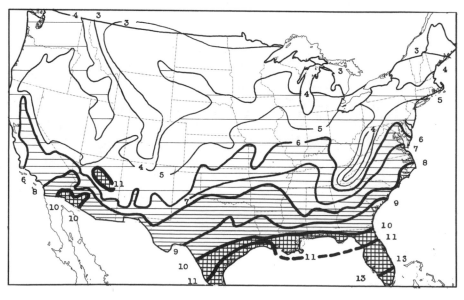

212

Average "temperature efficiency" for plant growth on days when the mean daily temperature is 40°F or higher (after Livingston and Shreve, Plate 39).

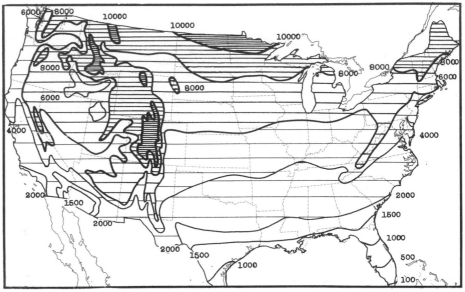

213

Annual normal total of (cold) degree days (sum of amounts by which the normal temperature of each day cooler than 65° is less than 65°).

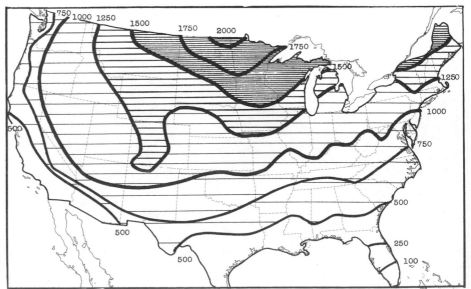

214

Normal number of (cold) degree days in January.

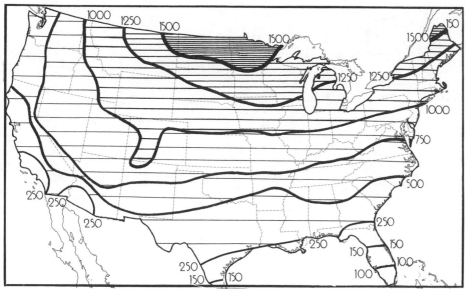

215
Normal number of (cold) degree days in February.

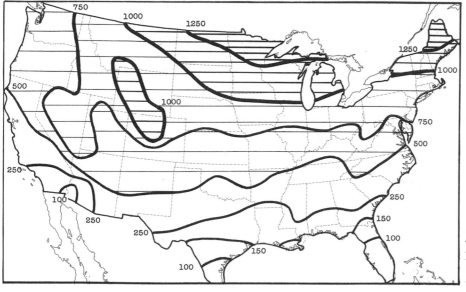
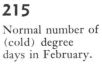

216
Normal number of (cold) degree days in March.

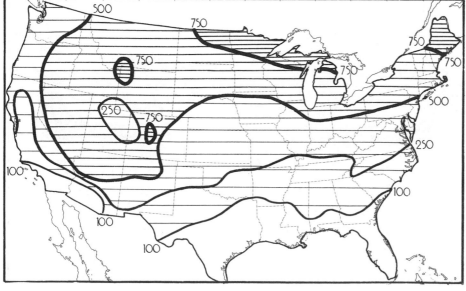
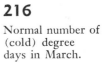

217
Normal number of (cold) degree days in April.

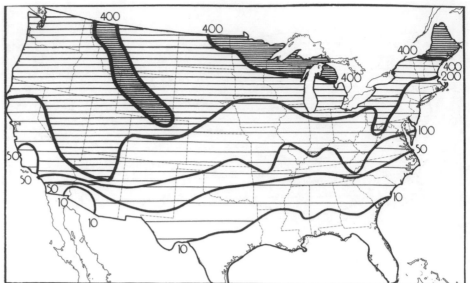

218

Normal number of (cold) degree days in May.

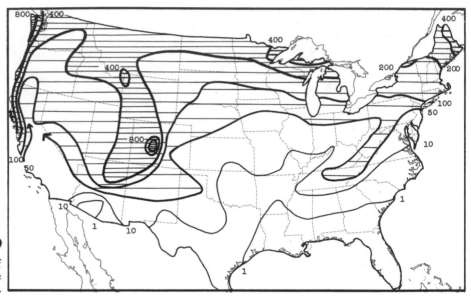

219

Normal number of (cold) degree days in summer.

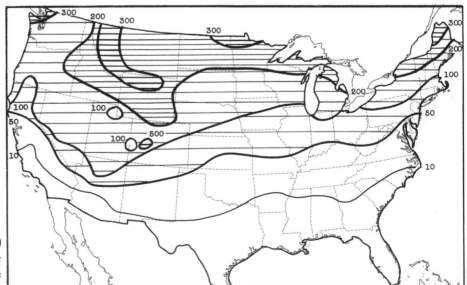

220

Normal number of (cold) degree days in September.

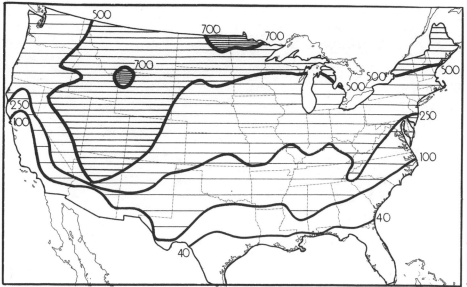

221

Normal number of (cold) degree days in October.

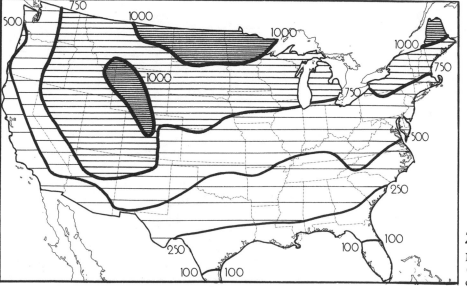
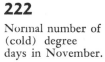

222

Normal number of (cold) degree days in November.

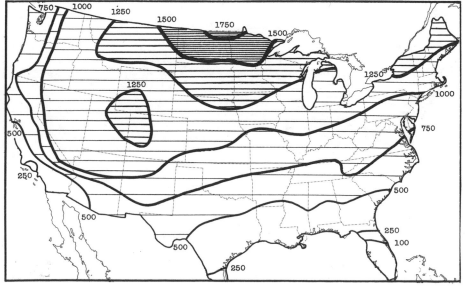

223

Normal number of (cold) degree days in December.

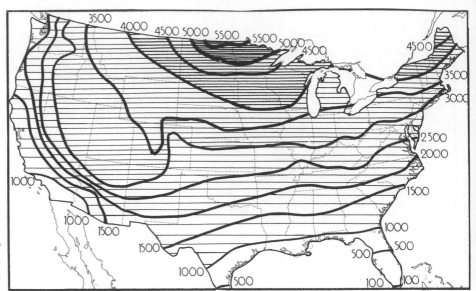

224

Normal number
of (cold) degree days
in winter.

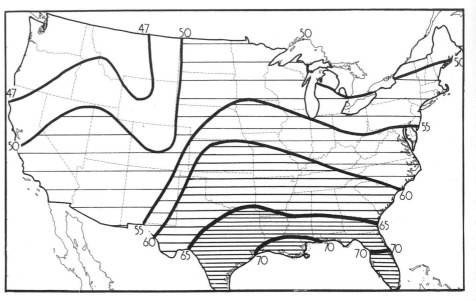

225

Normal percentage
of the year's
(cold) degree days
that occur in winter.

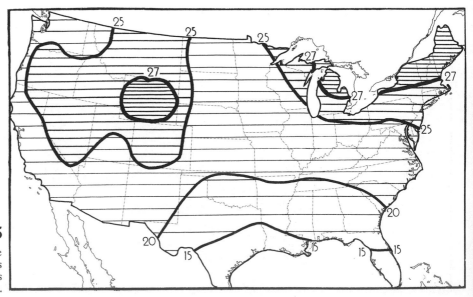

226

Normal percentage
of the year's
(cold) degree days
that occur in spring.

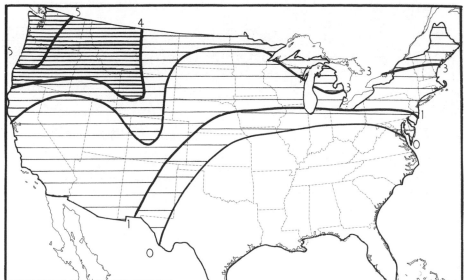

227

Normal percentage
of the year's
(cold) degree days
that occur in summer.

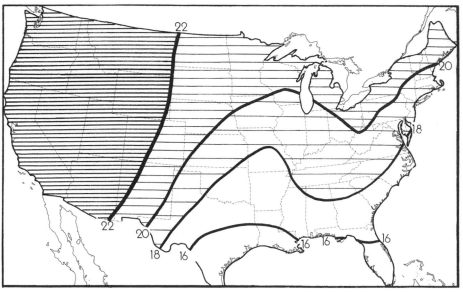

228

Normal percentage
of the year's
(cold) degree days
that occur in fall.

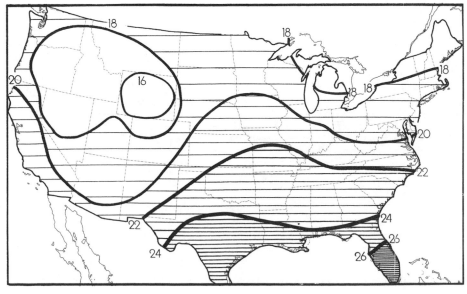

229

Normal percentage
of the year's
(cold) degree days
that occur in January.

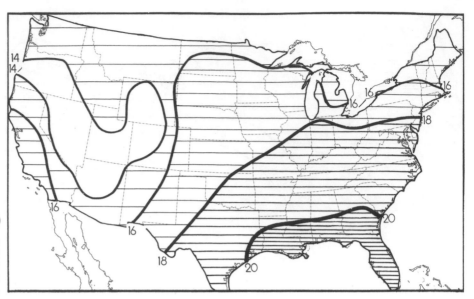

230

Normal percentage
of the year's
(cold) degree days
that occur in
February.

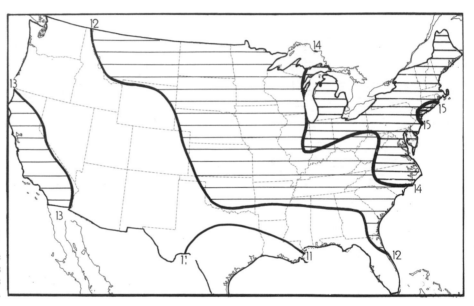

231

Normal percentage
of the year's
(cold) degree days
that occur in March.

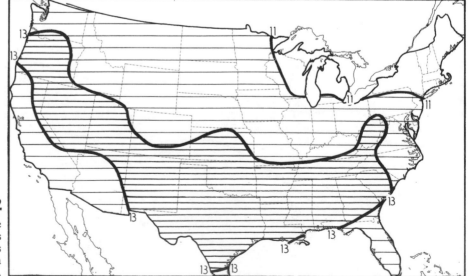

232

Normal percentage
of the year's
(cold) degree days
that occur in
November.

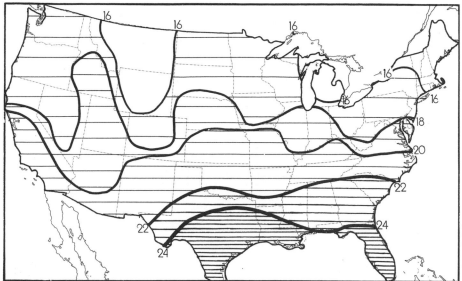

233

Normal percentage of the year's (cold) degree days that occur in December.

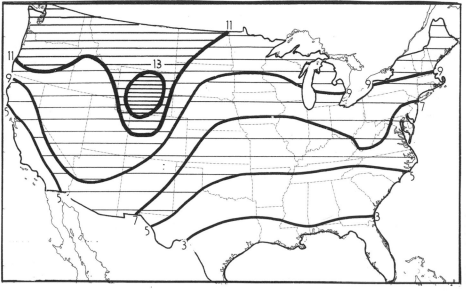

234

Normal percentage of the year's (cold) degree days that occur before November.

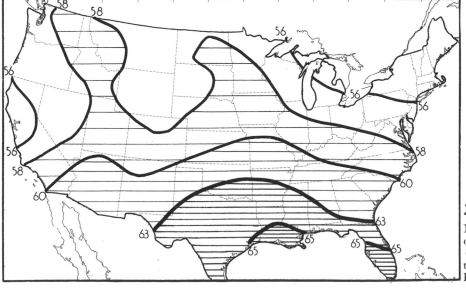

235

Normal percentage of the year's (cold) degree days that occur before February.

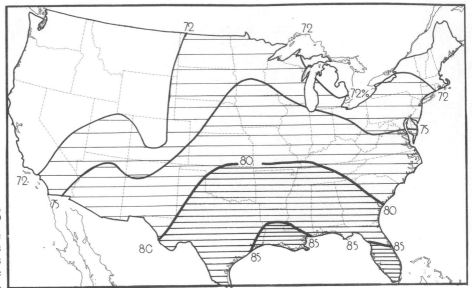

236

Normal percentage of the year's (cold) degree days that occur before March.

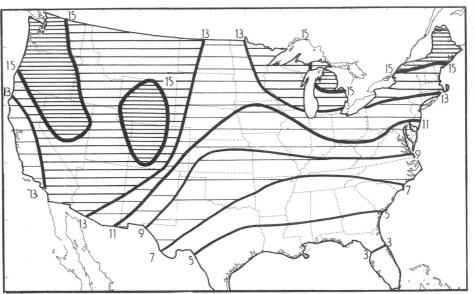

237

Normal percentage of the year's (cold) degree days that occur after March.

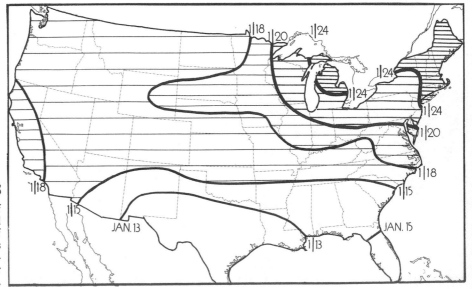

238

Date when half the normal annual number of (cold) degree days is reached (mid-season date for fuel requirement).

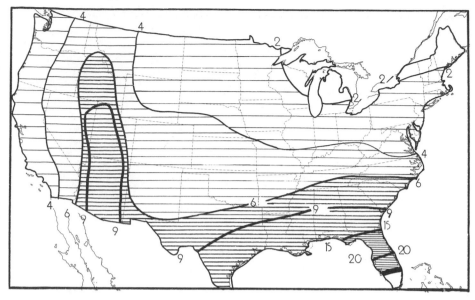

239

Average percentage by which those cold seasons that are colder than normal, as measured in (cold) degree-day units, depart from normal (based on 1927–1941).

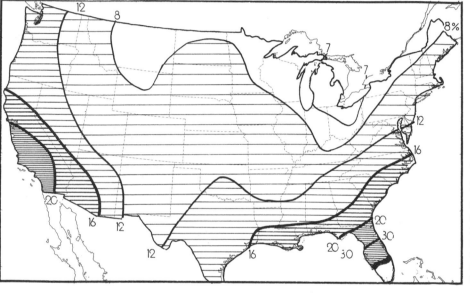

240

Average percentage by which those mild seasons that are less cold than normal, as measured in (cold) degree-day units, depart from normal (based on 1927–1941).

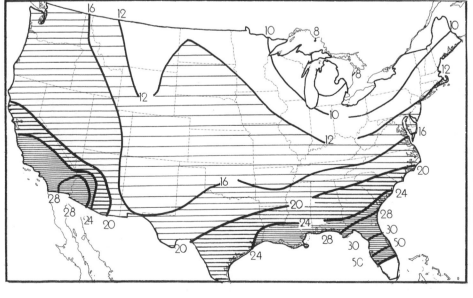

241

Average percentage range in annual totals of (cold) degree days (sums of average upward and downward departures from normal, 1927–1941).

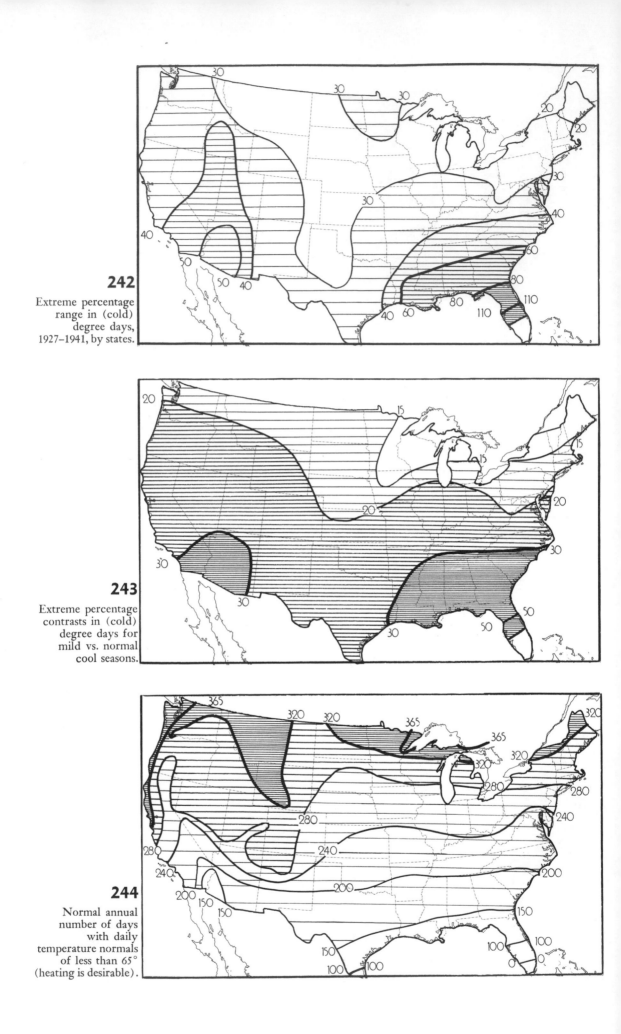

242

Extreme percentage range in (cold) degree days, 1927–1941, by states.

243

Extreme percentage contrasts in (cold) degree days for mild vs. normal cool seasons.

244

Normal annual number of days with daily temperature normals of less than 65° (heating is desirable).

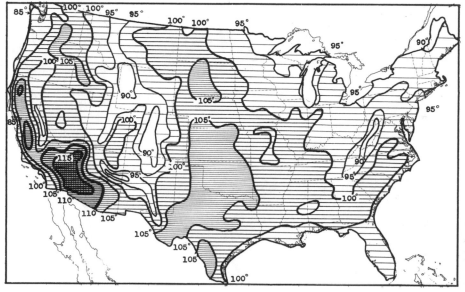

245

Highest temperature (°F) experienced in a normal year.

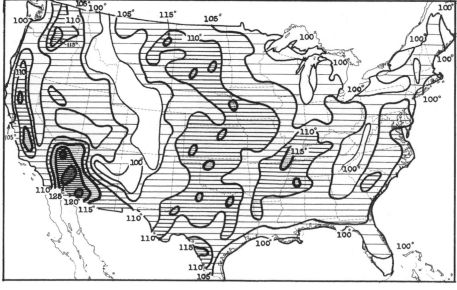

246

Highest temperature officially recorded, 1899–1938.

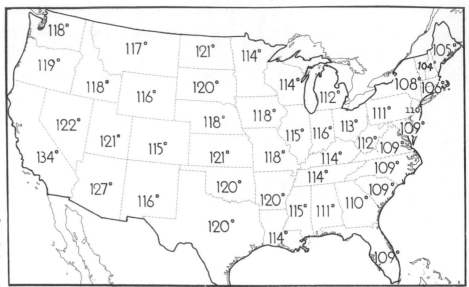

247

Highest summer temperature officially recorded in each state to 1945.

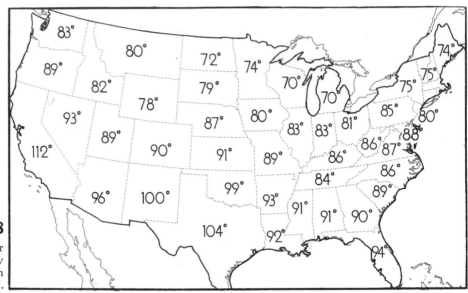

248

Highest winter temperature officially recorded in each state to 1945.

SOME SUPPLEMENTARY DATA ON HIGH TEMPERATURES

Figures 247 and 248 use U. S. Weather Bureau data assembled by J. R. Theaman of Indianapolis in his 1946 brochure, "Maximum temperatures for North America." The following supplementary data, therefrom, are of interest.

The national record of 134° was established on July 10, 1913, at the coöperative Weather Bureau Station Greenland Ranch, Inyo County, in Death Valley, California. On July 5–14 the maxima were 126°, 125°, 127°, 128°, 129°, 134°,129°, 130°, 131°, 127°. The record for August 19–30, 1924, is scarcely less spectacular. The minima were above 100° for 12 nights; on the 25th and 26th, they were 110°. The maxima for August 20–31 were above 110° each day and exceeded 119° on the 25th to 29th. The highest was 124°

on the 27th. In 1928 there were 159 days on which the temperature reached 100° or higher. For all of July 1917, the daily average of maximum and minimum temperatures was 107.2°. In the coolest year of 1912–1944, there were 111 days with maxima of 100° or higher. Presumably somewhat higher temperatures are experienced lower in Death Valley; Greenland Ranch Station is located 98 ft. above the valley floor. The thermometer shelter is situated in an irrigated alfalfa field, cooler because of the evaporation from the crop and ground than are areas in the nearby barren desert.

Temperatures in the Imperial Valley in extreme southeastern California bordering the Salton Sea (240 ft. below sea level) are occasionally only slightly less high than in Death Valley. Two stations have records of 130°; five others, records of 125–129°.

In southwestern Arizona, the record of 127° was established at Parker on July 7, 1905, on the Colorado River, where 126° was experienced on June 9, 1908, and on August 6, 1905. Nearby Mohawk and Maricopa have also had 126°.

East of the Rocky Mountains, the highest recorded summer temperatures are in the western plains, a dozen stations from Texas to North Dakota having records of 120°, mostly on July 18, 1936, or August 12, 1936.

East of the Mississippi River, the highest records are 116° at Collegeville near Rensselaer, northwestern Indiana, July 14, 1936; 115° at Greenville, Illinois, on July 12, 1936; and 115° at Holly Springs, Mississippi, on July 29, 1936. On the Atlantic Coast, Pennsylvania has had 111°; New Jersey and Georgia, 110°.

During the winter months (Fig. 248) the national record is 112° at Salton, California, January 21, 1896. Next come 104° at Fort Ringgold, Texas, February 26, 1902; 101° at Eagle Pass, Texas, February 21, 1917; 100° at Carlsbad, New Mexico, February 24, 1904; 99° at Arapaho, Oklahoma, February 24, 1918.

During the spring months, 124° was recorded at Salton, California, May 27, 1896; 121° at Aztec, Arizona, May 18, 1910; 118° at Volcano Springs, California, April 25, 1898; 115° at Fort McIntosh, Texas, May 7, 1927; 114° at Logan, Nevada, May 17, 1910; 113° at Redfield, South Dakota, May 30, 1934.

During the autumn months, 121° was reached at Greenland Ranch, California, September 7, 1932; 120° at Parker, Arizona, September 9, 1910; 117° there on October 3, 1905; 115° at Holdrege, Nebraska, September 7, 1897; 112° at Medora, North Dakota, September 3, 1912; 110° at Waukonis, Oklahoma, October 2, 1898; 105° at Ogilby, California, November 11, 1898.

The highest monthly means for July (Fig. 257) is based on the record to 1946 for each state as a whole and on an official map based on many individual stations. The following data, assembled by Theaman, supplement it significantly: Greenland Ranch, Death Valley, California, had a monthly mean of 107.2° for July 1917; Palm Springs, California, one of 104.9° for July 1894; Mohawk, Arizona, one of 104.3° for July 1899. In August, monthly means above 100° were experienced at Salton, California (107.4° in 1897), and at Ogilby, California (103.5° in 1895). June had a mean of 106.1° at Volcano Springs, California in 1896.

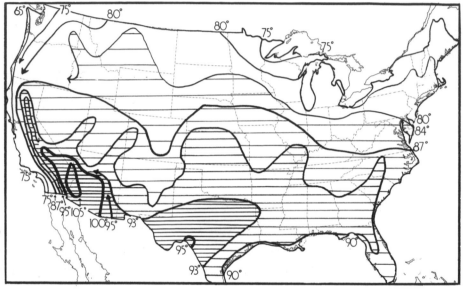

249

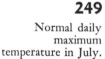

Normal daily
maximum
temperature in July.

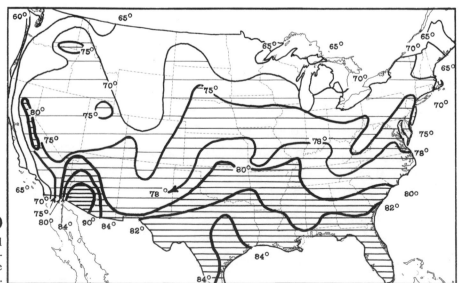

250

Highest normal
daily mean tem-
perature (average
of day and night).

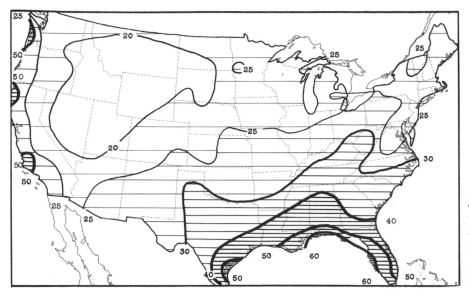

251
Normal duration of the summer's hottest weather (number of days with means within 0.5° of the maximum).

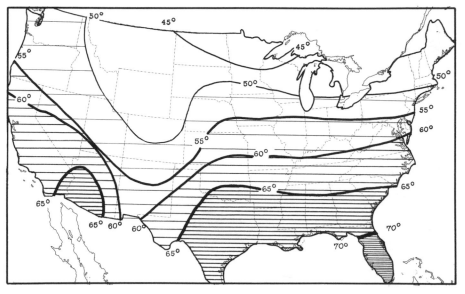

252
Highest mean annual temperature, 1902–1938 (based on state averages).

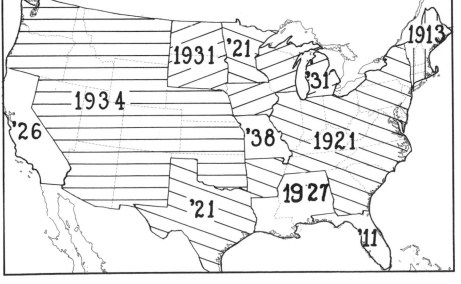

253
The warmest year, 1902–1938 (based on annual means and state averages).

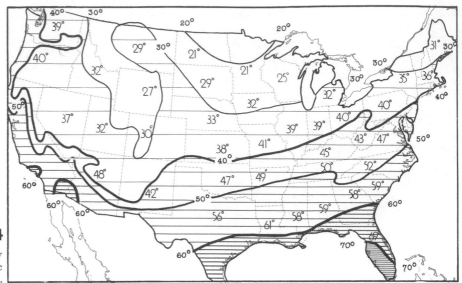

254

Highest January
mean temperature
recorded to 1945.

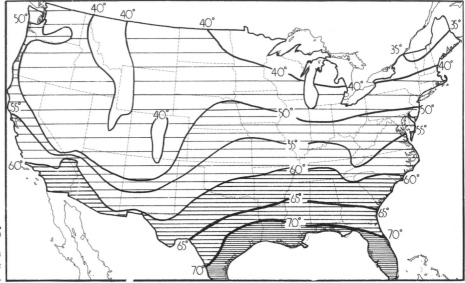

255

Highest March
mean temperature
recorded to 1945.

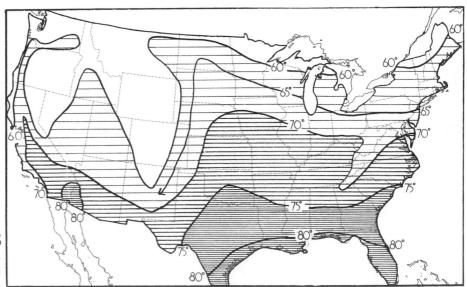

256

Highest May
mean temperature
recorded to 1945.

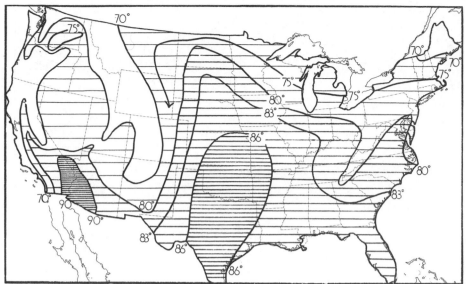

257
Highest July
mean temperature
recorded to 1945.

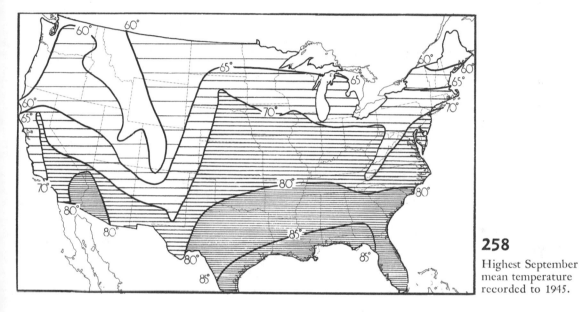

258
Highest September
mean temperature
recorded to 1945.

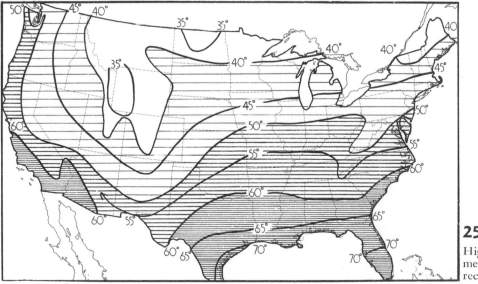

259
Highest November
mean temperature
recorded to 1945.

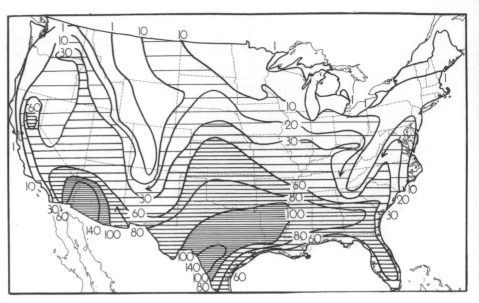

260

Normal annual
number of days
with maximum
temperatures of 90°
or higher.

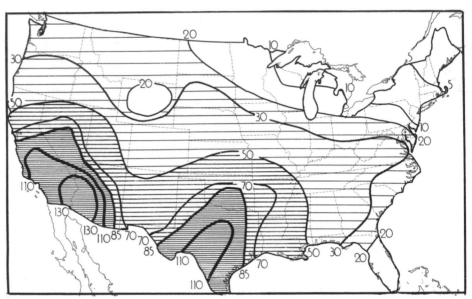

261

Number of days
with temperatures
above 100° in 1930.

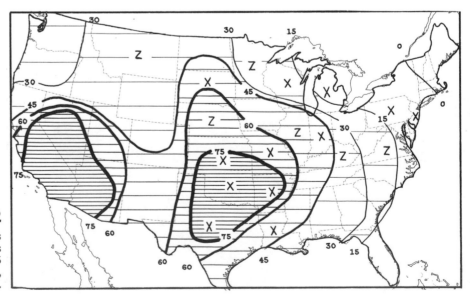

262

Number of days
with temperatures
above 100° in 1936
(X, a new record; Z,
old record equaled).

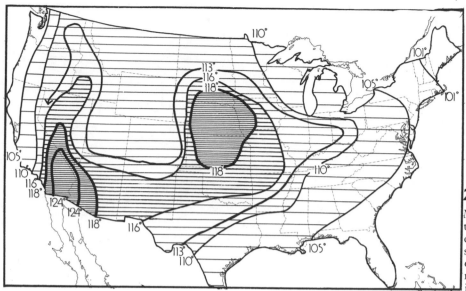

263

Maximum temperatures in an exceptionally hot summer, 1934 (based on the highest recorded in each state).

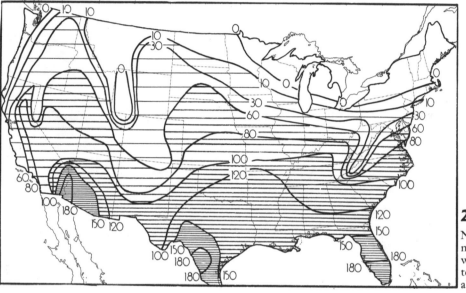

264

Normal annual number of days with daily maximum temperatures above 85°.

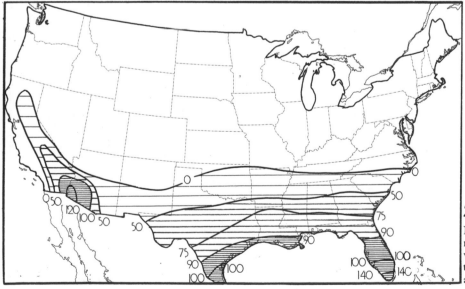

265

Normal annual number of days with daily normal temperatures above 80°.

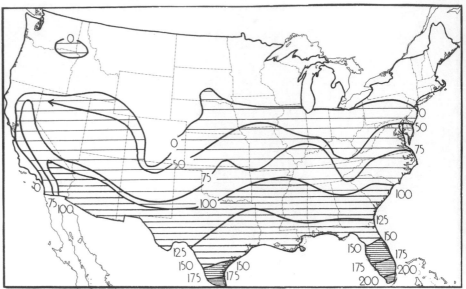

266

Normal annual number of days of very hot weather (day and night averaging 75° or higher).

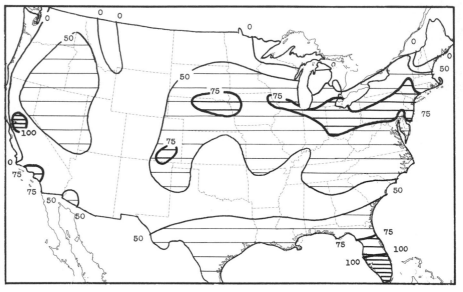

267

Normal annual number of days with normal mean temperatures of 68°–74.9°.

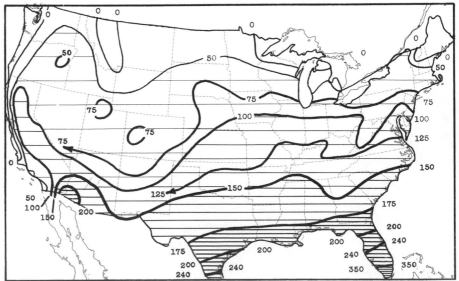

268

Normal annual number of days with normal mean temperatures of 68° or higher.

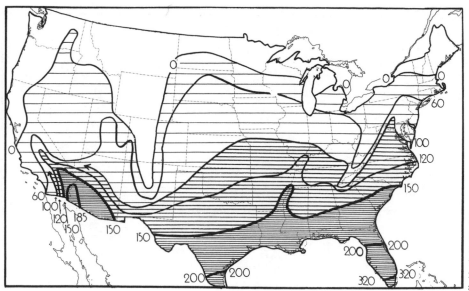

269

Normal annual number of days with daily normal mean temperatures above 70°.

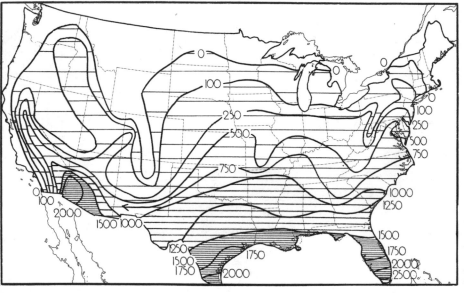

270

Annual average total of hot degree days (sum of amounts by which the normal temperature of each day with a normal temperature above 70° exceeds 70°).

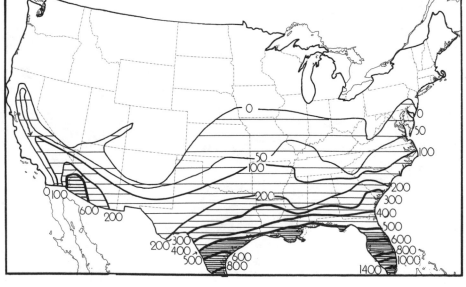

271

Normal number of hot degree days, September–May (outside of summer).

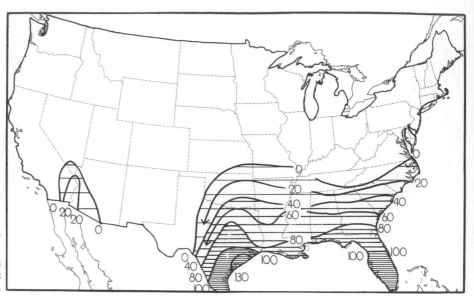

272

Normal annual
number of nights
with temperatures
constantly above 70°.

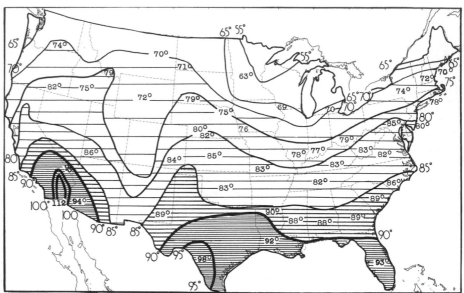

273

Highest January
temperature officially
recorded to 1945.

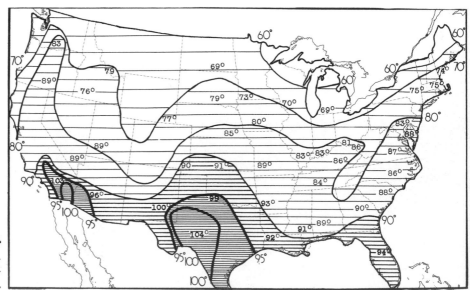

274

Highest February
temperature officially
recorded to 1945.

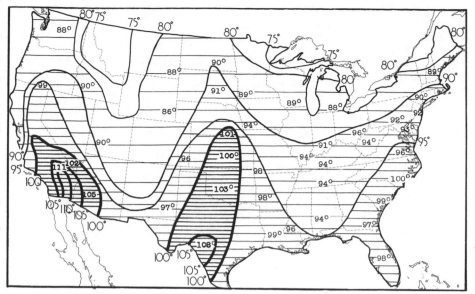

275

Highest March temperature officially recorded to 1945.

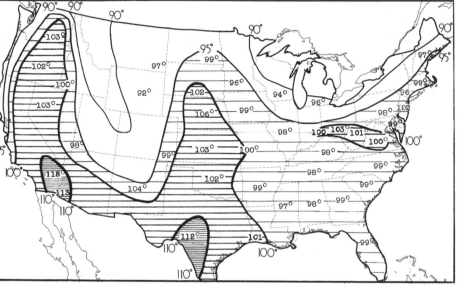

276

Highest April temperature officially recorded to 1945.

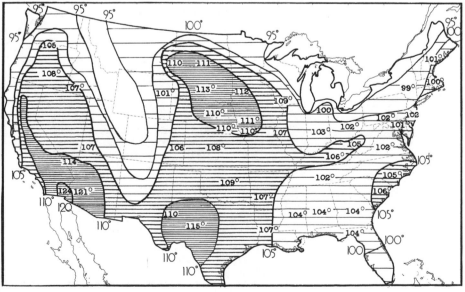

277

Highest May temperature officially recorded to 1945.

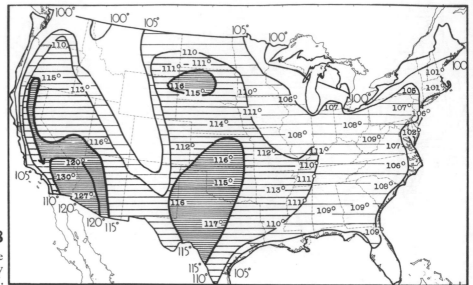

278
Highest June
temperature officially
recorded to 1945.

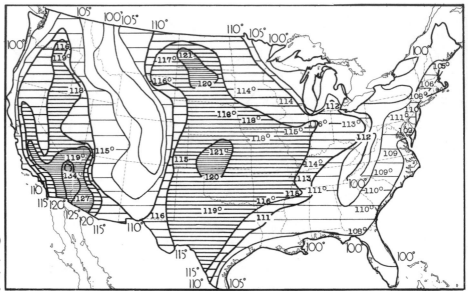

279
Highest July
temperature officially
recorded to 1945.

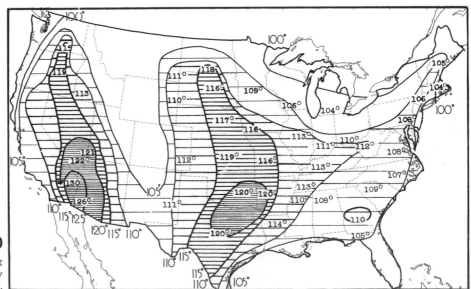

280
Highest August
temperature officially
recorded to 1945.

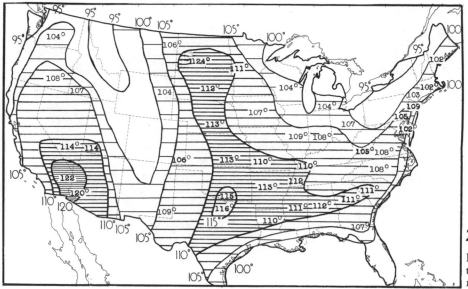

281

Highest September temperature officially recorded to 1945.

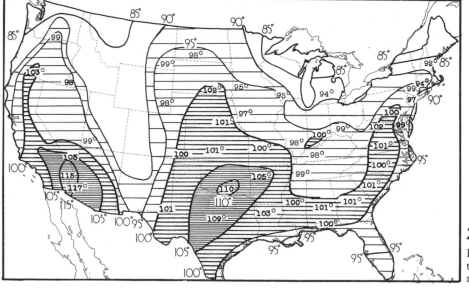

282

Highest October temperature officially recorded to 1945.

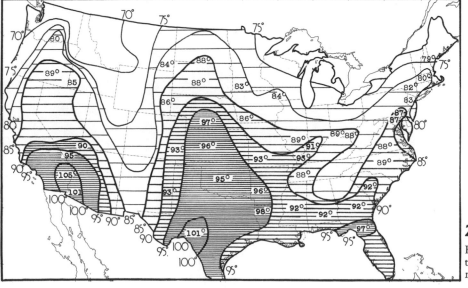

283

Highest November temperature officially recorded to 1945.

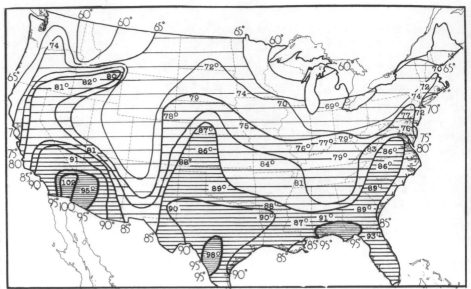

284

Highest December temperature officially recorded to 1945.

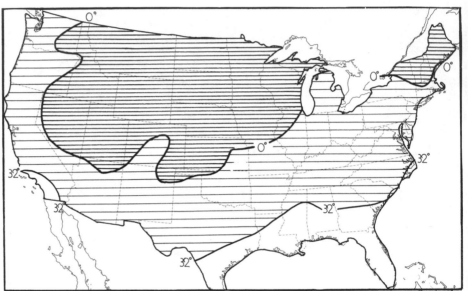

285

Southern limits of freezing and of zero in an exceptionally mild winter, 1931–1932.

9. RELATIVELY LOW TEMPERATURES; FROST FREQUENCY AND PENETRATION

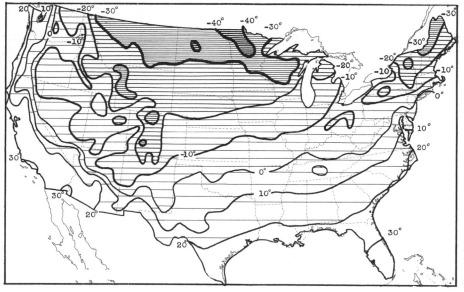

286

Lowest temperature experienced in a normal year.

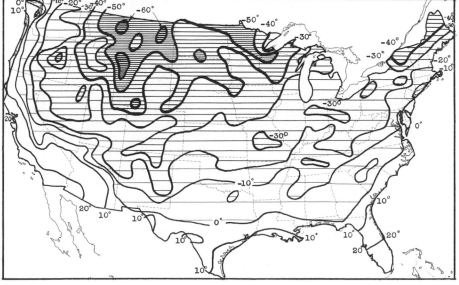

287

Lowest temperature officially recorded (1899–1938).

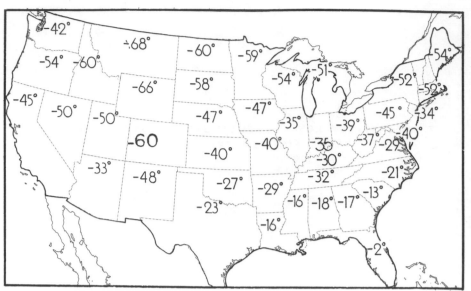

288

Lowest winter
temperature officially
recorded anywhere
in each state
(prior to 1952).

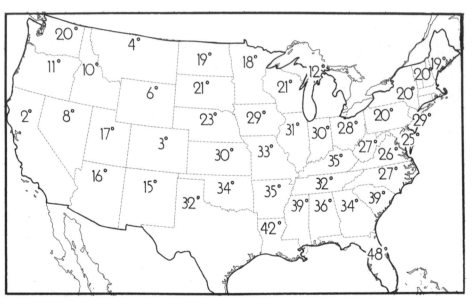

289

Lowest summer
temperature officially
recorded anywhere
in each state
(prior to 1945).

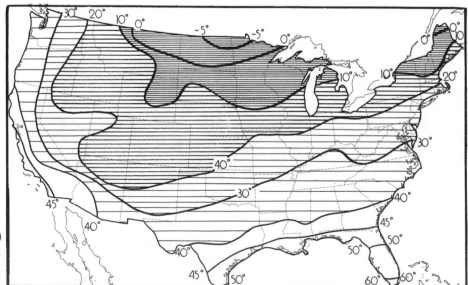

290

Normal January
daily minimum
temperature.

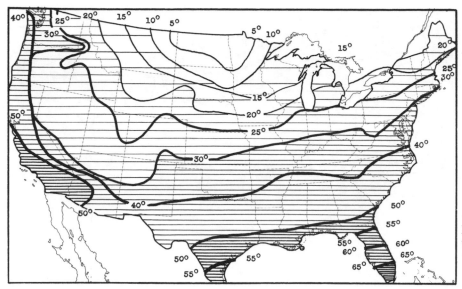

291

Lowest daily mean temperature in the smoothed annual course of temperature.

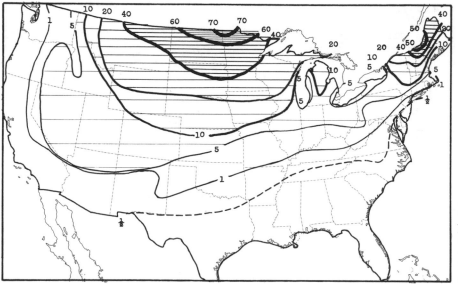

292

Normal annual number of days with minimum temperature of 0° or lower.

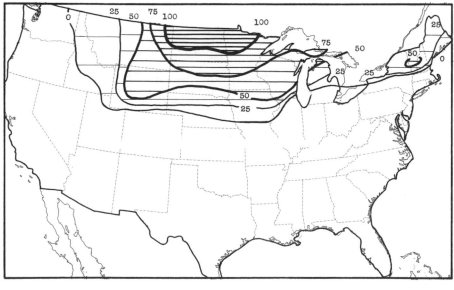

293

Normal annual number of days on which the mean temperature of the smoothed annual course of temperature is below 20°.

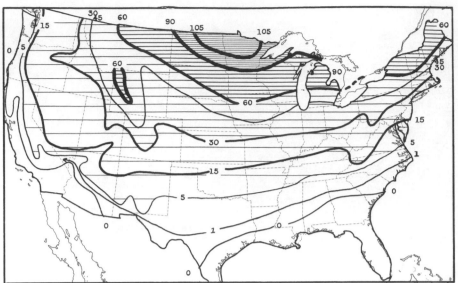

294

Normal annual number of days with temperature continuously below freezing.

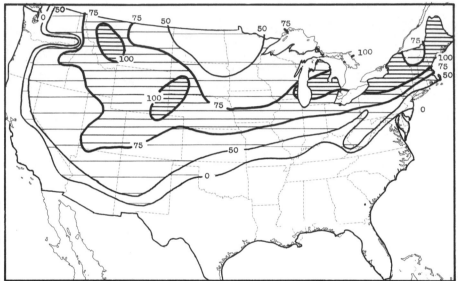

295

Normal annual number of days with normal mean temperatures of 20°–32°.

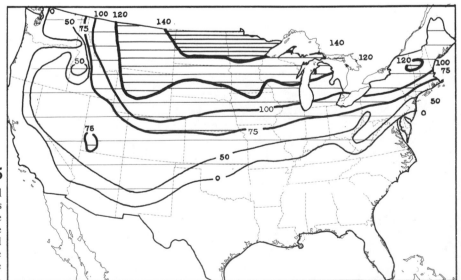

296

Normal annual number of days on which the mean temperature of the smoothed annual course of temperature is below 32°.

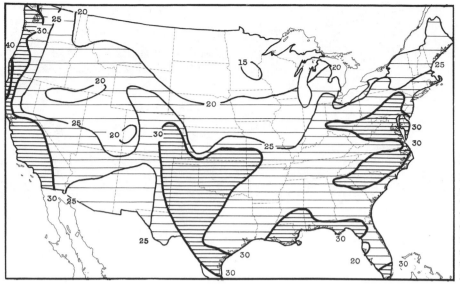

297

Normal annual number of days with normal mean temperature within 0.5° of the lowest in the smoothed annual course of temperature (shown in Fig. 291).

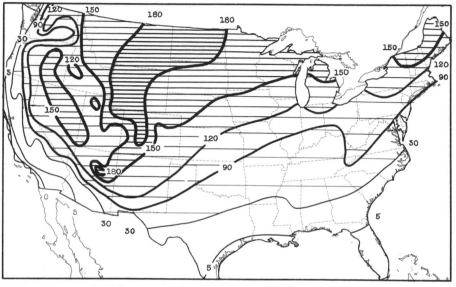

298

Normal annual number of nights with frost (minimum of 32° or lower).

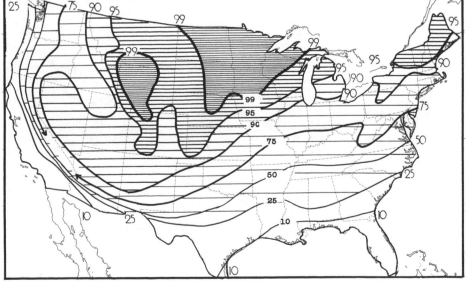

299

Percentage of nights with frost in mid-winter (January 15).

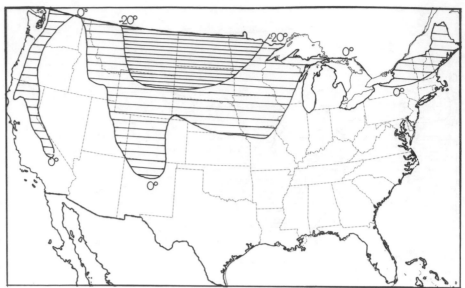

300

Areas where
January normally
has three or more
days with minimum
temperatures of
0°F, of –20°F.

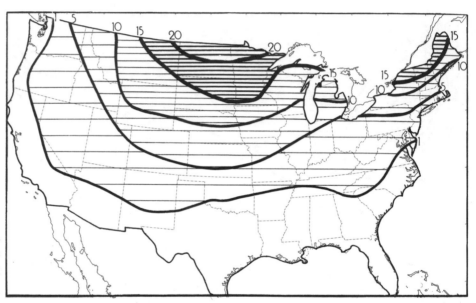

301

Normal number
of February nights
with minimum
temperature of
10° or lower.

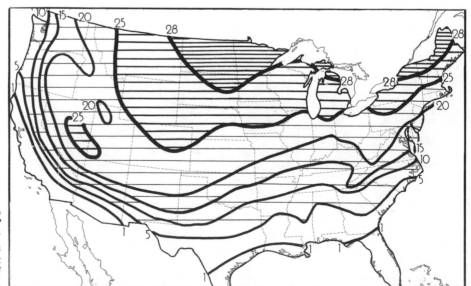

302

Normal number
of February nights
with frost
(minimum of
32° or lower).

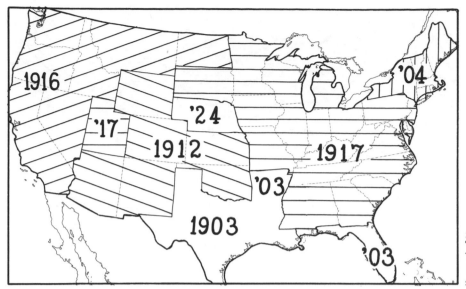

303

The coolest year, 1902–1938, based on state annual averages.

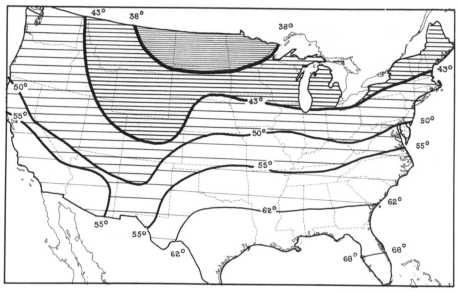

304

Lowest mean annual temperature, 1902–1938, based on state averages.

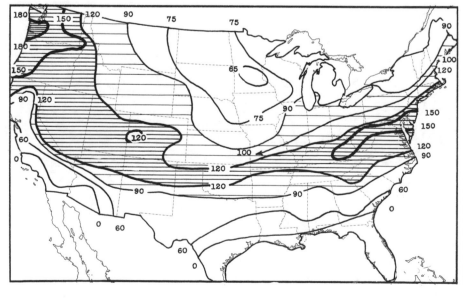

305

Normal annual number of days on which the mean temperature of the smoothed annual course of temperature is between 32° and 50°.

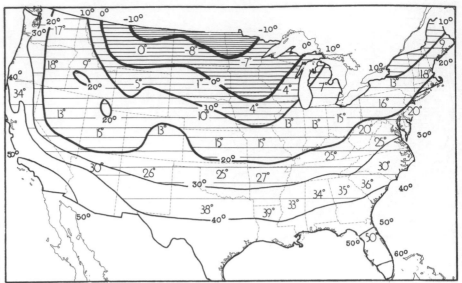

306

Lowest January
mean temperature;
state records to
1945 are shown.

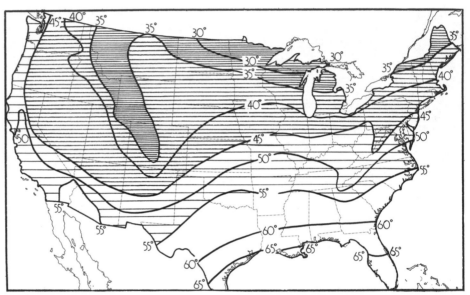

307

Lowest April
mean temperature.

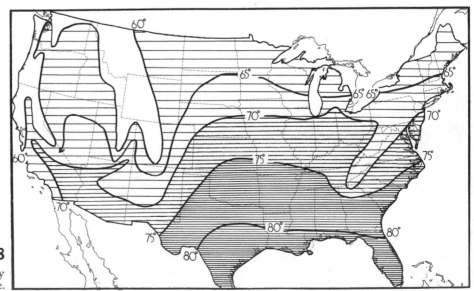

308

Lowest July
mean temperature.

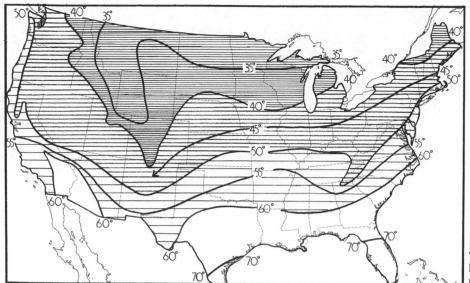

309
Lowest October
mean temperature.

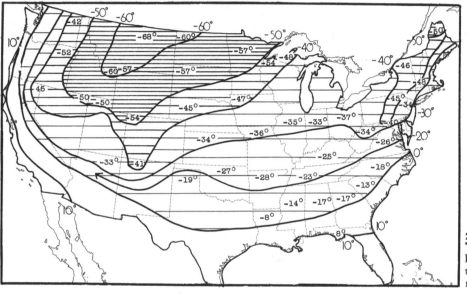

310
Lowest January
temperature officially
recorded to 1952.

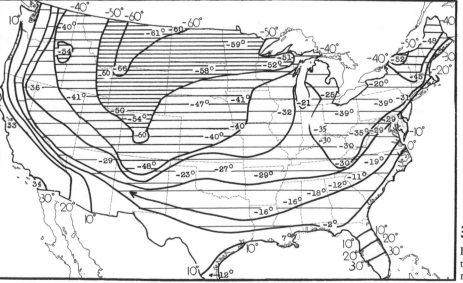

311
Lowest February
temperature officially
recorded to 1952.

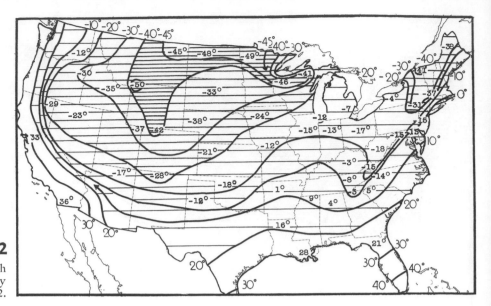

312

Lowest March
temperature officially
recorded to 1952.

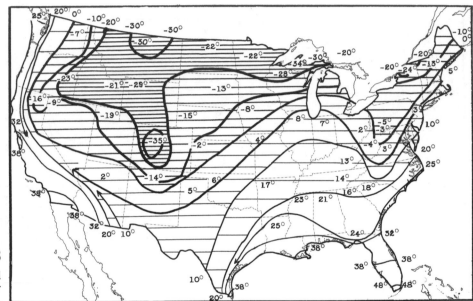

313

Lowest April
temperature officially
recorded to 1952.

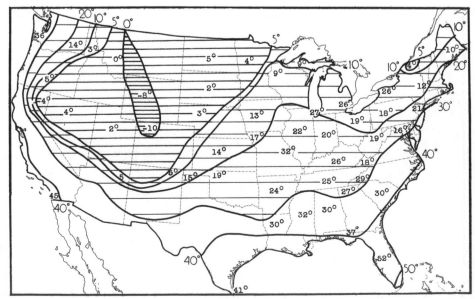

314

Lowest May
temperature officially
recorded to 1952.

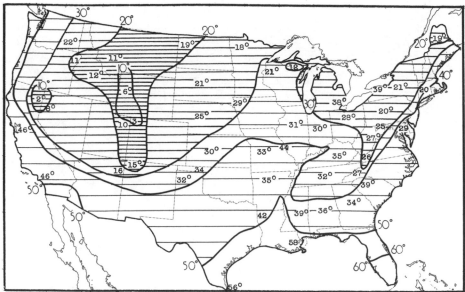

315
Lowest June
temperature officially
recorded to 1952.

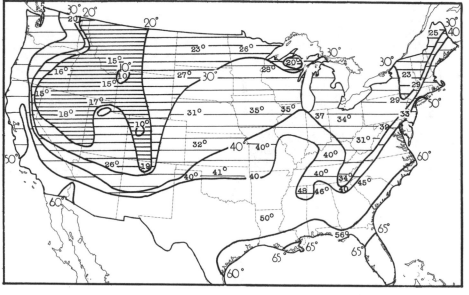

316
Lowest July
temperature officially
recorded to 1952.

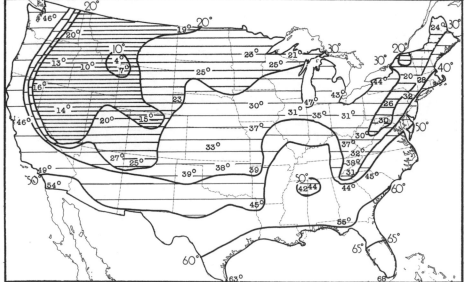

317
Lowest August
temperature officially
recorded to 1952.

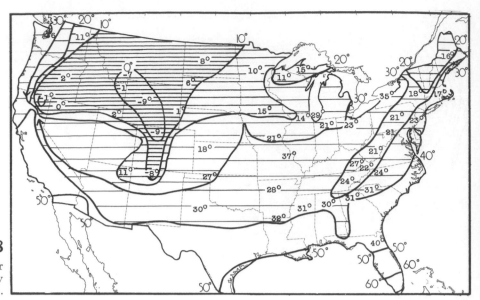

318

Lowest September temperature officially recorded to 1952.

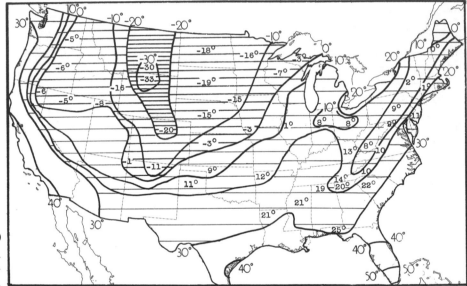

319

Lowest October temperature officially recorded to 1952.

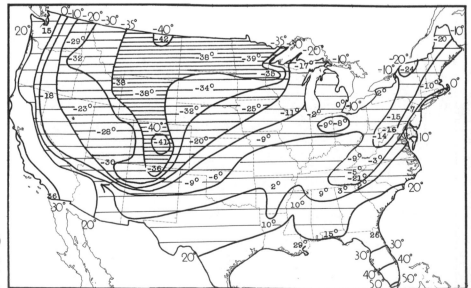

320

Lowest November temperature officially recorded to 1952.

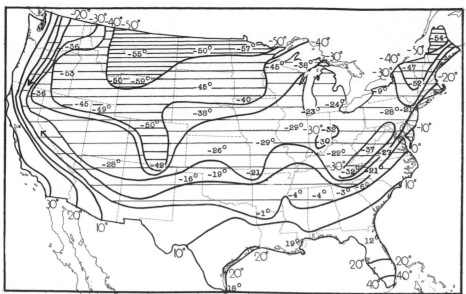

321

Lowest December temperature officially recorded to 1952.

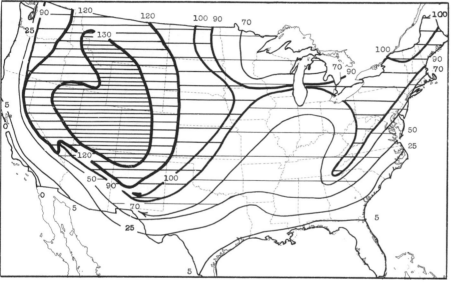

322

Average number of times per year of an alternation of freezing and thawing (based on the difference between the annual number of nights with frost and the number of days continuously below freezing, Figs. 294 and 298).

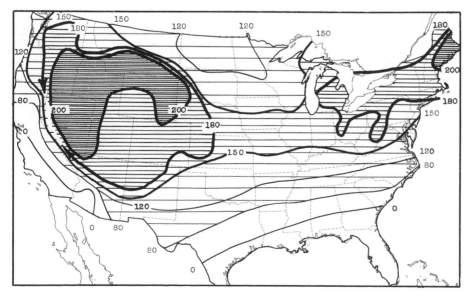

323

Potential freeze and thaw frequency as indicated by the number of days per year when the mean daily temperature in the smoothed annual course was between 20° (maximum could reach 32°) and 50° (minimum could reach 32°).

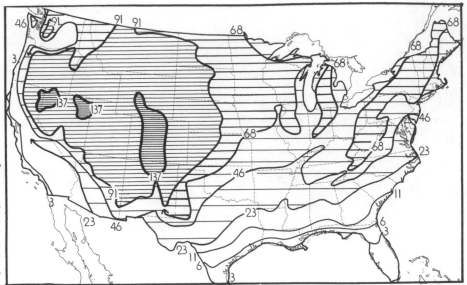

324

Freeze and thaw frequency; number of times per year when a temperature of 28° or lower was followed by one of 32° or higher (863 stations, 1914–1931).

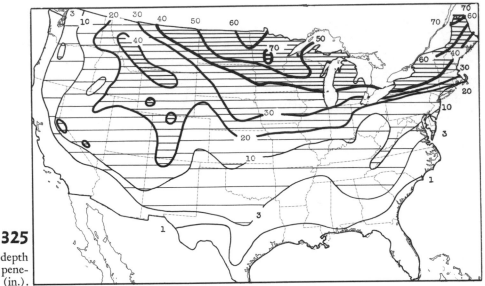

325

Average depth of frost penetration (in.).

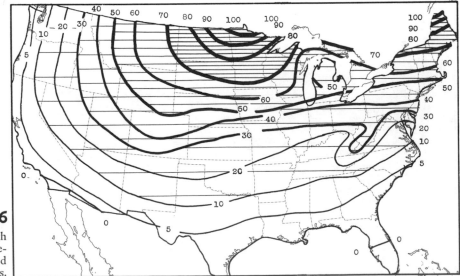

326

Extreme depth of frost penetration (in.), based on state averages.

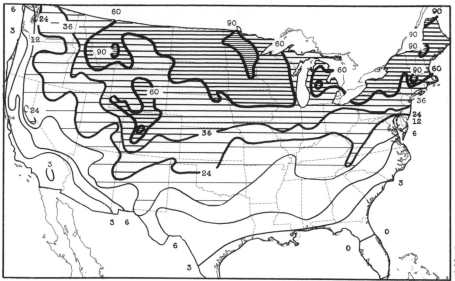

327
Same as Fig. 326,
but in more detail.

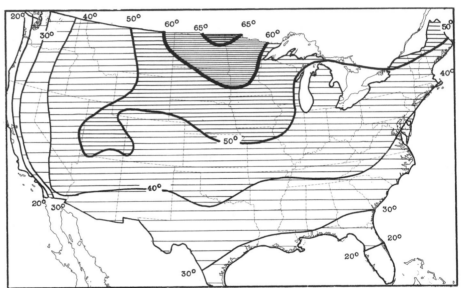

328

Difference between
normal January
and normal
July temperatures.

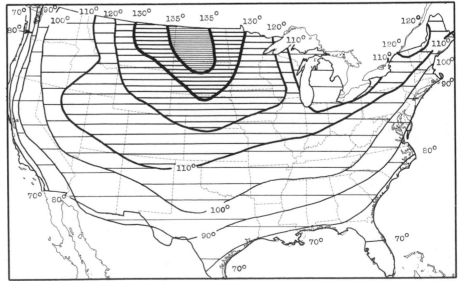

329

Normal absolute
annual range
of temperature
(normal annual
maximum minus
normal annual
minimum).

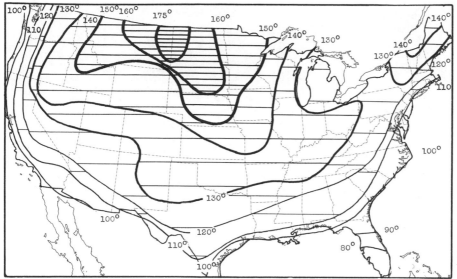

330

Absolute range of temperature (difference between highest and lowest temperatures officially recorded), at the stations with long records, 1899–1938.

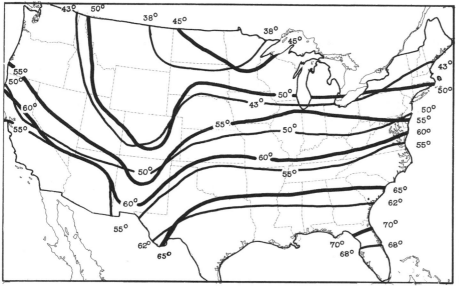

331

Highest and lowest mean annual temperatures, 1896–1938 (based on state averages).

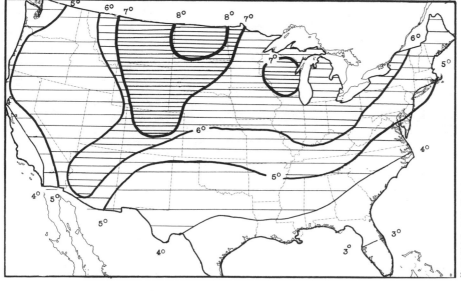

332

Difference between annual normal temperatures of the warmest and coldest years of record, mostly 1896–1902 to 1938 (based on state averages).

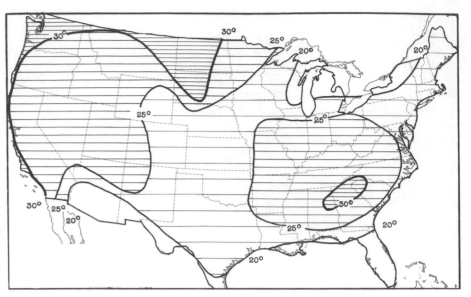

333

Difference between the normal absolute annual range and the absolute range.

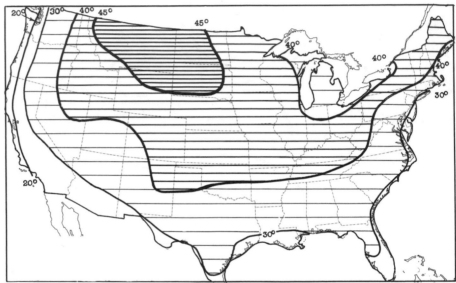

334

Difference between normal annual minimum and normal January temperatures.

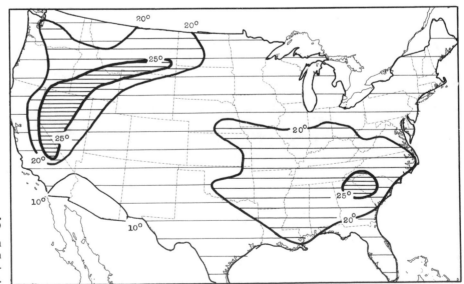

335

Difference between extreme minimum of record and normal annual minimum.

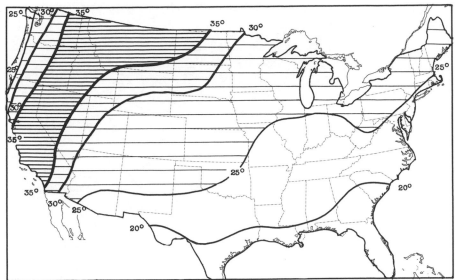

336

Difference between
normal annual
maximum and
normal July
temperatures.

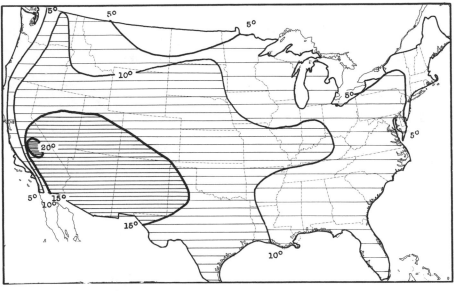
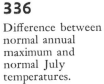

337

Normal July
difference between
wet-bulb and air
temperatures.

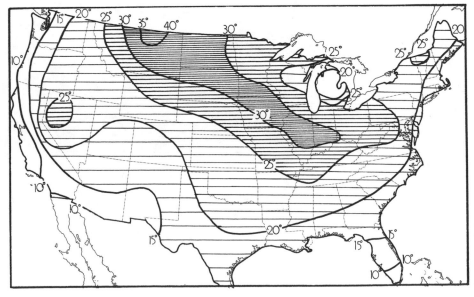

338

January extreme
range of monthly
mean temperature
(based on first-order
stations to 1931 and
state averages to 1945).

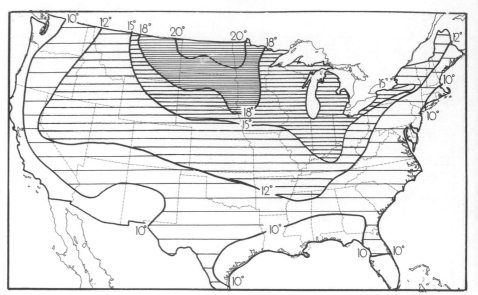

339

April extreme range of monthly mean temperature (based on first-order stations to 1931 and state averages to 1945).

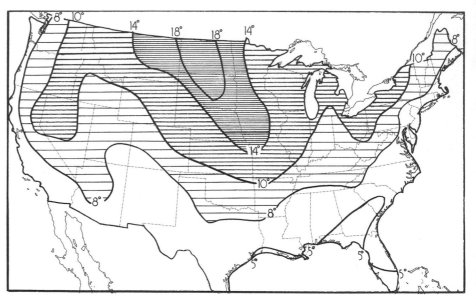

340

July extreme range of monthly mean temperature (based on first-order stations to 1931 and state averages to 1945).

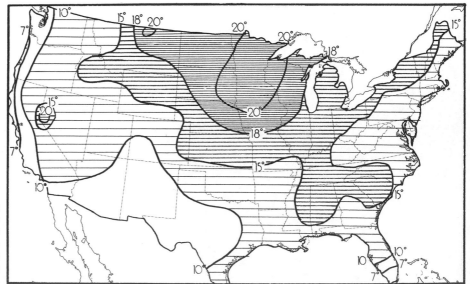

341

October extreme range of monthly mean temperature (based on first-order stations to 1931 and state averages to 1945).

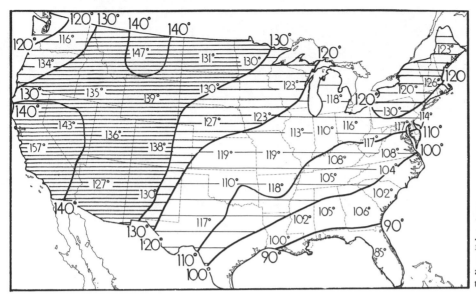

342

January absolute
range of temperature
(based on state high
and low records
to 1945).

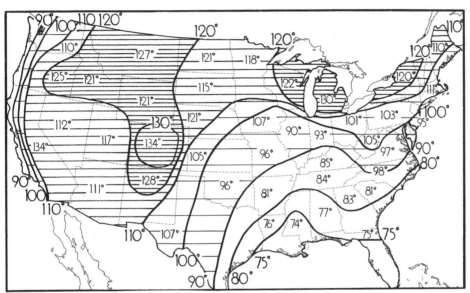

343

April absolute
range of temperature
(based on state high
and low records
to 1945).

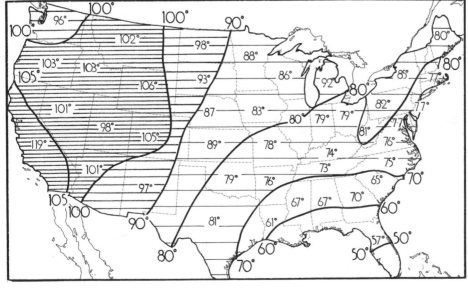

344

July absolute
range of temperature
(based on state high
and low records
to 1945).

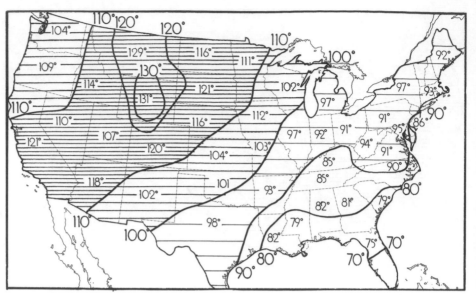

345

October absolute
range of temperature
(based on state high
and low records
to 1945).

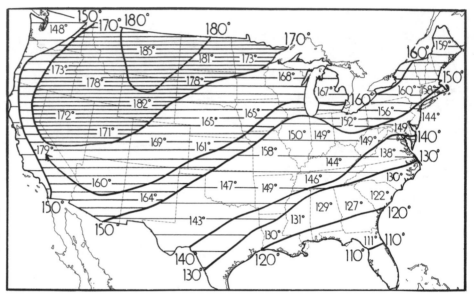

346

Annual absolute
range of temperature
(based on state high
and low records
to 1945).

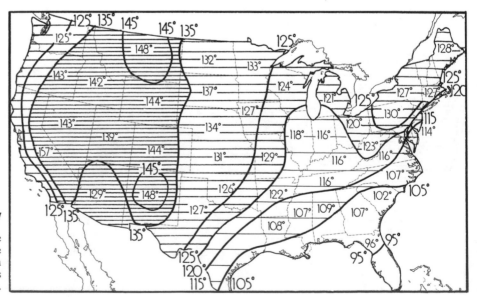

347

Winter absolute
range of temperature
(based on state high
and low records
to 1945).

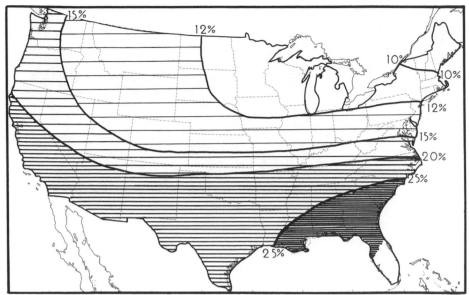

348
Average departure
from normal
(percentage either
above or below
normal) of the
annual number of
(cold) degree days
(42 years).

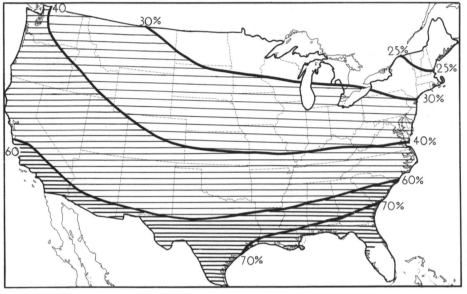

349
Extreme range of
annual (cold) degree
days in 42 years (per-
centage of normal).

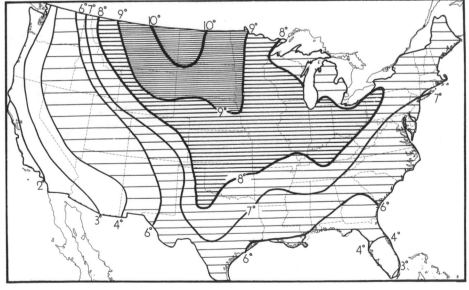

350
January normal
interdiurnal vari-
ability of temperature
(average difference
between mean
temperatures of one
day and the next).

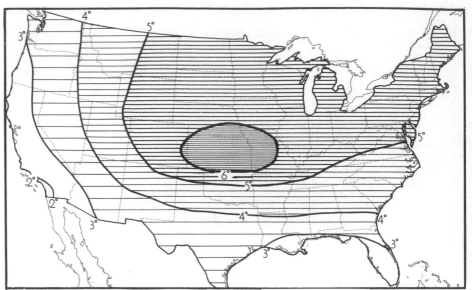

351

April normal
interdiurnal vari-
ability of temperature
(average difference
between mean
temperatures of one
day and the next).

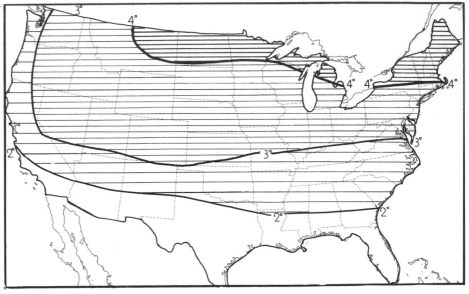

352

July normal
interdiurnal vari-
ability of temperature
(average difference
between mean
temperatures of one
day and the next).

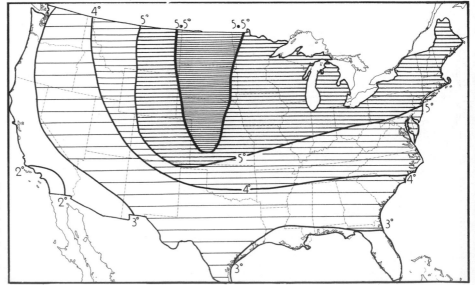

353

October normal
interdiurnal vari-
ability of temperature
(average difference
between mean
temperatures of one
day and the next).

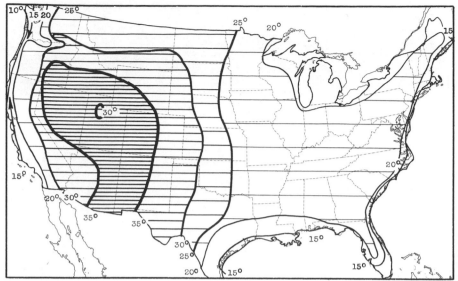

354

Normal daily range in temperature in official thermometer shelters.

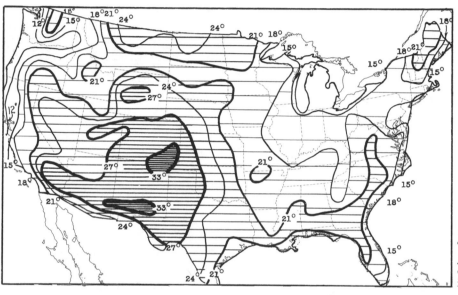

355

January normal daily range in temperature.

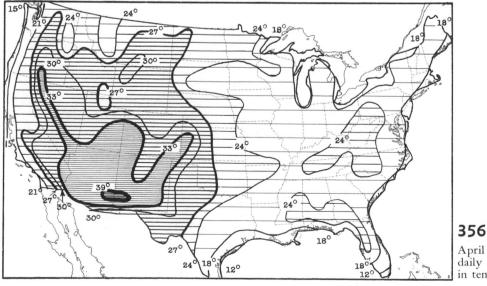

356

April normal daily range in temperature.

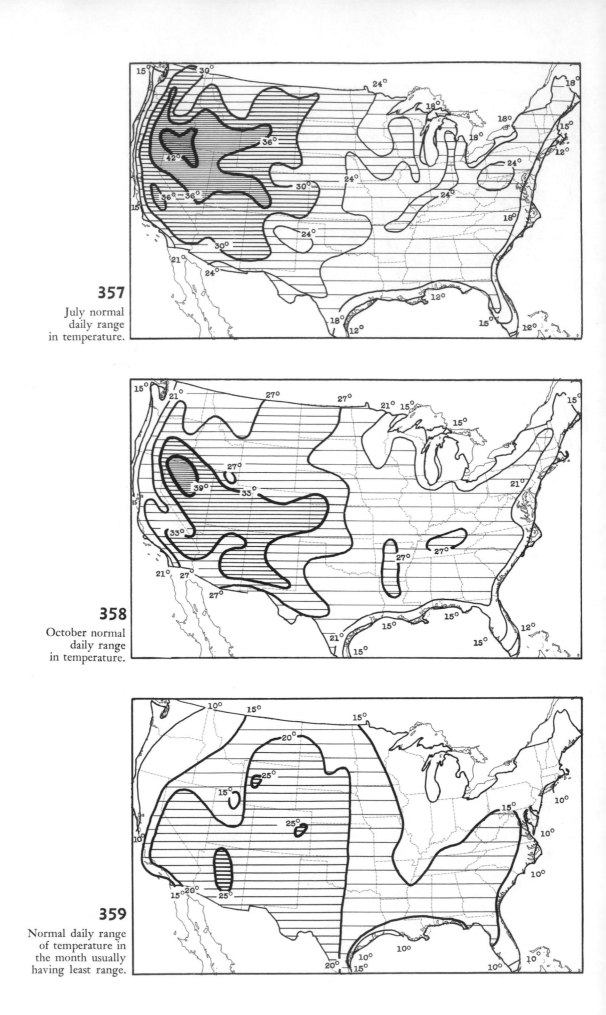

357
July normal
daily range
in temperature.

358
October normal
daily range
in temperature.

359
Normal daily range
of temperature in
the month usually
having least range.

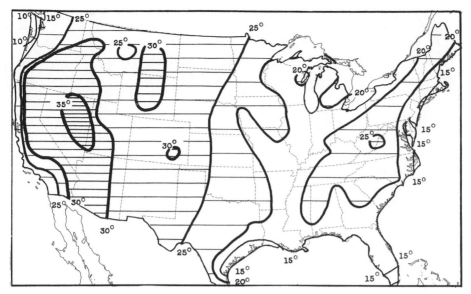

360

Normal daily range
of temperature in
the month usually
having greatest range.

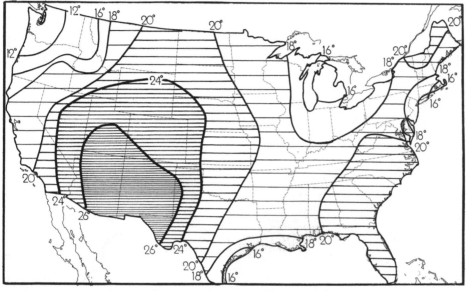

361

Normal daily range
in the normally
coldest week
(January 15–21).

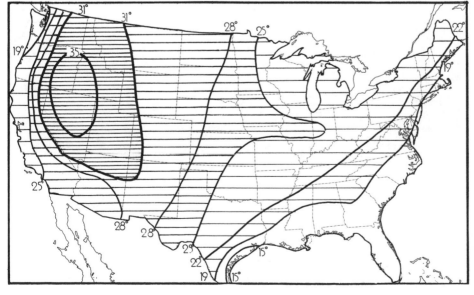

362

Normal daily range
in the normally
hottest week
(July 16–22).

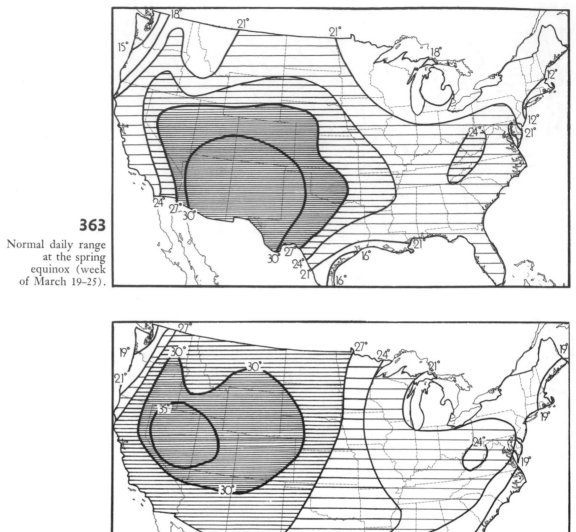

363

Normal daily range
at the spring
equinox (week
of March 19–25).

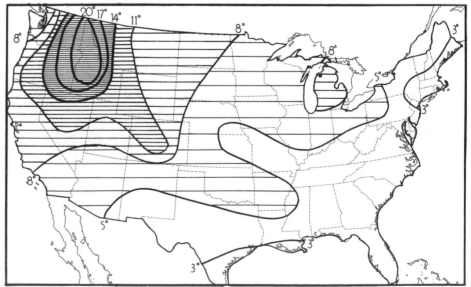

364

Normal daily range
at the autumnal
equinox (week of
September 17–25).

365

Range between the
normal daily ranges
of extreme weeks.

11. SUDDEN CHANGES OF TEMPERATURE
COLD WAVES, HOT WAVES, CHINOOKS

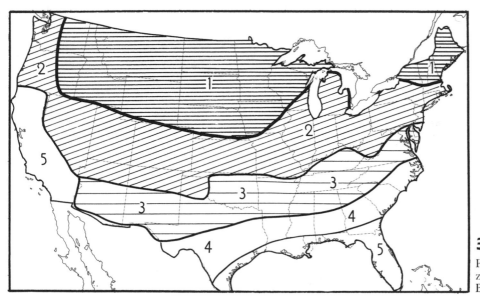

366
Five cold-wave zones, U. S. Weather Bureau definitions.

Weather Bureau definitions of cold waves.

Zone	Temperature drop in 24 hr required (F°)	Minimum temperature required (°F)	
		Winter	Other seasons
1	20	0	16
2	20	10	24
3	20	20	28
4	18	25	32
5	16	32	36

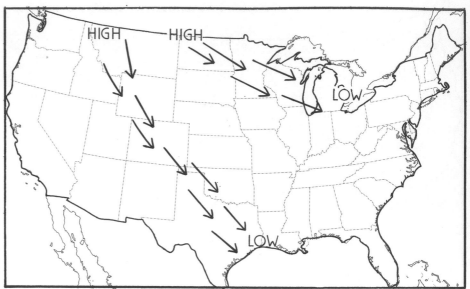

367

Two common
types of cold waves,
showing the location
of the highs
and lows when
cold-wave con-
ditions begin;
later the high
advances toward
the low.

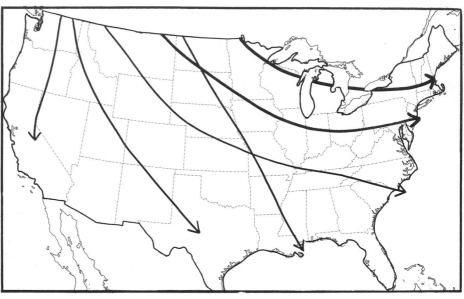

368

Approximate courses
followed by many
cold waves;
heavy lines show
the most common
courses.

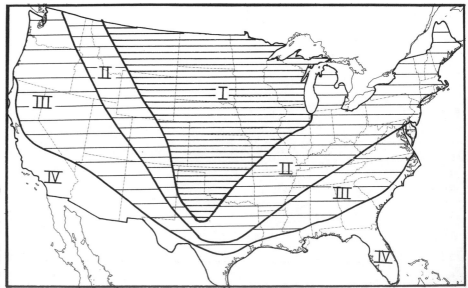

369

Cold waves:
relative frequency
of drops of 20°
or more within
24 hr, generalized
and preliminary (I,
frequent; IV, rare).

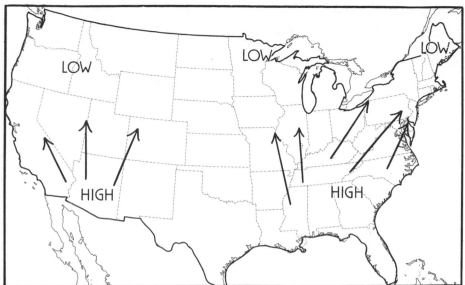

370

Two common types of hot waves, showing the location of highs and lows.

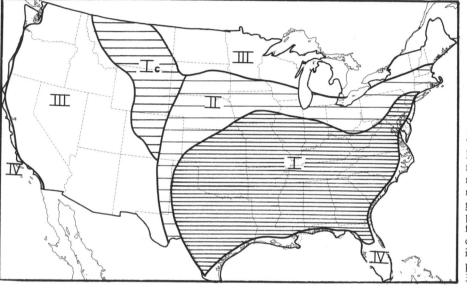

371

Hot waves: relative frequency of sudden rises of 20° or more within 24 hr, generalized and preliminary (I, frequent; IV, rare); chinooks are frequent in IC, occasionally producing a rise of 30° within an hour.

A CHINOOK DURING A COLD WAVE AT RAPID CITY, SOUTH DAKOTA

A self-registering thermograph record (reproduced in the Rapid City *Daily Journal* for Jan. 23, 1943) shows that at 7 A.M. the temperature was 0°; at 10:20 it was 5°; at 10:30, 42°; at 10:33, 20°; at 10:45, 55°; at 11:00, 10°; at 11:45, 60°; at noon, 13°; at 12:30 P.M. it was 15°; at 12:45, 50°; at 1:00, 15°; at 1:30, 60°; at 5:20, 60°; at 5:30, 15°; and from then on to midnight and beyond it was from 15° to 5°.

Four times between 10 A.M. and 6 P.M. the chinook shot the temperature up from near zero to between 50° and 60°. Three times the temperature remained relatively high for only a brief period, but once it remained high for nearly four hours, from 1:30 to 5:20 P.M.

The most sudden rise occurred at 11:45, 40° in less than 10 min. Twice during the day, the temperature dropped 35° within 5 min., once at noon and again at 5:20 p.m.

At the Rapid City Air Port (a few miles east of the city, which is on the eastern margin of the Black Hills, a mountainous outlier of the Rocky Mountains), the maximum temperature was 50° and the minimum was −2°; at Spearfish, some 100 miles to the northwest, near the north end of the Black Hills, the range was from 52° to −1°. At Philip, about 100 miles east of Rapid City, the range was only between 5° and −7°, since there was no chinook there.

12.   ATMOSPHERIC PRESSURE

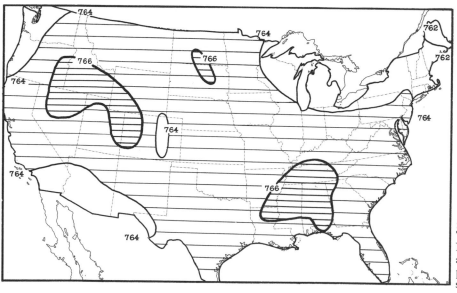

372

Normal January
atmospheric
pressure reduced to
sea level (mm).

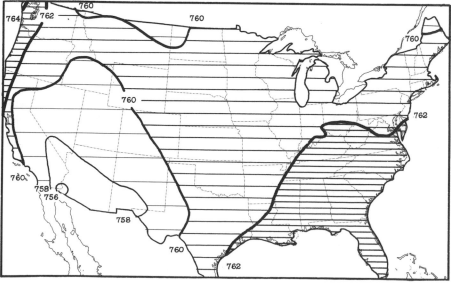

373

Normal July
atmospheric
pressure reduced to
sea level (mm).

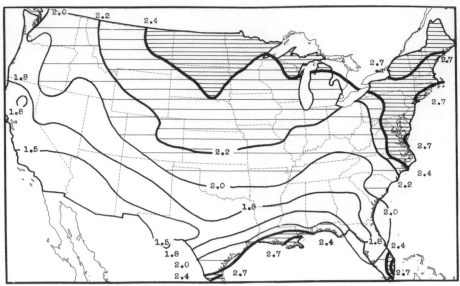

374

Atmospheric pressure range: difference (in.) between the highest and lowest official barometer readings, to 1940. (For normal atmospheric pressures in March, April, June, September, October, and December, see Figs. 377–384.)

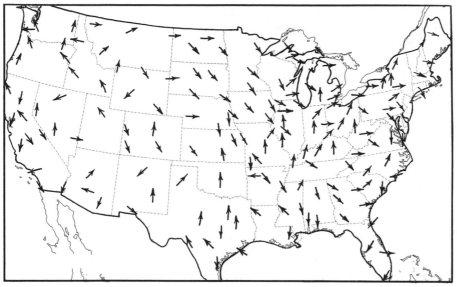

375
Normal surface
wind directions
in January.

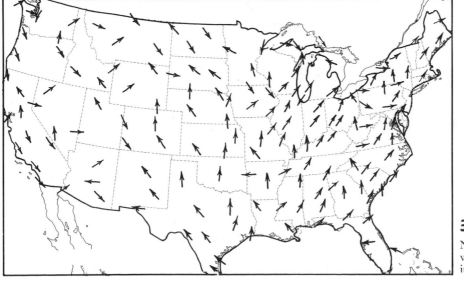

376
Normal surface
wind directions
in July.

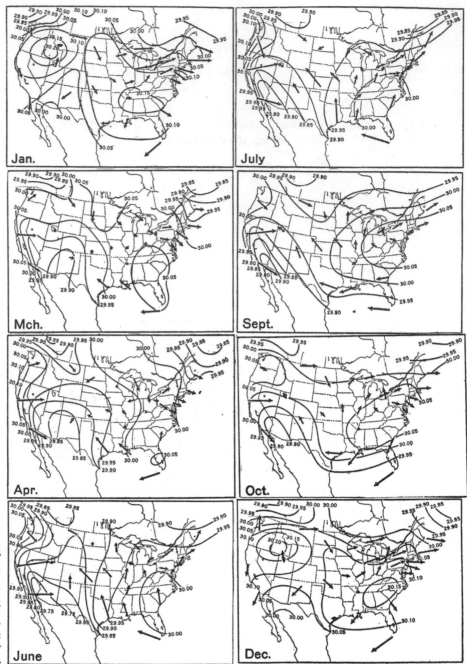

377-384

Net excess of wind from a given direction (shown by length of arrow) and average barometric pressure (shown by isobars), by months.

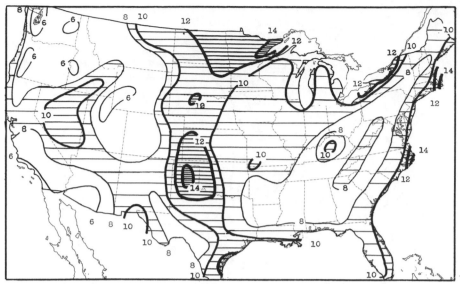

385
Average surface wind velocity (mi/hr).

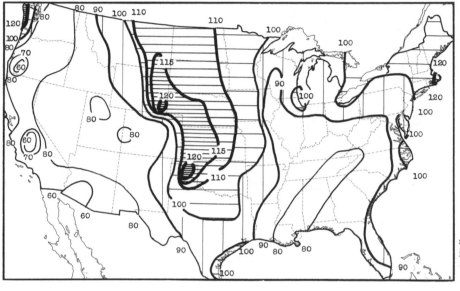

386
Relative velocity of wind over lakes and reservoirs (100 is the average velocity over a lake near Minneapolis).

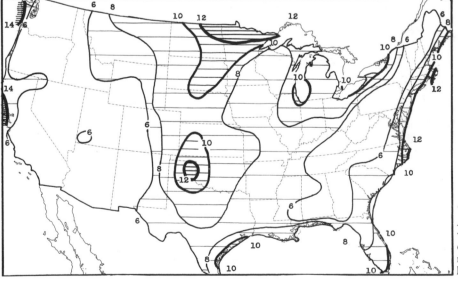

387
Average surface wind velocity at 6 A.M., local time, normally the hour of least wind.

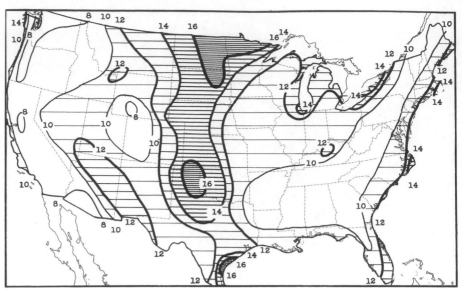

388

Average surface
wind velocity at
3 P.M., local time,
normally the hour
of most wind.

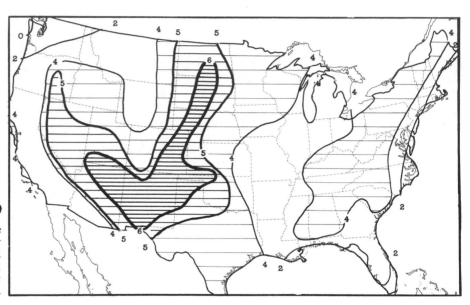

389

Average increase
in wind velocity
between 6 A.M.
and 3 P.M., local
time (average daily
range in velocity).

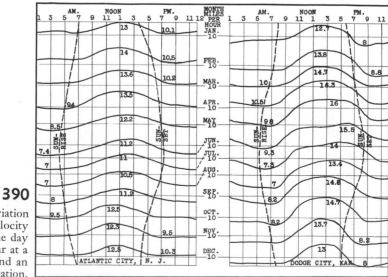

390

Average variation
in wind velocity
throughout the day
and year at a
coastal and an
inland station.

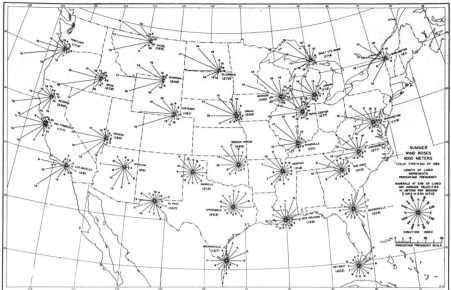

391

Relative frequency of winds from each direction at an altitude of 8000 m in summer.

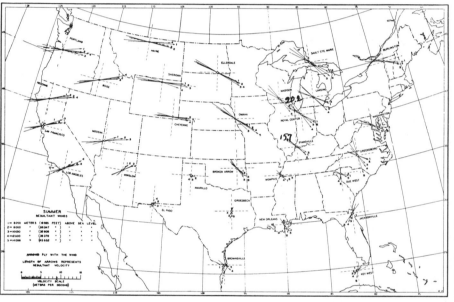

392

Winds at high altitudes in summer; length of arrows indicates resultant or net velocity.

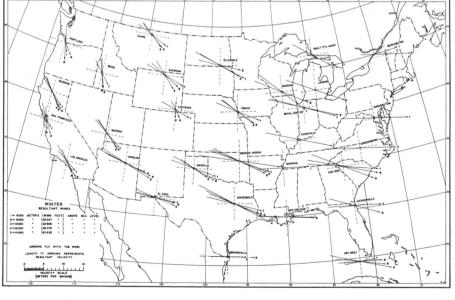

393

Winds at high altitudes in winter; length of arrows indicates resultant or net velocity.

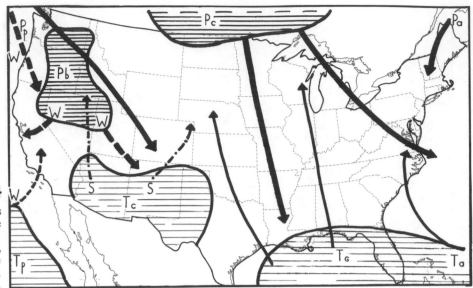

394

Air masses
affecting the
United States:
continuous line,
throughout the
year; *S*, summer;
W, winter.

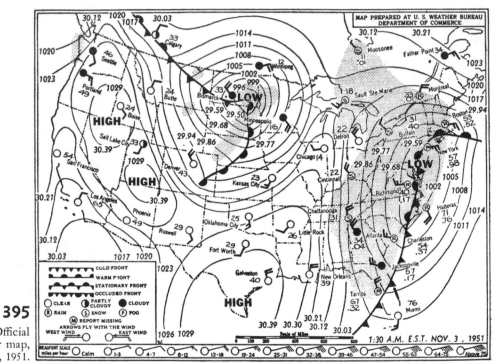

395

Official
weather map,
November 3, 1951.

14. STORMS: CYCLONES, THUNDERSTORMS, TORNADOES, HURRICANES, ANTICYCLONES

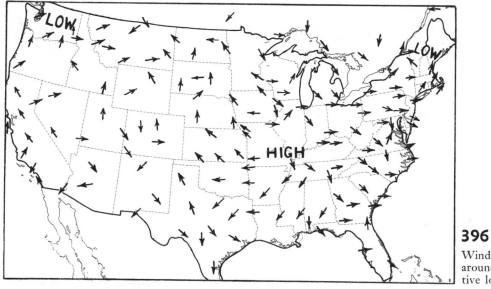

396
Wind direction around representative lows and a high.

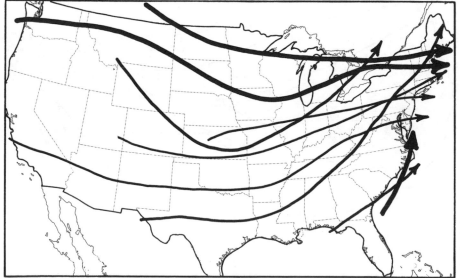

397
Tracks taken by many lows; width of line suggests relative abundance.

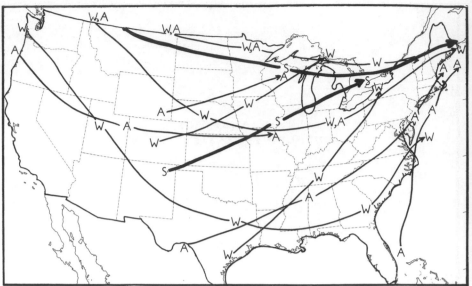

398

Approximate tracks
of many lows,
by seasons: *W*,
winter; *S*, summer;
A, fall-spring.

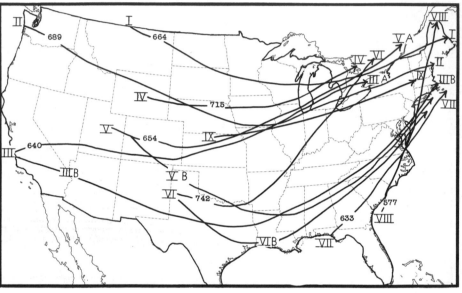

399

March: tracks
most frequently
taken by lows, by
types, and their
average daily
advance (mi).

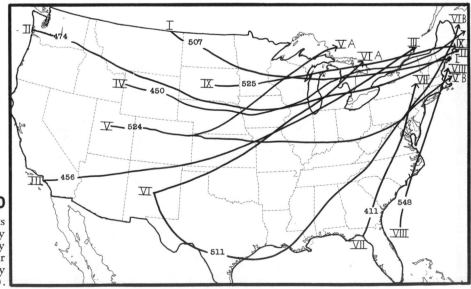

400

May: tracks
most frequently
taken by lows, by
types, and their
average daily
advance (mi).

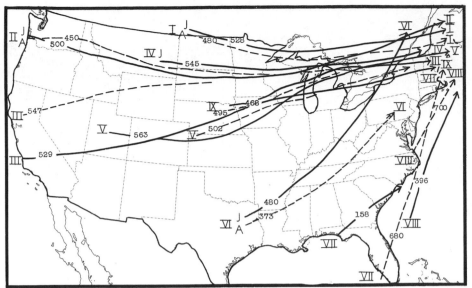

401

Tracks most frequently taken by lows in July (full line) and in August (dashed line), and their average daily advance (mi).

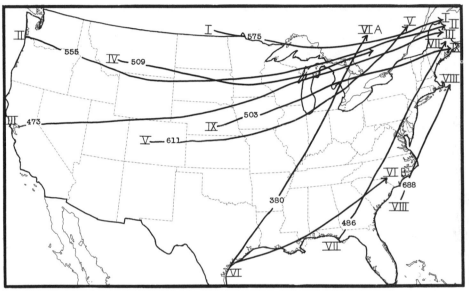

402

September: tracks most frequently taken by lows, by types, and their average daily advance (mi).

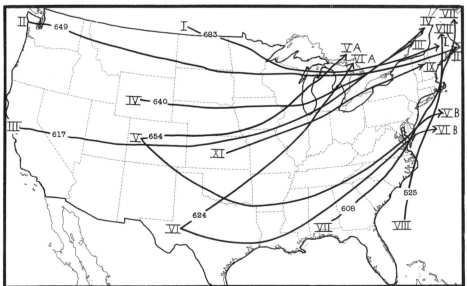

403

November: tracks most frequently taken by lows, by types, and their average daily advance (mi).

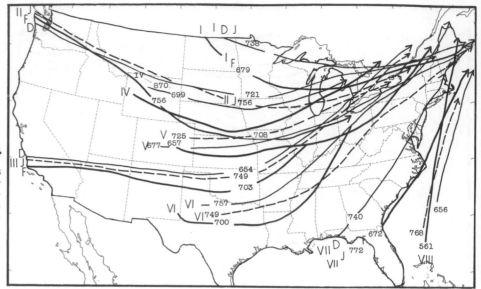

404

Winter: tracks most frequently taken by lows, by types, and their average daily advance (mi); heavy lines, January; light lines, February; dashed lines, December.

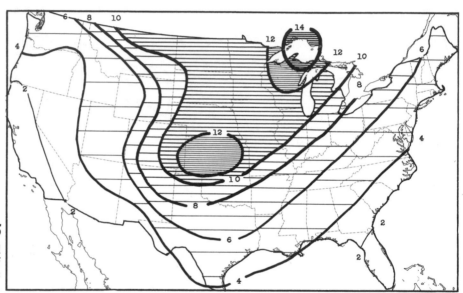

405

Normal annual number of cyclonic centers per 5° square.

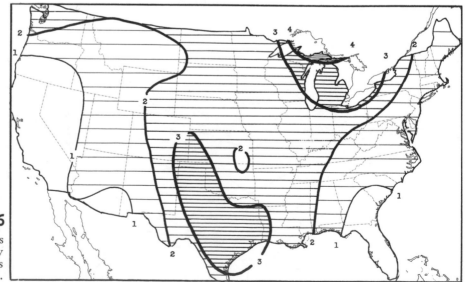

406

Frequency of lows in January (number of centers per 5° square).

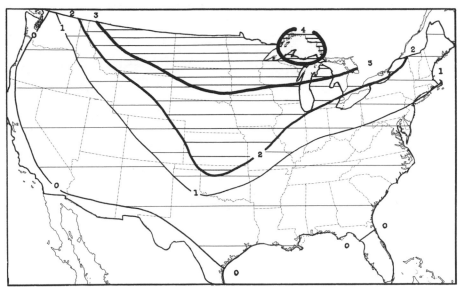

407

Frequency of lows in July (number of centers per 5° square).

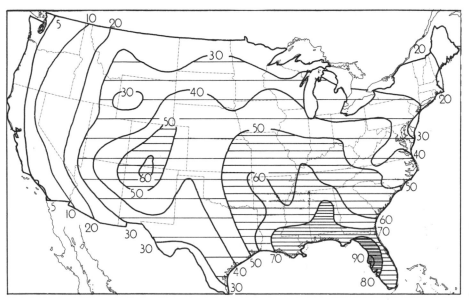

408

Annual number of thunderstorm days (with one or more thunderstorms in the vicinity).

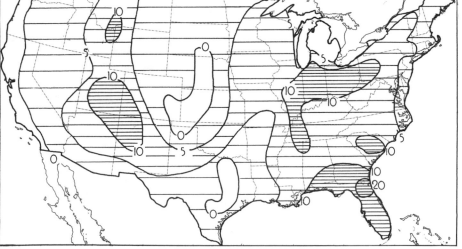

409

Annual frequency of two thunderstorms locally in 24 hr.

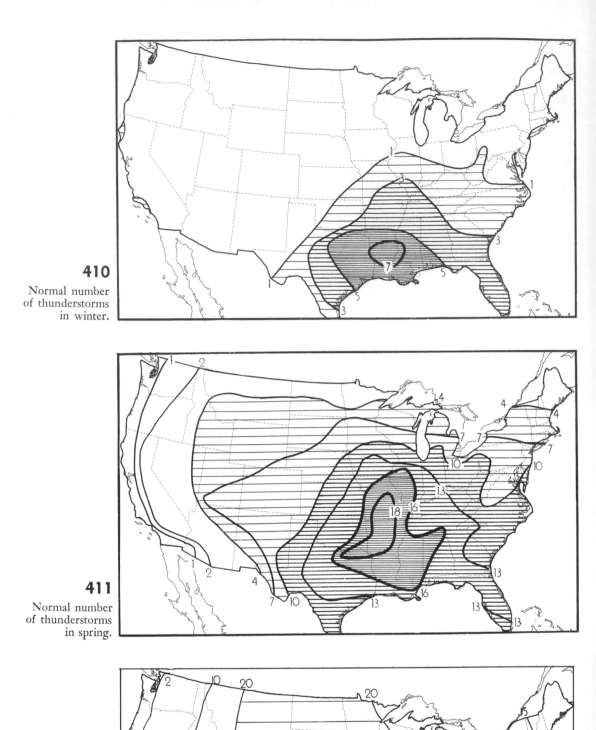

410

Normal number
of thunderstorms
in winter.

411

Normal number
of thunderstorms
in spring.

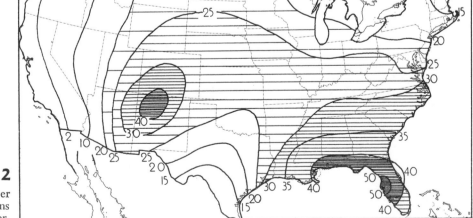

412

Normal number
of thunderstorms
in summer.

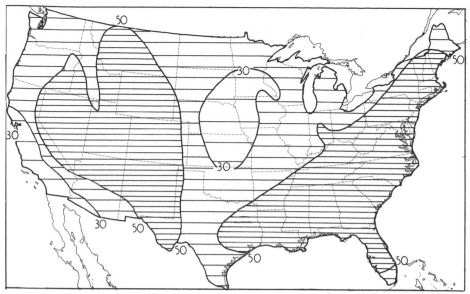

413

Percentage of the summer thunderstorms that occur between noon and 6 P.M., local time.

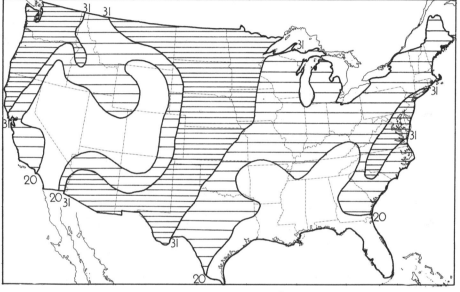

414

Percentage of the summer thunderstorms that occur between 6 P.M. and midnight, local time.

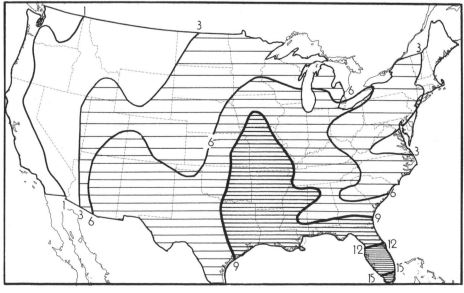

415

Normal number of thunderstorms in fall.

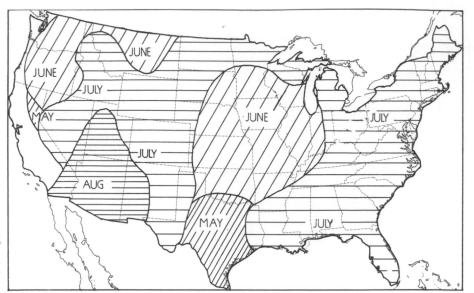

416

The month
normally having
most thunderstorms.

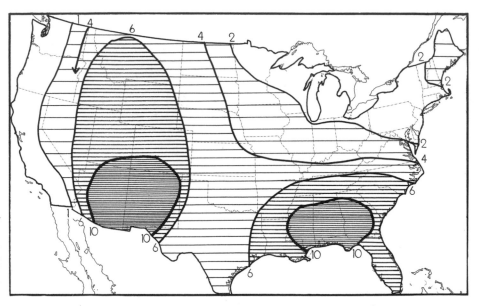

417

Average annual
number of human
deaths by lightning
per million
population.

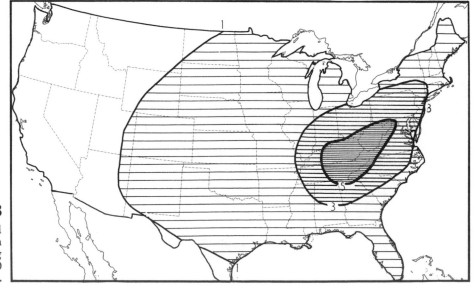

418

Average annual
number of human
deaths by lightning
per 10,000
square miles.

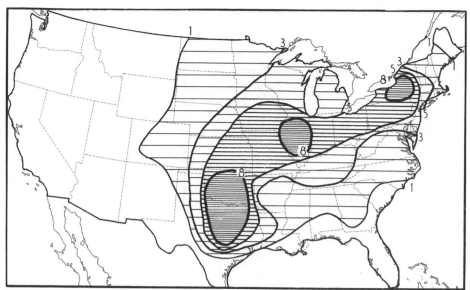

419

Average annual loss caused by lightning to farm buildings (millions of dollars per state).

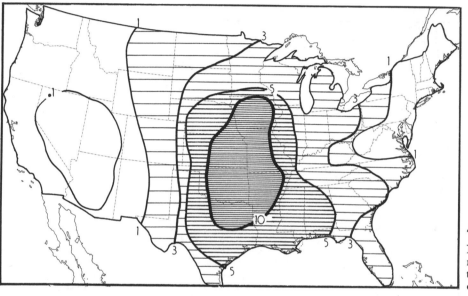

420

Normal annual number of tornadoes (based on state averages).

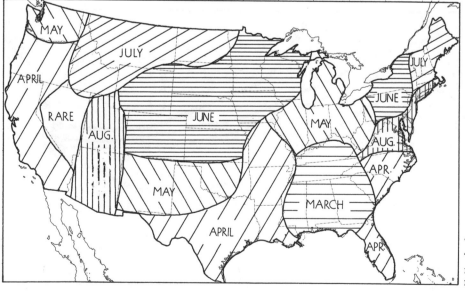

421

The month normally having most tornadoes.

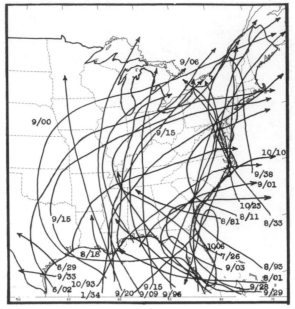

422

Some hurricane
tracks, dated as
to month and year.

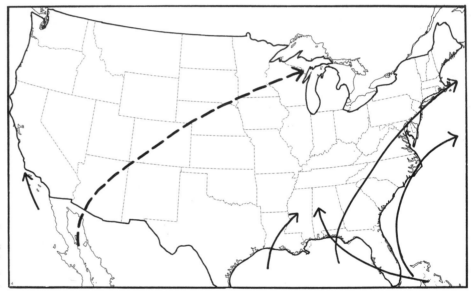

423

Generalized tracks
taken by many
American
tropical cyclones.

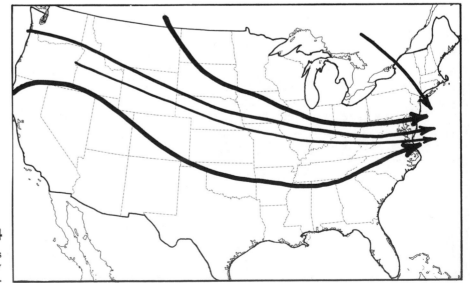

424

Generalized tracks
taken by many
highs or anticyclones.

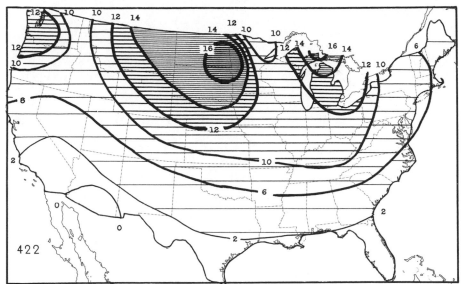

425

Normal annual number of anticyclonic centers per 5° square.

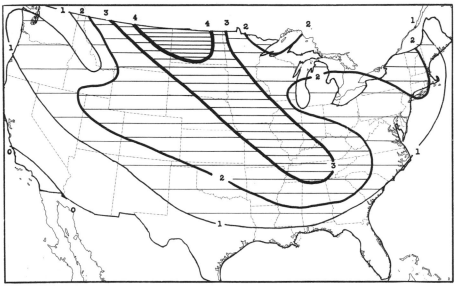

426

Frequency of anticyclones in January (number of centers per 5° square).

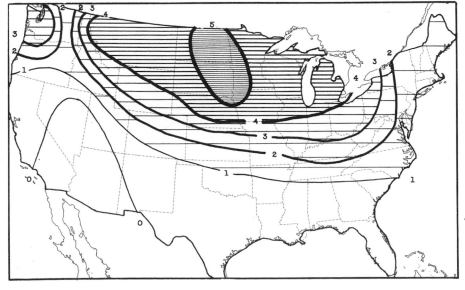

427

Frequency of anticyclones in July (number of centers per 5° square).

One of the worst storms of record in the United States, still referred to as "The Blizzard of 1888," occurred in the Northeastern States on March 11 to 14 of that year. It brought heavy snow, driven by winds of hurricane force which piled up drifts by actual measurements 20 to 40 feet high in some localities. In much of New England and parts of New York snow depths ranged from 30 to 50 inches. The storm forced complete suspension for several days of all railroad traffic entering the city of New York, while winds of 60 to 70 miles an hour along the coast caused heavy damage to shipping.— *U. S. Weather Bureau.*

In New York City even more snow — 25½ inches — fell on December 26, 1947. The great storm of November 25–26, 1950, known as the "Thanksgiving Day Storm," inflicted enormous damage from gales and floods to New York, New Jersey, and New England, and from snow and cold on the western slopes of the Appalachians, especially in western Pennsylvania and northeastern Ohio, where the snowfall locally exceeded 30 inches. Though the loss of life, 297, was half that of the New England hurricane of September 21, 1938, the damage, estimated at $400,000,000, approached that of 1938. The floods of the Missouri basin, however, in June and July 1951, following enormous rains, caused damage of nearly a billion dollars.

15. OTHER WINDS: SEA, LAKE, AND LAND BREEZES, VALLEY WINDS, SQUALLS, WHIRLWINDS

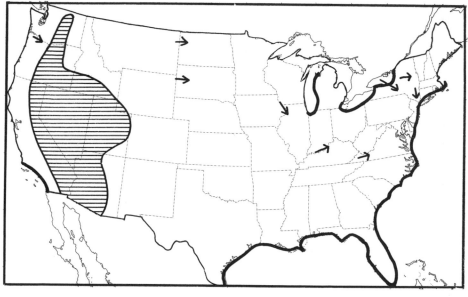

428

Parts of the country where sea and lake breezes are especially frequent; some places where the average wind direction clearly reflects topography (region of many whirlwinds lined).

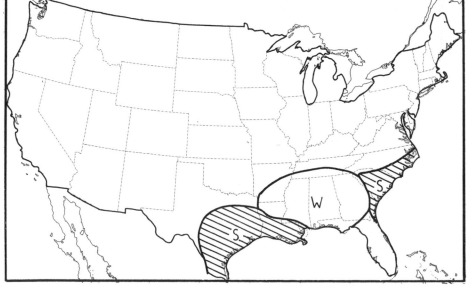

429

Areas where monsoonal winds are frequent in summer (*S*) and winter (*W*).

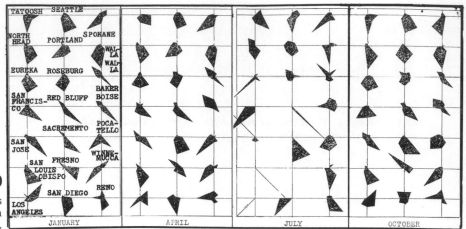

430

Wind directions
and precipitation
in the West.

Percentages of the average precipitation received with each wind direction at 21 scattered Western cities are shown. For example, San Diego gets its rain in January and April with south winds, in July with southwest winds, in October largely with north winds. Seattle gets its rain with south-southeast winds in January, April, and October, but partly with northeast and southwest winds in July.

PART III   SUNSHINE

16.   NORMAL AMOUNTS OF SUNSHINE, CLOUDINESS, FOG, RADIATION

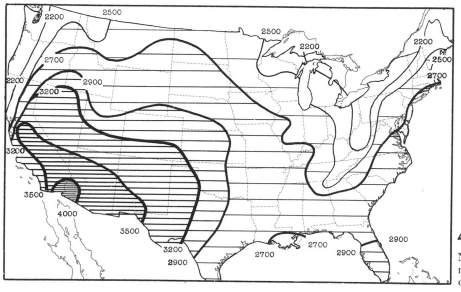

431
Normal annual number of hours of sunshine.

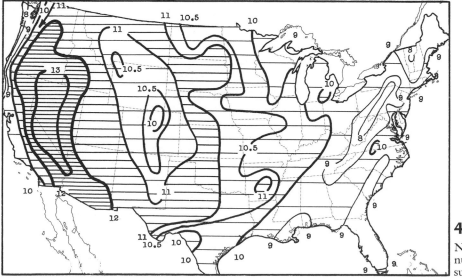

432
Normal daily number of hours of sunshine in summer.

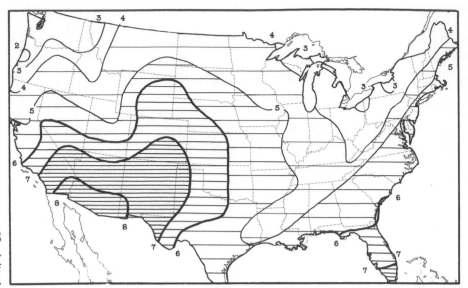

433

Normal daily
number of hours of
sunshine in winter.

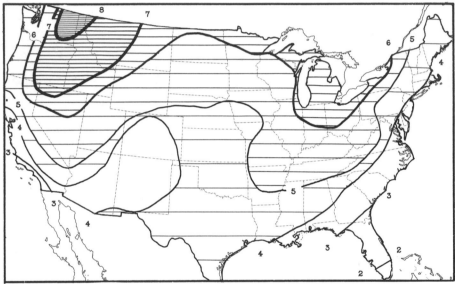

434

Summer and winter
sunshine contrasted:
normal number
of hours per day
by which summer
sunshine exceeds
that of winter.

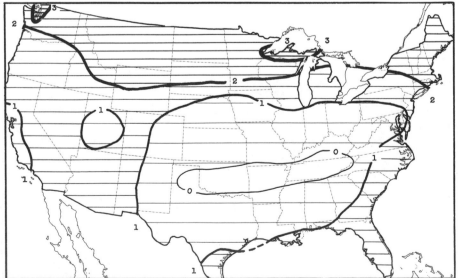

435

April and October
sunshine contrasted:
normal number of
hours per day by
which April
sunshine exceeds
that of October.

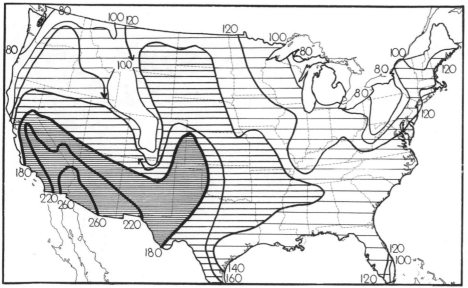

436

Normal annual
number of days
that are clear.

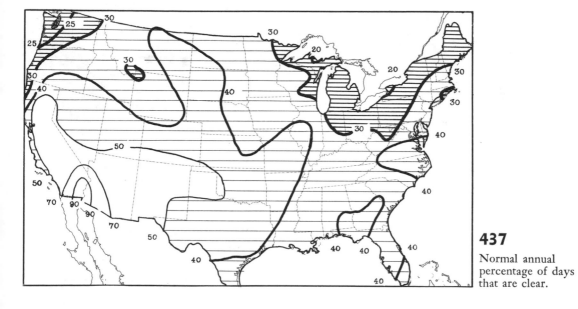

437

Normal annual
percentage of days
that are clear.

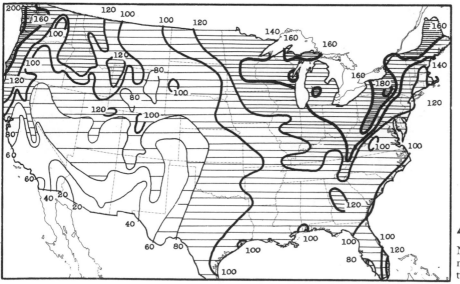

438

Normal annual
number of days
that are cloudy.

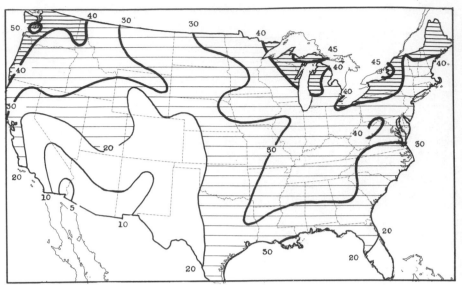

439

Normal annual
percentage of days
that are cloudy.

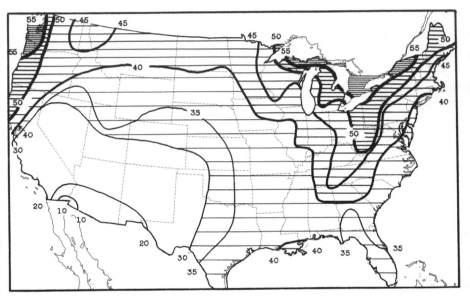

440

Normal annual
percentage of day-
time cloudiness.

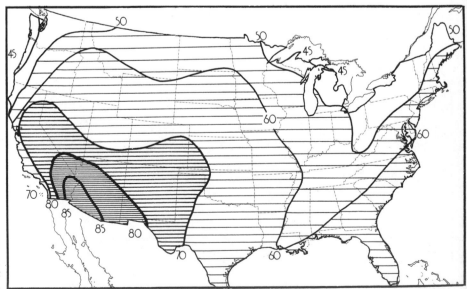

441

Normal annual
sunshine (percent
of possible).

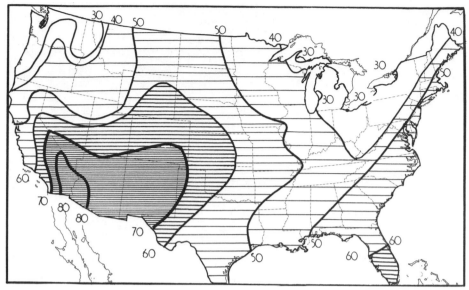

442
Normal winter
sunshine (percent
of possible).

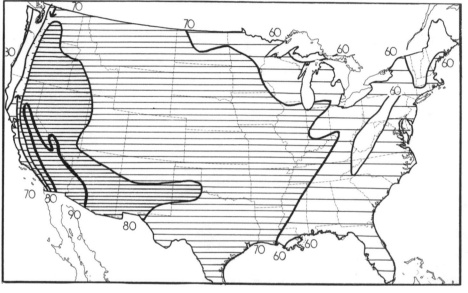

443
Normal summer
sunshine (percent
of possible).

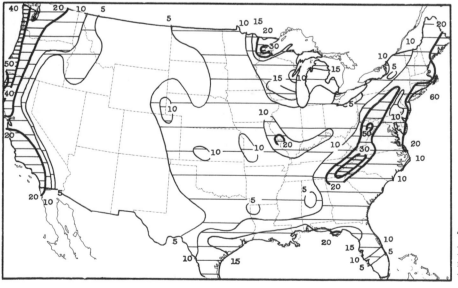

444
Normal annual
number of days
with dense fog.

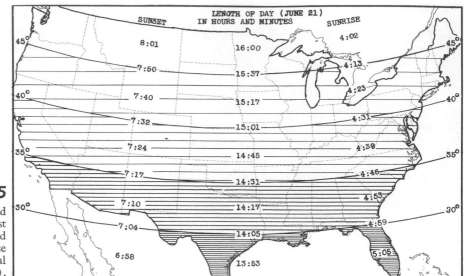

445

Length (hours and minutes) of longest day (June 21) and times of sunrise and sunset (local standard time).

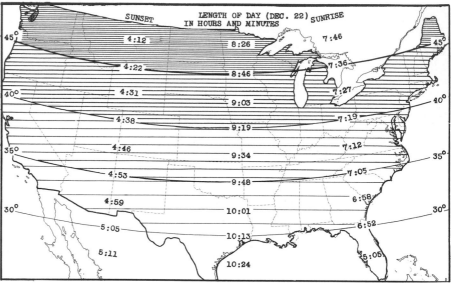

446

Length (hours and minutes) of shortest day (December 22) and time of sunrise and sunset (local standard time).

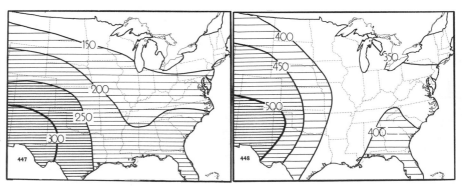

447, 448

Normal daily total solar radiation (langleys [≡gm cal/cm² of horizontal surface min]) received on January 21 (Fig. 447) and March 21 (Fig. 448).

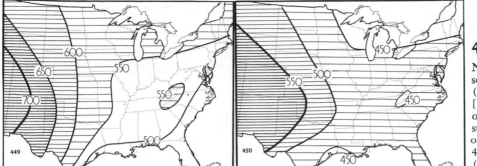

449, 450

Normal daily total solar radiation (langleys [≡gm cal/cm² of horizontal surface]) received on June 21 (Fig. 449) and August 21 (Fig 450).

451, 452

Normal daily total solar radiation (langleys [≡gm cal/cm² of horizontal surface]) received on October 21 (Fig. 451) and December 21 (Fig. 452).

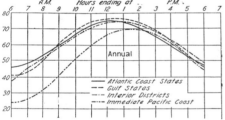
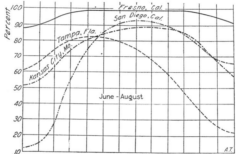

453

Contrasts in average sunshine hour by hour, for regions for the year and for selected stations during summer (percent of possible).

17. RELATIVE AND ABSOLUTE HUMIDITY AND VAPOR PRESSURE

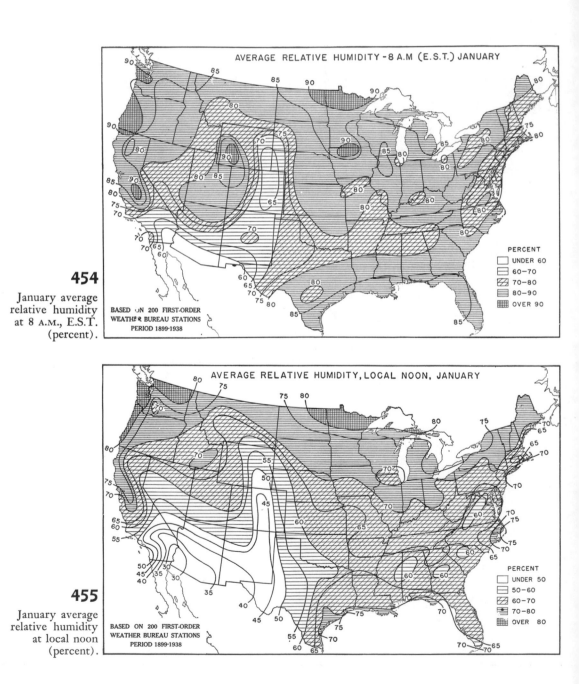

454

January average
relative humidity
at 8 A.M., E.S.T.
(percent).

455

January average
relative humidity
at local noon
(percent).

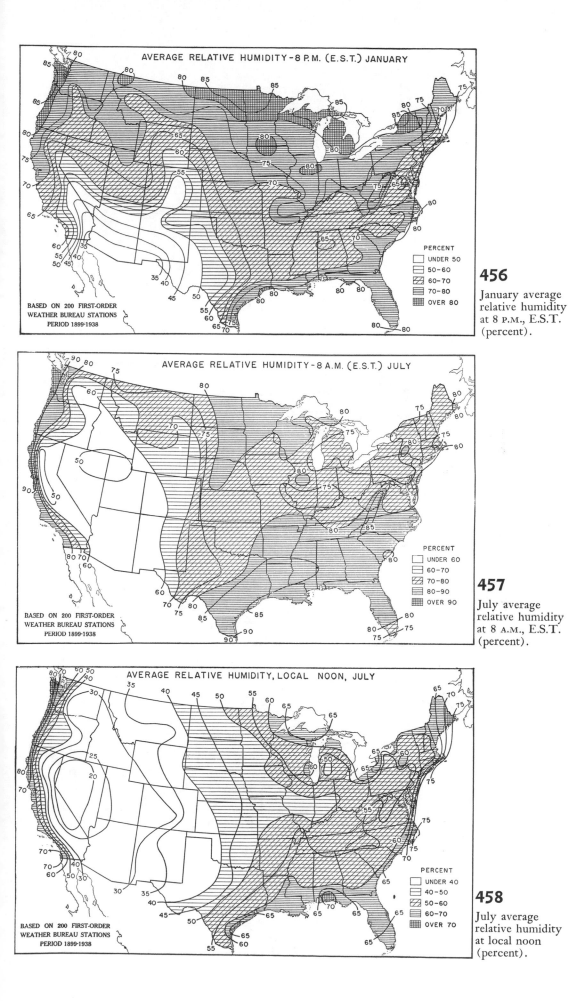

456
January average relative humidity at 8 P.M., E.S.T. (percent).

457
July average relative humidity at 8 A.M., E.S.T. (percent).

458
July average relative humidity at local noon (percent).

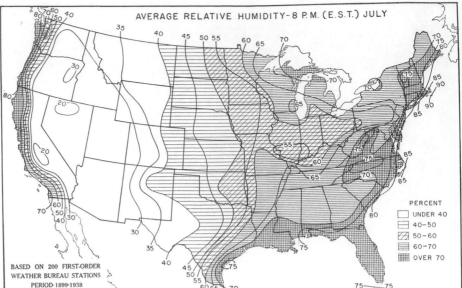

459

July average
relative humidity
at 8 P.M., E.S.T.
(percent).

460

Difference between
local noon average
relative humidity
in January and
July (percent);
January greatest,
lined; July
greatest, crossed.

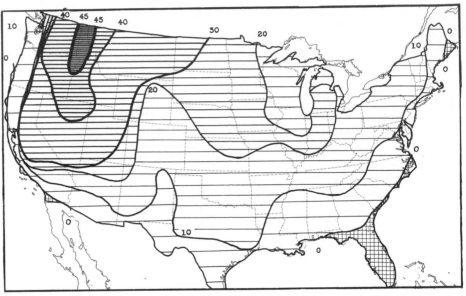

461

April average
minimum relative
humidity (percent).

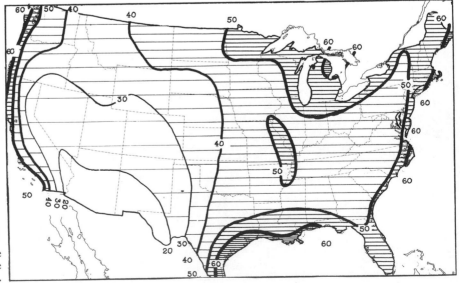

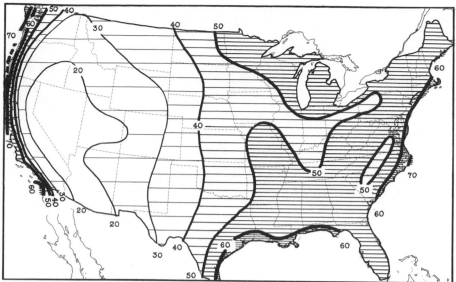

462

July average
minimum relative
humidity (percent).

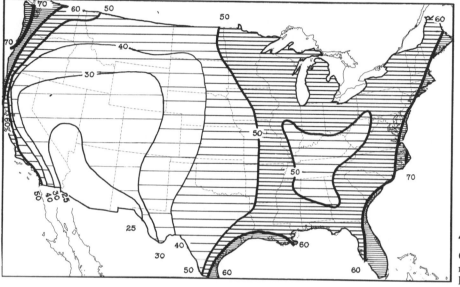

463

October average
minimum relative
humidity (percent).

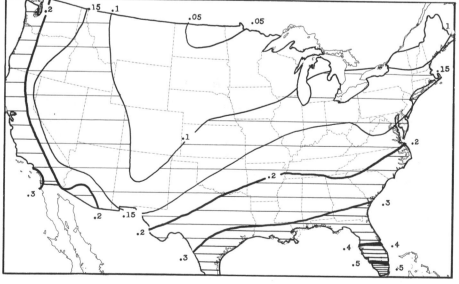

464

January average
vapor pressure
(in.-of-mercury).

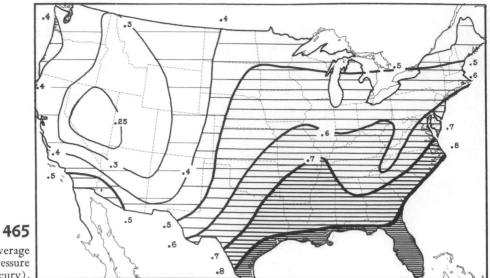

465

July average vapor pressure (in.-of-mercury).

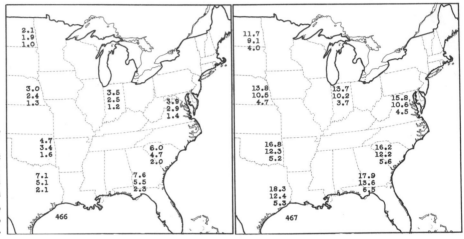

466, 467

Average absolute humidity (gm/m³) at the surface and at 1000 and 3000 m altitude (Fig. 466, winter; Fig. 467, summer).

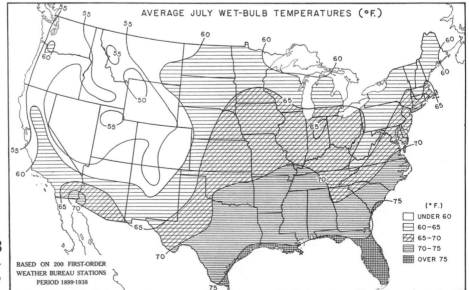

AVERAGE JULY WET-BULB TEMPERATURES (°F.)

BASED ON 200 FIRST-ORDER
WEATHER BUREAU STATIONS
PERIOD 1899-1938

(°F.)
UNDER 60
60-65
65-70
70-75
OVER 75

468

Average July wet-bulb temperatures.

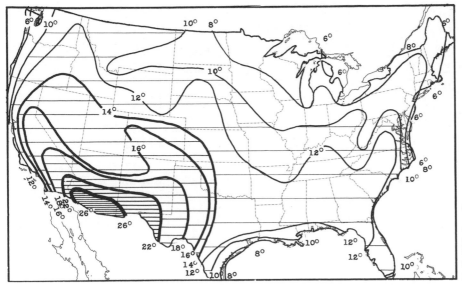

469

April average depression of wet-bulb temperature at time of minimum relative humidity.

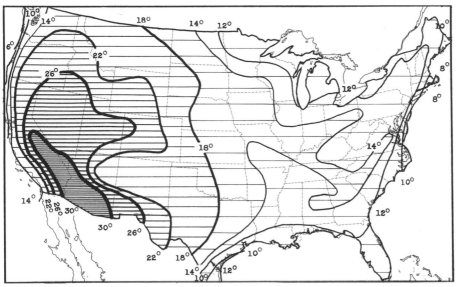

470

July average depression of wet-bulb temperature at time of minimum relative humidity.

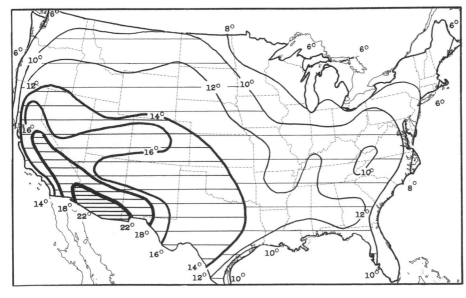

471

October average depression of wet-bulb temperature at time of minimum relative humidity.

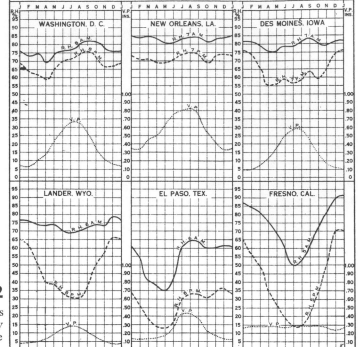

472

Annual changes of relative humidity and vapor pressure at six stations.

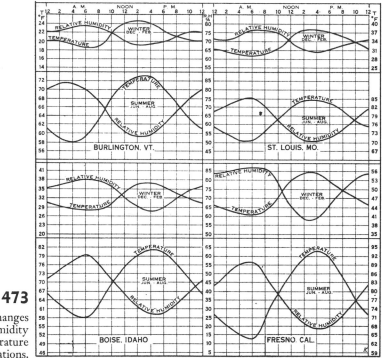

473

Hourly changes of relative humidity and temperature at four stations.

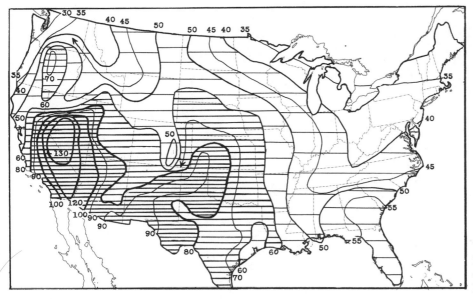

474

Normal annual
evaporation from
pans (in.).

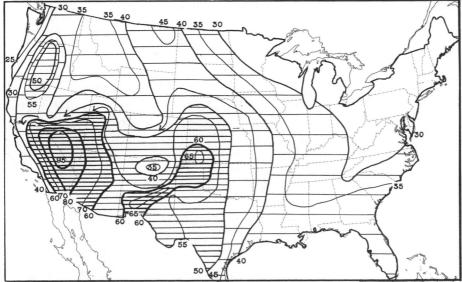

475

Normal May–October
evaporation from
pans (in.).

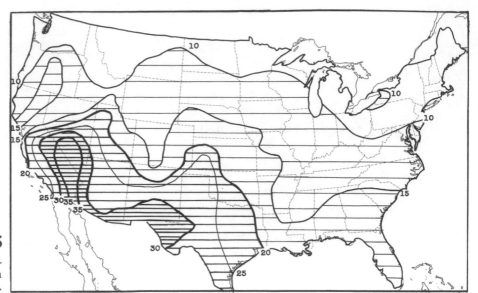

476

Normal November–
April evaporation
from pans (in.).

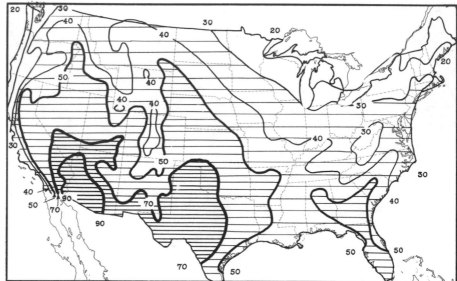

477

Normal annual
evaporation from
reservoirs and
shallow lakes (in.).

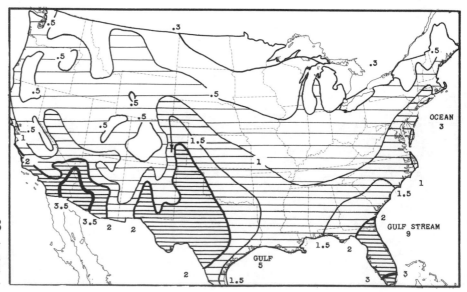

478

Normal January
evaporation from
reservoirs and
shallow lakes (in.).

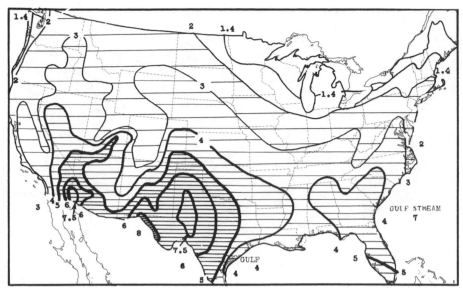

479

Normal April
evaporation from
reservoirs and
shallow lakes (in.).

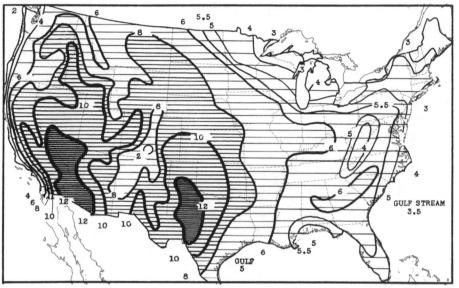

480

Normal July
evaporation from
reservoirs and
shallow lakes (in.).

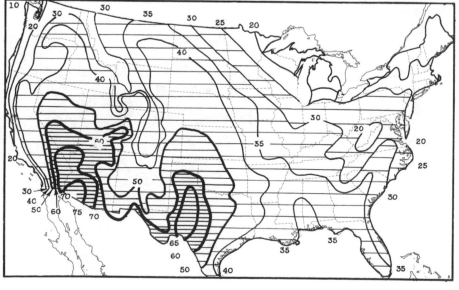

481

Normal April–
October evaporation
from reservoirs and
shallow lakes (in.).

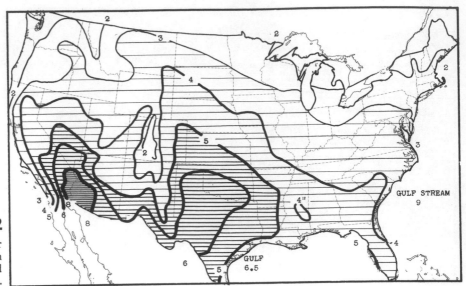

482

Normal October
evaporation from
reservoirs and
shallow lakes (in.).

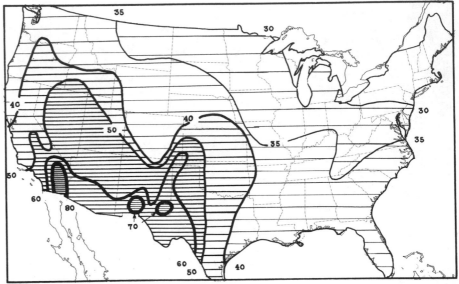

483

Normal evaporation
during the warm
season, April–
September
inclusive (in.).

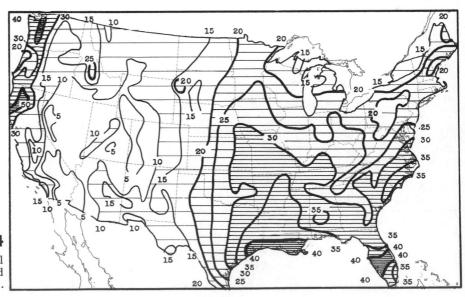

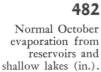

484

Normal annual
evaporation and
transpiration (in.).

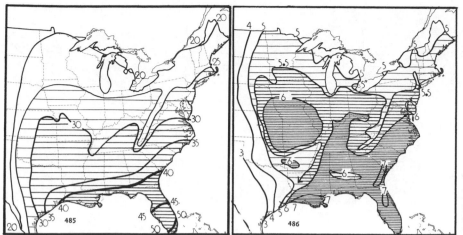

485, 486

Normal annual (Fig. 485) and July (Fig. 486) evaporation and transpiration (in.).

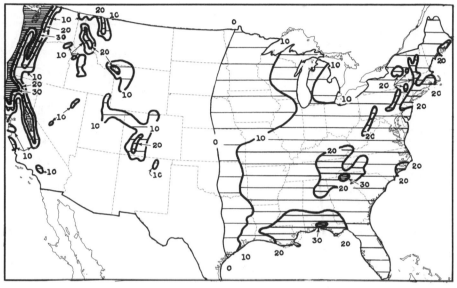

487

Normal annual excess of precipitation over evaporation (in.).

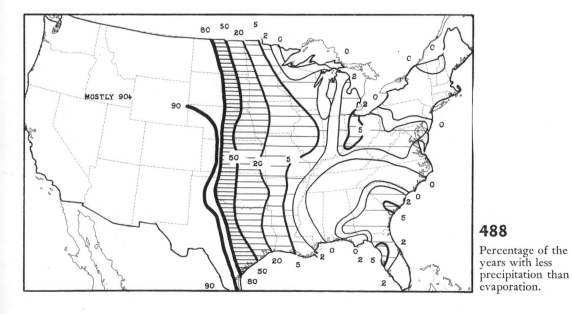

488

Percentage of the years with less precipitation than evaporation.

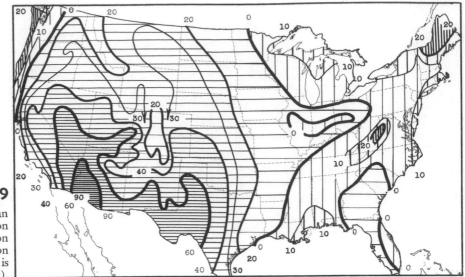

489

Difference in mean
annual evaporation
and precipitation
(in.) (precipitation
in excess is
lined vertically).

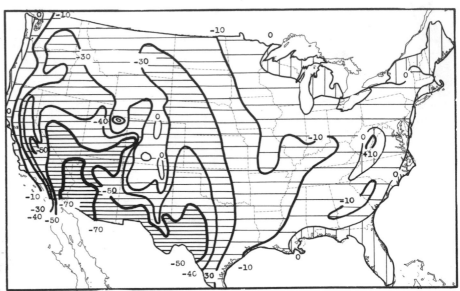

490

Mean difference
(in.) between
precipitation and
evaporation of
April to October.

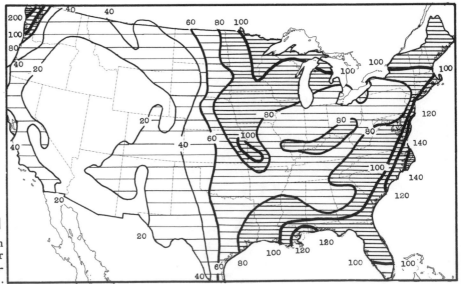

491

Ratio of precipitation
to evaporation for
the normal frost-
free season (percent).

PART V   PRECIPITATION

19. NORMAL AMOUNTS OF PRECIPITATION: ANNUAL, SEASONAL, MONTHLY, SEMIMONTHLY, DAILY

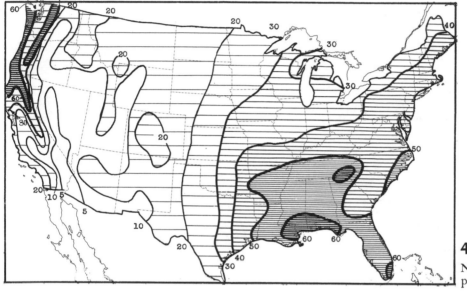

492
Normal annual
precipitation (in.).

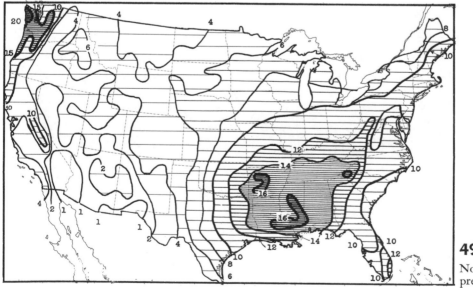

493
Normal spring
precipitation (in.).

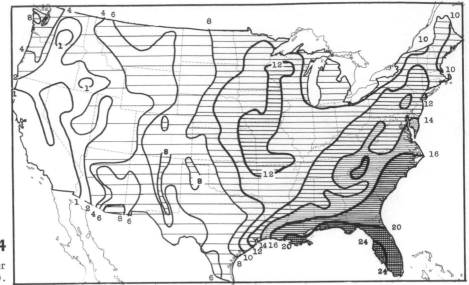

494

Normal summer
precipitation (in.).

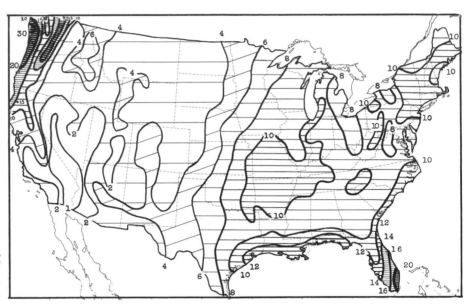

495

Normal fall
precipitation (in.).

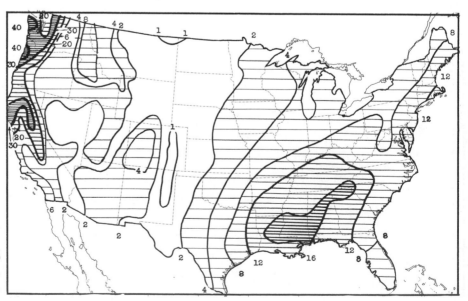

496

Normal winter
precipitation (in.).

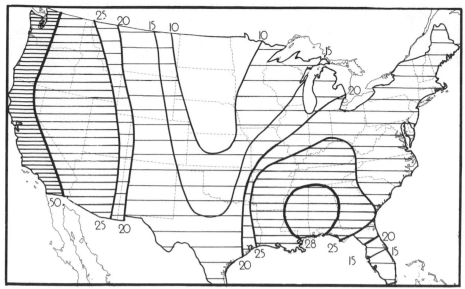

497

Percentage of the normal annual total precipitation that normally occurs in winter (based on state averages for 57 years).

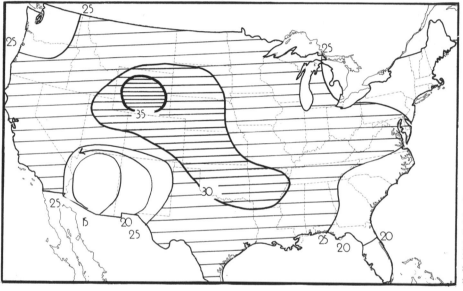

498

Percentage of the normal annual total precipitation that normally occurs in spring (based on state averages for 57 years).

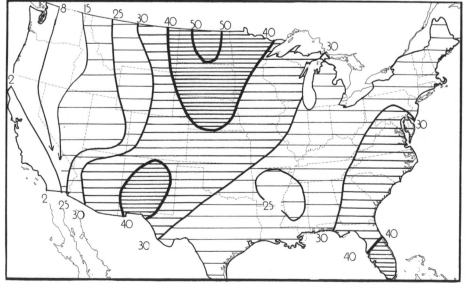

499

Percentage of the normal annual total precipitation that normally occurs in summer (based on state averages for 57 years).

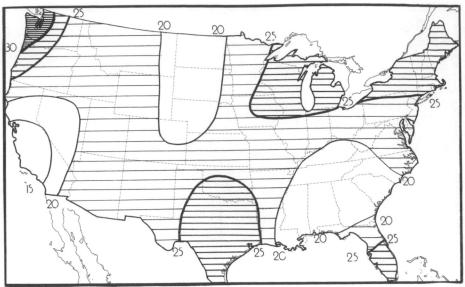

500

Percentage of the normal annual total precipitation that normally occurs in autumn (based on state averages for 57 years).

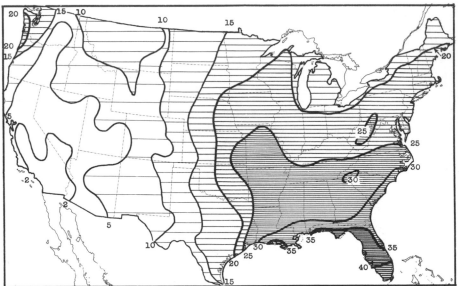

501

Normal precipitation (in.) during the crop-growing season, April to September, inclusive.

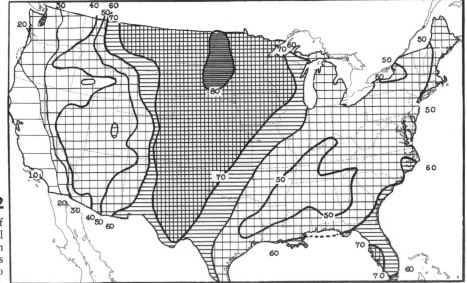

502

Percentage of the normal annual total precipitation that normally occurs from April to September, inclusive.

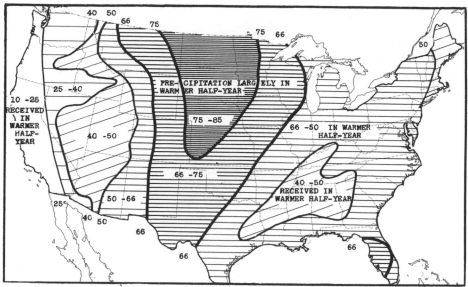

503

Percentage of the normal annual total precipitation that normally occurs in the warmer half year.

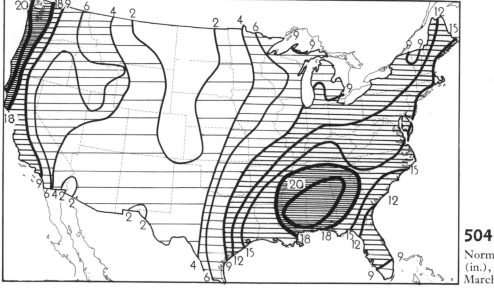

504

Normal precipitation (in.), December to March, inclusive.

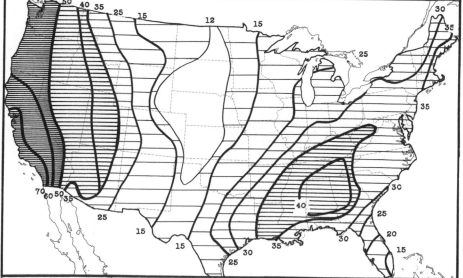

505

Percentage of the normal annual total precipitation that normally occurs from December to March, inclusive.

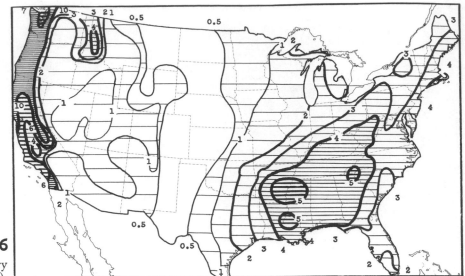

506
Normal January
precipitation (in.).

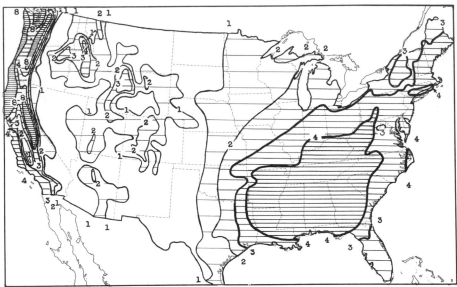

507
Normal March
precipitation (in.).

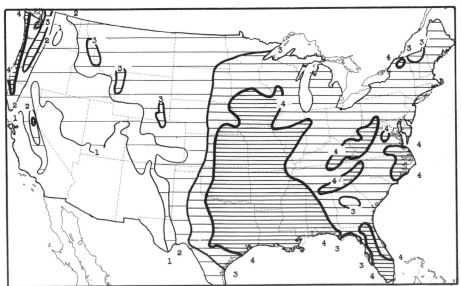

508
Normal May
precipitation (in.).

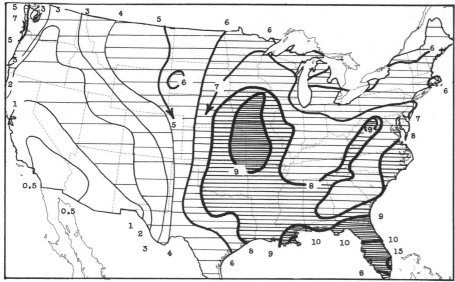

509
Normal May–June
precipitation (in.).

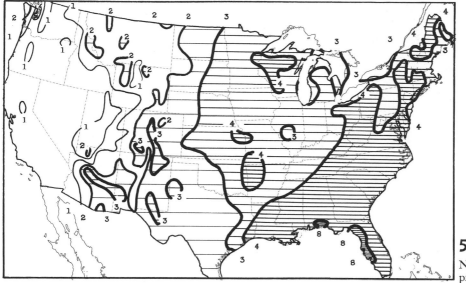

510
Normal July
precipitation (in.).

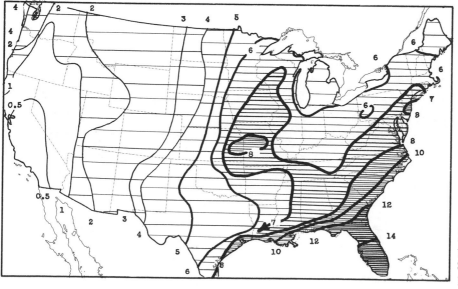

511
Normal August–
September
precipitation (in.).

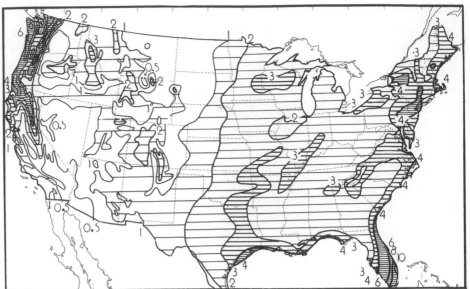

512

Normal October
precipitation (in.).

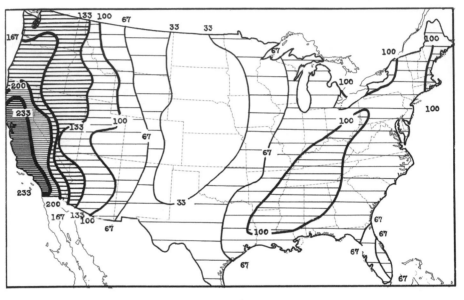

513

Ratio of the
normal January
precipitation to
one-twelfth of
the normal annual
precipitation
(percent).

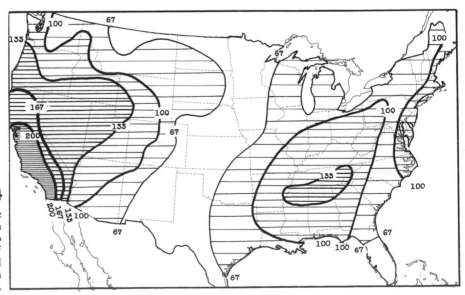

514

Ratio of the
normal March
precipitation to
one-twelfth of
the normal annual
precipitation
(percent).

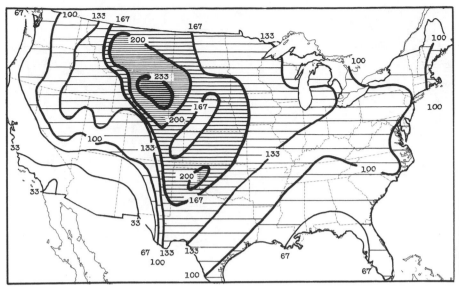

515

Ratio of the normal May precipitation to one-twelfth of the normal annual precipitation (percent).

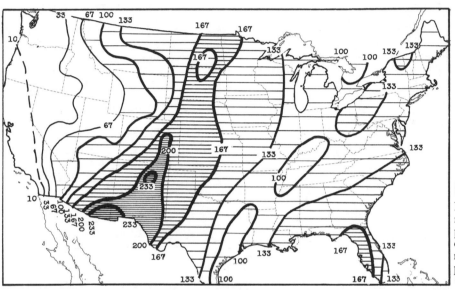

516

Ratio of the normal July precipitation to one-twelfth of the normal annual precipitation (percent).

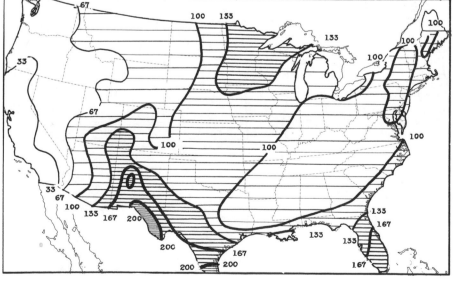

517

Ratio of the normal September precipitation to one-twelfth of the normal annual precipitation (percent).

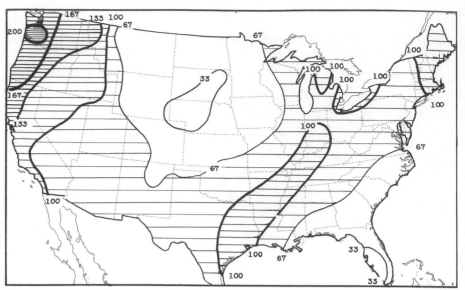

518

Ratio of the normal November precipitation to one-twelfth of the normal annual precipitation (percent).

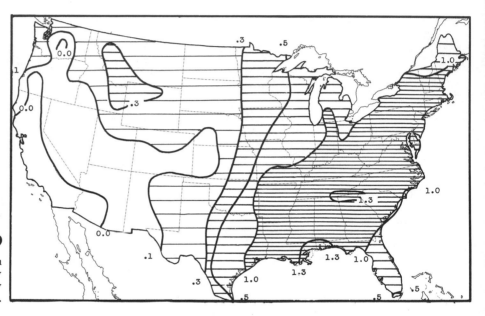

519

Total precipitation in the normally driest 14-day period (in.).

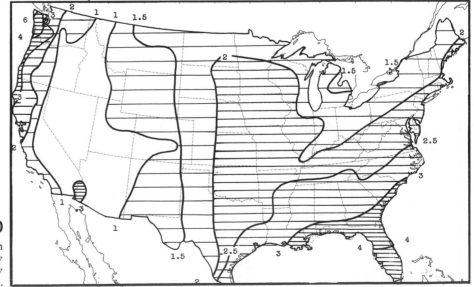

520

Total precipitation in the normally wettest 14-day period (in.).

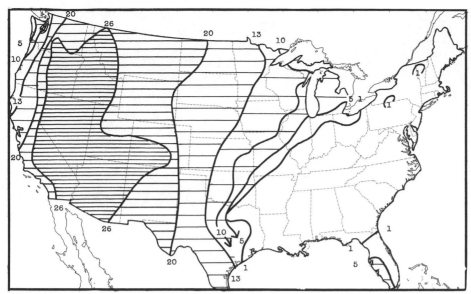

521

Normal annual number of 14-day periods during which less than 1.0 in. of precipitation occurs.

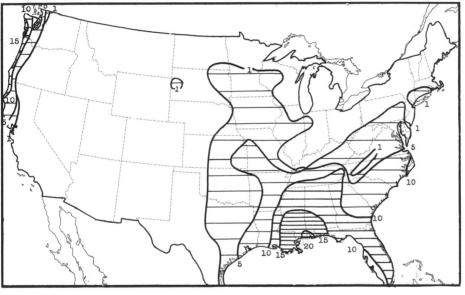

522

Normal annual number of 14-day periods during which more than 2.0 in. of precipitation occurs.

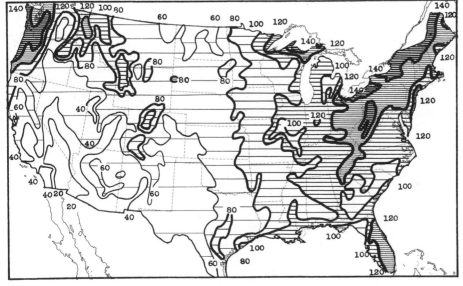

523

Normal annual number of days on which 0.01 in. or more of precipitation occurs.

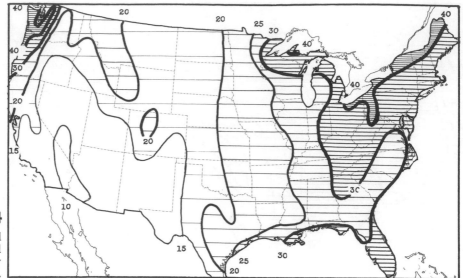

524

Normal annual
daily rainfall
probability
(percent).

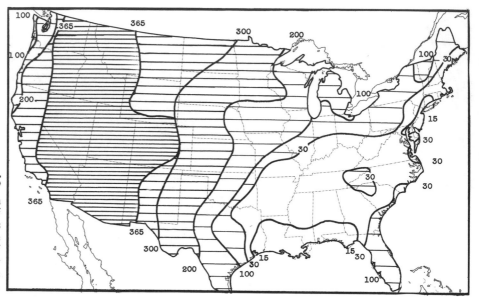

525

Maximum
number of
consecutive days
during which the
annual curve of
normal daily
precipitation is
below 0.1 in.

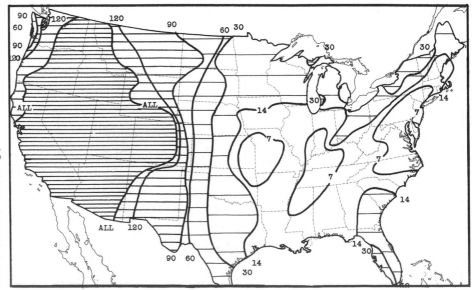

526

Maximum
number of
consecutive days
in the spring-
summer half year
during which the
annual curve of
normal daily
precipitation is
below 0.1 in.

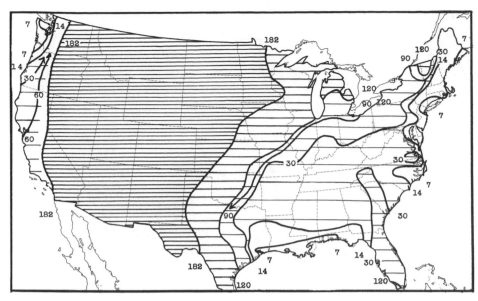

527

Maximum number of consecutive days in the fall-winter half year during which the annual curve of normal daily precipitation is below 0.1 in.

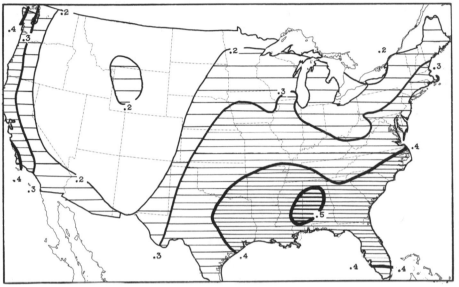

528

Normal annual precipitation per day with precipitation of 0.01 in. or more.

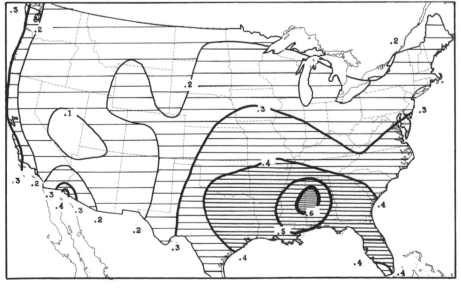

529

Normal precipitation per day in spring with precipitation of 0.01 in. or more.

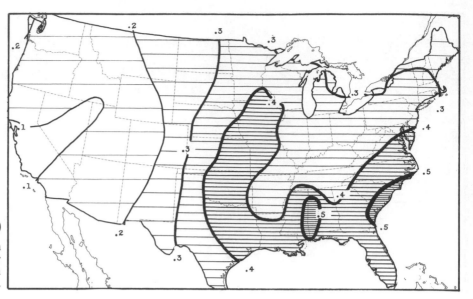

530

Normal precipitation
per day in summer
with precipitation
of 0.01 or more.

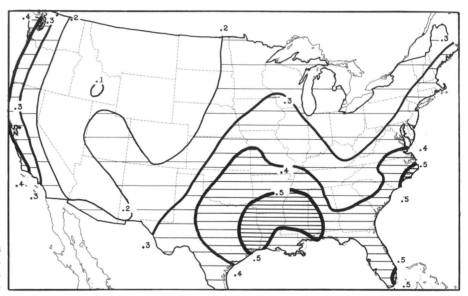

531

Normal precipitation
per day in fall
with precipitation
of 0.01 or more.

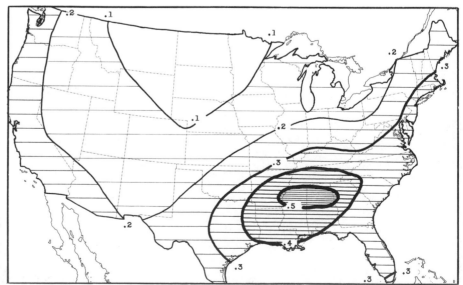

532

Normal precipitation
per day in winter
with precipitation
of 0.01 or more.

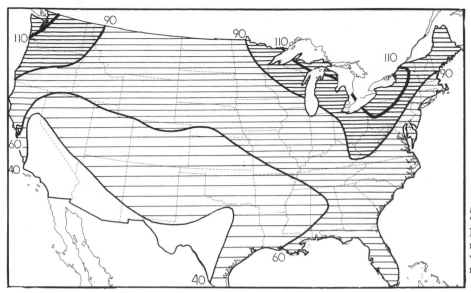

533

Normal annual
number of days
with light to
moderate rainfall
(0.01–0.25 in.).

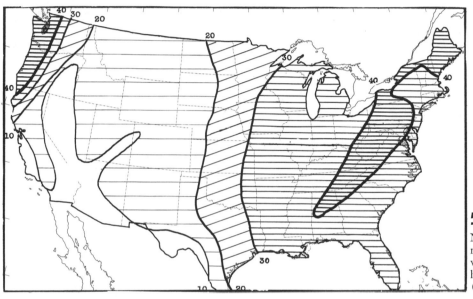

534

Normal annual
number of days
with moderately
heavy rainfall
(0.25–0.5 in.).

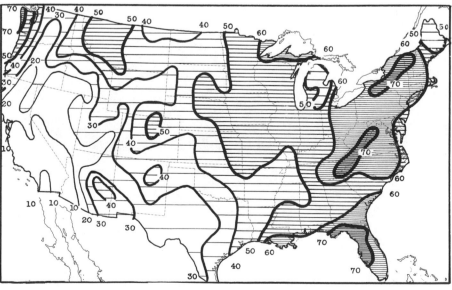

535

Normal number of
days in the
half year April–
September with
precipitation of
0.01 in. or more.

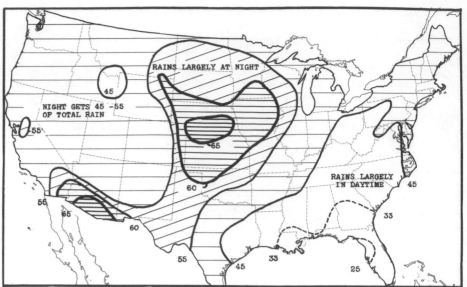

536

Percentage of
total rain that
falls between
6 P.M. and 6 A.M.
in the half year
April to September.

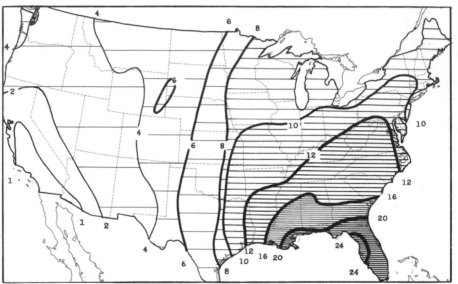

537

Normal total day-
time (6 A.M.–6 P.M.)
precipitation (in.)
for the half year
April to September.

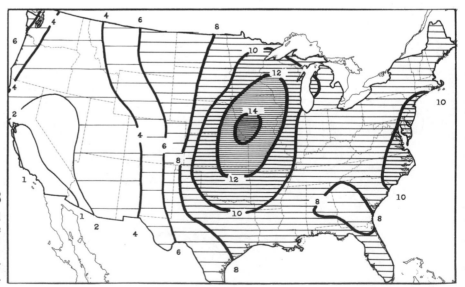

538

Normal total
nighttime
(6 P.M.–6 A.M.)
precipitation (in.)
for the half year
April to September.

20. NORMAL AMOUNT OF PRECIPITATION RECEIVED IN ALTERNATE WEEKS

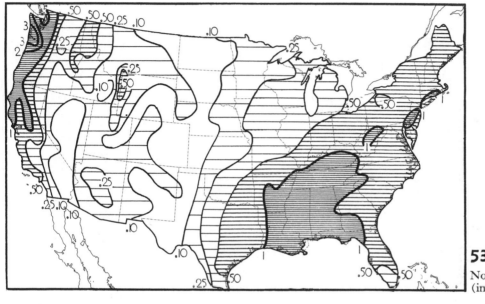

539

Normal precipitation
(in.), January 1–7.

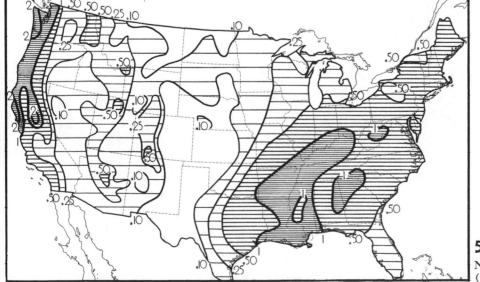

540

Normal precipitation
(in.), January 15–21.

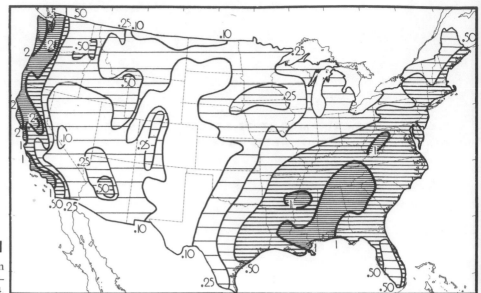

541

Normal precipitation
(in.), January 29–
February 4.

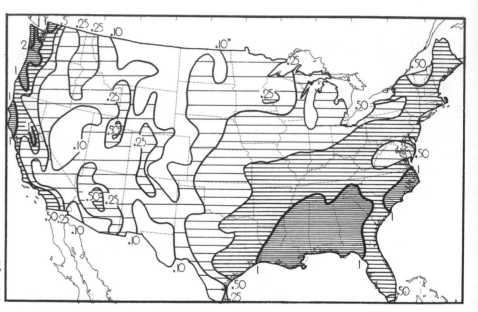

542

Normal precipitation
(in.), February 12–18.

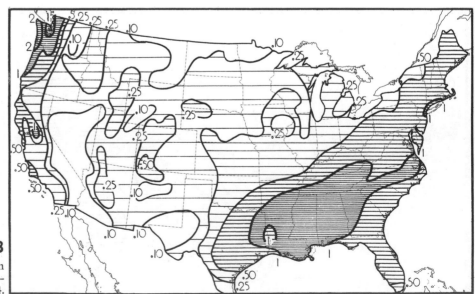

543

Normal precipitation
(in.), February 26–
March 4.

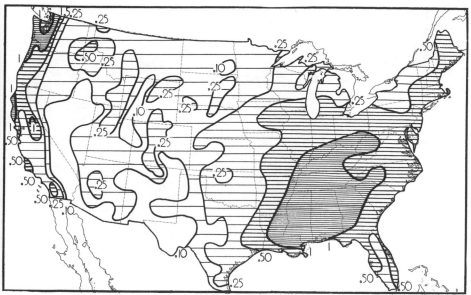

544

Normal precipitation (in.), March 12–19.

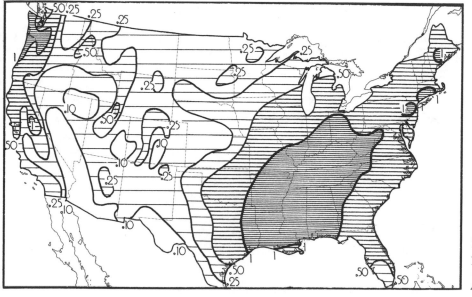

545

Normal precipitation (in.), March 26–April 1.

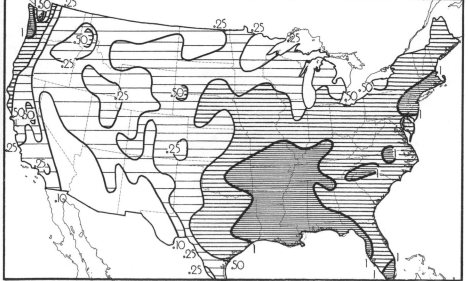

546

Normal precipitation (in.), April 9–15.

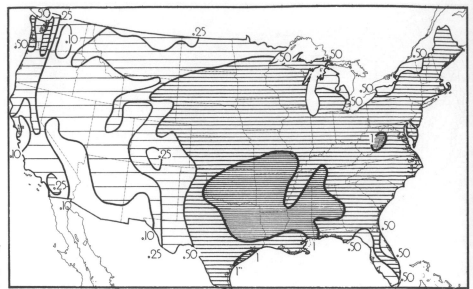

547
Normal precipitation
(in.), April 23–29.

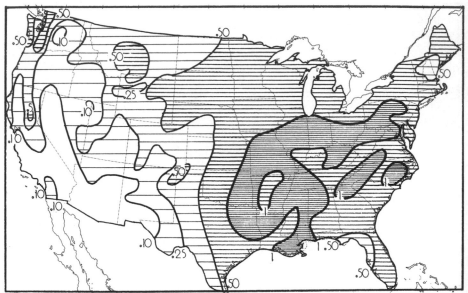

548
Normal precipitation
(in.), May 7–13.

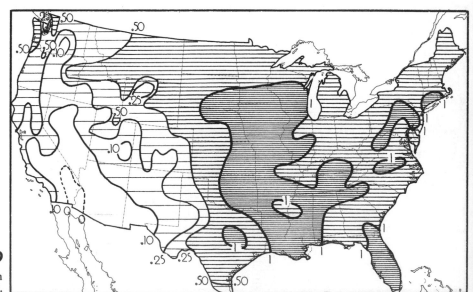

549
Normal precipitation
(in.), May 21–27.

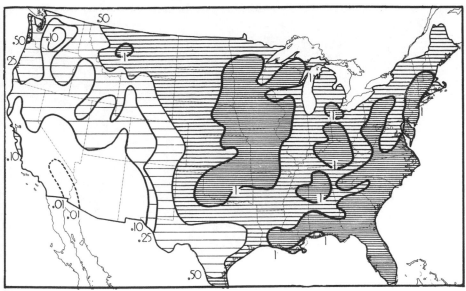

550

Normal precipitation
(in.), June 4–10.

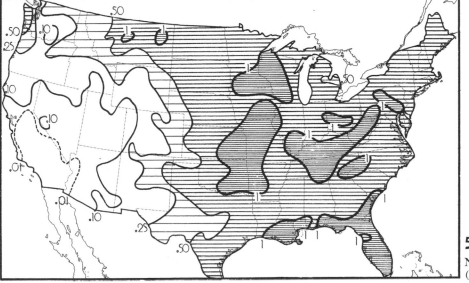

551

Normal precipitation
(in.), June 18–24.

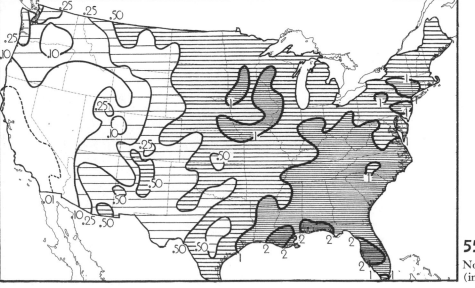

552

Normal precipitation
(in.), July 2–8.

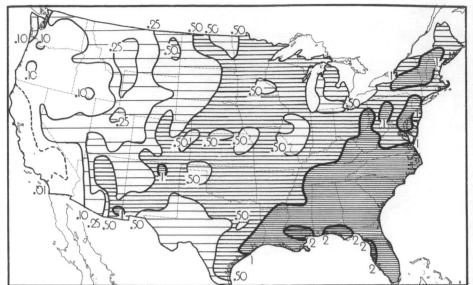

553

Normal precipitation
(in.), July 16–22.

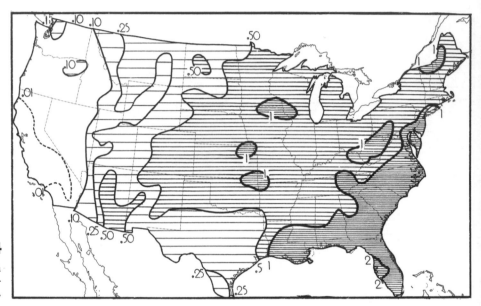

554

Normal precipitation
(in.), July 30–
August 5.

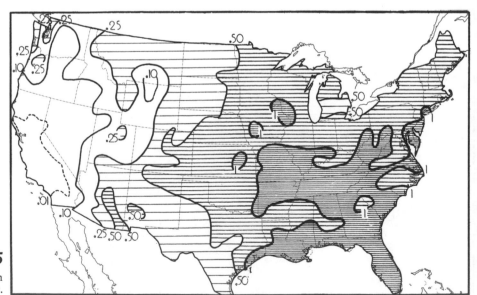

555

Normal precipitation
(in.), August 13–19.

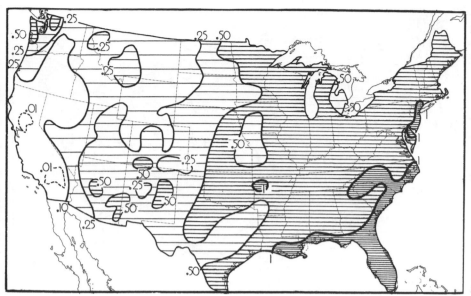

556

Normal precipitation (in.), August 27–September 2.

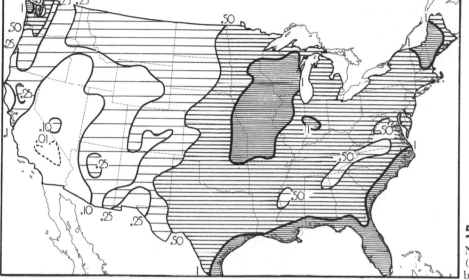

557

Normal precipitation (in.), September 10–16.

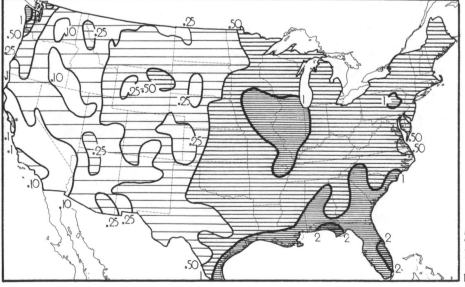

558

Normal precipitation (in.), September 24–30.

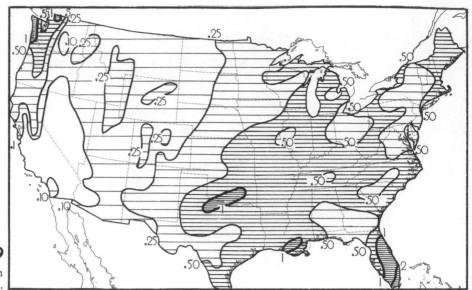

559
Normal precipitation
(in.), October 8–14.

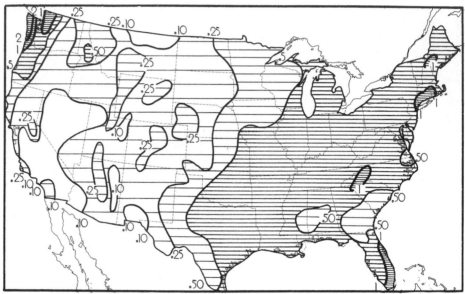

560
Normal precipitation
(in.), October 22–28.

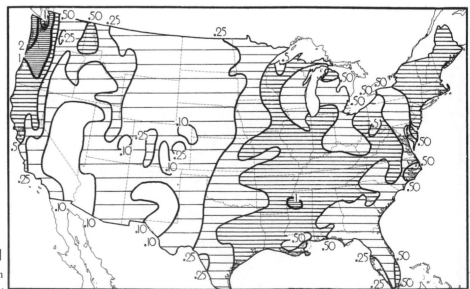

561
Normal precipitation
(in.), November 5–11.

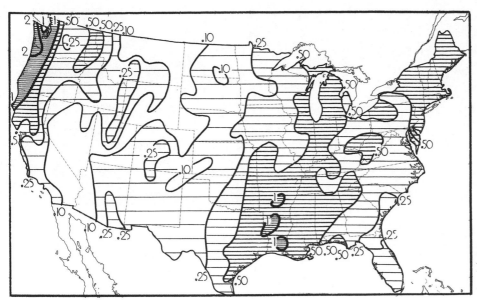

562
Normal precipitation (in.), November 19–25.

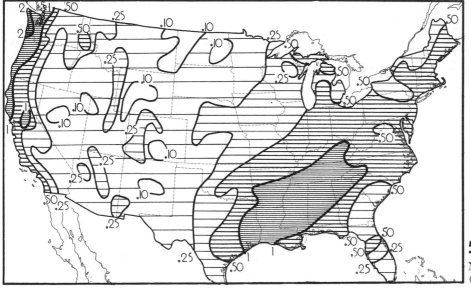

563
Normal precipitation (in.), December 3–9.

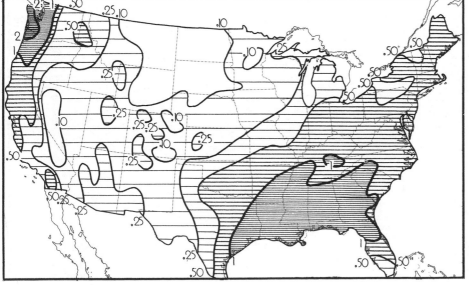

564
Normal precipitation (in.), December 17–23.

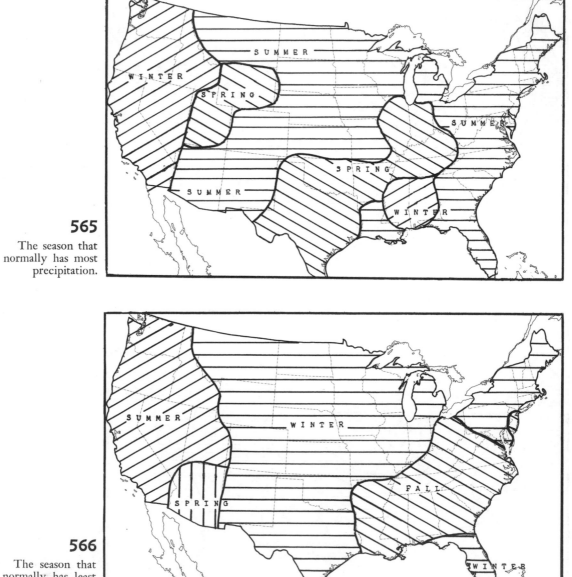

565

The season that normally has most precipitation.

566

The season that normally has least precipitation.

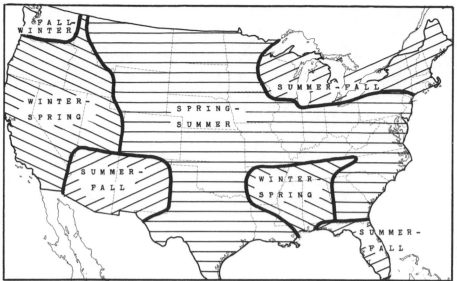

567
The half year
that normally has
most precipitation.

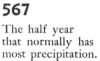

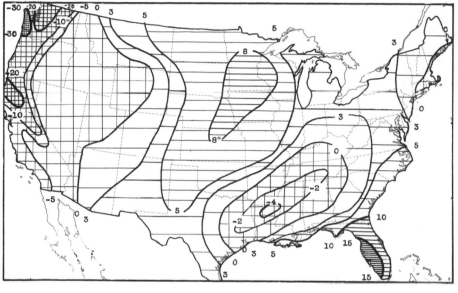

568
Summer versus
winter precipitation
(in.); summer excess,
lined; winter excess,
crossed.

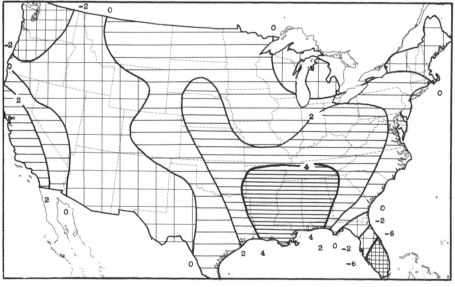

569
Spring versus fall
precipitation (in.);
spring excess, lined;
autumn excess,
crossed.

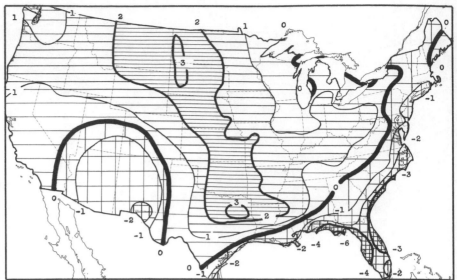

570

May–June versus August–September precipitation (in.); May–June excess, lined; August–September excess, crossed.

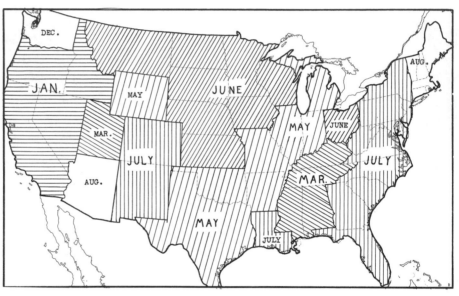

571

The wettest month of the year, normally (state averages).

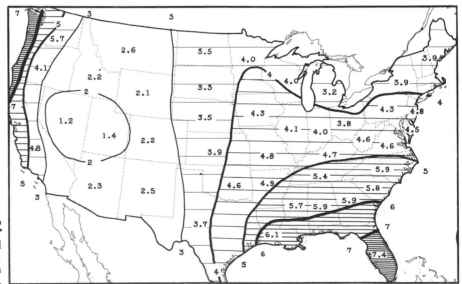

572

Normal total precipitation (in.) in the month normally wettest.

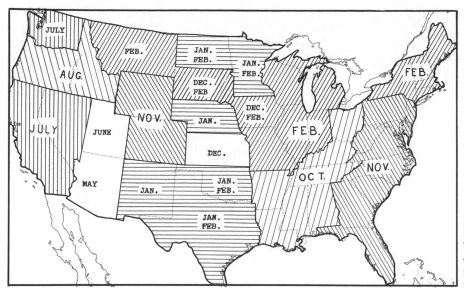

573

The driest month of the year, normally (state averages).

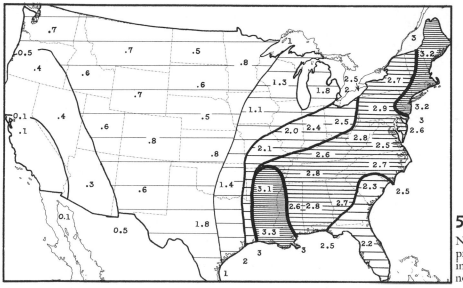

574

Normal total precipitation (in.) in the month normally driest.

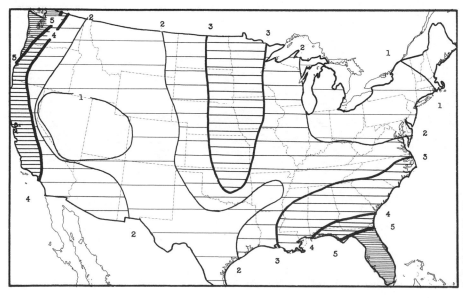

575

Differences in precipitation (in.), between the normally wettest and driest months of the year.

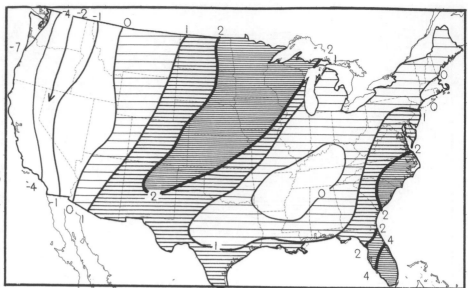

576

Normal July
excess of
precipitation (in.)
over that usually
received in
January; where
January is the
wetter, unshaded.

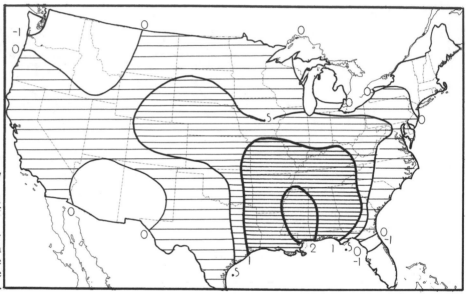

577

Normal April
excess of
precipitation (in.)
over that usually
received in
October; where
October is the
wetter, unshaded.

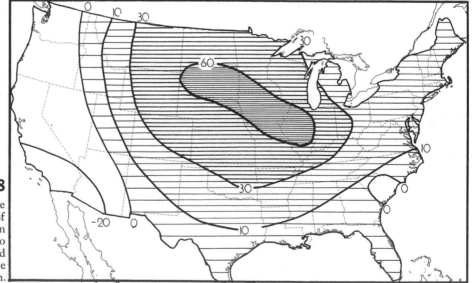

578

Average percentage
increase of
precipitation from
February to
March; unshaded
areas receive
less in March.

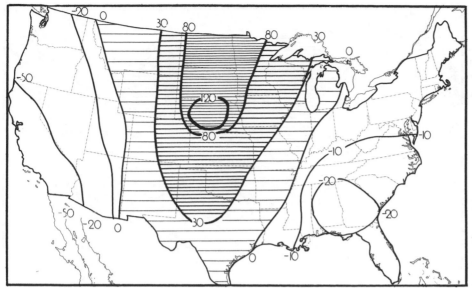

579

Average percentage increase of precipitation from March to April; unshaded areas receive less in April.

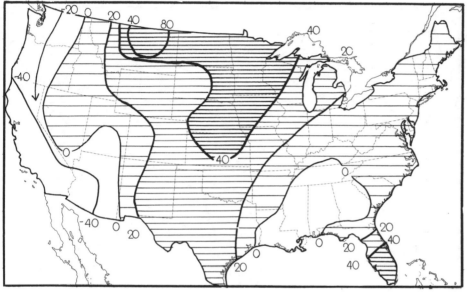

580

Average percentage increase of precipitation from April to May; unshaded areas receive less in May.

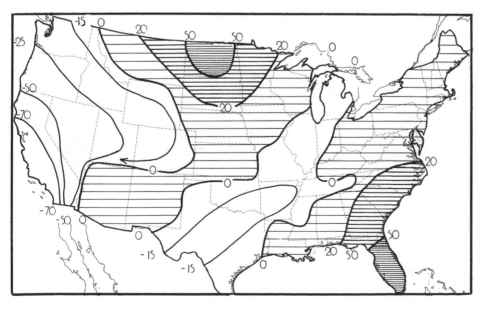

581

Average percentage increase of precipitation from May to June; unshaded areas receive less in June.

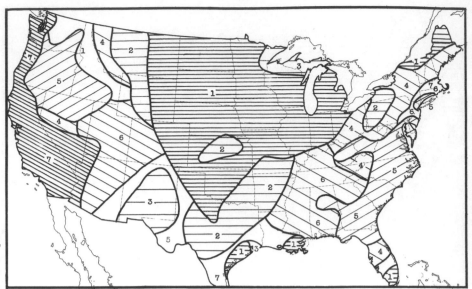

582

The normally
driest 14-day
period of spring.

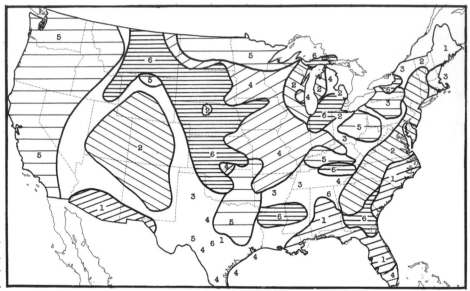

583

The normally
driest 14-day
period of summer.

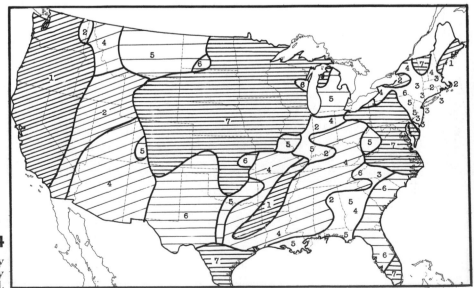

584

The normally
driest 14-day
period of fall.

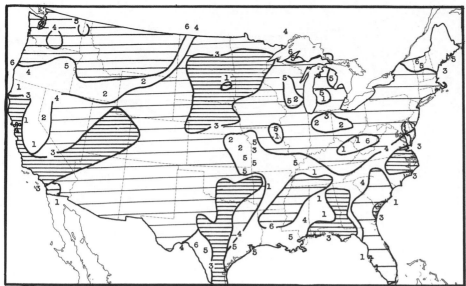

585
The normally
driest 14-day
period of winter.

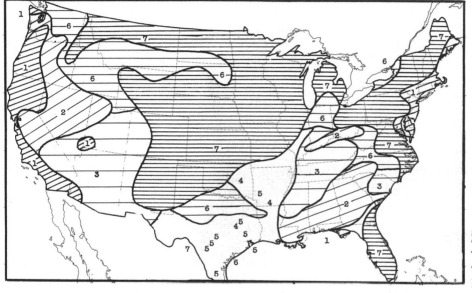

586
The normally
wettest 14-day
period of spring.

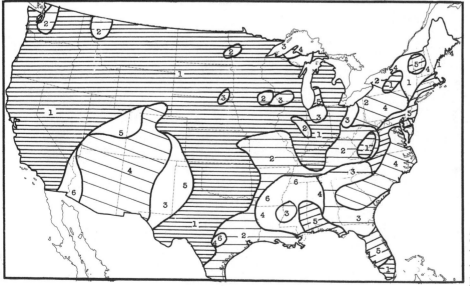

587
The normally
wettest 14-day
period of summer.

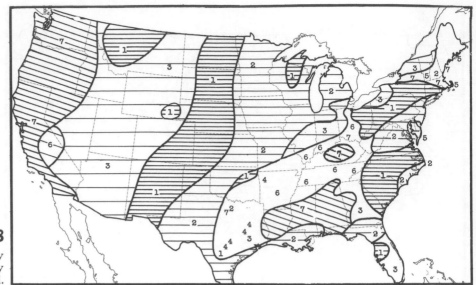

588

The normally wettest 14-day period of fall.

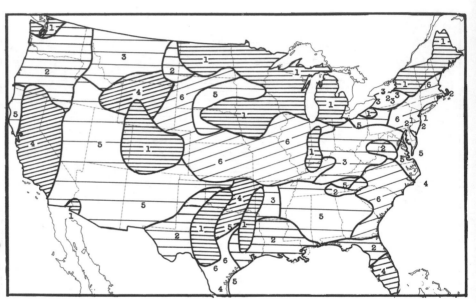

589

The normally wettest 14-day period of winter.

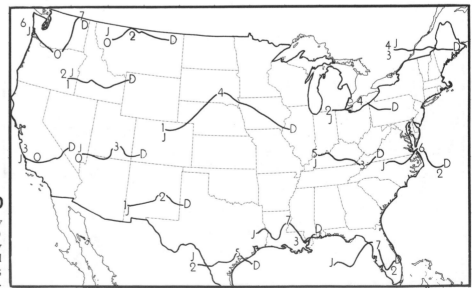

590

Normal monthly precipitation (in.) as shown by curves for selected states; *J*, January; *D*, December.

RAINFALL TYPES. AS SHOWN BY THE PERCENTAGE OF THE ANNUAL WHICH OCCURS MONTHLY.

591

Normal monthly precipitation (percent of annual precipitation) as shown by bar graphs for selected states.

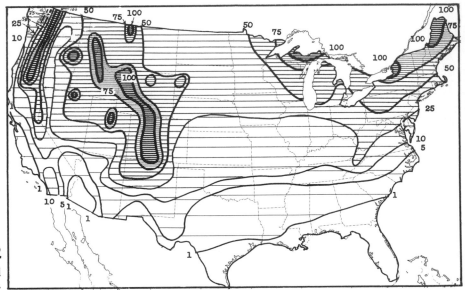

592

Normal annual
snowfall (in.).

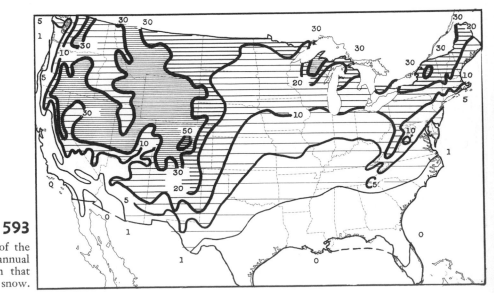

593

Percentage of the
normal annual
precipitation that
falls as snow.

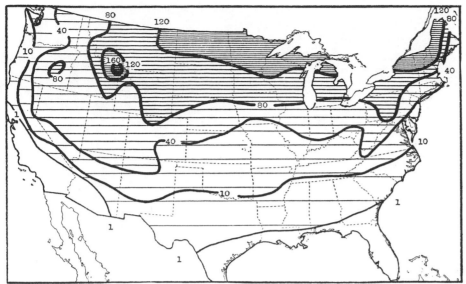

594

Normal number of days with snow cover (1 in.).

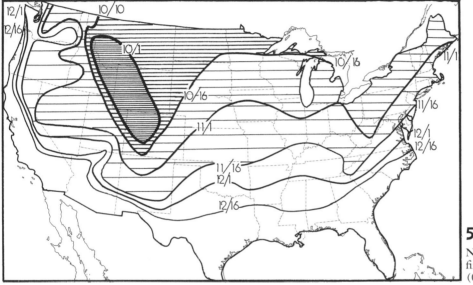

595

Normal date of first snowfall (0.1 in.) in fall.

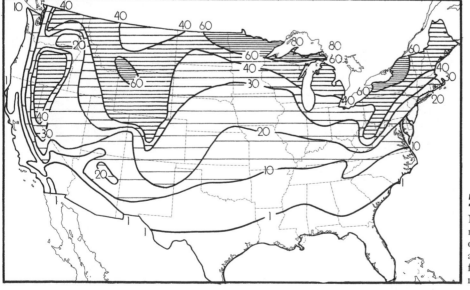

596

Normal annual number of days on which appreciable snow falls (0.01 in. or more melted).

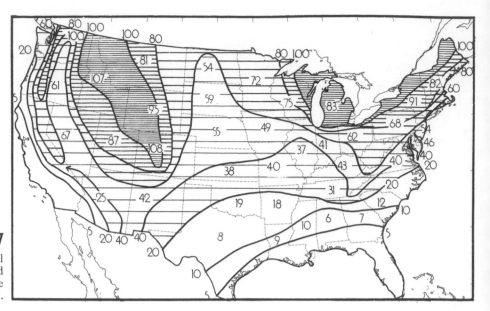

597

Heaviest annual snowfall of record (in.), based on state averages to 1945.

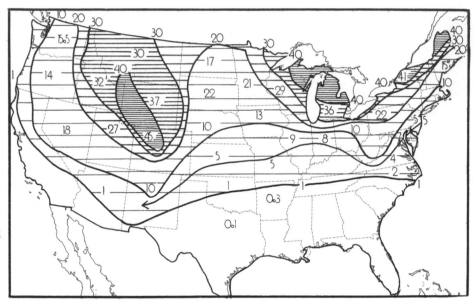

598

Least annual snowfall of record (in.), based on state averages to 1945.

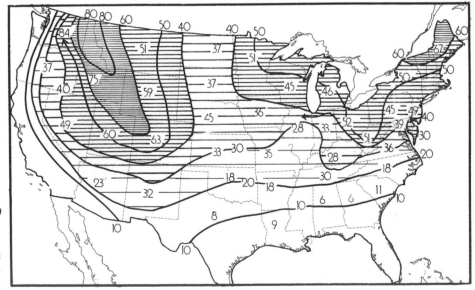

599

Snowfall range: difference (in.) between totals shown in Figs. 597 and 598.

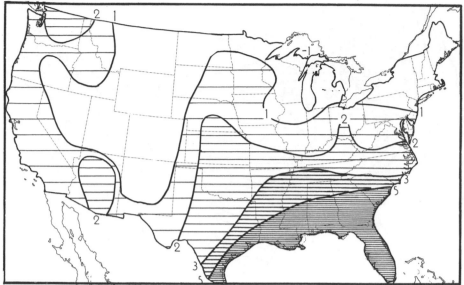

600

Snowfall range compared with normal annual snowfall (1, equal; 5, range 5 times normal annual amount).

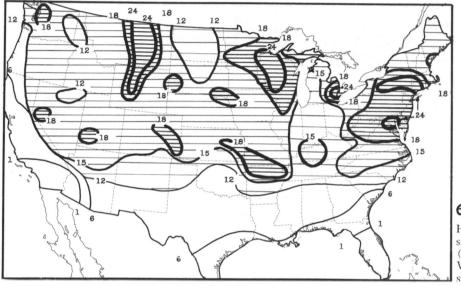

601

Heaviest 24-hr snowfall of record (in.) at first-order Weather Bureau stations (to 1931).

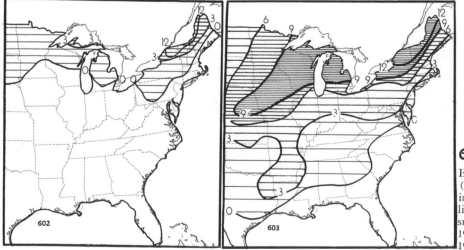

602, 603

Extent and depth (in.) of snow cover in Januaries with little and with much snow (January 24, 1944; January 22, 1940).

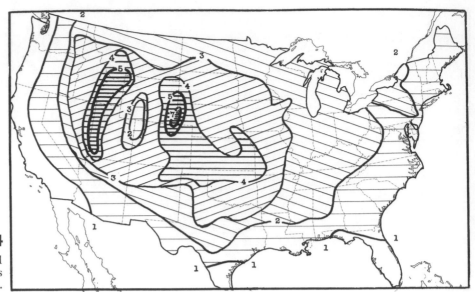

604

Normal annual
number of days
with hail.

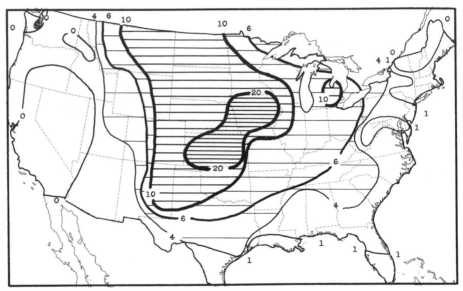

605

Normal number of
hailstorms per
growing season
(based on state
averages).

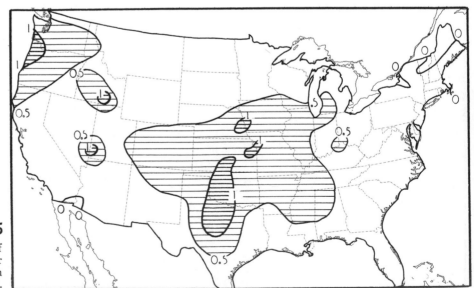

606

Normal number of
hailstorms per
sizeable area in
April.

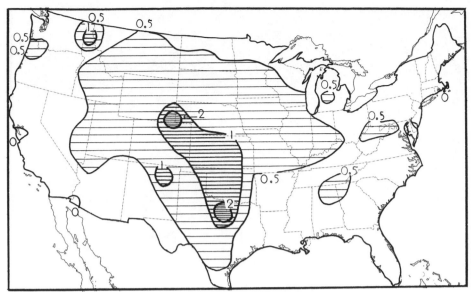

607

Normal number of
hailstorms per
sizeable area in
May.

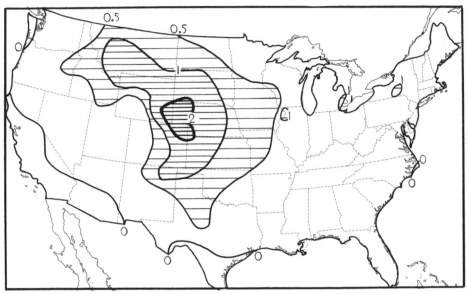

608

Normal number of
hailstorms per
sizeable area in
June.

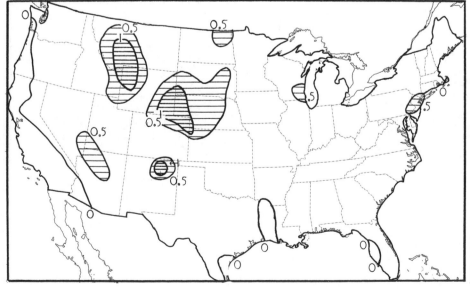

609

Normal number of
hailstorms per
sizeable area in
July.

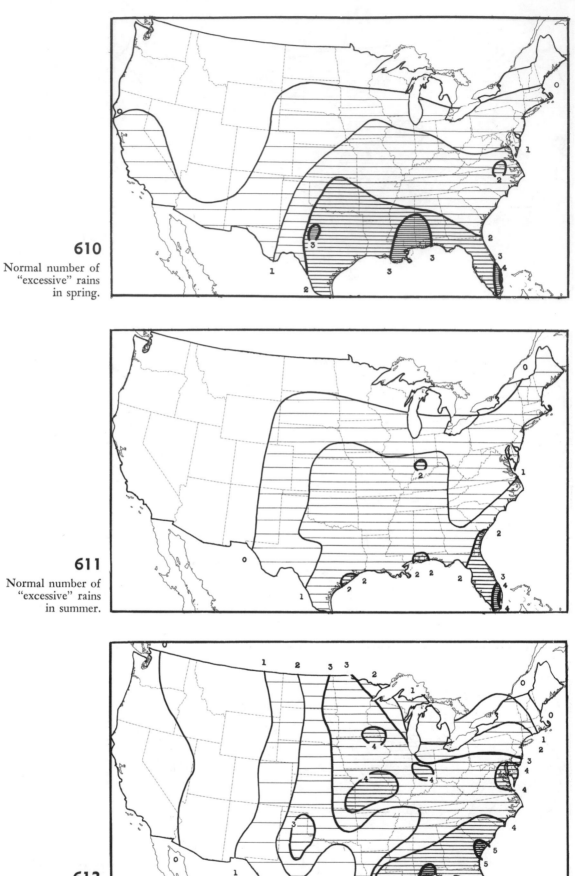

610

Normal number of "excessive" rains in spring.

611

Normal number of "excessive" rains in summer.

612

Normal number of "excessive" rains in fall.

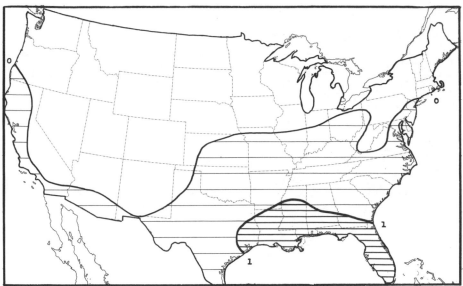

613

Normal number of "excessive" rains in winter.

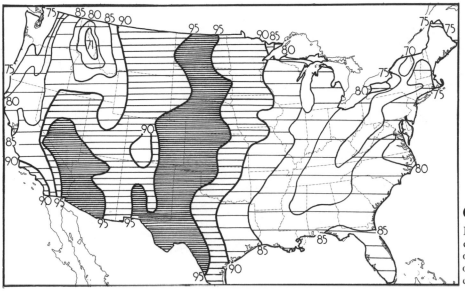

614

Probabilities (percent) in January of less than 0.1 in. of precipitation during the next 48 hr.

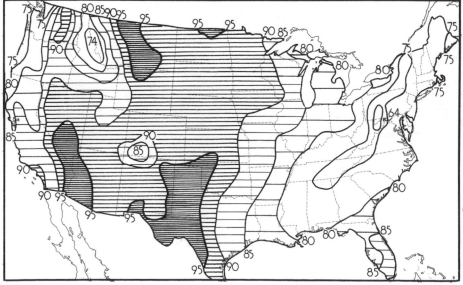

615

Probabilities (percent) in February of less than 0.1 in. of precipitation during the next 48 hr.

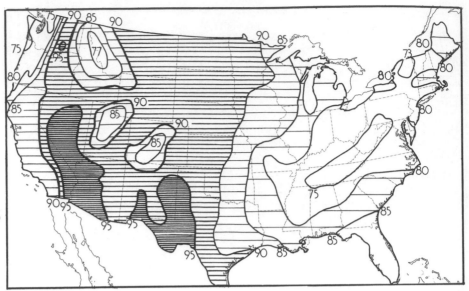

616

Probabilities (per-
cent) in March
of less than 0.1 in.
of precipitation
during the next 48 hr.

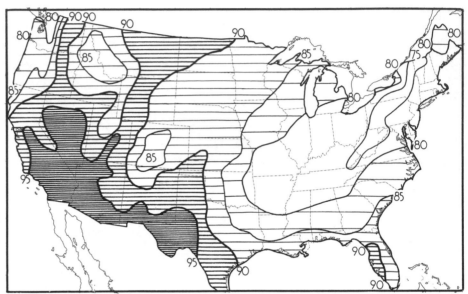

617

Probabilities (per-
cent) in April
of less than 0.1 in.
of precipitation
during the next 48 hr.

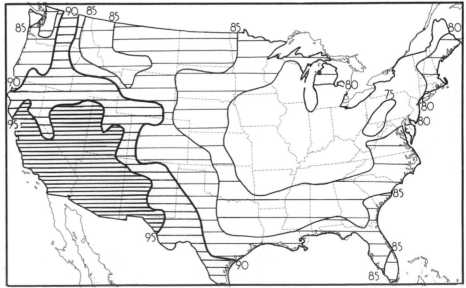

618

Probabilities (per-
cent) in May
of less than 0.1 in.
of precipitation
during the next 48 hr.

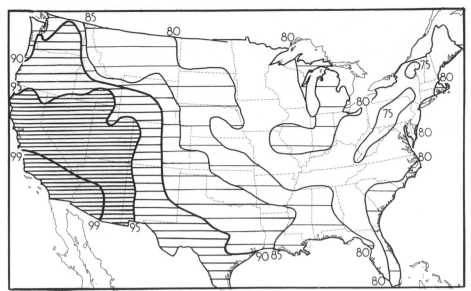

619

Probabilities (percent) in June
of less than 0.1 in.
of precipitation
during the next 48 hr.

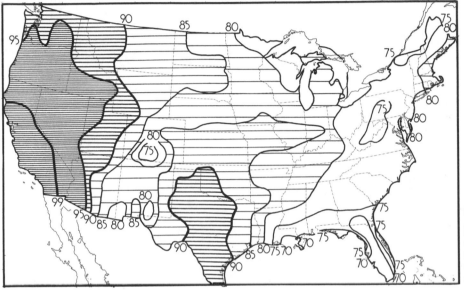

620

Probabilities (percent) in July
of less than 0.1 in.
of precipitation
during the next 48 hr.

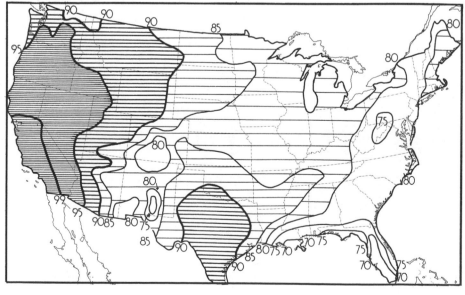

621

Probabilities (percent) in August
of less than 0.1 in.
of precipitation
during the next 48 hr.

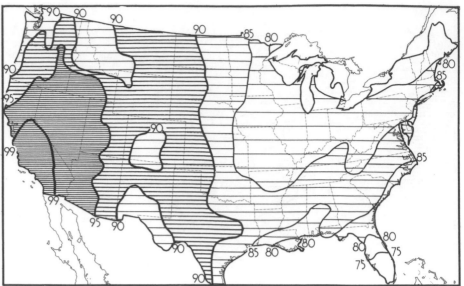

622

Probabilities (percent) in September of less than 0.1 in. of precipitation during the next 48 hr.

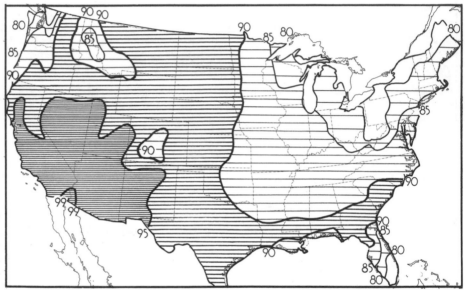

623

Probabilities (percent) in October of less than 0.1 in. of precipitation during the next 48 hr.

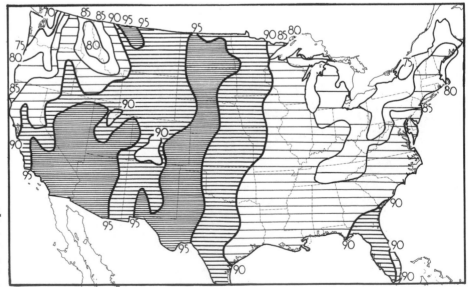

624

Probabilities (percent) in November of less than 0.1 in. of precipitation during the next 48 hr.

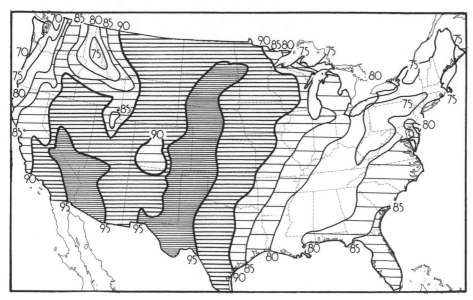

625
Probabilities (percent) in December of less than 0.1 in. of precipitation during the next 48 hr.

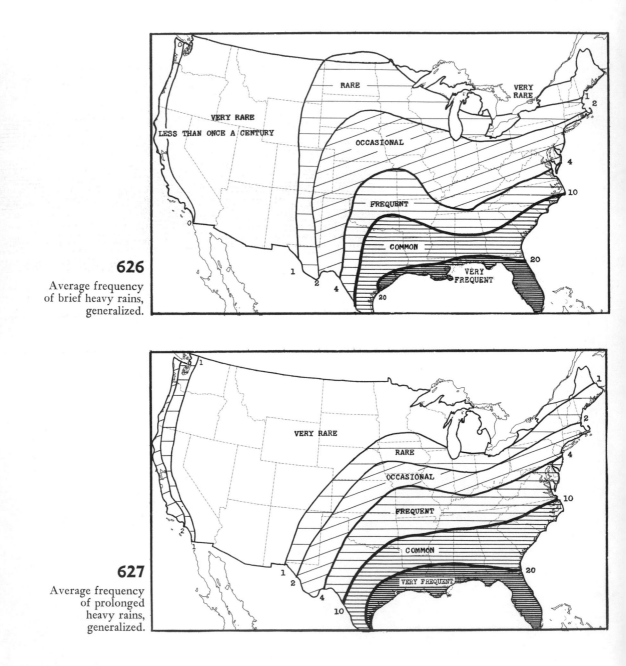

626
Average frequency
of brief heavy rains,
generalized.

627
Average frequency
of prolonged
heavy rains,
generalized.

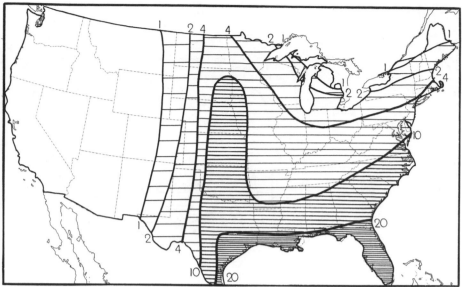

628

Number per century
of rainfalls of
1 in. in 10 min.

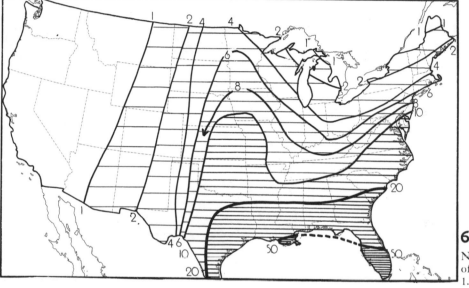

629

Number per century
of rainfalls of
1.25 in. in 15 min.

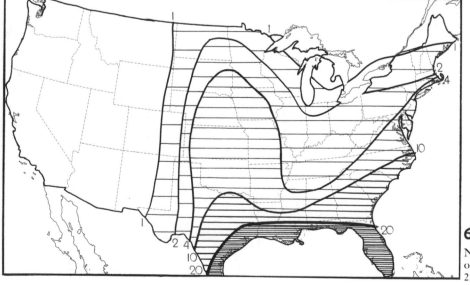

630

Number per century
of rainfalls of
2.00 in 30 min.

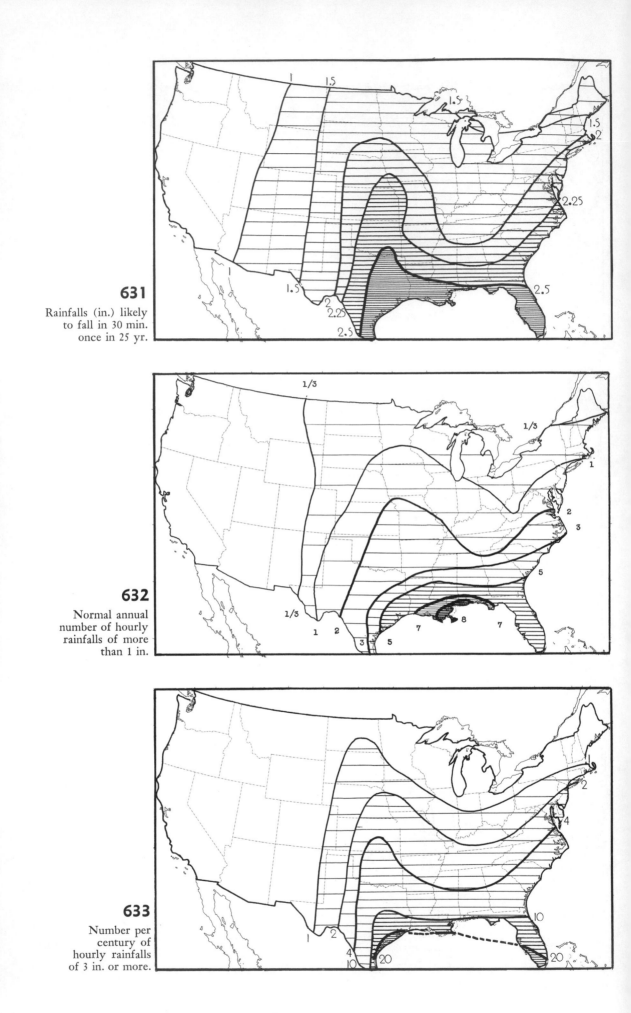

631
Rainfalls (in.) likely
to fall in 30 min.
once in 25 yr.

632
Normal annual
number of hourly
rainfalls of more
than 1 in.

633
Number per
century of
hourly rainfalls
of 3 in. or more.

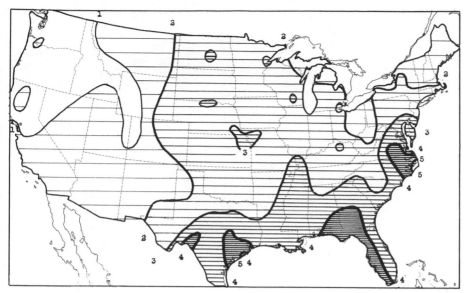

634
Heaviest hourly
rainfall (in.)
likely in 40 yr
(conservative, as
based on main
stations only).

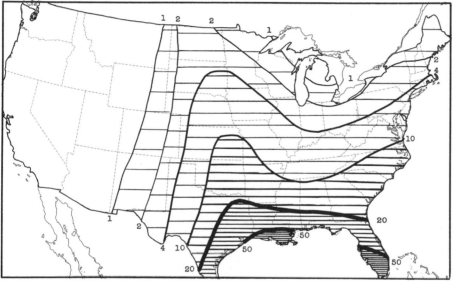

635
Number per century
of 2-hr rainfalls
of 3 in. or more.

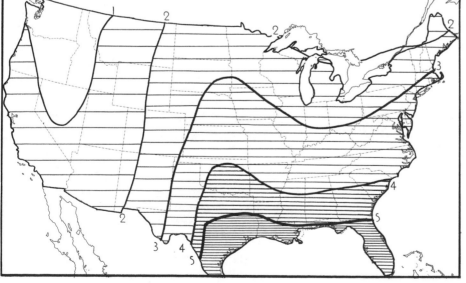

636
Two-hour rainfalls
(in.) likely once
in 25 yr.

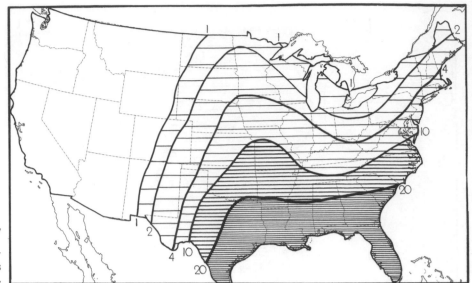

637

Number per century
of 8-hr rainfalls
of 4 in. or more.

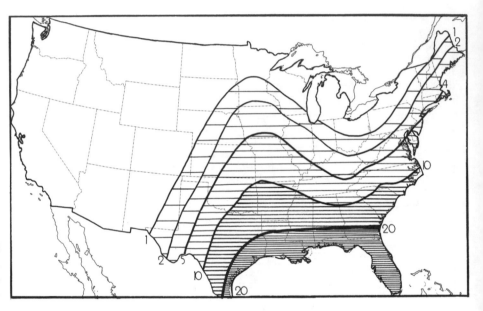

638

Number per century
of 16-hr rainfalls
of 5 in. or more.

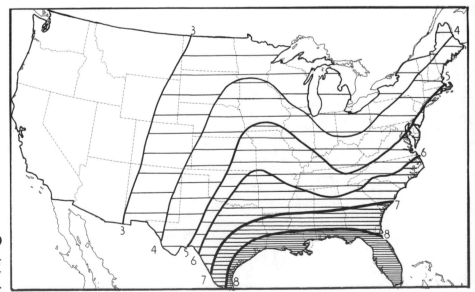

639

Sixteen-hour
rainfalls (in.) likely
once in 25 yr.

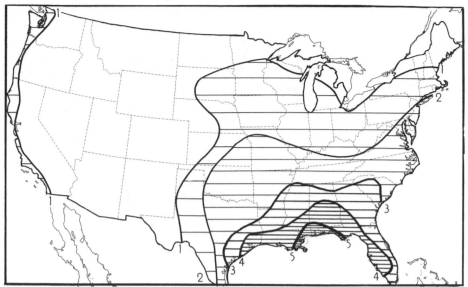

640

Normal annual
number of days
with rainfalls
of 2 in. or more.

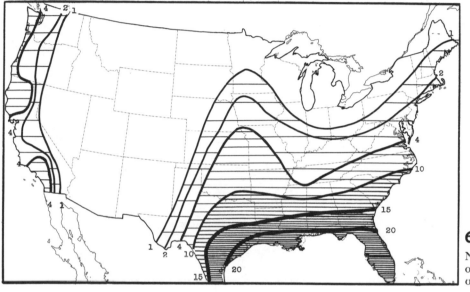

641

Number per century
of 24-hr rainfalls
of 6 in. or more.

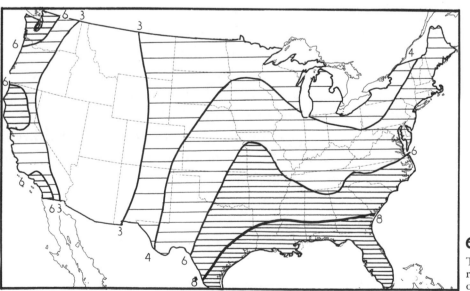

642

Twenty-four-hour
rainfalls (in.) likely
once in 25 yr.

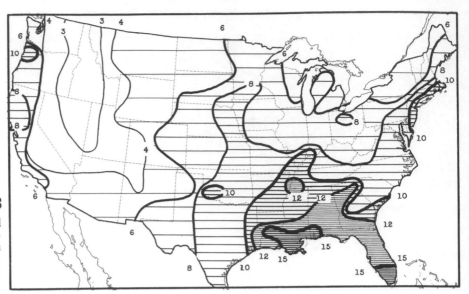

643

Heaviest rainfall (in.) in 72 consecutive hours at 200 first-order stations (prior to 1931).

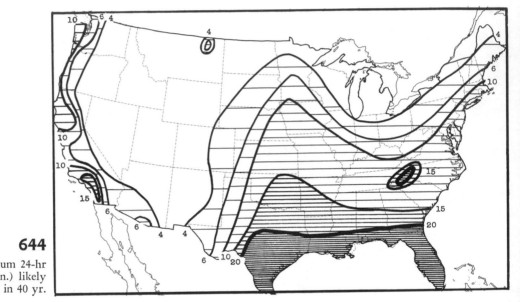

644

Maximum 24-hr rainfall (in.) likely in 40 yr.

RAINFALL RECORDS

Figure 644, showing the maximum rainfall to be expected each half century, is based on scattered records during the 50 years ending with 1944. Since the individual records of about 293 days with more than 10 in. of rainfall, mostly in a single decade, were assembled by the present writer and published in the *Monthly Weather Review*, John R. Theaman of Indianapolis has assembled several score earlier and later records, especially for the Southern and Pacific States, and has privately published them. The nine highest official records to 1945 are: Hooge's Camp, California, 25.83 in. in 24 hr. on January 22–23, 1943; Santa Anita Springs, California, 24.10 in. on the same day; New Smyrna, Florida, 23.22 in. on October 10–11, 1924; Taylor, Texas, 23.11 in. on September 9–10, 1921; Alta Pass, North Carolina, 22.22 in. on July 15–16, 1922; Alexandria, Louisiana, 21.2

in. on June 15–16, 1886; Montell, Texas, 20.6 in. on June 28–29, 1913; Smithville, Texas, 20.40 in. on June 29–30, 1940; Elba, Alabama, 20.0 in. on March 14–15, 1929. For the northern half of the United States, the highest records appear to be Tuckerton, New Jersey, 14.8 in. on August 19–20, 1939; Jewell, Maryland, 14.75 in. on July 26–27, 1897; Larabee and Primghar, Iowa, 13.00 in. on June 24, 1891, and July 14–15, 1900; Neosha Falls, Kansas, 13.0 in. on September 12, 1926; Greeley Center, Nebraska, 12.0 in. on June 5, 1896; Quinault, Washington, 12.0 in. on January 21, 1935.

Unofficial records and estimates of torrential rainfalls have more recently been assembled by the Hydrometeorological Section of the Army Engineers (published, mimeographed, as Technical Papers of the Weather Bureau, April 1947). Those in charge of this study conclude that rainfall totals much greater than the official ones mentioned above and mapped in Fig. 644, occasionally occur. Indeed, a chart of the "maximum possible rainfall in 24 hours" indicates that nearly 40 in. has occurred in 24 hr. near Thrall, Texas on September 9, 1921, and about 30 in. near Smithport, Pennsylvania on July 18, 1942.

In "Hydrometeorological Report No. 23" (mimeographed), June 1947, these experts chart estimated maximum possible rainfalls in 6 hr. for small areas (10 square miles) which are greater than the officially recorded 24-hr. totals. They show a total of more than 26 to 30 in. in 6 hr. from central Texas to Virginia and north in the Appalachians into Pennsylvania. In 24 hr., the maximum possible in small areas is given as about one-fourth greater than for 6 hr., with totals as great as 25 in. theoretically possible in northern Nebraska, Illinois, southern Michigan, and Massachusetts, and with more than 35 in. possible in 24 hr. in the South, from western Texas to South Carolina. The totals for a somewhat larger area (500 square miles) are notably less than for 10 square miles but are estimated at 20 in. in 24 hr. for southern Iowa, northern Indiana, and Maryland, and at about 30 in. in southern Louisiana and adjacent Texas and Mississippi. The calculated possible maximum totals in 48 hr. for areas of 500 square miles are 21 in. in southeastern Nebraska, northern Illinois, northern Ohio, and central Pennsylvania; 30 in. is given for southern Oklahoma to southern South Carolina and 34 in. for southeast Texas to western Florida.

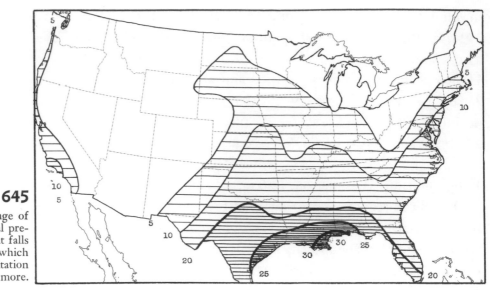

645

Percentage of the annual precipitation that falls on days on which the precipitation is 2.5 in. or more.

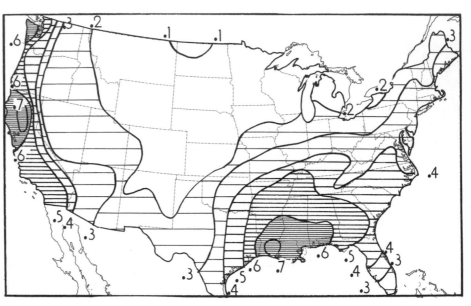

646

Normal precipitation (in.) on a day having measurable precipitation, January 1–28.

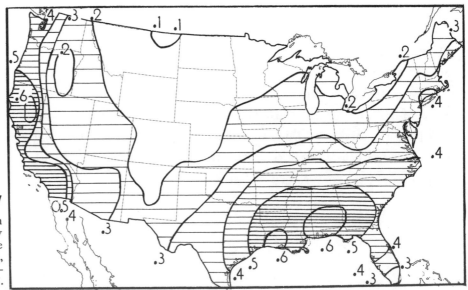

647

Normal precipitation (in.) on a day having measurable precipitation, January 29–February 25.

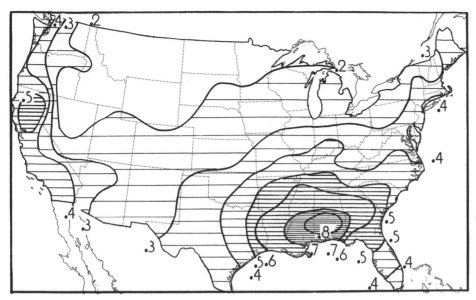

648

Normal precipitation (in.) on a day having measurable precipitation, February 26–March 25.

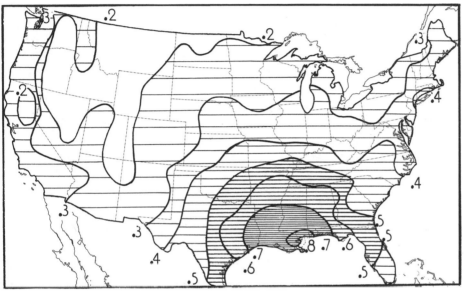

649

Normal precipitation (in.) on a day having measurable precipitation, March 26–April 22.

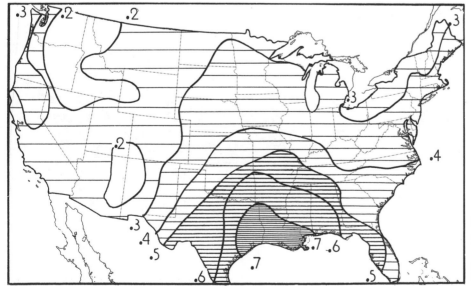

650

Normal precipitation (in.) on a day having measurable precipitation, April 23–May 20.

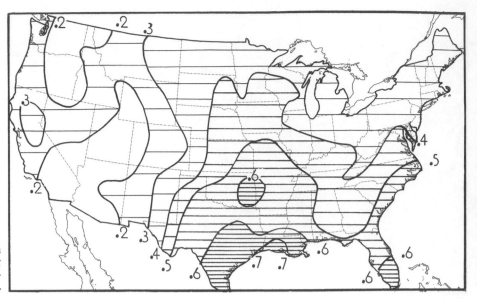

651

Normal precipitation (in.) on a day having measurable precipitation, May 21–June 17.

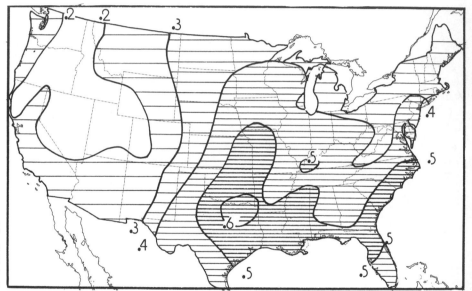

652

Normal precipitation (in.) on a day having measurable precipitation, June 18–July 15.

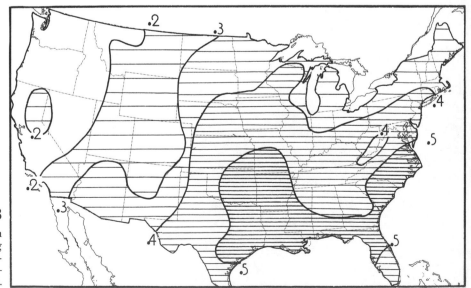

653

Normal precipitation (in.) on a day having measurable precipitation, July 16–August 12.

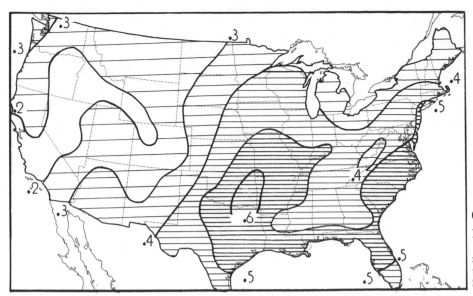

654

Normal precipitation (in.) on a day having measurable precipitation, August 13–September 9.

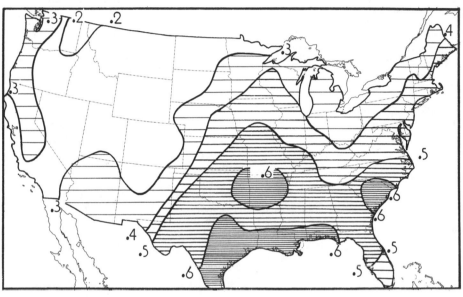

655

Normal precipitation (in.) on a day having measurable precipitation, September 10–October 7.

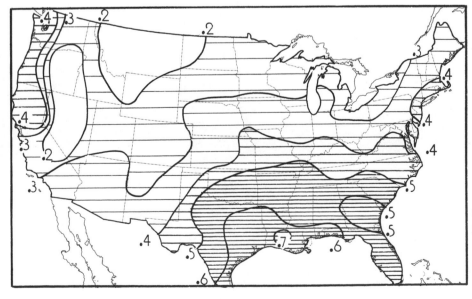

656

Normal precipitation (in.) on a day having measurable precipitation, October 8–November 4.

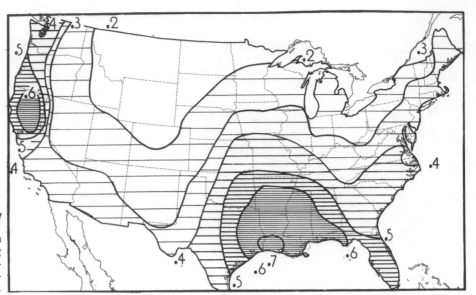

657

Normal precipitation (in.) on a day having measurable precipitation, November 5–December 2.

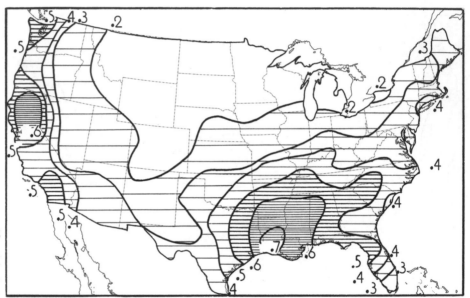

658

Normal precipitation (in.) on a day having measurable precipitation, December 3–31.

24. NORMAL RUNOFF AND ABSORPTION
(GROUND-WATER RECHARGE)

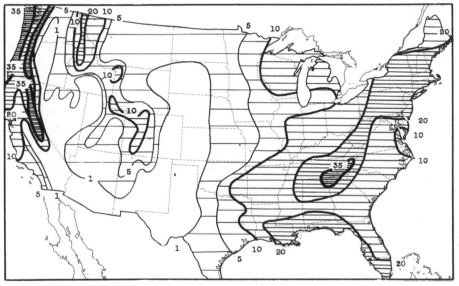

659
Normal annual runoff (in.).

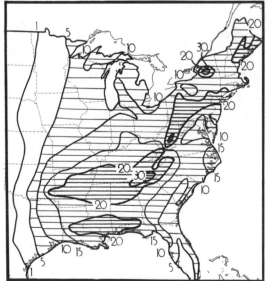

660
Normal annual runoff (in.), eastern United States.

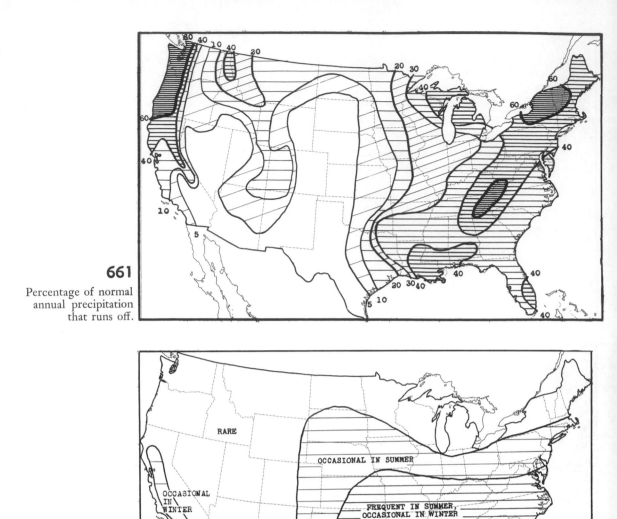

661
Percentage of normal annual precipitation that runs off.

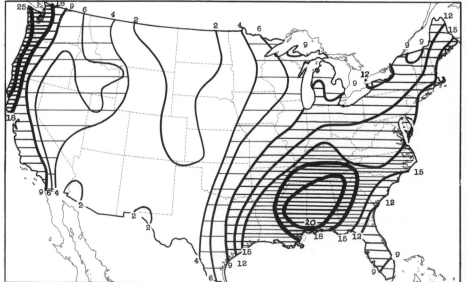

662
Frequency of very hard rains (see also Fig. 626).

663
Normal precipitation (in.), December to March, inclusive.

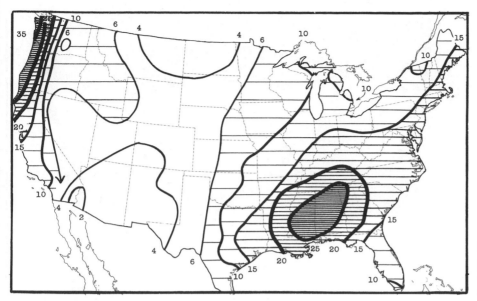

664

Normal precipitation (in.), December to April, inclusive.

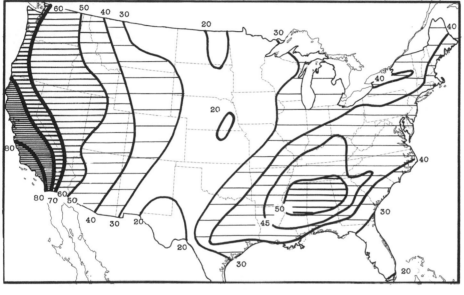

665

Percentage of the normal annual precipitation that falls from December to April, inclusive.

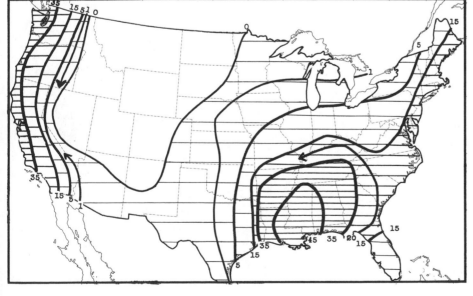

666

Percentage of the months during the cooler half year (November–April, inclusive) for which the normal precipitation is 5 in. or more.

667

Normal annual
number of months
that are dry,
temperature as
well as precipitation
being considered.

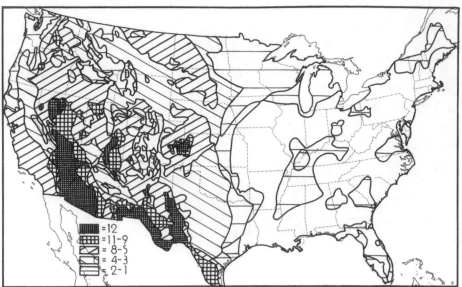

= 12
= 11-9
= 8-5
= 4-3
= 2-1

668

Normal annual
number of months
that are wet,
temperature as
well as precipitation
being considered.

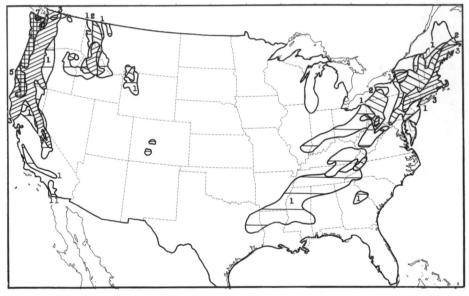

669

Normal annual
water loss (in.)
by runoff and
evaporation (the
rest of the precip-
itation enters
the ground).

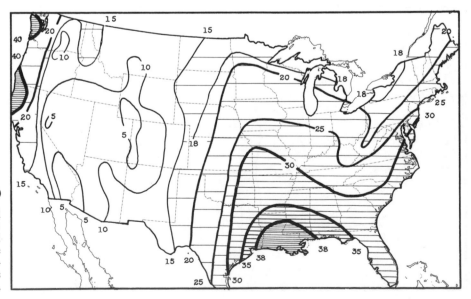

25. EXCEPTIONALLY WET YEARS, SEASONS, MONTHS, SPELLS: AMOUNTS

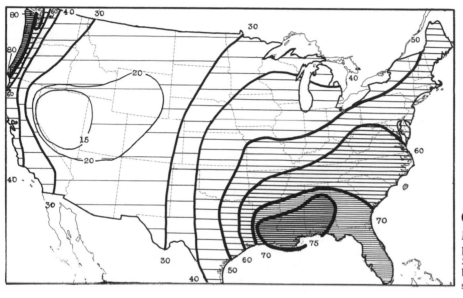

670

Maximum annual
precipitation (in.) in
50 years (1889–1938),
based on
state averages.

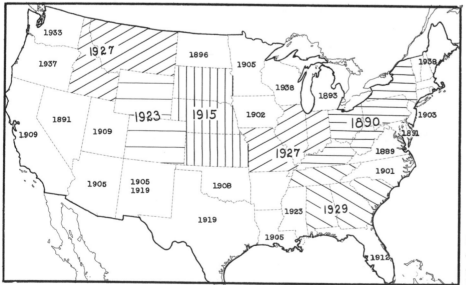

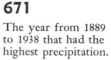

671

The year from 1889
to 1938 that had the
highest precipitation.

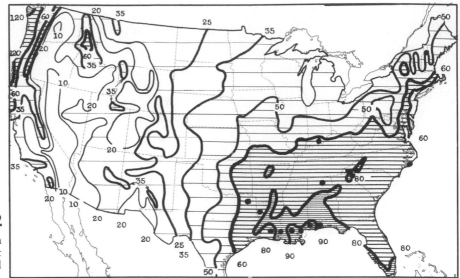

672

Total precipitation (in.) in the wettest year studied, based on scattered stations.

SUPPLEMENTARY STATEMENT CONCERNING MAXIMUM ANNUAL PRECIPITATION

Figure 672, after one by Lackey, has been supplemented by the addition of 15 large dots in the eastern half of the country, which represent 15 coöperative Weather Bureau Stations which have received 100 in. or more of precipitation in one year. Fort Barrancas, in extreme western Florida, received 127 and 125 in. in 1877 and 1878. A nearby Florida station got 102 in. in 1912. A nearby Alabama station got 106.6 in. in 1853. In southern Mississippi and Louisiana, totals of 101, 104, 107, and 105 in. have been received, two of them in 1940. This coastal strip is occasionally the rainiest in the Eastern United States. Next wettest is the southern end of the Appalachian Mountains, where four stations have repeatedly received more than 100 in. Two in Macon County, North Carolina, Rockhouse and Highlands, got totals of 113.8, 111, 110, 106, 105, and 105 in. between 1901 and 1930. A nearby South Carolina station received 101.6 in. in 1932 and 97 in. in 1929; in northern Georgia, Diamond received 101.6 in. in 1899, and nearby Clayton, 98 in. in 1929 and 94 in. in 1906.

Other eastern records include Hatteras, North Carolina, on the coast, 102 in. in 1877; Clarksville, Texas, 109.4 in. in 1873; five stations in Arkansas, 90 to 93 in. In southern Indiana, Marengo got 97.4 in. in 1890 and 103 in. in the year ending October 31, 1890.

For Florida, in addition to the three northwestern records of 102 to 127 in., three stations in southern Florida have received 90 to 94 in.

Mount Washington, New Hampshire (elevation 6,293 ft.) received 121.1 in. in 1881, 114.5 in. in 1878, and 100.8 in. in 1884.

In western Washington and Oregon several stations have received annual totals in excess of 125 in. Three have records in excess of 150 in.: Wynooche Oxbow, Washington, 184.6 (1931), 171, 162, 151 in.; Glenora, Oregon, 167, 156, 151 in., and Clearwater, Washington, 152 in.

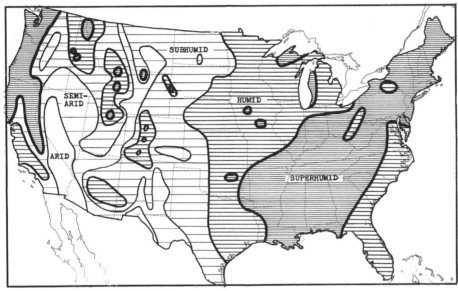

673

Precipitation type in the wettest year from 1900 to 1939, temperature as well as precipitation being considered.

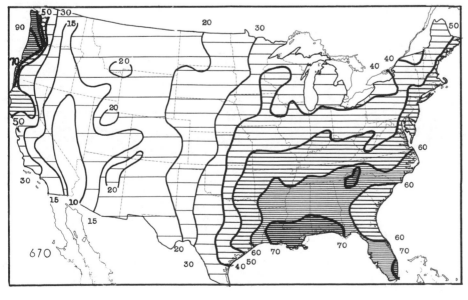

674

Total precipitation (in.) in so wet a year that only one-eighth of the years received more.

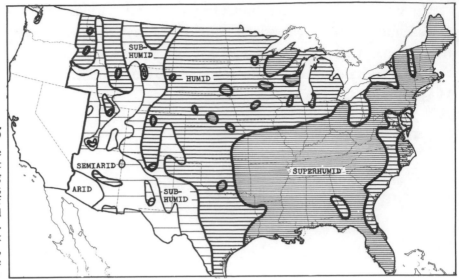

675

Precipitation type
of the wettest
crop growing
season, 1900–1939;
maximum extent of
the superhumid and
humid climates.
(For the blank
Pacific Coast area,
requisite data are
not available.)

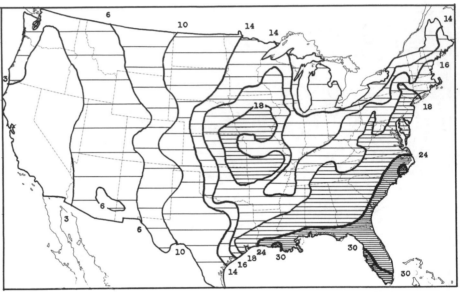

676

Total precipitation
(in.) in so wet a
summer that only
one-eighth of the
summers
receive more.

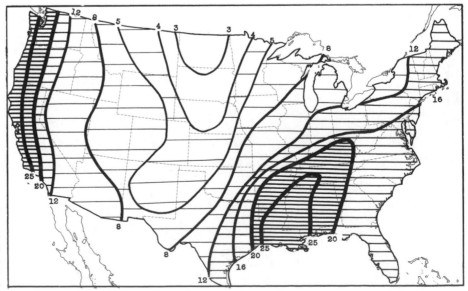

677

Total precipitation
(in.) in the wettest
winter of 50 years,
based on
state averages.

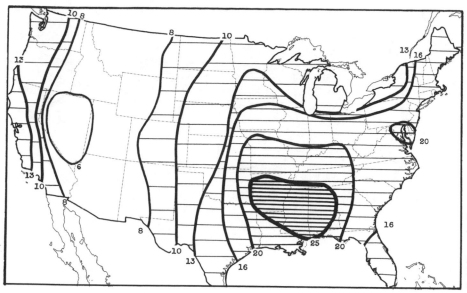

678

Total precipitation
(in.) in the wettest
spring of 50 years,
based on
state averages.

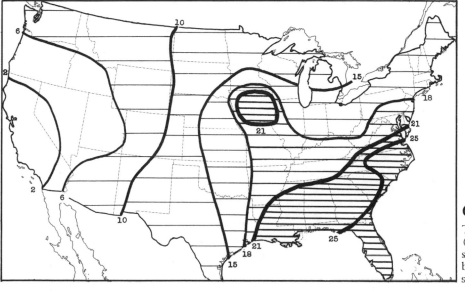

679

Total precipitation
(in.) in the wettest
summer of 50 years,
based on
state averages.

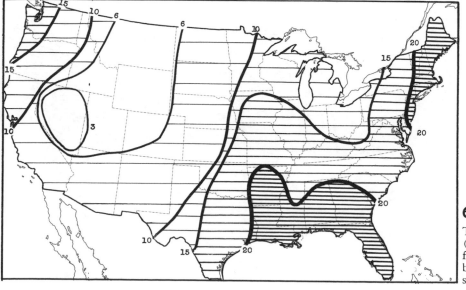

680

Total precipitation
(in.) in the wettest
fall of 50 years,
based on
state averages.

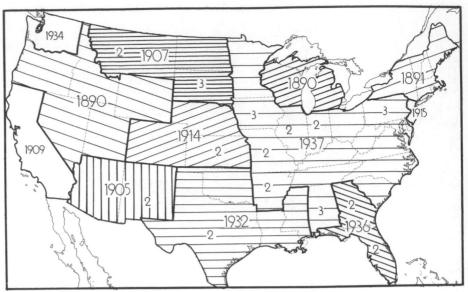

681

The winter that was generally the wettest: the first, second, or third wettest of 50 years (state average). Areas numbered 2 or 3 were the second or third wettest in the indicated winter.

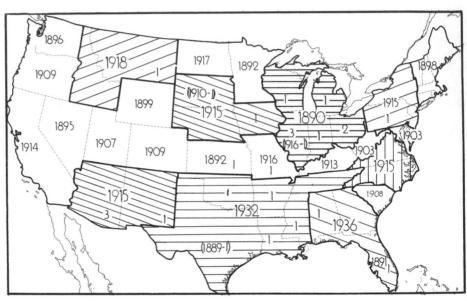

682

The second wettest winter of 50 years. States with 1 or 3 had indicated winter as wettest or third wettest. (For the three states when the winter of greatest precipitation is not given here or in Fig. 681 it is inserted in parentheses.)

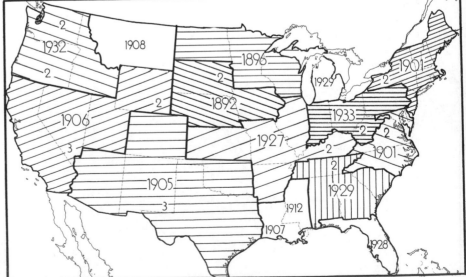

683

The wettest spring, generally, of 50 years. The 2 or 3 in a state means that the indicated spring ranked second or third.

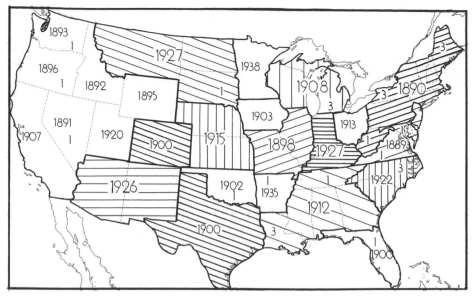

684

The second wettest spring, generally, of 50 years. The 1 or 3 in the state means that the indicated spring ranked first or third in wetness.

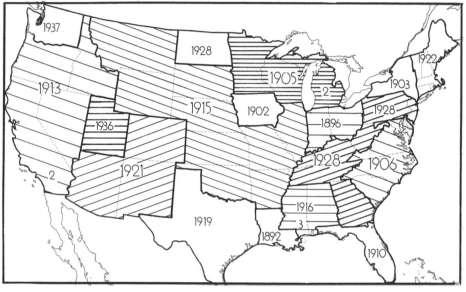

685

The wettest summer, generally, in 50 years. The 2 or 3 in a state indicates that summer was second or third wettest.

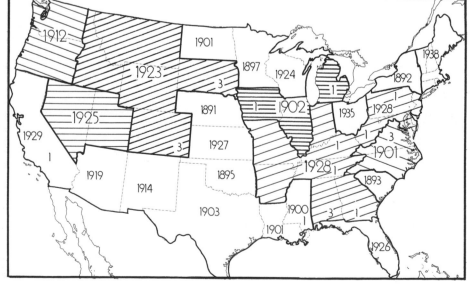

686

The second wettest summer, generally, in 50 years. States with 1 or 3 were the wettest or third wettest in that year.

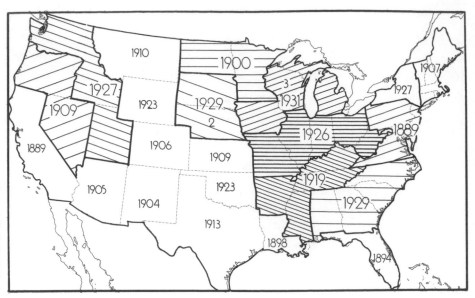

687

The wettest fall, generally, in 50 years. In states with 2 or 3, the indicated autumn ranked second or third.

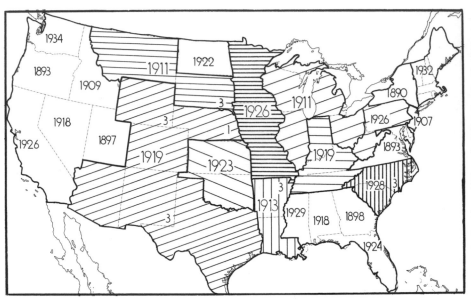

688

The second wettest fall, generally, in 50 years. In states with 1 or 3 the indicated autumn ranked first or third in wetness.

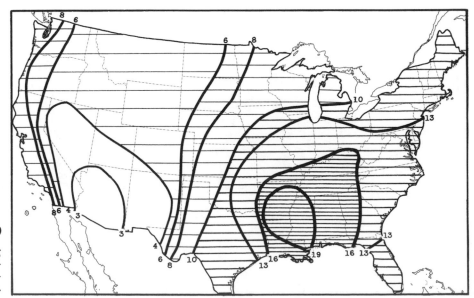

689

Common spring maximum precipitation (in.); only one-fifth receive more.

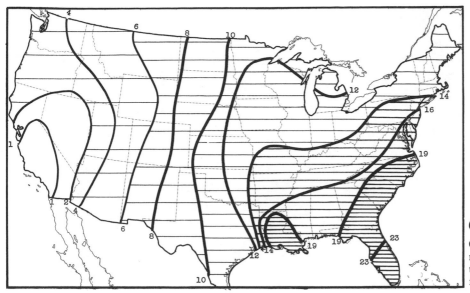

690

Common summer maximum precipitation (in.); only one-fifth receive more.

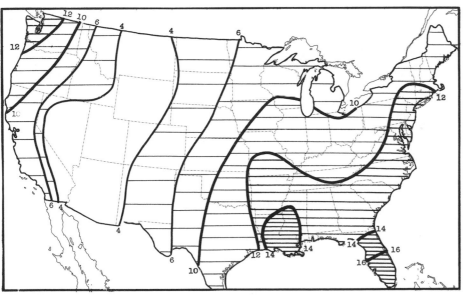

691

Common fall maximum precipitation (in.); only one-fifth receive more.

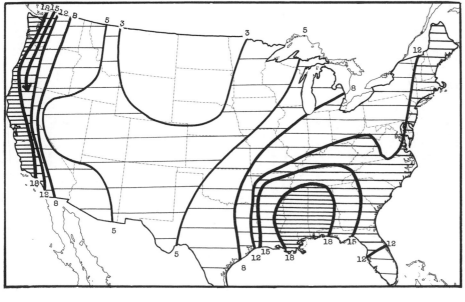

692

Common winter maximum precipitation (in.); only one-fifth receive more.

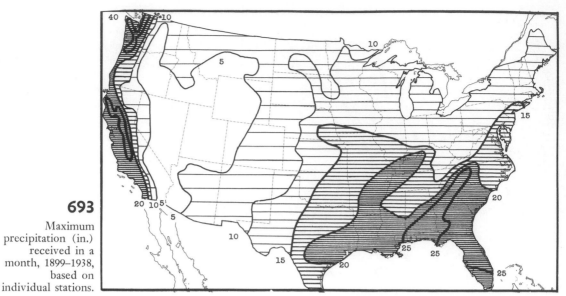

693

Maximum
precipitation (in.)
received in a
month, 1899–1938,
based on
individual stations.

SOME MAXIMUM MONTHLY TOTALS OF PRECIPITATION

Twelve California stations received from 50 to 71 in. in January 1909; four Washington stations, 51 to 57 in. in December 1930; two Oregon, two other California stations, and one Washington station got 50 to 64 in. in some other month. Totals in excess of 25 in. have been received locally in the Southeast in areas shown to have received 20–25 in. Examples are: McKinley, Texas, 34.8 in. in May 1881; in Louisiana, five stations got 30 to 38 in. in August 1940; one got 36.9 in. in June 1886; seven others got 25 to 30 in. in some month of 1881–1933; in South Carolina, Kingtree got 31.1 in. in July 1916; and in Florida, New Smyrna got 39.1 in. in October 1924.

In the 25-in.-plus zone of Fig. 693 totals are from 30 in. in Mississippi and Georgia to 35 in. in Alabama and 36.4 in. in North Carolina (July 1916).

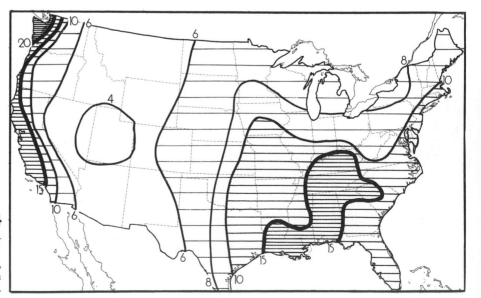

694

Greatest monthly
precipitation (in.)
of record to 1940,
based on
state averages.

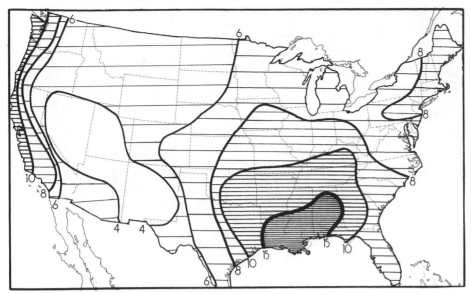

695

Greatest monthly spring precipitation (in.) of record to 1940, based on state averages.

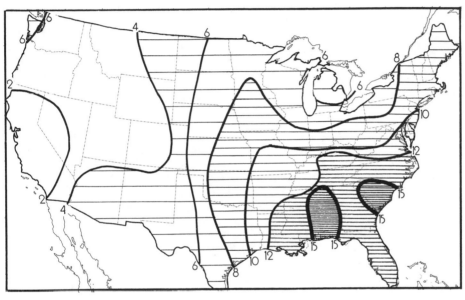

696

Greatest monthly summer precipitation (in.) of record to 1940, based on state averages.

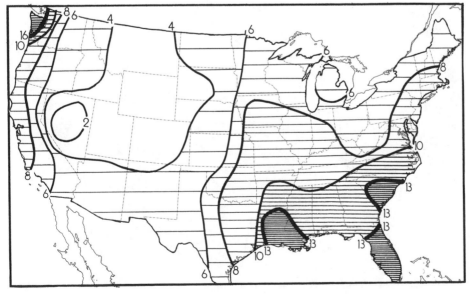

697

Greatest monthly fall precipitation (in.) of record to 1940, based on state averages.

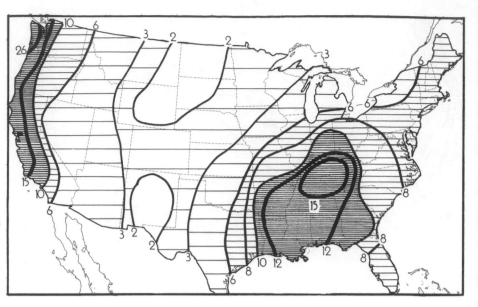

698

Greatest monthly
winter precipita-
tion (in.) of record
to 1940, based on
state averages.

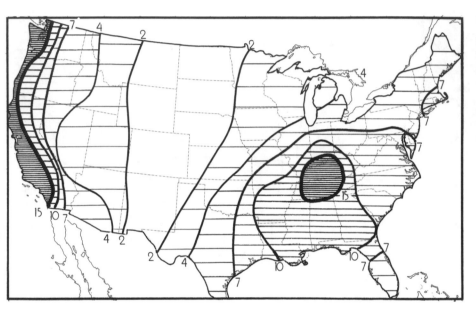

699

Greatest January
precipitation (in.)
in 50 years, based
on state averages.

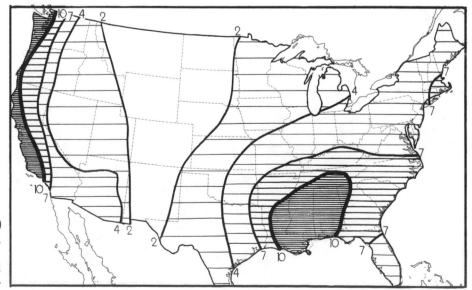

700

Greatest February
precipitation (in.)
in 50 years, based
on state averages.

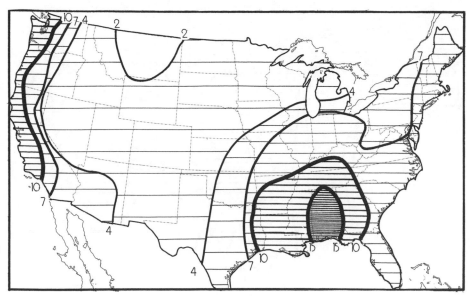

701

Greatest March precipitation (in.) in 50 years, based on state averages.

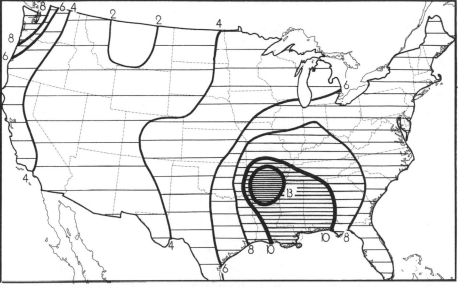

702

Greatest April precipitation (in.) in 50 years, based on state averages.

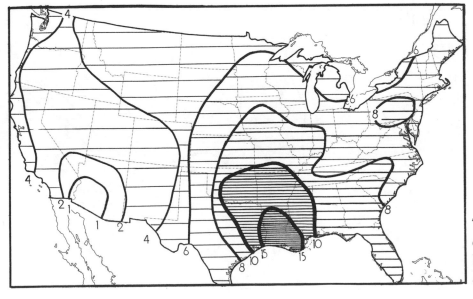

703

Greatest May precipitation (in.) in 50 years, based on state averages.

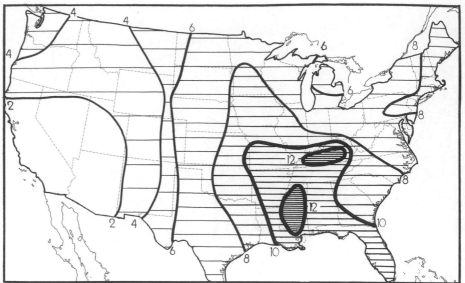

704

Greatest June
precipitation (in.) in
50 years, based
on state averages.

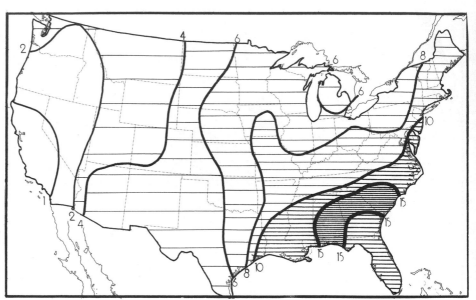

705

Greatest July
precipitation (in.) in
50 years, based
on state averages.

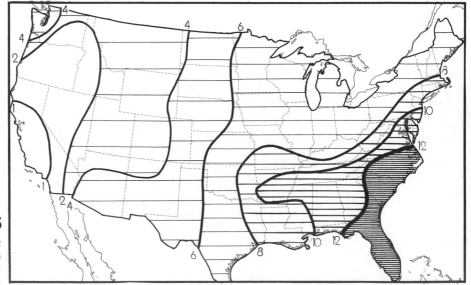

706

Greatest August
precipitation (in.) in
50 years, based
on state averages.

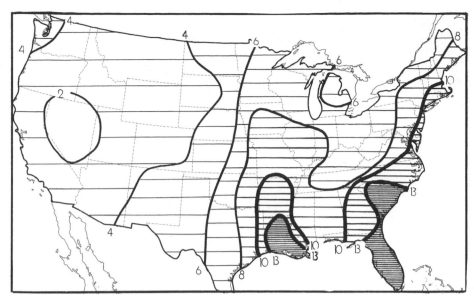

707

Greatest September
precipitation (in.) in
50 years, based
on state averages.

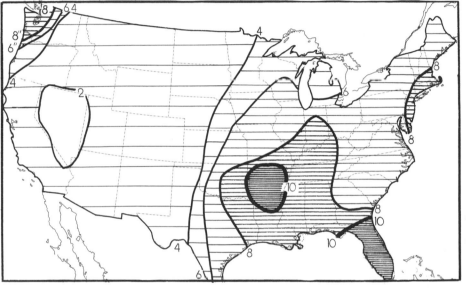

708

Greatest October
precipitation (in.) in
50 years, based
on state averages.

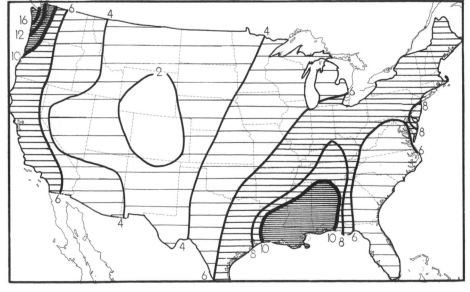

709

Greatest November
precipitation (in.) in
50 years, based
on state averages.

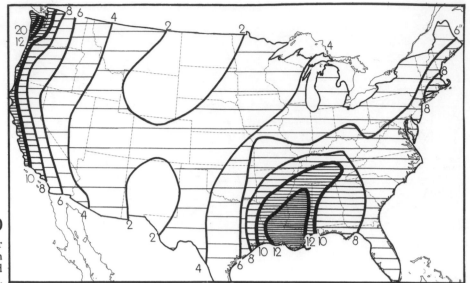

710

Greatest December
precipitation (in.) in
50 years, based
on state averages.

26. EXCEPTIONALLY DRY YEARS, SEASONS, MONTHS, SPELLS: AMOUNTS

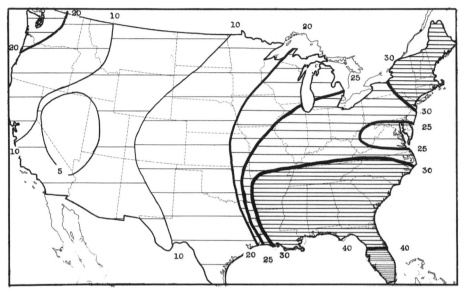

711

Least annual pre-
cipitation (in.) in 50
years (1889–1938),
based on
state averages.

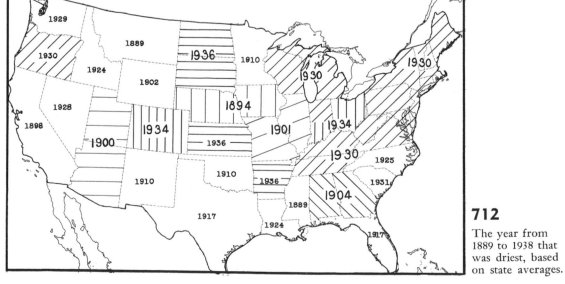

712

The year from
1889 to 1938 that
was driest, based
on state averages.

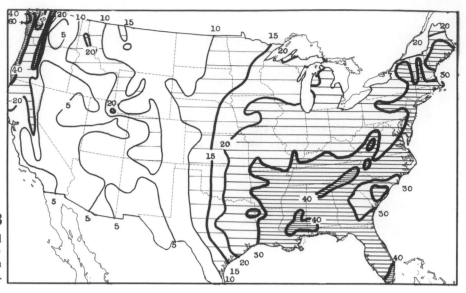

713

Least annual precipitation (in.) to 1930, based on scattered stations.

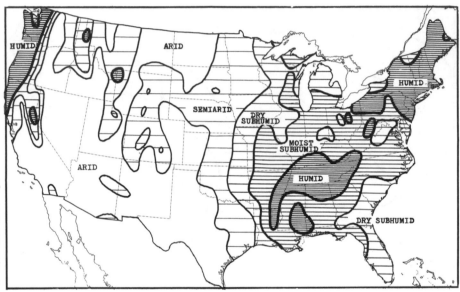

714

Climatic type in the driest year from 1900 to 1939; maximum extent of dry types, minimum extent of humid types.

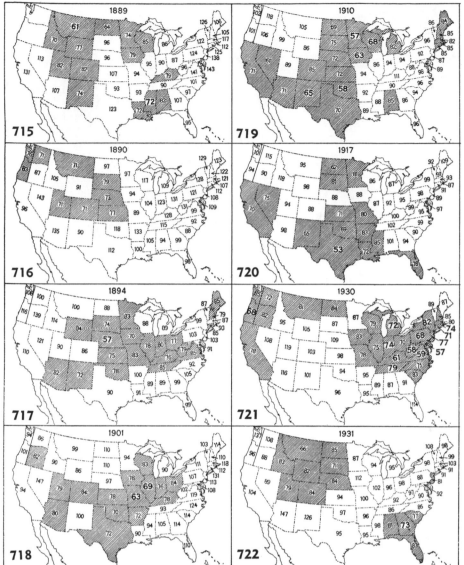

715-722

Drought areas during each of eight major drought years (shaded). The numerals show the percentage of the normal precipitation that was received.

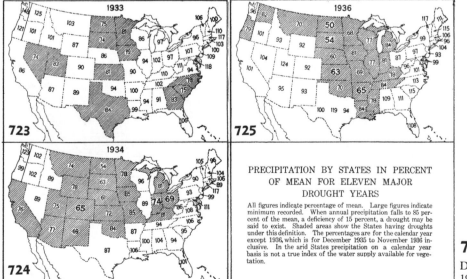

PRECIPITATION BY STATES IN PERCENT
OF MEAN FOR ELEVEN MAJOR
DROUGHT YEARS

All figures indicate percentage of mean. Large figures indicate minimum recorded. When annual precipitation falls to 85 percent of the mean, a deficiency of 15 percent, a drought may be said to exist. Shaded areas show the States having droughts under this definition. The percentages are for the calendar year except 1936, which is for December 1935 to November 1936 inclusive. In the arid States precipitation on a calendar year basis is not a true index of the water supply available for vegetation.

723-725

Drought areas during 1933, 1934, 1935.

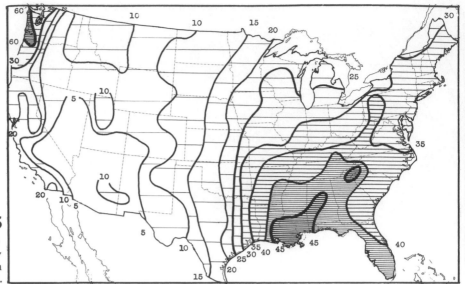

726

Precipitation (in.)
in a year so dry
that only one-eighth
have less precipitation.

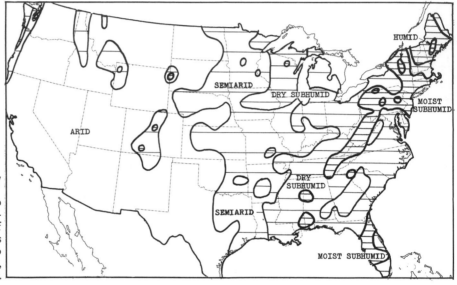

727

Driest crop
season: the max-
imum extent of
dry climatic types
from March to
August, inclusive,
1900–1939.

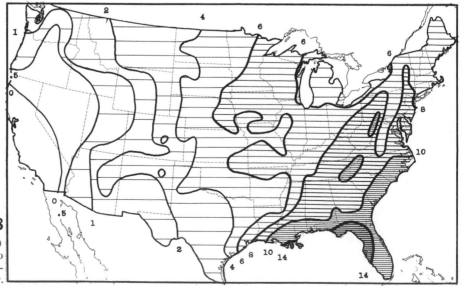

728

Total rainfall (in.)
in a summer so
dry that only one-
eighth are drier.

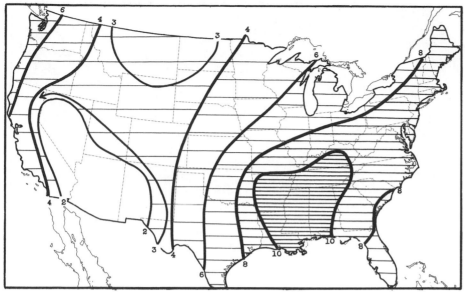

729

Precipitation (in.)
in a spring so dry
that only one-fifth
are drier, based
on state averages.

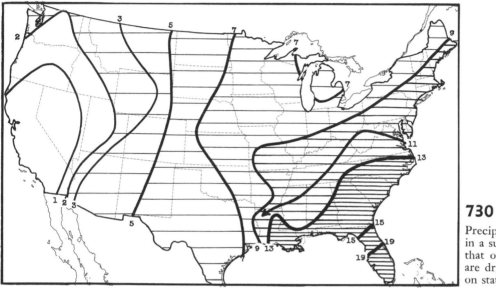

730

Precipitation (in.)
in a summer so dry
that only one-fifth
are drier, based
on state averages.

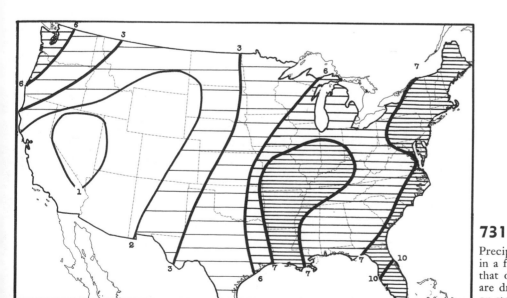

731

Precipitation (in.)
in a fall so dry
that only one-fifth
are drier, based
on state averages.

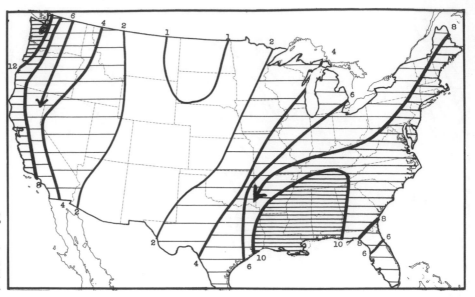

732

Precipitation (in.) in a winter so dry that only one-fifth are drier, based on state averages.

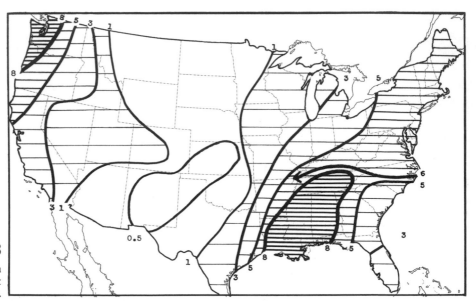

733

Total precipitation (in.) in the driest winter of 50 years.

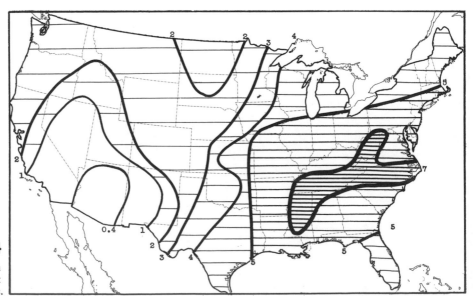

734

Total precipitation (in.) in the driest spring of 50 years.

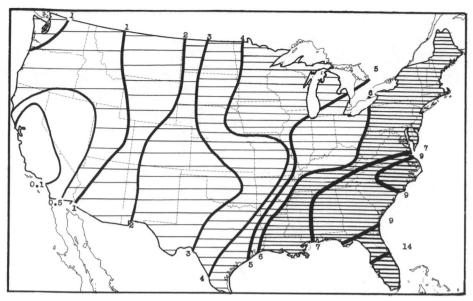

735

Total precipitation (in.) in the driest summer of 50 years.

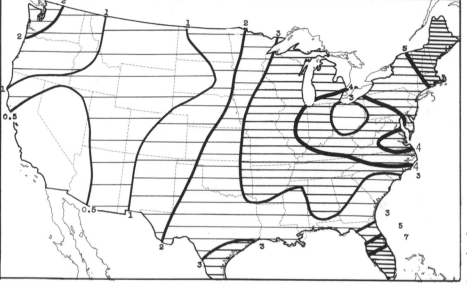

736

Total precipitation (in.) in the driest fall of 50 years.

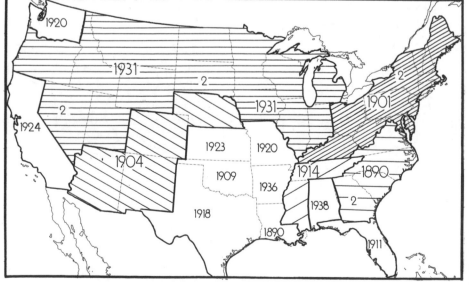

737

The driest winter of 50 years, based on state averages.

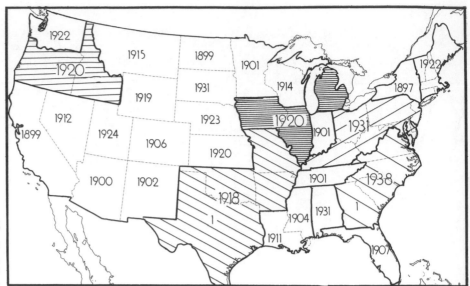

738

The second driest
winter of 50 years,
based on
state averages.

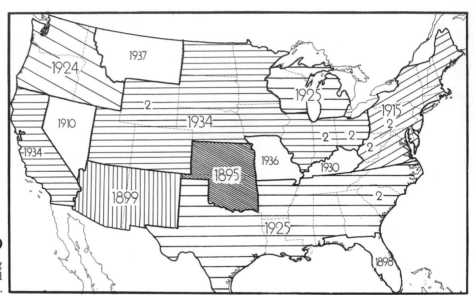

739

The driest spring
of 50 years, based
on state averages.

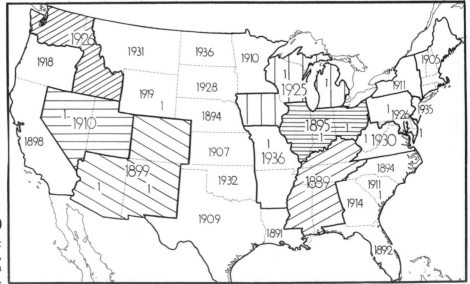

740

The second driest
spring of 50 years,
based on
state averages.

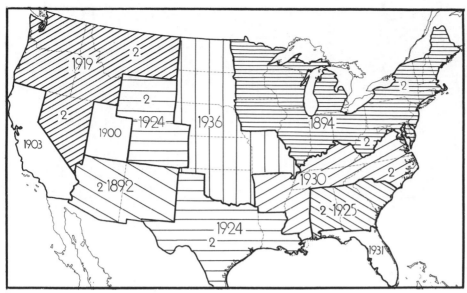

741

The driest summer
of 50 years, based
on state averages.

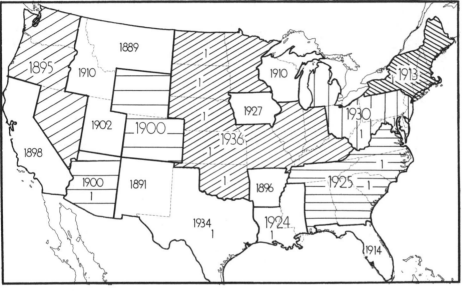

742

The second driest
summer of 50 years,
based on
state averages.

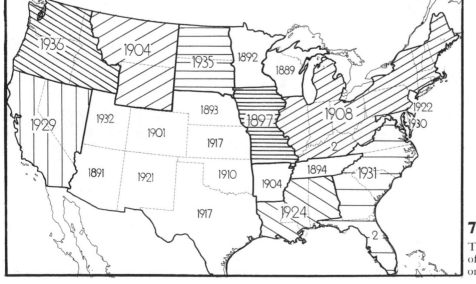

743

The driest fall
of 50 years, based
on state averages.

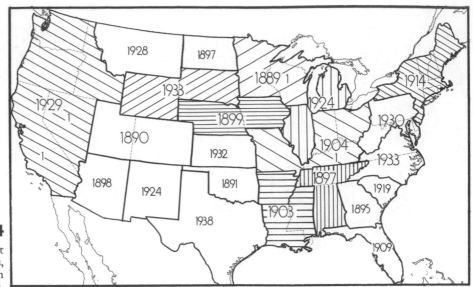

744

The second driest
fall of 50 years,
based on
state averages.

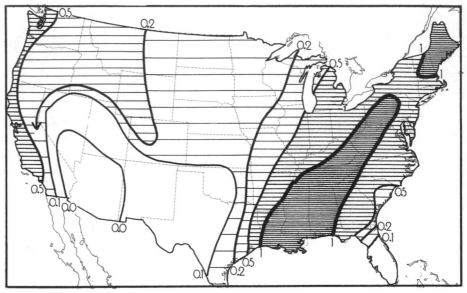

745

Total precipitation
(in.) in the driest
winter month of
50 years, based
on state averages.

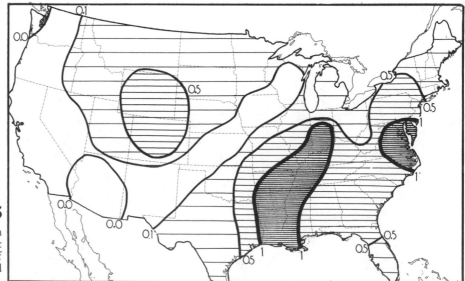

746

Total precipitation
(in.) in the driest
spring month of
50 years, based
on state averages.

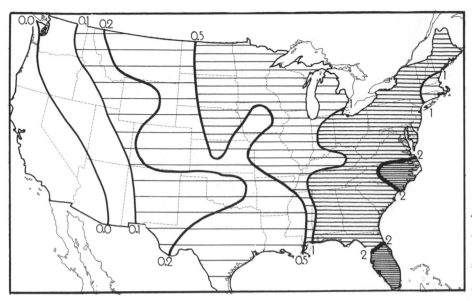

747

Total precipitation
(in.) in the driest
summer month of
50 years, based
on state averages.

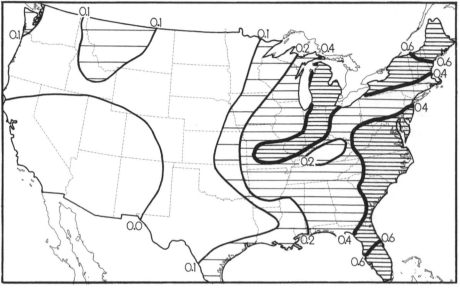

748

Total precipitation
(in.) in the driest
fall month of
50 years, based
on state averages.

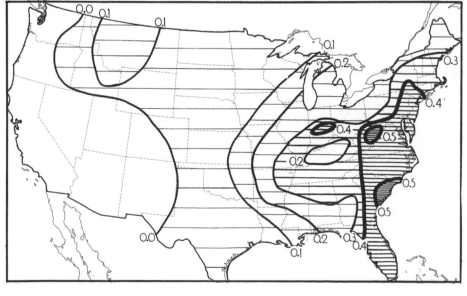

749

Minimum monthly
precipitation (in.) in
50 years, based
on state averages.

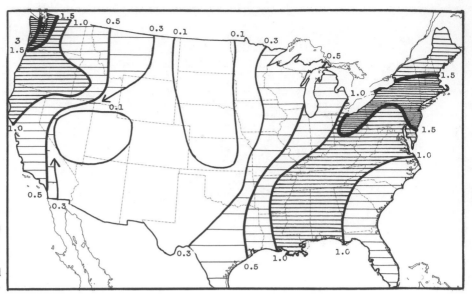

750

Minimum January
precipitation (in.)
in 50 years, based
on state averages.

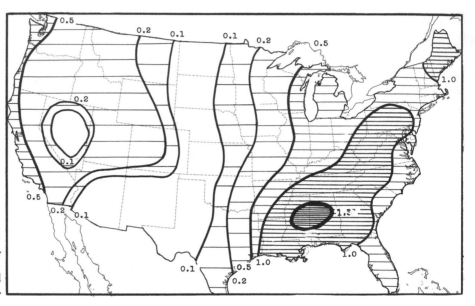

751

Minimum February
precipitation (in.)
in 50 years, based
on state averages.

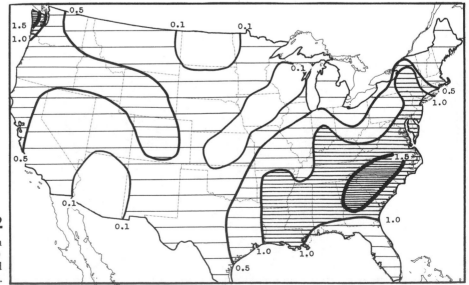

752

Minimum March
precipitation (in.)
in 50 years, based
on state averages.

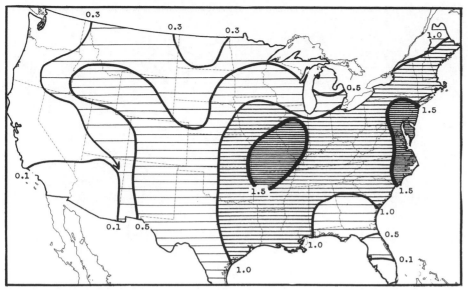

753

Minimum April
precipitation (in.)
in 50 years, based
on state averages.

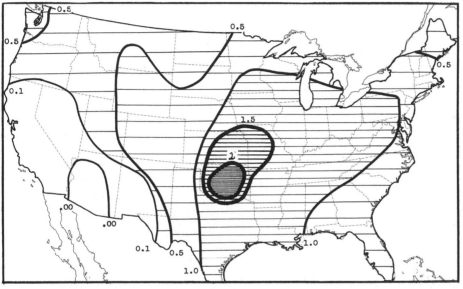

754

Minimum May
precipitation (in.)
in 50 years, based
on state averages.

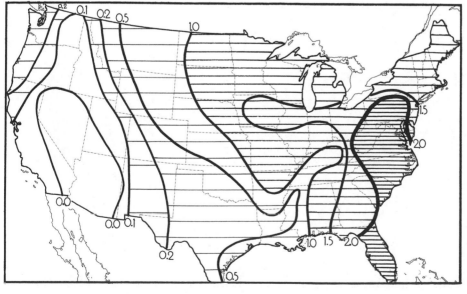

755

Minimum June
precipitation (in.)
in 50 years, based
on state averages.

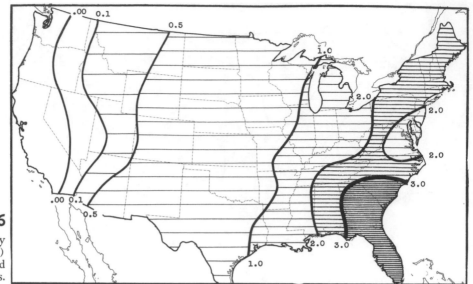

756

Minimum July
precipitation (in.)
in 50 years, based
on state averages.

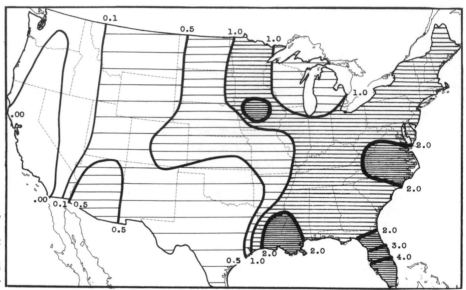

757

Minimum August
precipitation (in.)
in 50 years, based
on state averages.

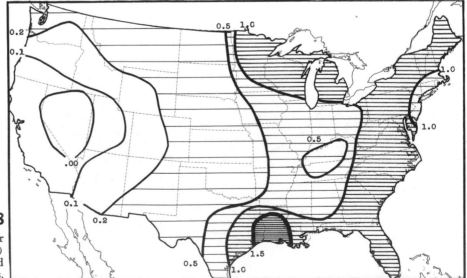

758

Minimum September
precipitation (in.)
in 50 years, based
on state averages.

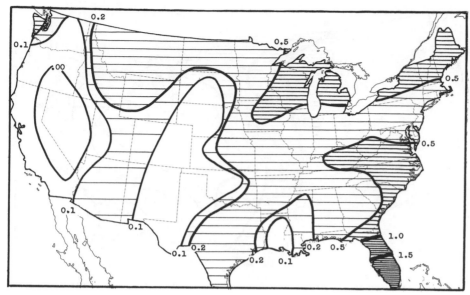

759

Minimum October
precipitation (in.)
in 50 years, based
on state averages.

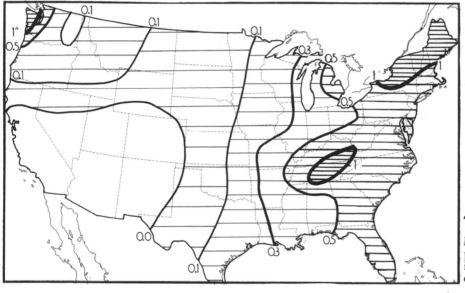

760

Minimum November
precipitation (in.)
in 50 years, based
on state averages.

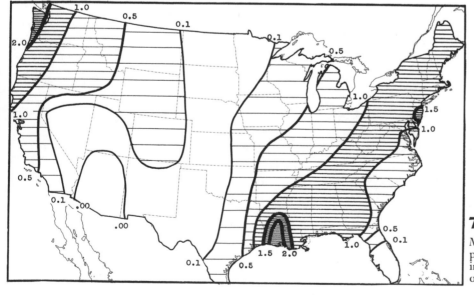

761

Minimum December
precipitation (in.)
in 50 years, based
on state averages.

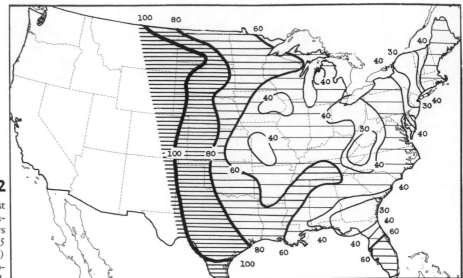

762

The greatest number of consecutive dry days (with less than 0.25 in. of precipitation) from March to September 1895–1914.

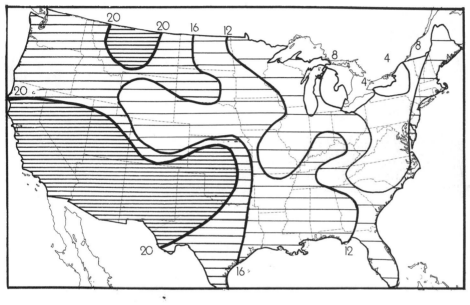

763
Frequency of dry
years: percentage
with less than
85 percent of normal
precipitation, based
on state averages
for 50 years.

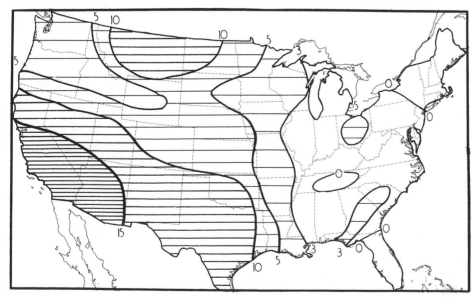

764
Frequency of
distinctly dry years:
percentage with less
than three-fourths of
normal precipitation,
based on state
averages for 50 years.

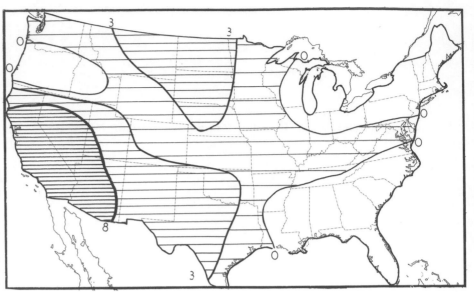

765

Frequency of very dry years: percentage with less than two-thirds of normal precipitation, based on state averages for 50 years.

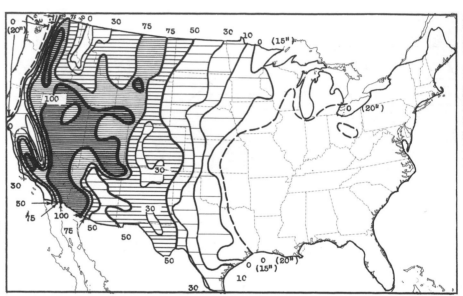

766

Percentage of the years having less than 15 in. of precipitation (50 years).

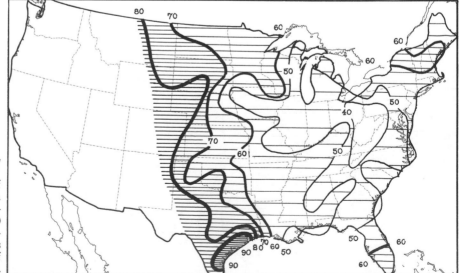

767

Percentage of the growing season (March–September) with 30 or more consecutive days with less than 0.25 in. of precipitation in 24 hr.

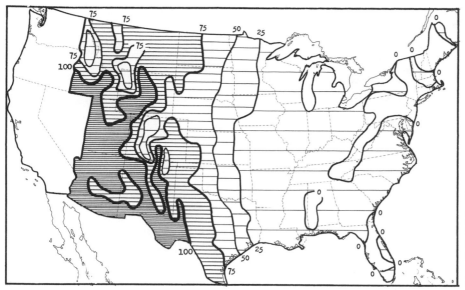

768

Frequency (percent) of dry subhumid, semiarid, or arid crop-growing seasons (March–August, 1900–1939).

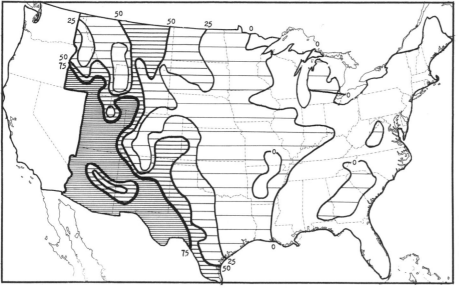

769

Frequency (percent) of semiarid or arid crop-growing seasons (March–August).

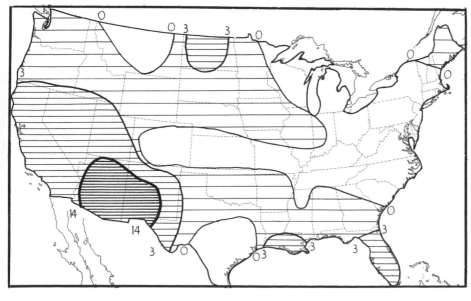

770

Frequency of dry springs: percentage with less than half of normal precipitation based on state averages for 50 years.

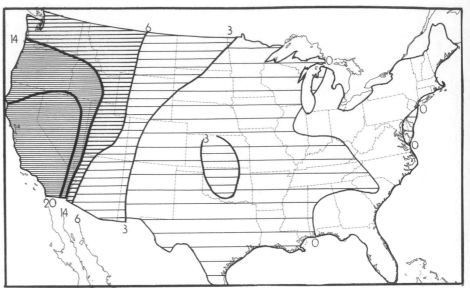

771

Frequency of
dry summers: per-
centage with less
than half of
normal precipitation,
based on state
averages for 50 years.

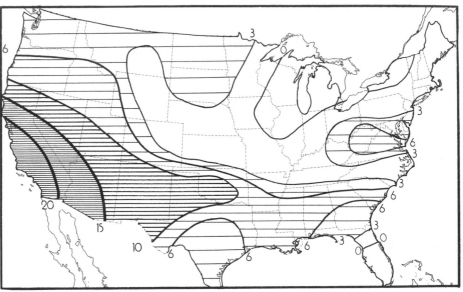

772

Frequency of
dry falls: percentage
with less than
half of normal
precipitation, based
on state averages.

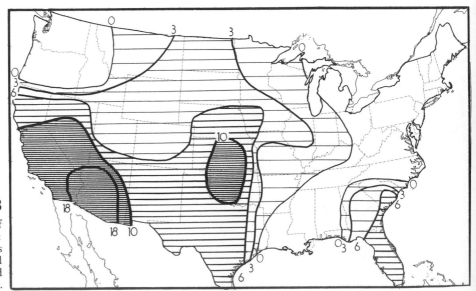

773

Frequency of
dry winters:
percentage with
less than half of
normal precipitation,
based on
state averages.

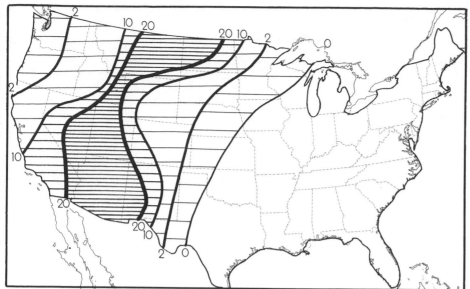

774

Percentage of the springs receiving less than 3 in. of precipitation, based on state averages for the driest 10 of 50 years.

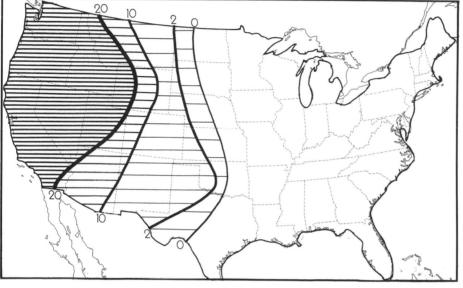

775

Percentage of the summers receiving less than 3 in. of precipitation, based on state averages for the driest 10 of 50 years.

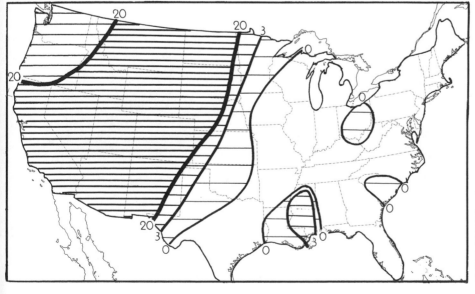

776

Percentage of the autumns receiving less than 3 in. of precipitation, based on state averages for the driest 10 of 50 years.

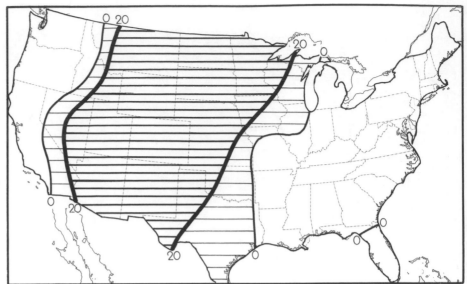

777

Percentage of the
winters receiving
less than 3 in.
of precipitation,
based on state
averages for the
driest 10 of 50 years.

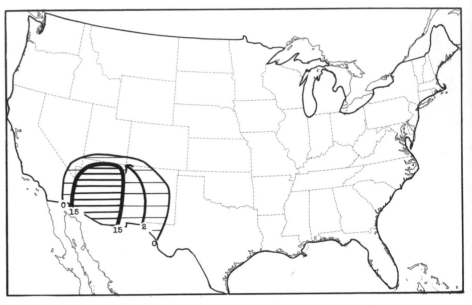

778

Frequency of
extremely dry springs:
percentage receiving
less than 1 in.
of precipitation.

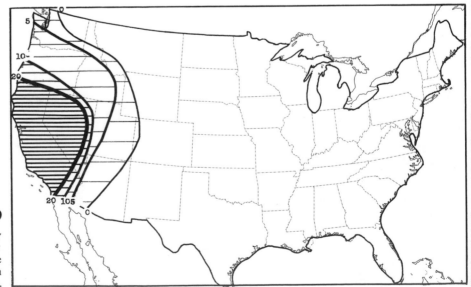

779

Frequency
of extremely dry
summers: percentage
receiving less than
1 in. of precipitation.

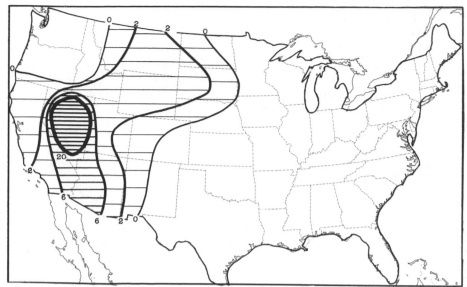

780
Frequency of
extremely dry falls:
percentage receiving
less than 1 in. of
precipitation.

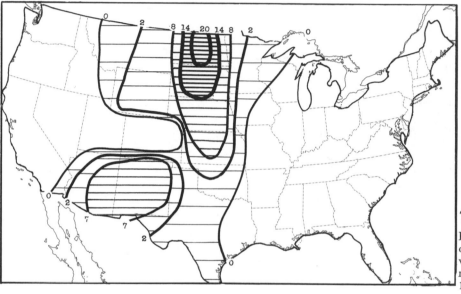

781
Percentage
of extremely dry
winters: percentage
receiving less than
1 in. of precipitation.

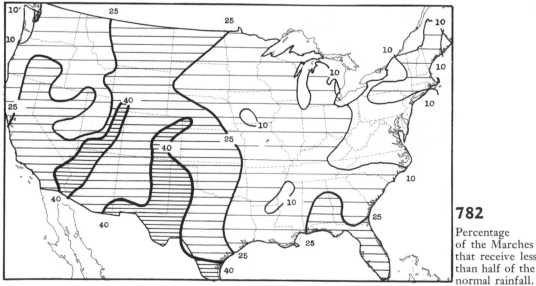

782
Percentage
of the Marches
that receive less
than half of the
normal rainfall.

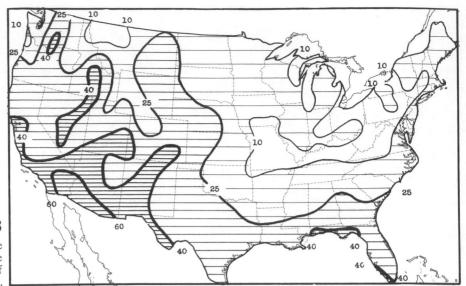

783

Percentage of the
Aprils that receive
less than half of
the normal rainfall.

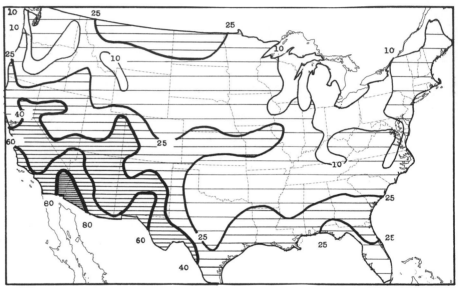

784

Percentage of the
Mays that receive
less than half of
the normal
precipitation.

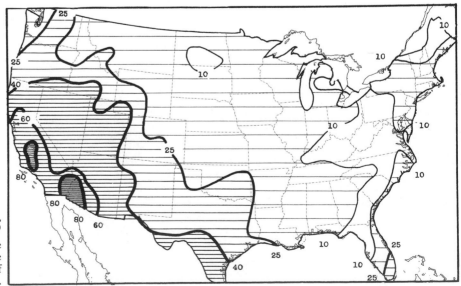

785

Percentage of the
Junes that receive
less than half of
the normal rainfall.

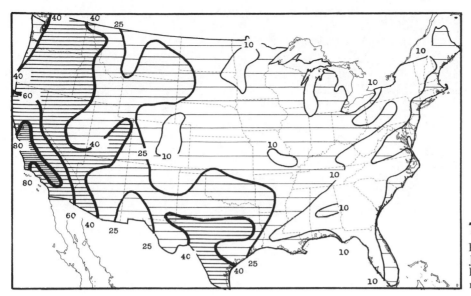

786

Percentage of the
Julies that receive
less than half of the
normal rainfall.

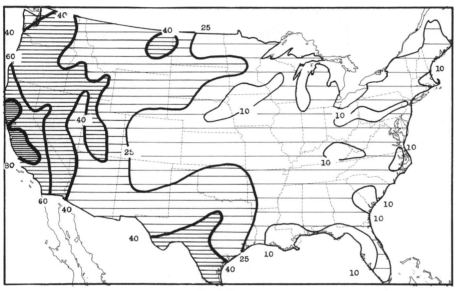

787

Percentage of the
Augusts that receive
less than half of the
normal rainfall.

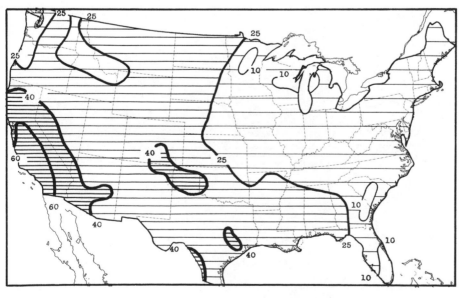

788

Percentage of the
Septembers that
receive less than half
of the normal rainfall.

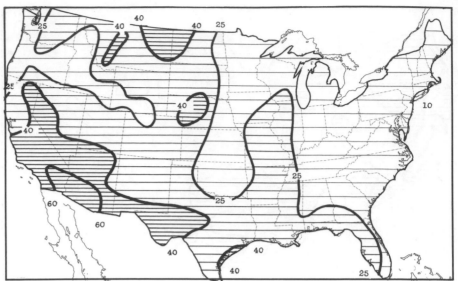

789

Percentage of the
Octobers that receive
less than half of
the normal rainfall.

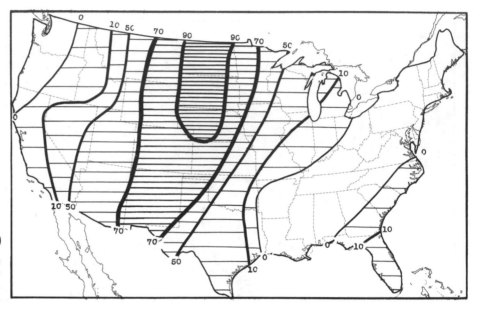

790

Percentage of the
Januaries that receive
less than 1 in.
of precipitation.

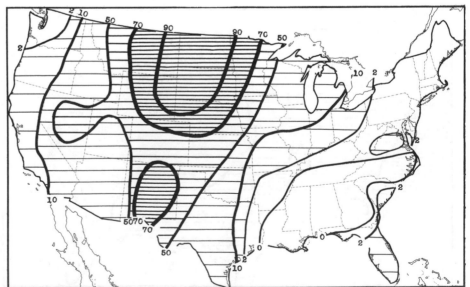

791

Percentage of the
Februaries that
receive less than
1 in. of
precipitation.

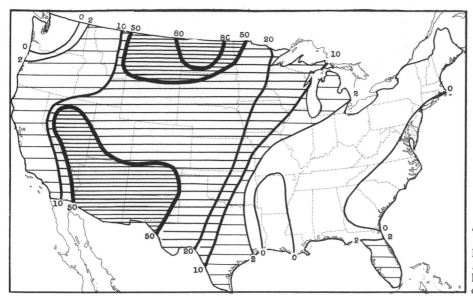

792

Percentage of the
Marches that receive
less than 1 in.
of precipitation.

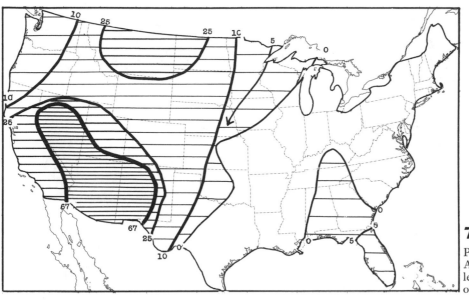

793

Percentage of the
Aprils that receive
less than 1 in.
of precipitation.

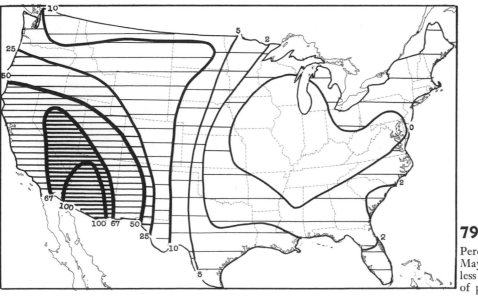

794

Percentage of the
Mays that receive
less than 1 in.
of precipitation.

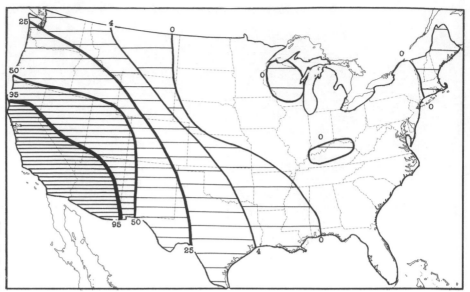

795

Percentage of the
Junes that receive
less than 1 in.
of precipitation.

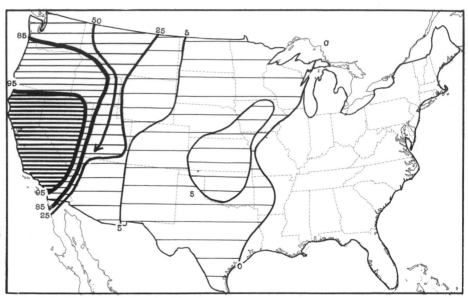

796

Percentage of the
Julies that receive
less than 1 in.
of precipitation.

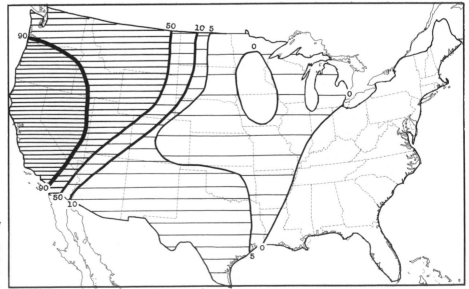

797

Percentage of the
Augusts that receive
less than 1 in.
of precipitation.

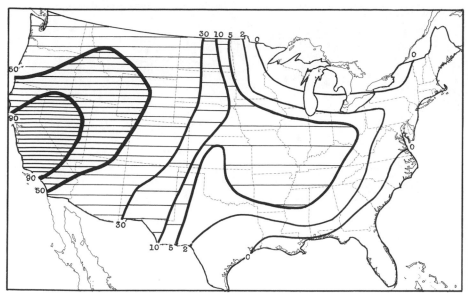

798

Percentage of the
Septembers that
receive less than 1 in.
of precipitation.

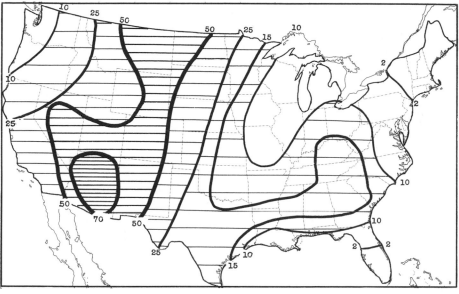

799

Percentage of the
Octobers that receive
less than 1 in.
of precipitation.

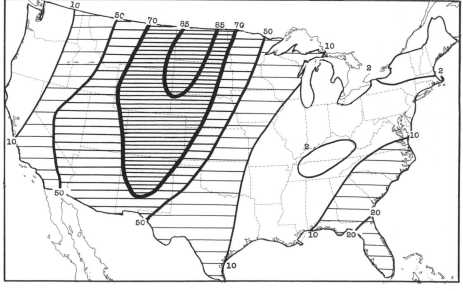

800

Percentage of the
Novembers that
receive less than 1 in.
of precipitation.

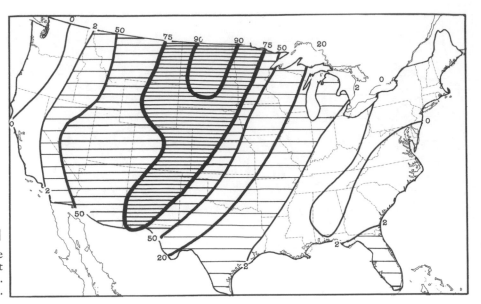

801

Percentage of the
Decembers that
receive less than 1 in.
of precipitation.

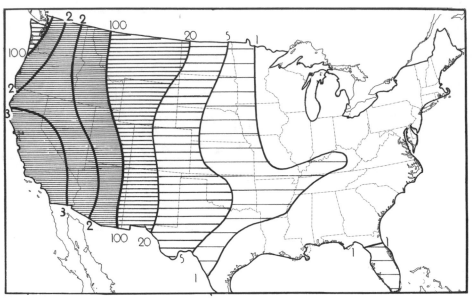

802

Frequency of
months with less
than 0.5 in. of rain
from April to
September: per-
centage of the years
with one such month.
West of the
easternmost line
2, except beyond
the second line 2 in
the northwest,
there are two such
months per average
year; west of
line 3 there are
three much months.

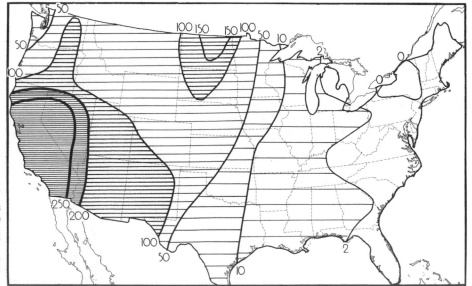

803

Number of months
in 50 years (600
months) that had
a precipitation of
less than 0.5 in.,
based on
state averages.

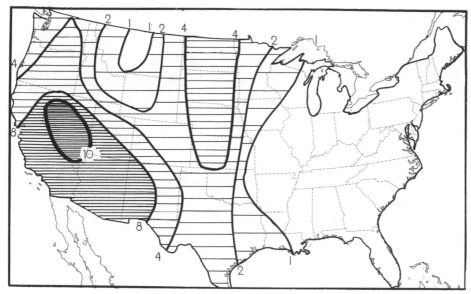

804

Number of months
per year that have
been almost rainless
(0.1 in. or less,
state average) at least
once in 50 years.

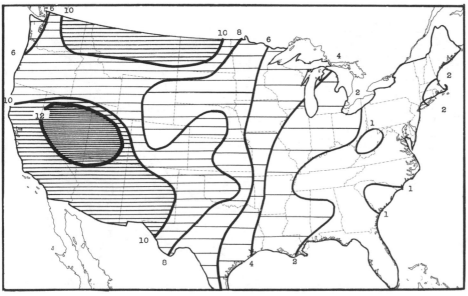

805

Number of months
per year in which
precipitation has
been less than 0.5 in.
(state average) at least
once in 50 years.

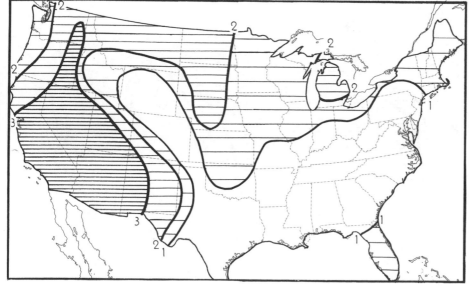

806

Number of months
in spring in which
precipitation has
been less than 0.5
in. (state average)
at least once in
50 years. (The un-
shaded areas never
have been that dry.)

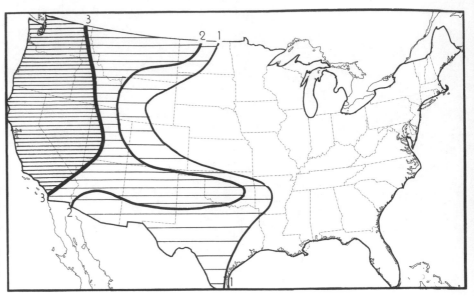

807

Number of months in summer in which precipitation has been less than 0.5 in. (state average) at least once in 50 years. (The unshaded areas never have been that dry.)

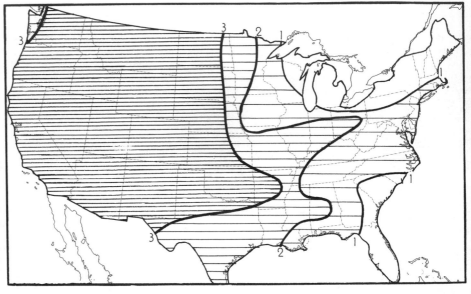

808

Number of months in fall in which precipitation has been less than 0.5 in. (state average) at least once in 50 years. (The unshaded areas never have been that dry.)

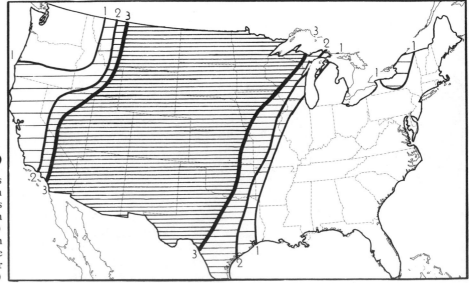

809

Number of months of winter in which precipitation has been less than 0.5 in. (state average) at least once in 50 years. (The unshaded areas never have been that dry.)

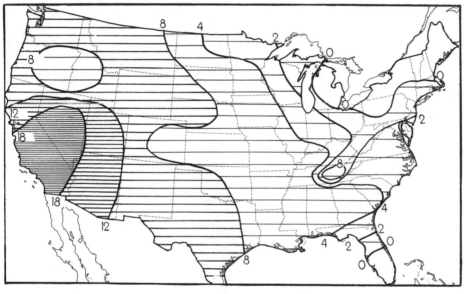

810

Frequency of wet years: percentage in which the precipitation is 125 percent of normal or more.

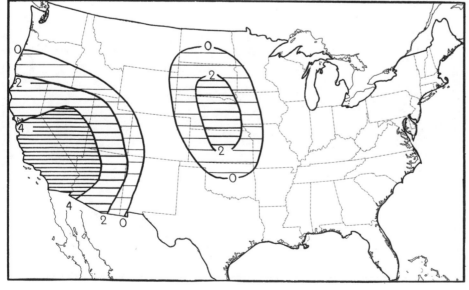

811

Frequency of very wet years: percentage in which the precipitation is 150 percent of normal or more.

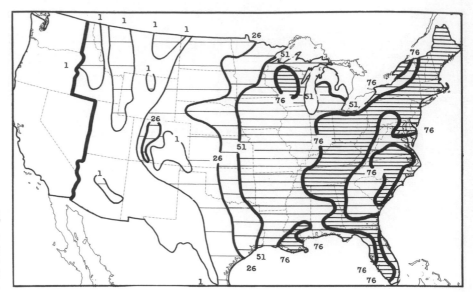

812

Percentage of the crop-growing seasons (March–August) that are humid.

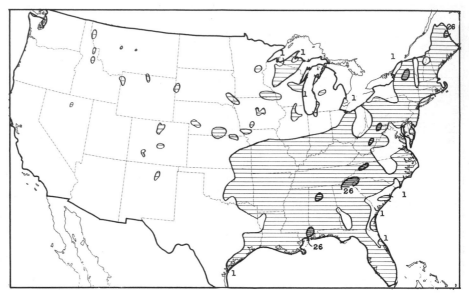

813

Percentage of the crop-growing seasons (March–August that are superhumid.

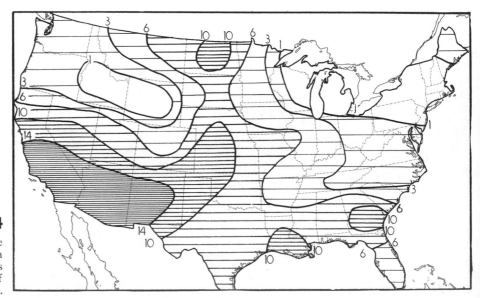

814

Percentage of the springs in which the precipitation is 150 percent of normal or more.

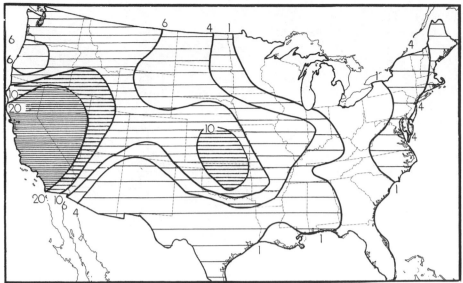

815

Percentage of the
summers in which
the precipitation is
150 percent of
normal or more.

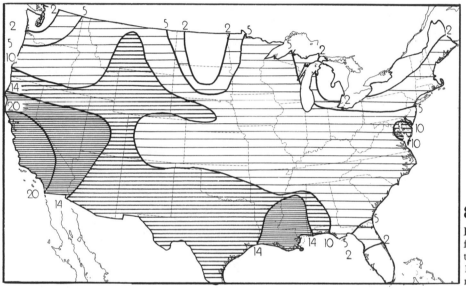

816

Percentage of the
falls in which
the precipitation is
150 percent of
normal or more.

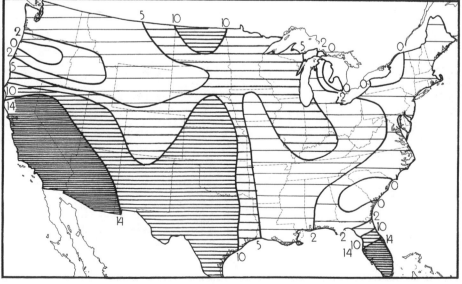

817

Percentage of the
winters in which
the precipitation is
150 percent of
normal or more.

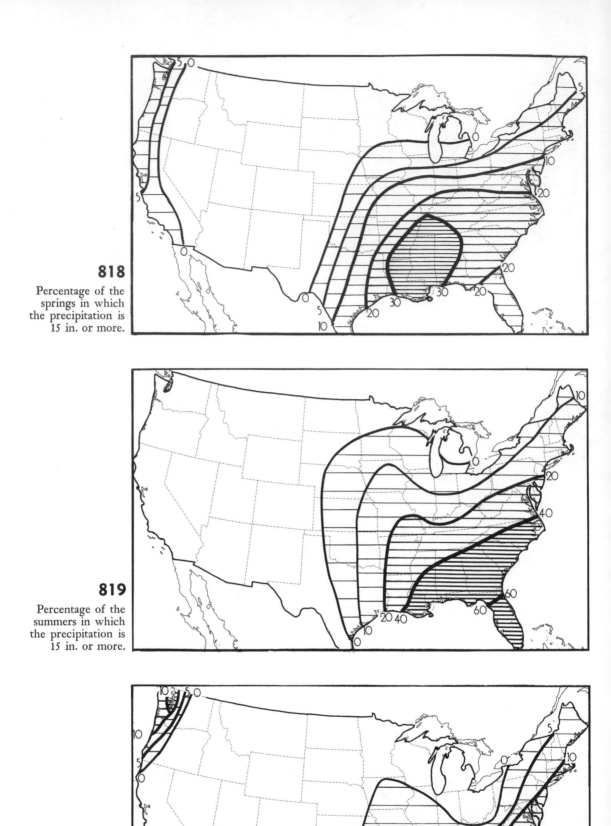

818

Percentage of the
springs in which
the precipitation is
15 in. or more.

819

Percentage of the
summers in which
the precipitation is
15 in. or more.

820

Percentage of the
falls in which
the precipitation is
15 in. or more.

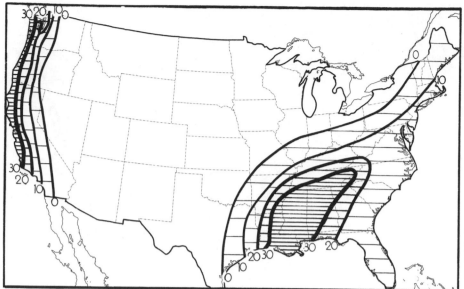

821

Percentage of the winters in which the precipitation is 15 in. or more.

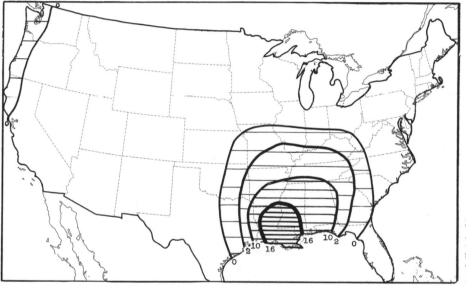

822

Percentage of the springs in which the precipitation is 20 in. or more.

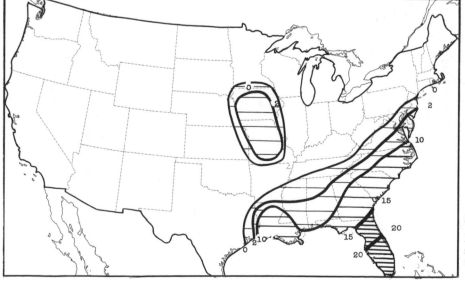

823

Percentage of the summers in which the precipitation is 20 in. or more.

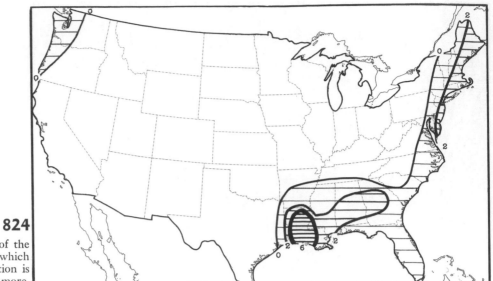

824

Percentage of the falls in which the precipitation is 20 in. or more.

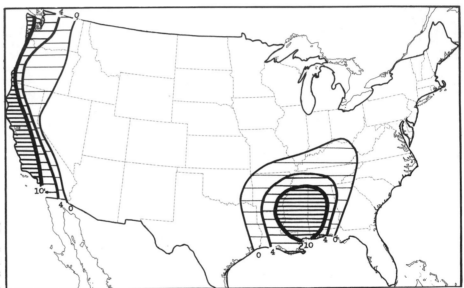

825

Percentage of the winters in which the precipitation is 20 in. or more.

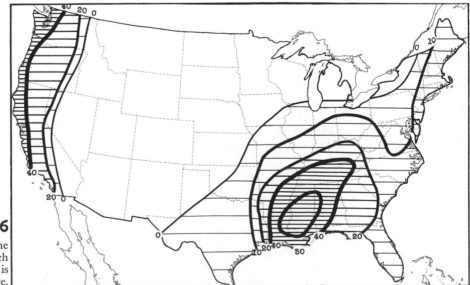

826

Percentage of the Januaries in which the precipitation is 5 in. or more.

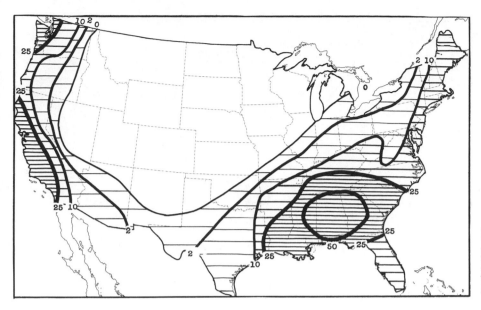

827

Percentage of the
Februaries in which
the precipitation is
5 in. or more.

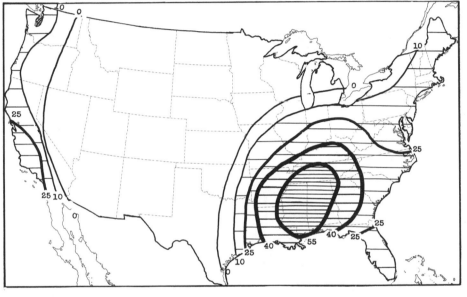

828

Percentage of the
Marches in which
the precipitation is
5 in. or more.

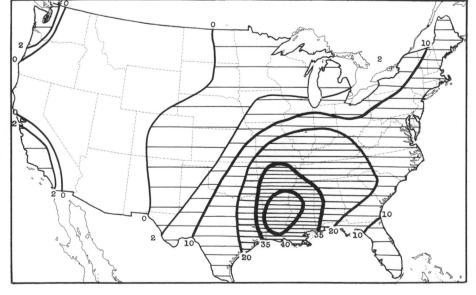

829

Percentage of the
Aprils in which
the precipitation is
5 in. or more.

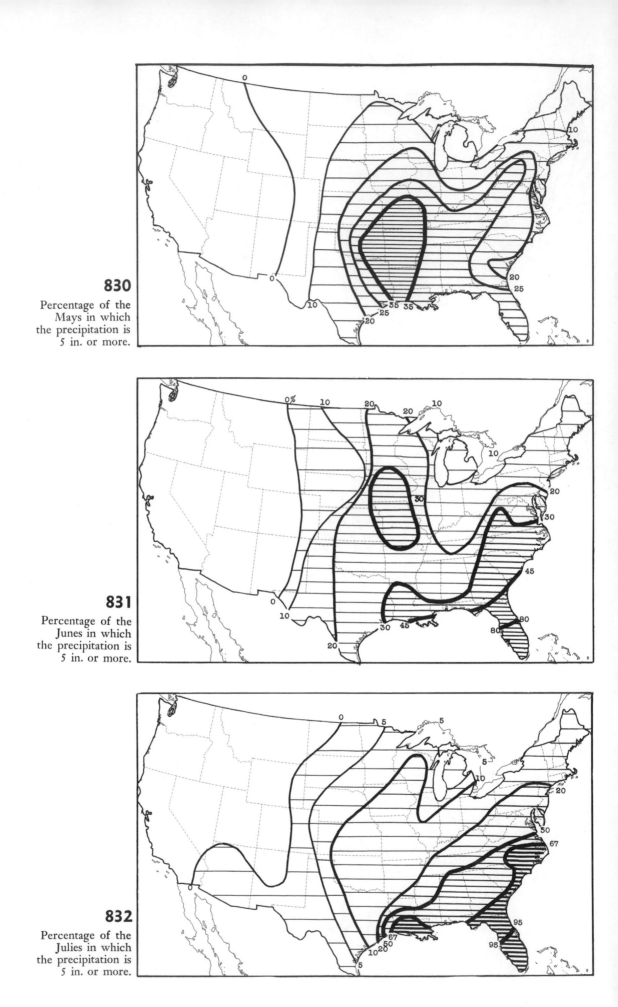

830

Percentage of the
Mays in which
the precipitation is
5 in. or more.

831

Percentage of the
Junes in which
the precipitation is
5 in. or more.

832

Percentage of the
Julies in which
the precipitation is
5 in. or more.

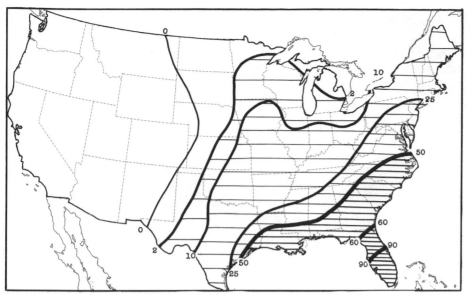

833

Percentage of the
Augusts in which
the precipitation is
5 in. or more.

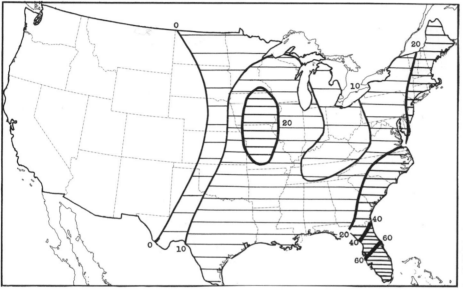

834

Percentage of the
Septembers in which
the precipitation is
5 in. or more.

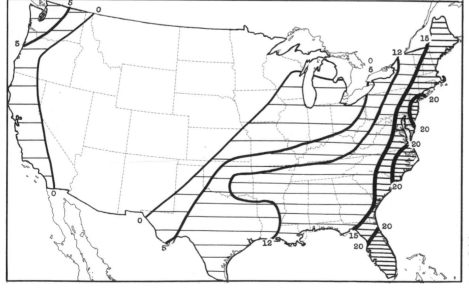

835

Percentage of the
Octobers in which
the precipitation is
5 in. or more.

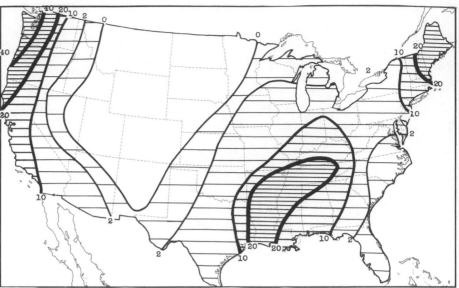

836

Percentage of the Novembers in which the precipitation is 5 in. or more.

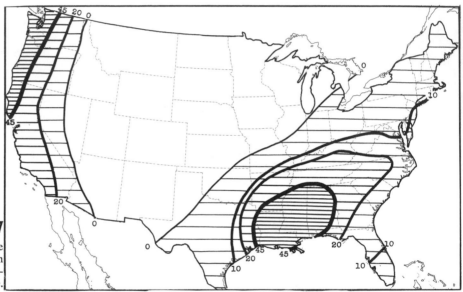

837

Percentage of the Decembers in which the precipitation is 5 in. or more.

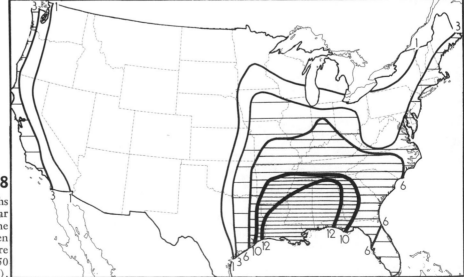

838

Number of months of the year in which the precipitation has been 8 in. or more at least once in 50 years (state averages).

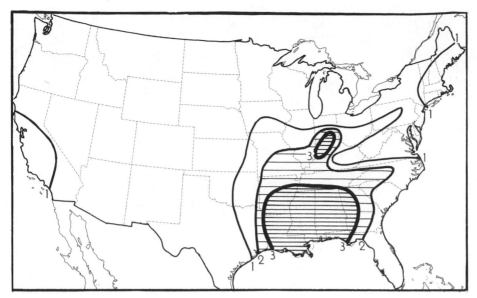

839

Number of the
spring months
with precipitation of
8 in. or more at
least once in 50 years
(state averages).

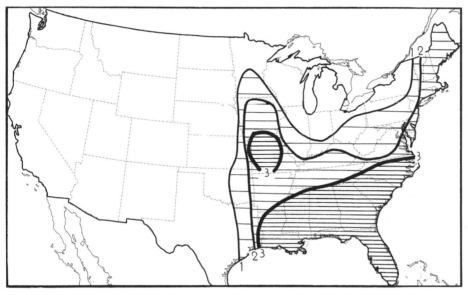

840

Number of the
summer months
with precipitation of
8 in. or more at
least once in 50 years
(state averages).

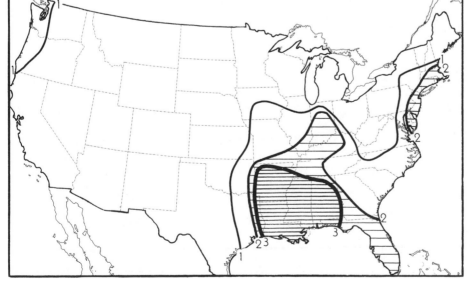

841

Number of the
fall months
with precipitation of
8 in. or more at
least once in 50 years
(state averages).

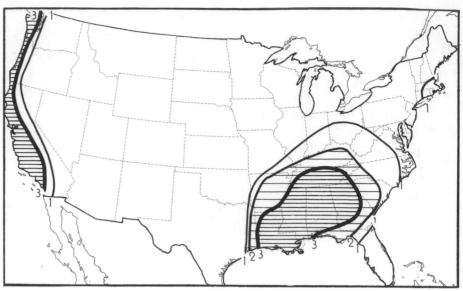

842

Number of the winter months with precipitation of 8 in. or more at least once in 50 years (state averages).

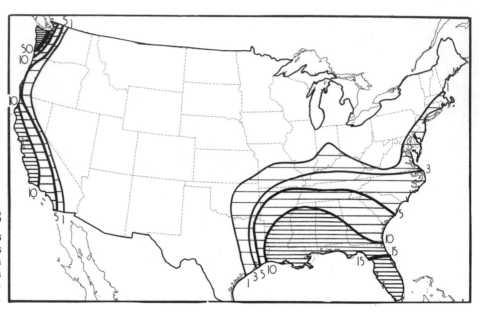

843

Number of times in 50 years that some month had a precipitation of 10 in. or more (state averages).

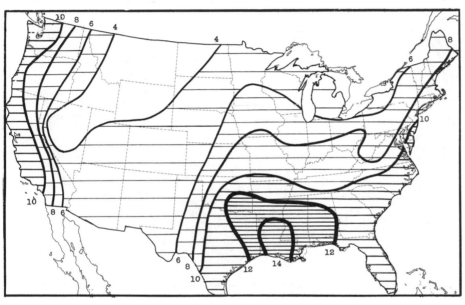

844

Range (in.) in
annual precipitation
in three-fifths of the
years (one-fifth
are wetter, one-fifth
are drier).

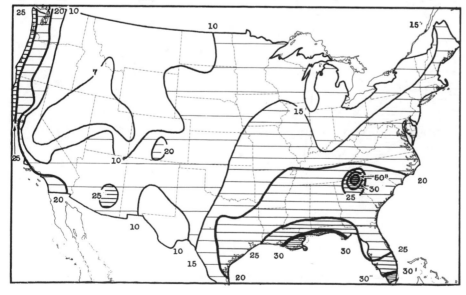

845

Range (in.)
in annual precipita-
tion in three-fourths
of the years (one-
eighth are wetter,
one-eighth are drier).

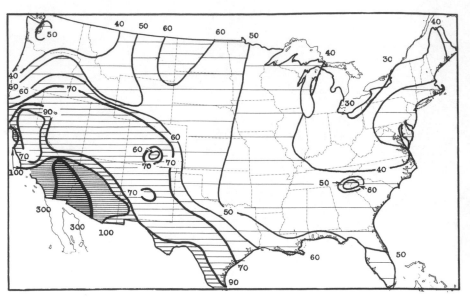

846

Percentage deviation from the normal annual precipitation in three-fourths of the years (one-eighth are wetter, one-eighth are drier).

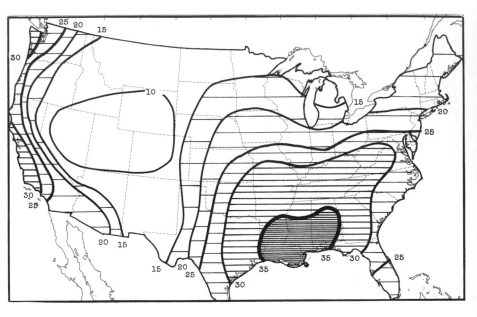

847

Extreme range (in.) in annual precipitation: (wettest vs. driest years of a half century).

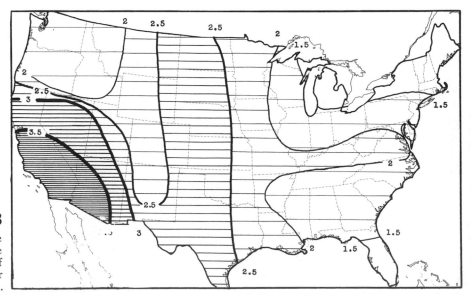

848

Ratio of the precipitation of the wettest to that of the driest year (1889–1938).

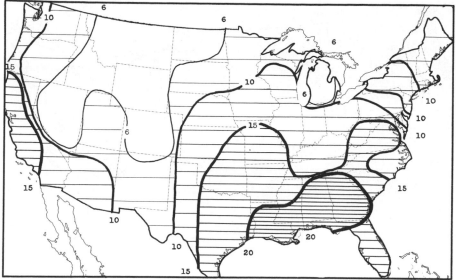

849
Excess of precipitation (in.) of the wettest year over the normal (1889–1938).

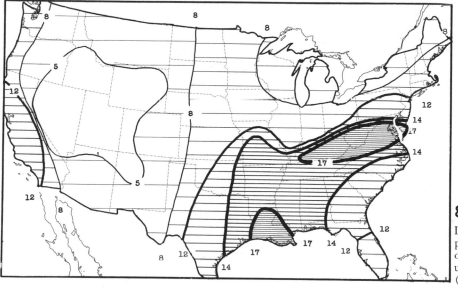

850
Deficiency of precipitation (in.) of the driest year under the normal (1889–1938).

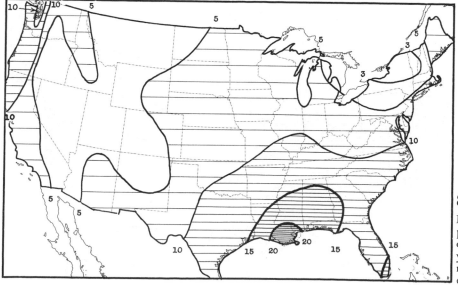

851
Excess of precipitation (in.) of a relatively wet year over the normal (only one-eighth are wetter).

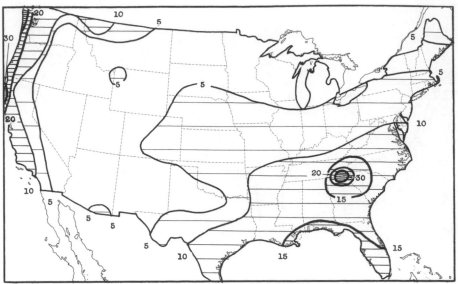

852

Deficiency of precipitation (in.) of a relatively dry year under the normal (only one-eighth are drier).

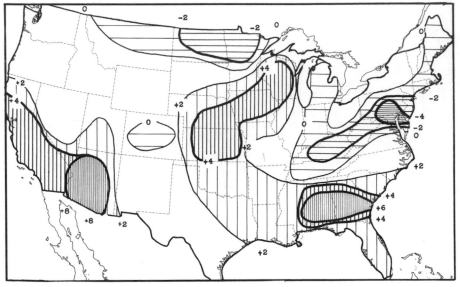

853

Precipitation deviation (in.) from normal of the wettest and driest years (1889–1938). In vertically shaded areas, the precipitation of the wettest year deviated more from the normal than did that of the driest year.

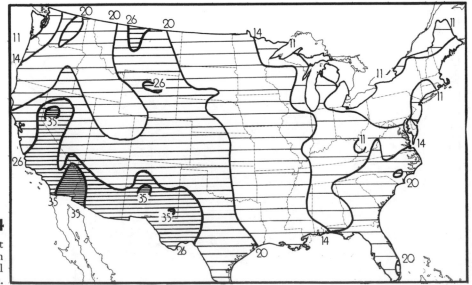

854

Average percent deviation from normal annual precipitation.

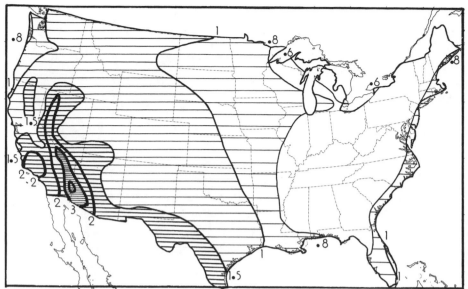

855

Ratio of extreme range (50 years) of annual precipitation to the normal annual precipitation.

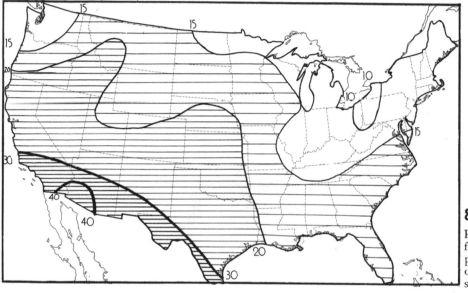

856

Percentage variability from normal of precipitation (based on 52 scattered stations).

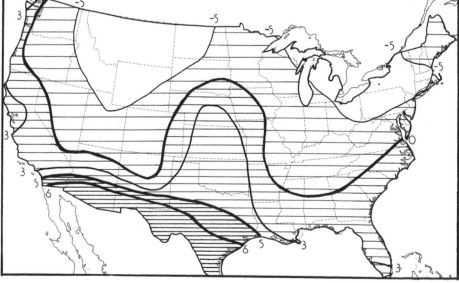

857

Deviation of relative variability of precipitation (in.) from normal relative variability.

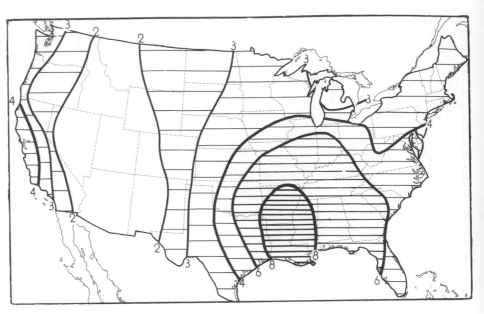

858

Range (in.) in
spring precipitation
in three-fifths of
the years (one-
fifth are wetter,
one-fifth are drier).

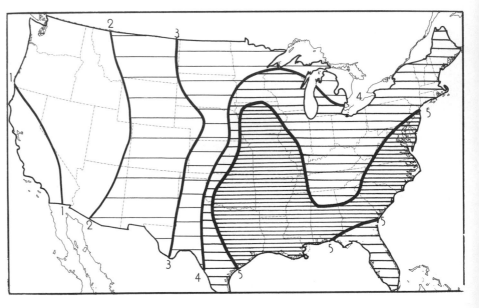

859

Range (in.) in
summer precipitation
in three-fifths of
the years (one-
fifth are wetter,
one-fifth are drier).

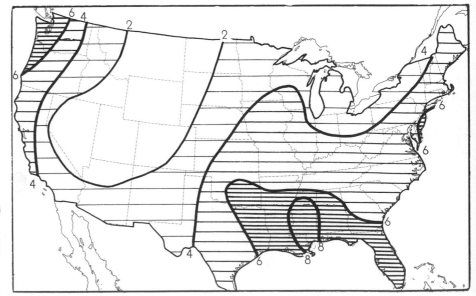

860

Range (in.) in
fall precipitation
in three-fifths of
the years (one-
fifth are wetter,
one-fifth are drier).

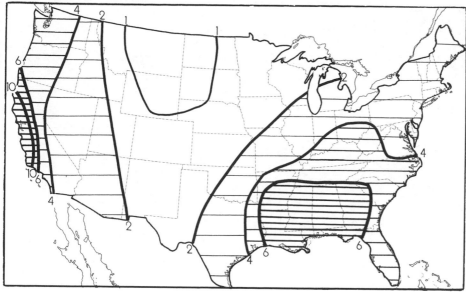

861

Range (in.) in winter precipitation in three-fifths of the years (one-fifth are wetter, one-fifth are drier).

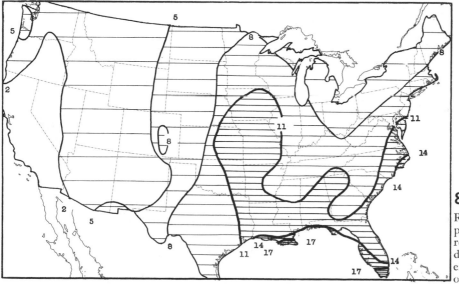

862

Range (in.) in precipitation between relatively wet and dry summers (one-eighth are wetter, one-eighth are drier).

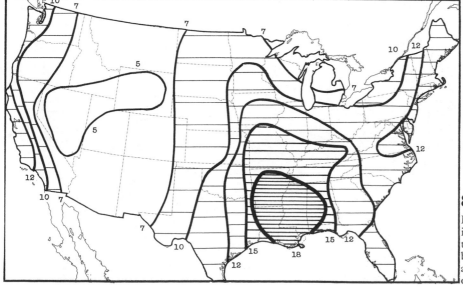

863

Extreme range (in.) in spring precipitation: difference between greatest and least totals of 50 years.

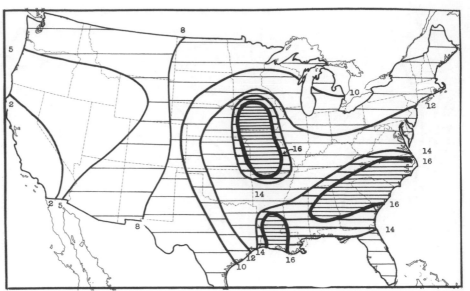

864

Extreme range (in.)
in summer precip-
itation: difference
between greatest
and least totals
of 50 years.

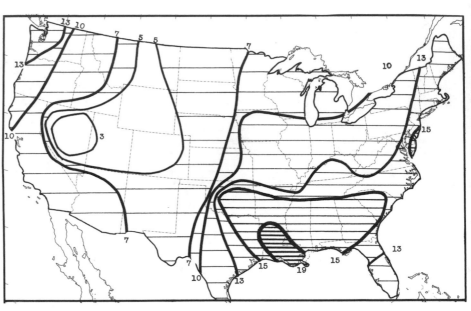

865

Extreme range (in.)
in fall precipitation:
difference between
greatest and least
totals of 50 years.

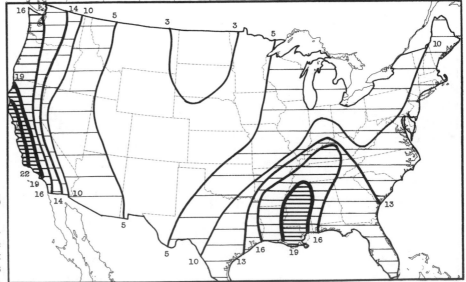

866

Extreme range (in.)
in winter precipita-
tion: difference
between greatest
and least totals
of 50 years.

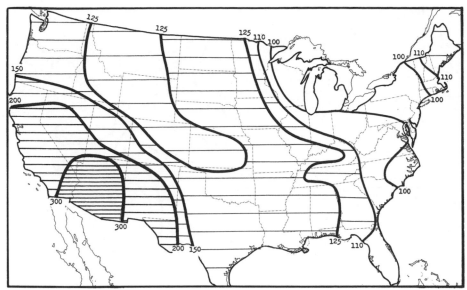

867

Range of
spring precipitation
in percent of normal
precipitation (200,
range double normal
precipitation).

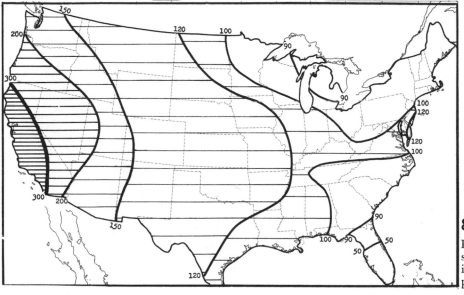

868

Range of
summer precipitation
in percent of normal
precipitation.

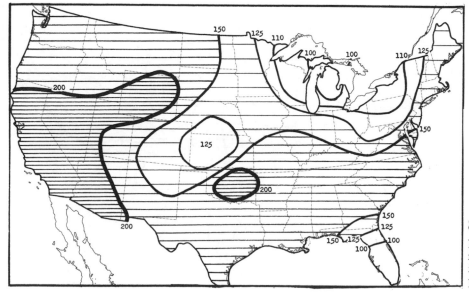

869

Range of
fall precipitation
in percent of normal
precipitation.

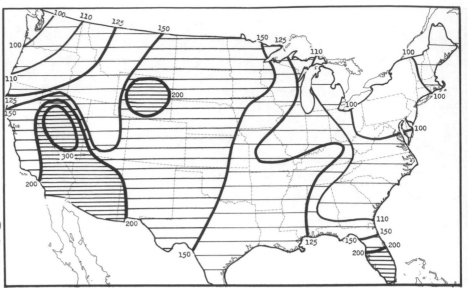

870

Range of
winter precipitation
in percent of normal
precipitation.

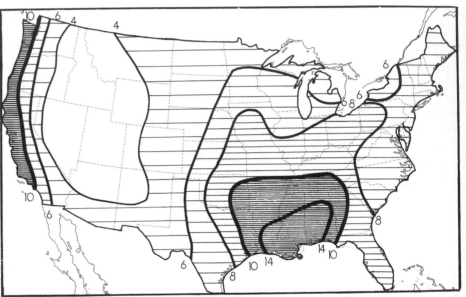

871

Extreme range
(in.) of monthly
precipitation in the
spring (1889–1938).

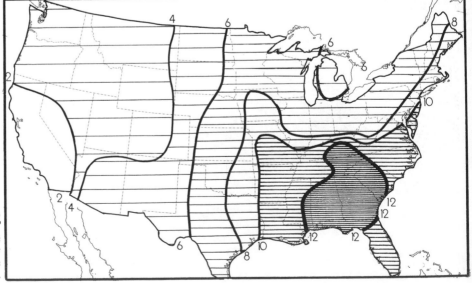

872

Extreme range
(in.) of monthly
precipitation in the
summer (1889–1938).

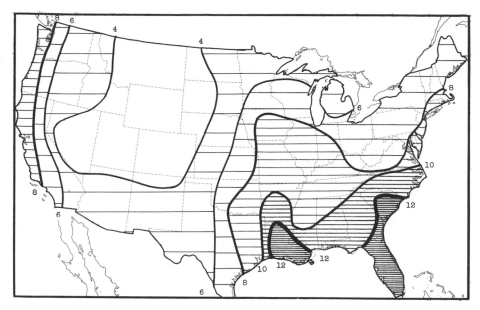

873

Extreme range (in.) of monthly precipitation in the fall (1889–1938).

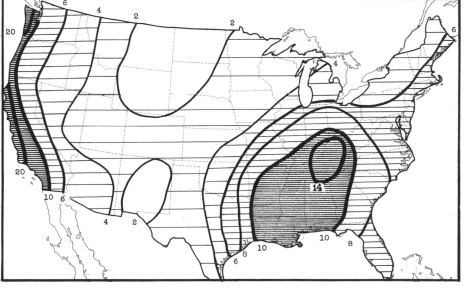

874

Extreme range (in.) of monthly precipitation in the winter (1889–1938).

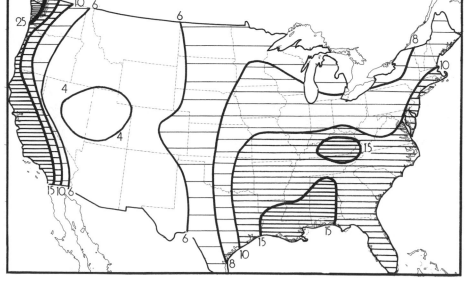

875

Extreme range (in.) of monthly precipitation (1889–1938).

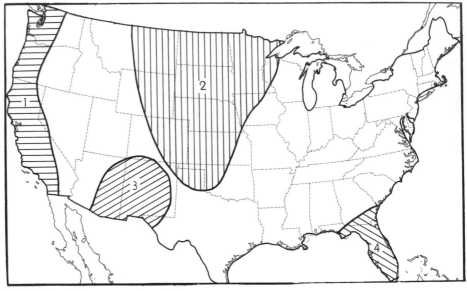

876

Areas with conspicuous seasonal contrasts in total precipitation: 1, dry in summer; 2, dry in winter; 3, dry except for part of summer; 4, much wetter in summer than in winter.

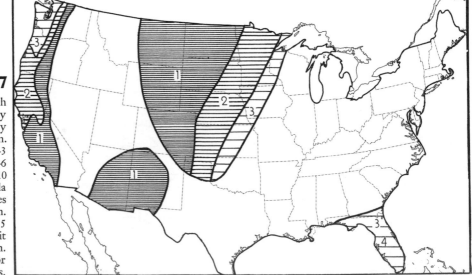

877

Average length of the relatively wet season (weekly normals of 0.5 in. or more): 1, 1–3 months; 2, 4–6 months; 3, 7–10 months; 4, Florida normally receives more than 1 in. a week for 5 months, much of it more than 2 in. per week for at least 6 weeks.

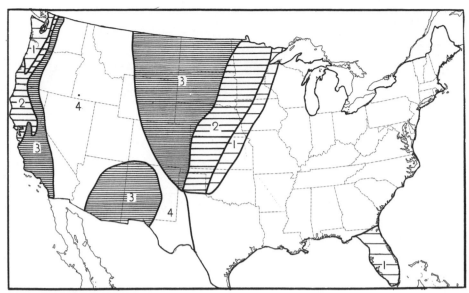

878

Average length of the relatively dry season (weekly normals of less than 0.5 in.): 1, 2–5 months; 2, 6 or 7 months; 3, 8–10 months; 4, 11 or 12 months.

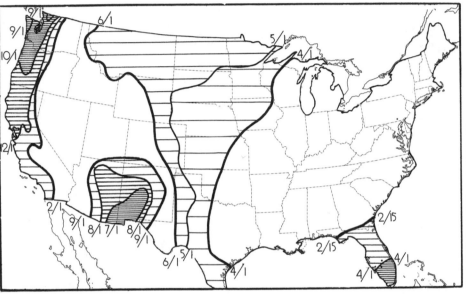

879

Normal date of beginning of the rainy season (weekly normals exceeding 0.5 in.). In the unshaded area of the west, no week normally has as much as 0.5 in.; in the east, every week normally has more than 0.5 in.

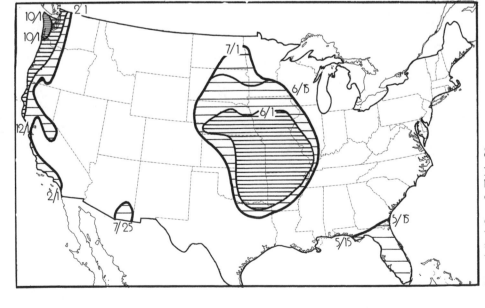

880

Normal date of beginning of the distinctly wet season (weekly normals exceeding 1 in.). The western unshaded area does not have weekly normals of 1 in.; the eastern one has them irregularly.

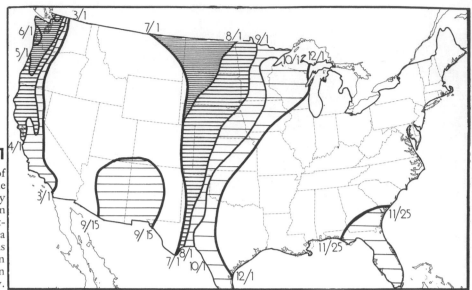

881

Normal date of beginning of the dry season (weekly normals less than 0.5 in.). The western unshaded area frequently has normals less than 0.5 in., the eastern area, rarely.

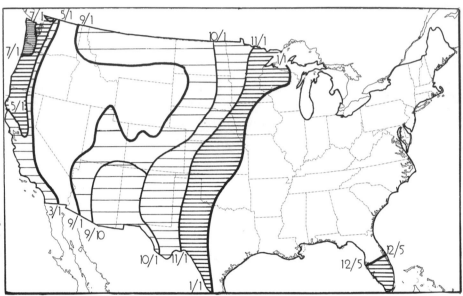

882

Normal date of beginning of the distinctly dry season (weekly normals less than 0.25 in.)

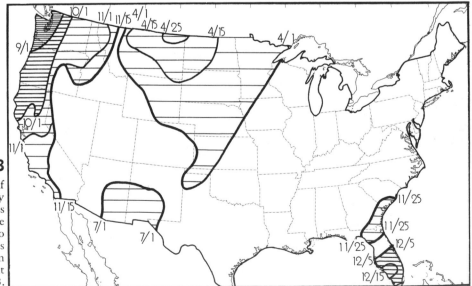

883

Normal date of ending of distinctly dry season (less than 0.25 in.). The season with no rain normally ends in southwestern California about August 23.

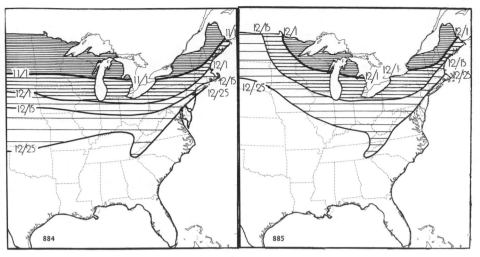

884

Normal date of first snow cover (1 in. or more). (For the date of the first measurable snowfall see Fig. 595.)

885

Normal date of first considerable snow cover (3 in. or more).

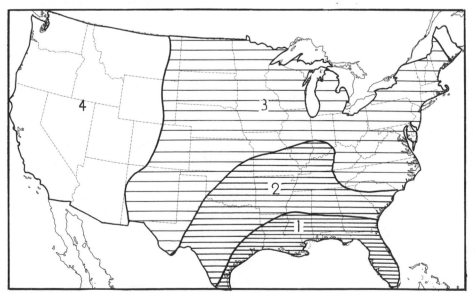

886

Normal date of first snow cover of 6 in. or more, based on those years with that much snow, few except in the north.

887

Normal date of last 3-in. snow cover.

888

Normal date of last snow cover (for other snow maps see Figs. 594, 597).

889

"Excessive" rains, seasonal distribution: 1, during 9 months or more; 2, 6–8 months; 3, occasional in summer; 4, lacking or very rare (excessive rains are vaguely defined but include 1 in. in 1 hr, 1.5 in 2 hr).

890

Date when "excessive" rains become occasional (10 per month in 30 years, averaging one-third per month).

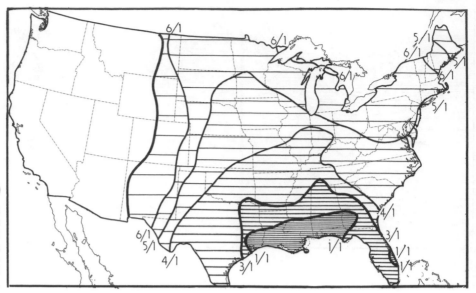

891

Approximate ending date of season of occasional "excessive" rains.

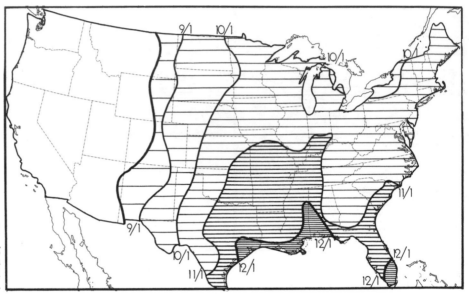

892

Date when "excessive" rains become frequent (averaging 1 or more per month).

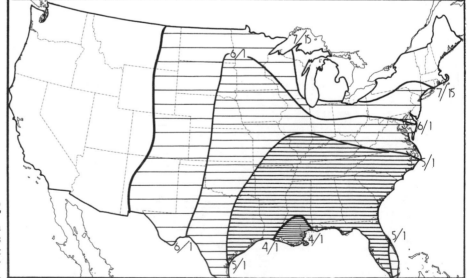

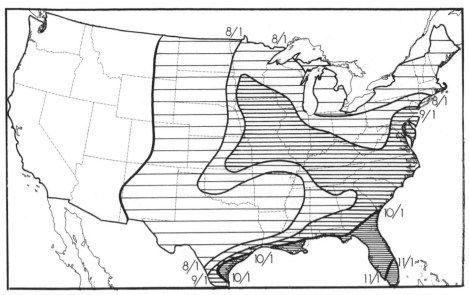

893

Date when "excessive" rains become infrequent (averaging fewer than 1 per month). (For maps of the average number of "excessive" rains in each quarter year, see Figs. 610–613.)

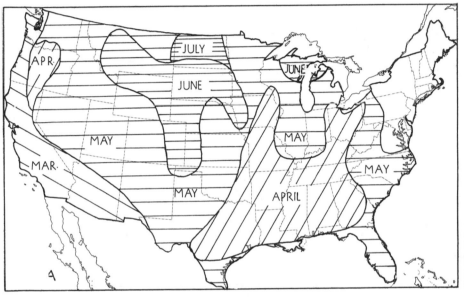

894

Hail: the month normally having most hailstorms.

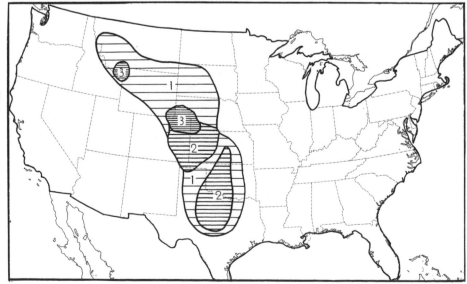

895

Hail: average length of season having 1 or more hailstorms per month. 1, less than 1 month; 2, 1 or 2 months; 3, 3 or 4 months.

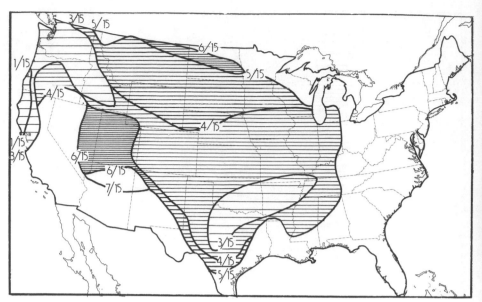

896

Average date of
beginning of season
with occasional
hailstorms.

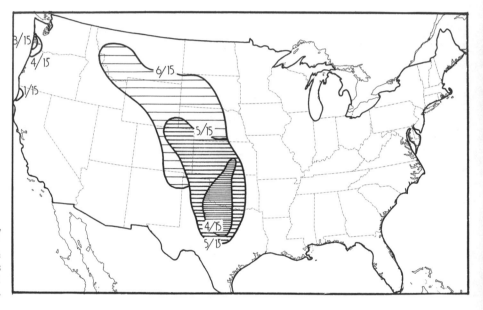

897

Average date
when hailstorms
become frequent (1
or more per month).

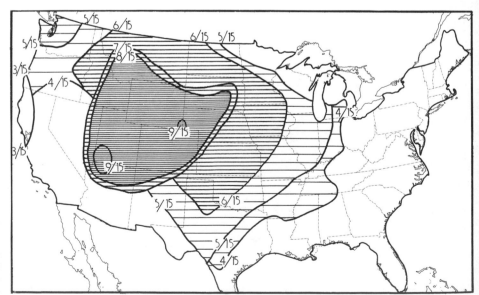

898

Average date
when hailstorms
become infrequent
(for length of hail
season, see Fig. 895).

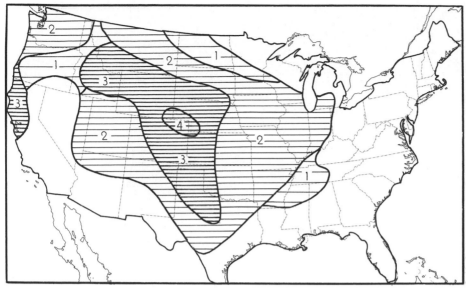

899

Hail regions based on the length of the season having hailstorms. In the blank area and in 1, hailstorms normally occur very rarely; in 2 they nearly all occur in one month; in 3 they occur in 2 or 3 months; in 4 they occur in 4 or 5 months. (For maps of the average number of hailstorms per month, see Figs. 606–609.)

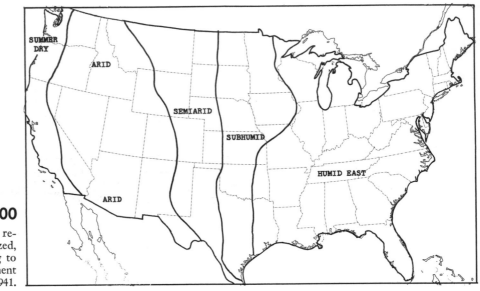

900

Precipitation regions, generalized, according to U. S. Department of Agriculture, 1941.

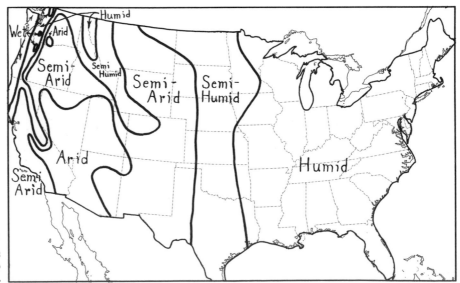

901

"Moisture" belts according to McDougal, 1927.

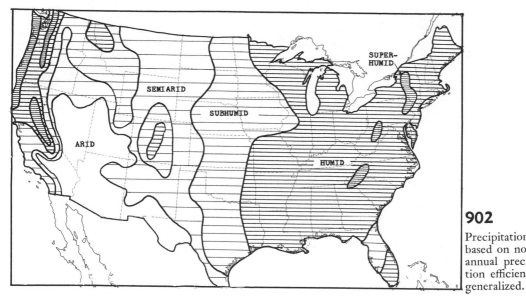

902
Precipitation regions based on normal annual precipitation efficiency, generalized.

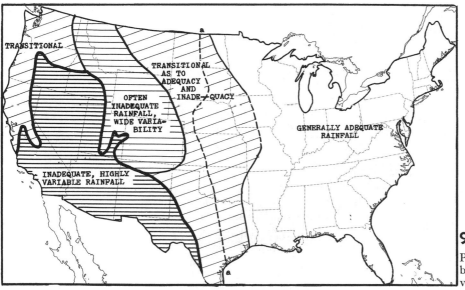

903
Precipitation regions based on precipitation variability.

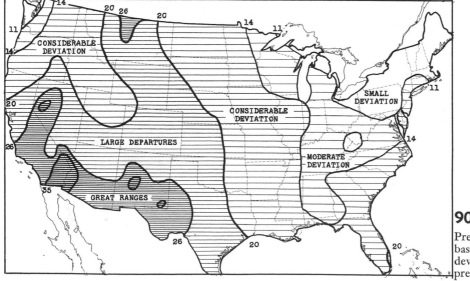

904
Precipitation regions based on normal deviation of annual precipitation.

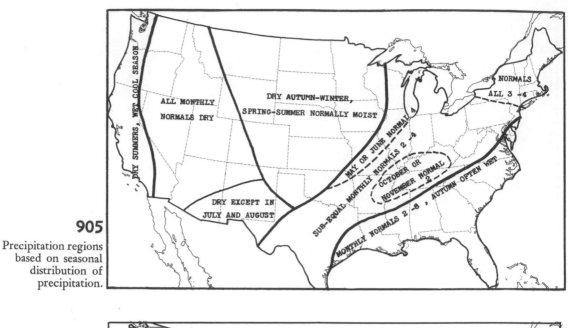

905
Precipitation regions
based on seasonal
distribution of
precipitation.

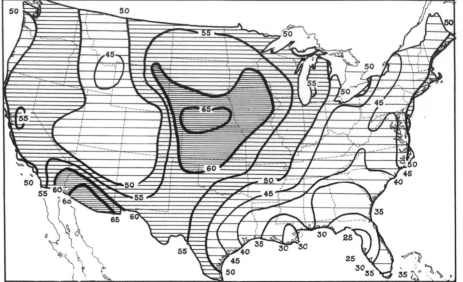

906
Precipitation regions
based on percentage
of warm-season rain
falling at night.

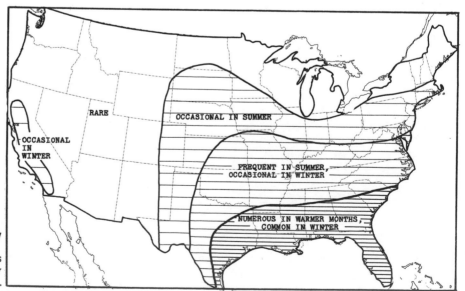

907
Precipitation regions
based on frequency
of "excessive" rains.

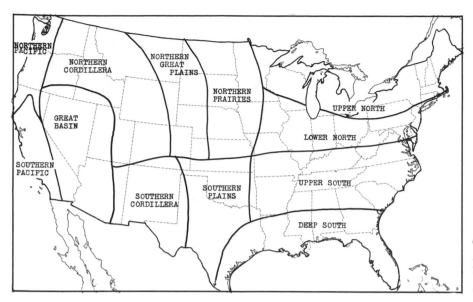

908
Precipitation regions
based on many pre-
cipitation criteria.

Within the map:

NORTHERN
PACIFIC

NORTHERN
CORDILLERA

NORTHERN
GREAT
PLAINS

NORTHERN
PRAIRIES

UPPER NORTH

GREAT
BASIN

LOWER NORTH

SOUTHERN
PACIFIC

UPPER SOUTH

SOUTHERN
CORDILLERA

SOUTHERN
PLAINS

DEEP SOUTH

32. SOME CONSEQUENCES OF CLIMATE AND WEATHER
ON AGRICULTURE AND HEALTH

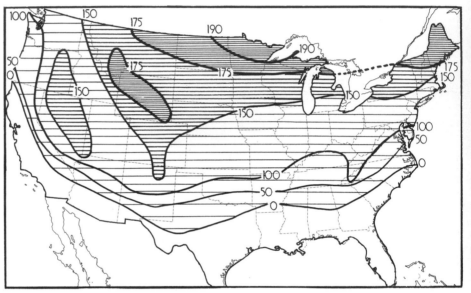

909

Duration of period
with little or no
plant growth:
annual number of
days with daily
normal temperature
below 43°.

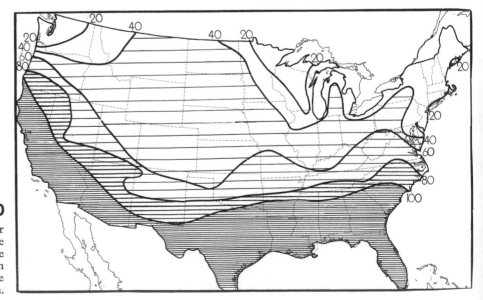

910

Normal number
of days that the
length of the
vegetative season
exceeds that of the
frost-free season.

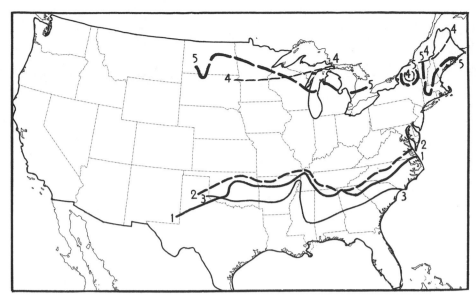

911

Five isotherms of special significance as corresponding to limits of extensive production of certain crops: 1, southern limit of winter wheat (68° April 15–June 15); 2, northern limit of cotton (200 days frostless season); 3, 4, southern and northern limits of apples (respectively, summer temperature, 79°; winter temperature, 13°); 5, northern limit of corn for grain (summer temperature, 66°).

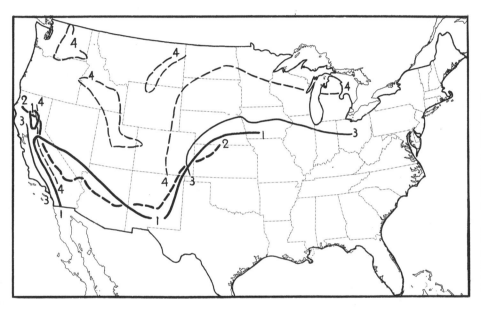

912

Four additional isotherms close to the limits of chief production of important crops: 1, 2, northern limits of grain sorghum (respectively, summer 75°, 160-day growing season); 3, 4, warmer and cooler margins of sugar beets (summer temperature respectively 67°, 72°).

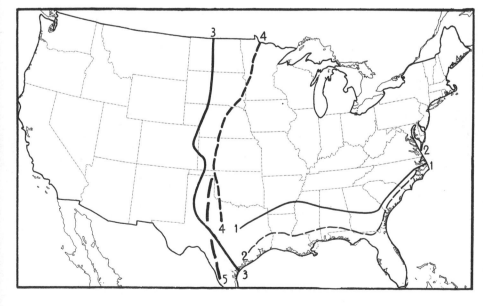

913

Five isohyets of special significance as corresponding to limits of extensive production of certain crops: 1, southern limit of wheat (55 in. annual precipitation except near eastern and western ends, where it is 50 in.); 2, southern limit of cotton (fall rainfall exceeds 10 in.); 3, western limit of corn for grain (summer rainfall less than 8 in.); 4, western limit of eastern apples (annual precipitation less than 18 in.); 5, western limit of eastern cotton (annual precipitation less than 18 in.).

914

Four additional isohyets close to the limits of chief production of important crops: 1, 2, eastern limit of any and of much grain sorghum (annual precipitation, 40 in., 25 in.); 3, western limit of grain sorghum; 4, northern limit of red and yellow leached soils (April–September precipitation, 25 in.; western limit is about 20 in. annual precipitation).

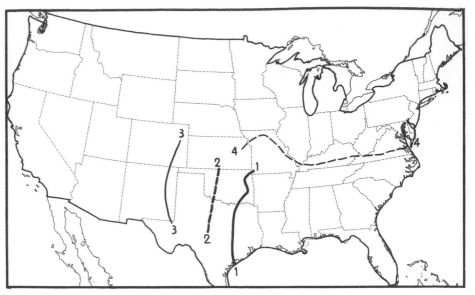

915

Date when seeding of spring wheat and winter oats usually is general.

916

Date when seeding of spring oats usually is general.

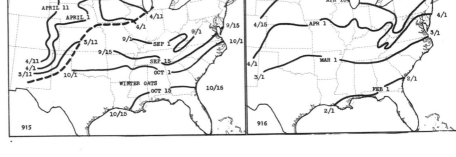

917

Date when corn planting usually begins.

918

Date when potato planting usually is general.

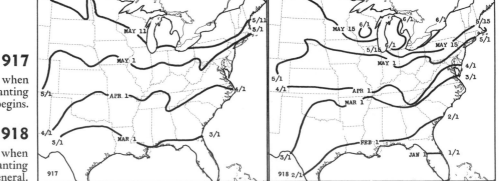

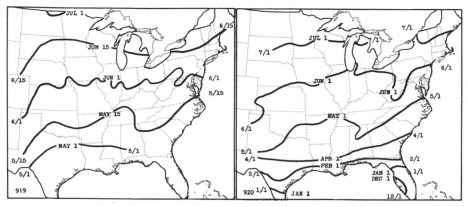

919
Date when
alfalfa first cutting
usually is general.

920
Date when
strawberry picking
usually begins.

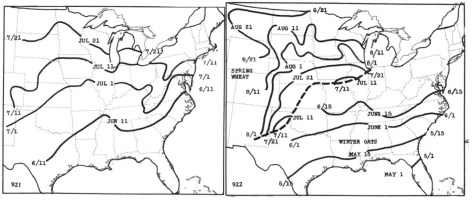

921
Date when
winter-wheat harvest
usually is general.

922
Date when
spring-wheat and
winter-oats harvest
usually is general.

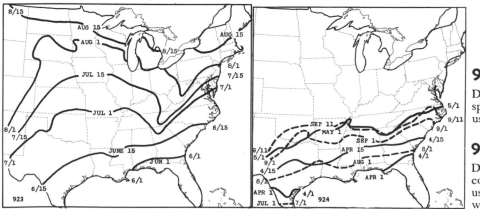

923
Date when
spring-oats harvest
usually is general.

924
Date when
cotton planting
usually is general and
when picking begins.

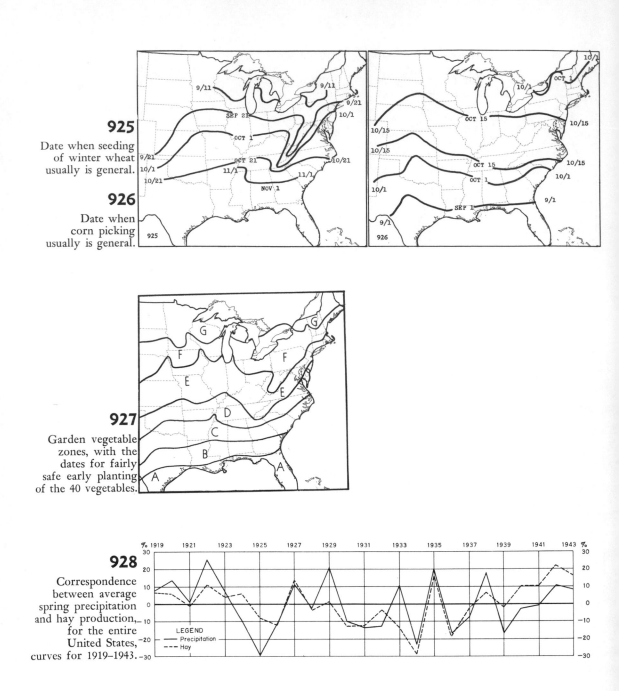

925 Date when seeding of winter wheat usually is general.

926 Date when corn picking usually is general.

927 Garden vegetable zones, with the dates for fairly safe early planting of the 40 vegetables.

928 Correspondence between average spring precipitation and hay production, for the entire United States, curves for 1919–1943.

LEGEND
—— Precipitation
----- Hay

Earliest safe date for planting vegetable seed

for the middle of each zone of Fig. 927

	Zone*				
Crop	B	C	D	E	F
Asparagus	Feb. 15	May 7	Apr. 1	Apr. 27	May 7
Beans, lima	Mar. 23	Apr. 7	May 7	May 22	June 1
Beans, snap	Mar. 7	Mar. 22	Apr. 15	May 7	May 22
Beets	Feb. 22	Mar. 7	Apr. 1	Apr. 22	May 7
Broccoli	Feb. 1	Feb. 22	Mar. 7	Apr. 1	Apr. 22
Brussels Sprouts	Feb. 1	Feb. 22	Mar. 7	Apr. 1	Apr. 22
Cabbage	Feb. 1	Feb. 22	Mar. 7	Apr. 1	Apr. 22
Carrots	Feb. 22	Mar. 7	Mar. 22	Apr. 15	May 7
Cauliflower	Feb. 1	Feb. 22	Mar. 7	Apr. 1	Apr. 22
Celery	Feb. 1	Feb. 22	Mar. 7	Apr. 1	Apr. 22
Chard	Feb. 1	Feb. 22	Mar. 7	Apr. 1	Apr. 22
Chives	Feb. 7	Feb. 22	Mar. 7	Apr. 1	Apr. 22
Corn, sweet	Mar. 8	Mar. 22	Apr. 15	May 1	May 15
Cress	Feb. 22	Mar. 7	Mar. 22	Apr. 15	May 7
Cucumbers	Mar. 23	Apr. 7	Apr. 22	May 15	June 1
Eggplant	Mar. 22	Apr. 7	Apr. 22	May 15	June 1
Endive	Feb. 22	Mar. 7	Mar. 22	Apr. 15	May 7
Garlic	Feb. 7	Feb. 22	Mar. 7	Apr. 1	Apr. 15
Kale	Feb. 7	Feb. 22	Mar. 7	Apr. 1	Apr. 22
Kohlrabi	Feb. 22	Mar. 7	Mar. 22	Apr. 15	May 7
Leek	Feb. 7	Feb. 22	Mar. 7	Apr. 1	Apr. 15
Lettuce	—	Mar. 1	Apr. 1	Apr. 15	Apr. 22
Muskmelon	—	—	Apr. 1	May 15	June 7
Mustard	—	Feb. 1	Apr. 1	Apr. 15	Apr. 22
Okra	Mar. 7	Mar. 22	Apr. 22	May 7	May 22
Onion plants	Feb. 7	Feb. 22	Mar. 7	Apr. 1	Apr. 15
Onion seed	Feb. 22	Mar. 7	Mar. 22	Apr. 15	May 7
Parsley	Feb. 22	Mar. 7	Mar. 22	Apr. 15	May 7
Parsnip	Feb. 22	Mar. 7	Mar. 22	Apr. 15	May 7
Peas	Feb. 1	Feb. 22	Mar. 7	Apr. 1	Apr. 22
Potatoes	Feb. 1	Feb. 7	Mar. 1	Apr. 1	Apr. 22
Pumpkins	—	—	Apr. 22	May 7	June 7
Radishes	—	Feb. 1	Mar. 7	Apr. 1	Apr. 22
Rhubarb	—	—	Apr. 1	Apr. 15	May 1
Rutabaga	—	Mar. 1	Mar. 15	Apr. 1	Apr. 22
Salsify	Feb. 22	Mar. 7	Apr. 1	Apr. 22	May 7
Spinach	Feb. 22	Mar. 7	Mar. 15	Apr. 1	Apr. 22
Squash	Mar. 22	Apr. 7	Apr. 22	May 15	June 7
Sweet potatoes	Mar. 7	Mar. 22	May 7	May 22	June 7
Tomato plants	Mar. 7	Mar. 22	May 7	May 22	June 7
Turnips	Mar. 15	Mar. 22	Apr. 1	Apr. 7	Apr. 22
Watermelon	Mar. 22	Apr. 7	May 1	May 15	June 7

* In zone A planting is safe at any time; in zone G frost may occur in any month.

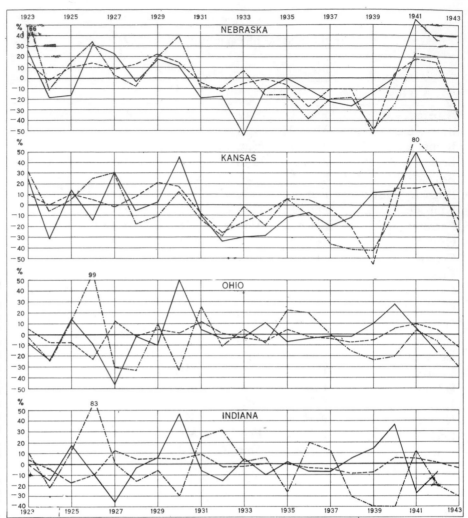

929

Correspondence between average August–October rainfall and winter-wheat conditions on December 1, and the state average yield in the following harvest: curves of percentage departure from the 20-year average (full line, yield; dashed line, December 1 wheat condition; dash-dot line, August–October rainfall).

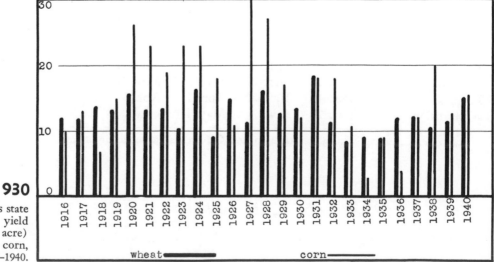

930

Kansas state average yield (bushels per acre) of wheat and corn, 1916–1940.

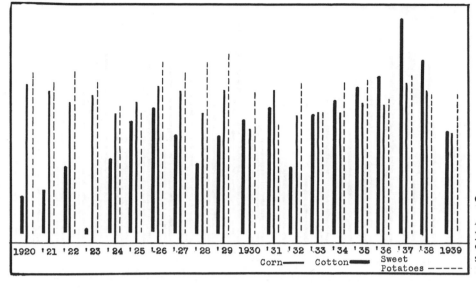

931

Alabama state average yield per acre of corn, cotton, and sweet potatoes, 1920–1939.

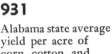

1920 '21 '22 '23 '24 '25 '26 '27 '28 '29 1930 '31 '32 '33 '34 '35 '36 '37 '38 1939

Corn——— Cotton——— Sweet Potatoes ———–

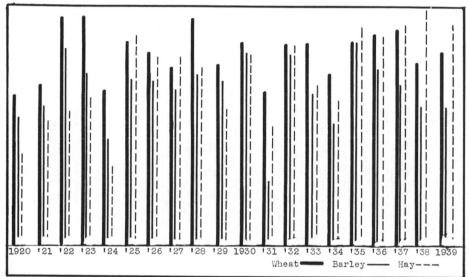

932

California state average yield per acre of wheat, barley, and hay, 1920–1939.

1920 '21 '22 '23 '24 '25 '26 '27 '28 '29 1930 '31 '32 '33 '34 '35 '36 '37 '38 1939

Wheat——— Barley——— Hay–––

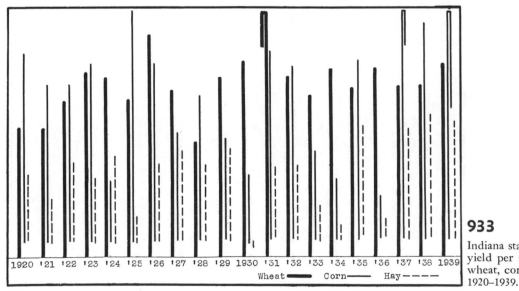

933

Indiana state average yield per acre of wheat, corn, and hay, 1920–1939.

1920 '21 '22 '23 '24 '25 '26 '27 '28 '29 1930 '31 '32 '33 '34 '35 '36 '37 '38 1939

Wheat——— Corn——— Hay–––

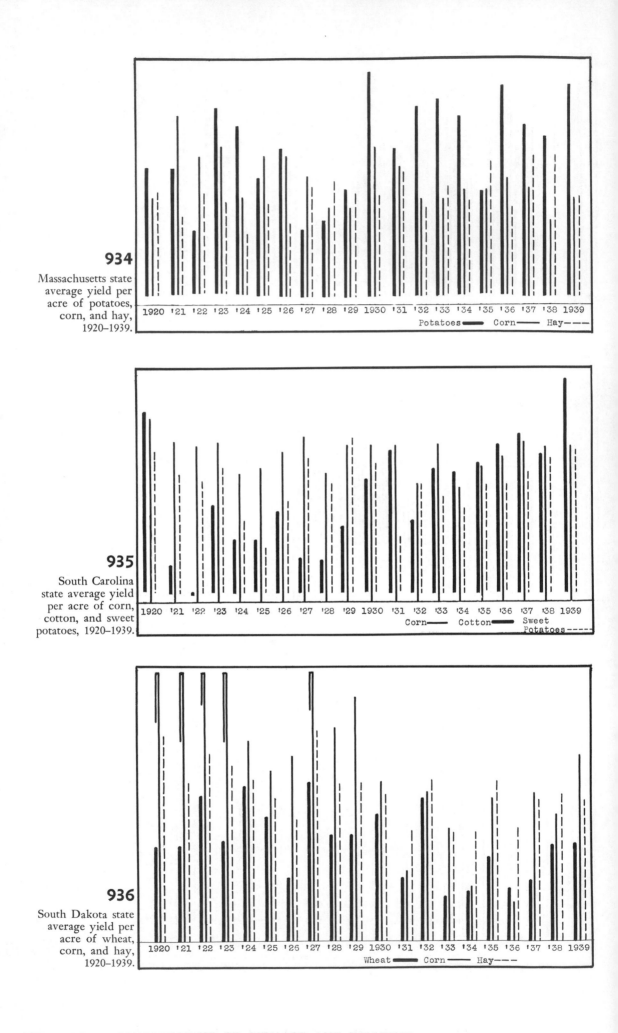

934

Massachusetts state average yield per acre of potatoes, corn, and hay, 1920–1939.

| | | | | | | | | | | | | | | | | | | | |
| 1920 | '21 | '22 | '23 | '24 | '25 | '26 | '27 | '28 | '29 | 1930 | '31 | '32 | '33 | '34 | '35 | '36 | '37 | '38 | 1939 |

Potatoes ■■■ Corn ——— Hay – – –

935

South Carolina state average yield per acre of corn, cotton, and sweet potatoes, 1920–1939.

| | | | | | | | | | | | | | | | | | | | |
| 1920 | '21 | '22 | '23 | '24 | '25 | '26 | '27 | '28 | '29 | 1930 | '31 | '32 | '33 | '34 | '35 | '36 | '37 | '38 | 1939 |

Corn ——— Cotton ■■■ Sweet Potatoes – – –

936

South Dakota state average yield per acre of wheat, corn, and hay, 1920–1939.

| | | | | | | | | | | | | | | | | | | | |
| 1920 | '21 | '22 | '23 | '24 | '25 | '26 | '27 | '28 | '29 | 1930 | '31 | '32 | '33 | '34 | '35 | '36 | '37 | '38 | 1939 |

Wheat ■■■ Corn ——— Hay – – –

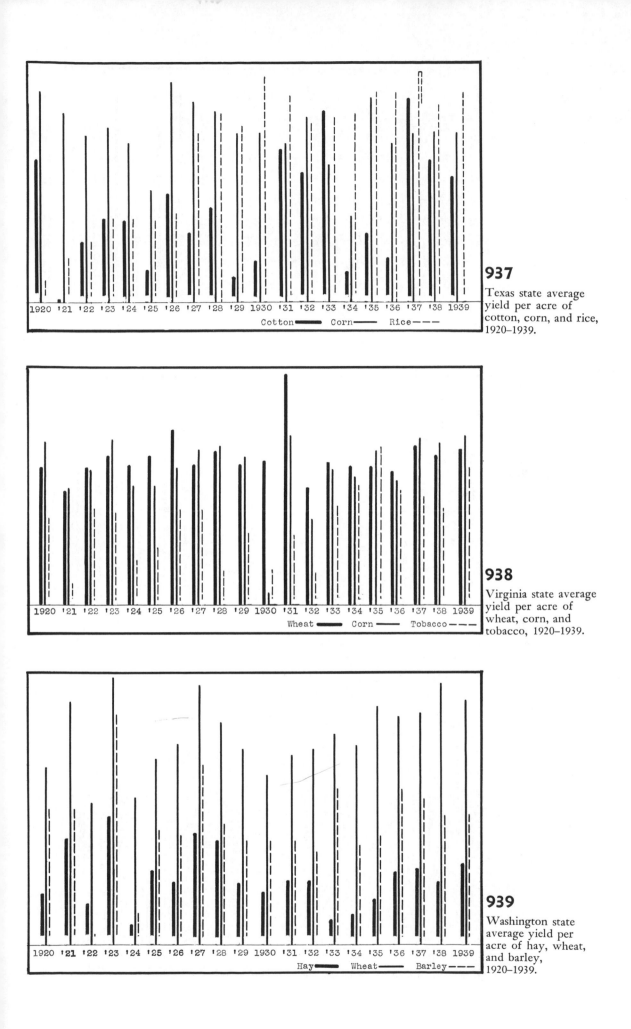

937
Texas state average yield per acre of cotton, corn, and rice, 1920–1939.

938
Virginia state average yield per acre of wheat, corn, and tobacco, 1920–1939.

939
Washington state average yield per acre of hay, wheat, and barley, 1920–1939.

The state average yields in the 20 years 1920–1939 varied as follows (bushels per acre for the grains and potatoes, tons per acre for hay, pounds per acre for cotton and tobacco): *California:* wheat, 14.5–21.5; barley, 18–31; hay, 2.0–2.7; *Indiana:* corn, 25.5–51.5; wheat, 10.5–25.9; hay, 0.8–1.4; *Massachusetts:* corn, 38–48; potatoes, 85–162; hay, 1.1–1.5; *South Carolina:* corn, 10.5–15; cotton, 140–340; sweet potatoes, 55–107; *South Dakota:* corn, 3.4–32.0; wheat, 4.3–14.9; hay, 0.5–1.0; *Texas:* corn, 8.2–21.0; rice, 34–57; cotton, 101–197; *Virginia:* corn, 11–25.5; wheat, 10.8–22; tobacco, 551–874; *Washington:* wheat, 13.6–25.3; barley, 21–42; hay, 1.4–1.8.

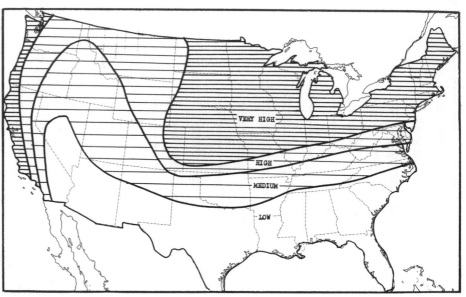

940

Climatic efficiency as suggested by contrasts in human energy and health.

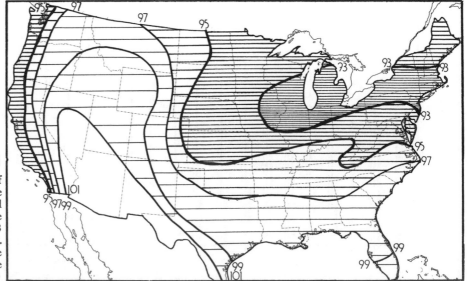

941

Distribution of health on the basis of seasonal variations of the death rate in 33 cities, 1900–1915. (The lower the numbers, the better the health.)

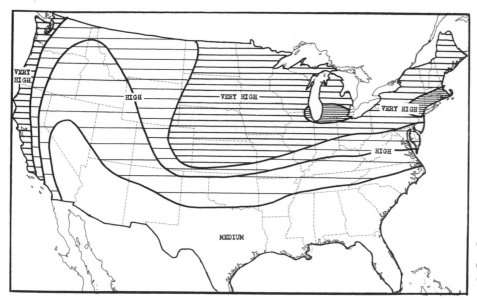

942

Climatic energy
on the basis of output
per factory worker.

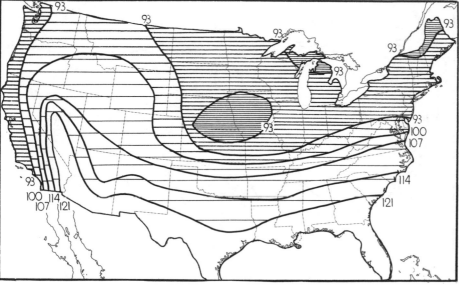

943

Climate and health
as suggested by
difference in human
death rates. (The
numbers are percent-
ages of the average
death rate for the
entire country,
according to life-
insurance statistics.)

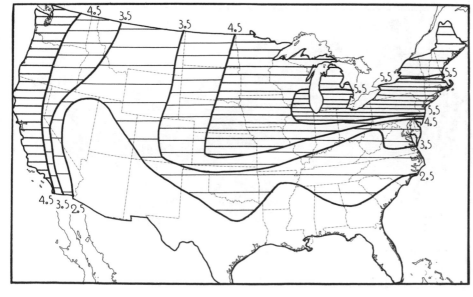

944

Civilization contrasts.
(Each of 23
Americans rated
each state according
to a dozen criteria
of civilization on a
scale of 1 to 6,
6 being highest. The
numbers shown are
the averages of
the ratings.)

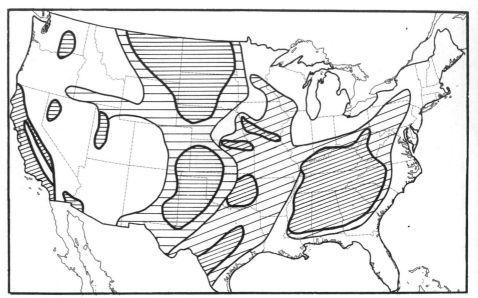

945

A generalized map showing the chief large areas of much soil erosion by wind (horizontal shading) or runoff (slanting shading).

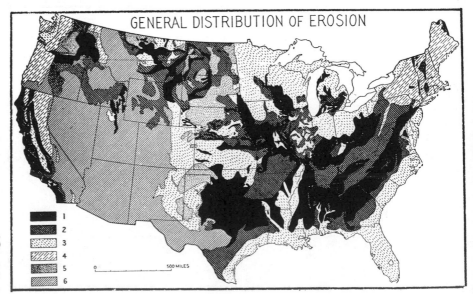

GENERAL DISTRIBUTION OF EROSION

946

Soil erosion, greatest in 1, little in 3, least in 6.

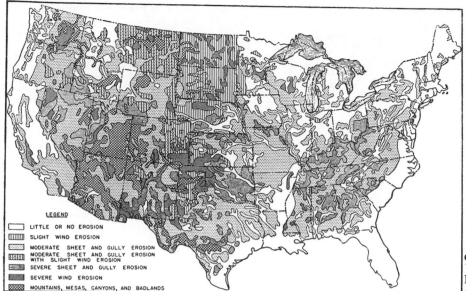

947
Principal areas
of soil erosion.

LEGEND
- LITTLE OR NO EROSION
- SLIGHT WIND EROSION
- MODERATE SHEET AND GULLY EROSION
- MODERATE SHEET AND GULLY EROSION WITH SLIGHT WIND EROSION
- SEVERE SHEET AND GULLY EROSION
- SEVERE WIND EROSION
- MOUNTAINS, MESAS, CANYONS, AND BADLANDS

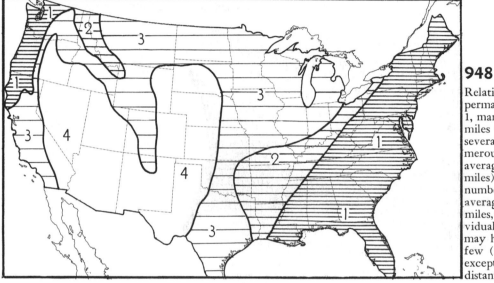

948
Relative number of
permanent streams:
1, many (few square
miles without
several); 2, nu-
merous (scores per
average 100 square
miles); 3, moderate
numbers (dozens per
average 100 square
miles, though indi-
vidual square miles
may have none); 4,
few (locally none,
except streams from
distant mountains).

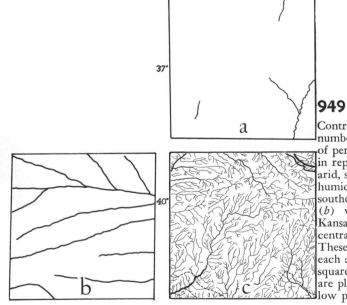

949
Contrasts in the
number and length
of permanent streams
in representative
arid, semiarid and
humid climates: (a)
southeastern Nevada;
(b) west central
Kansas; (c) east
central Indiana.
These areas are
each about 100
square miles; two
are plains, one a
low plateau.

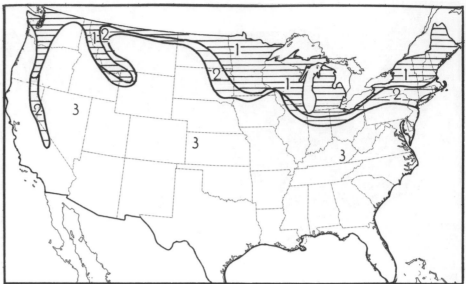

950

Relative number or extent of lakes: 1, many or large; 2, few and small; 3, almost lacking, except rare oxbows along large rivers, ponds in limestone sinkholes, and a few other types, such as Great Salt Lake.

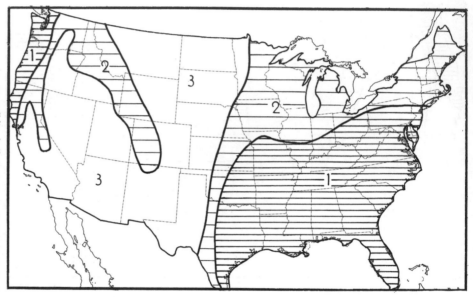

951

Contrasts in the average slope of somewhat comparable uplands (the average angle from streams to the divides between streams): 1, relatively great; 2, moderate; 3, small, although cliffs and other steep slopes occur, often separated by miles of gentle slope.

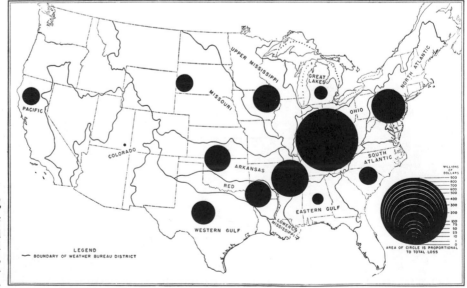

952

Distribution of estimated flood losses by regional drainage divisions, July 1, 1902–December 31, 1937.

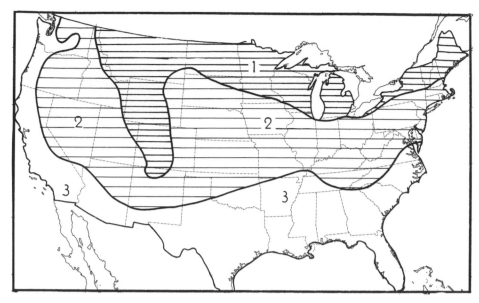

953

Ice contrasts: 1, region where ice action on the shores of lakes and rivers is often notable and where the ground freezes deeply; 2, region where frost action (freeze and thaw) is considerable, though ice on water bodies is of minor importance; 3, region where frost action is relatively unimportant in modifying the land.

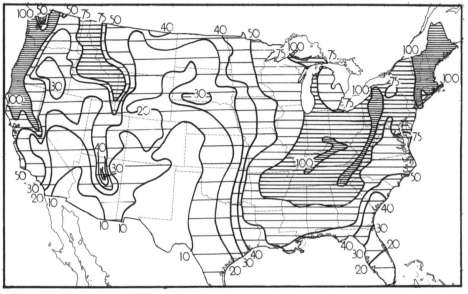

954

Average soil moisture (percent of saturation) in January, according to Angstrom's coefficient.

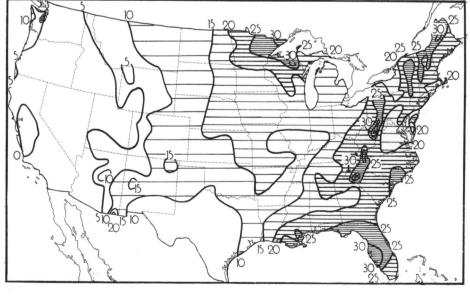

955

Average soil moisture (percent of saturation) in July, according to Angstrom's coefficient.

34. CLIMATIC REGIONS, ON VARIOUS CRITERIA

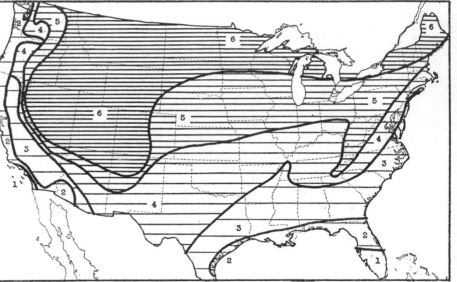

956

Regions based on frequency and severity of freezing: 1, frost rare; 2, freezes rare; 3, freezes frequent, soil usually freezes 1–4 in. annually; 4, soil normally freezes 6–18 in., frosts occur 5–7 months; 5, soil normally freezes 18–36 in., only 3 or 4 months without frost; 6, soil usually freezes 3–6 ft., frosts in all months, or all but 1 or 2.

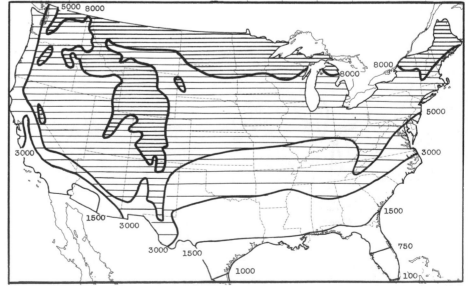

957

Regions based on the annual normal total of (cold) degree days. (For a more detailed map of (cold) degree days, see Fig. 213.)

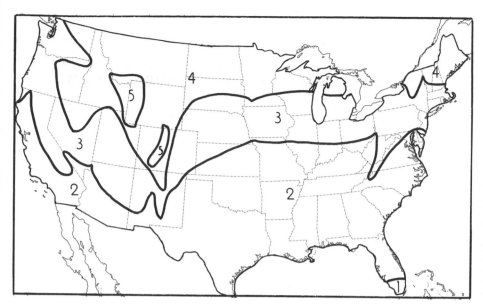

958

Temperature efficiency provinces: 1, warm-phase mesothermal; 2, mesothermal; 3, warm-phase micro-thermal; 4, micro-thermal; 5, taiga.

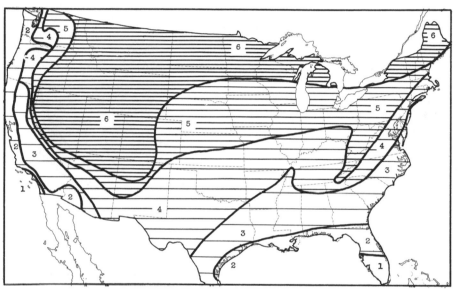

959

Temperature regions, based on average January temperatures: 1, tropical; 2, occasionally tropical; 3, regularly meso-thermal; 4, occasion-ally mesothermal; 5, occasionally micro-thermal; 6, regularly microthermal.

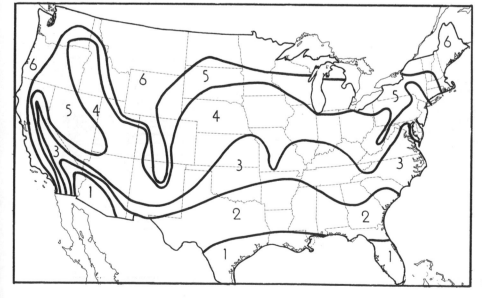

960

Regions based on the annual normal total of hot degree days: 1, temperature normally above 70°; 2, temperature above 70° most of the year; 3, hot weather normal for nearly half of the year; 4, hot summers; 5, rare spells of hot weather; 6, daily normals never above 70°. (For a more detailed map, see Fig. 270.)

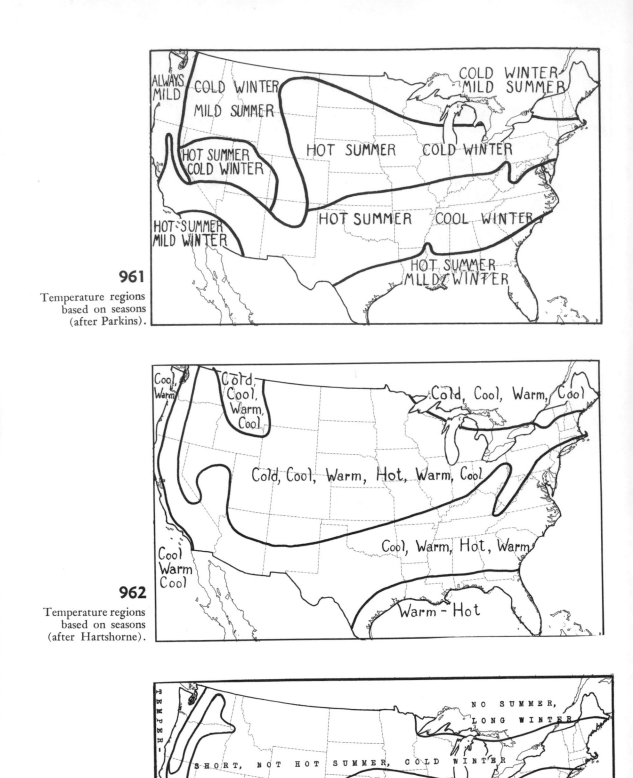

961

Temperature regions
based on seasons
(after Parkins).

962

Temperature regions
based on seasons
(after Hartshorne).

963

Temperature regions
based on seasons
(Visher).

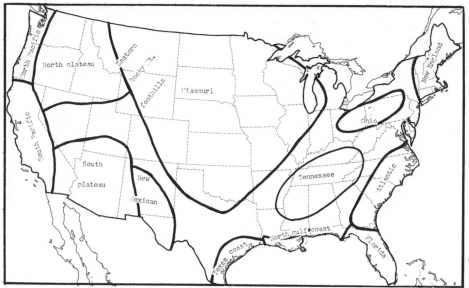

964

Rainfall types.

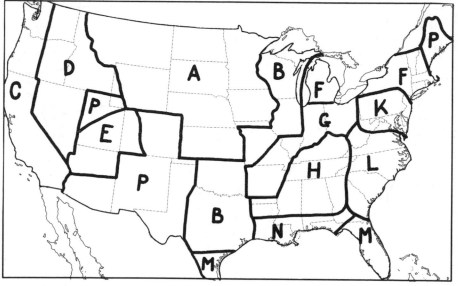

965

Rainfall regions, based on the season of maximum and minimum.

Sections	Months bringing		Average precipitation (in.)	Range of intensity (pluviometric coeff.)
	Principal maximum intensity	Principal minimum intensity		
A	June	January	23	161
B	June	January	33	96
C	January	July	31	194
D	January	July	13	117
E	February	June	14	112
F	July	January	38	34
G	May	October	42	57
H	March	October	50	65
K	July	November	44	39
L	August	November	48	75
M	September	January	25	142
N	—	October	55	85
P	Miscellaneous areas			

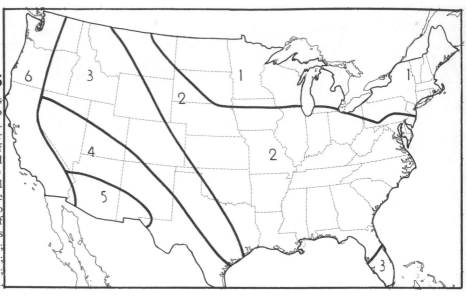

966

Humidity provinces according to Lang's formula. Lang's rain factor is the ratio of normal annual precipitation (mm) to normal annual mean temperature (°C). The map gives values of the rain factor as follows: 1, > 100; 2, 61–100; 3, 41–60; 4, 21–40; 5, < 20; 6, no data.

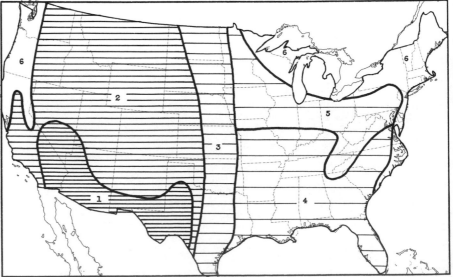

967

Humidity provinces according to Meyer's formula. Meyer's N. S. quotient is the ratio of precipitation (mm) to the absolute saturation deficit of the air. The map gives values of the N. S. quotient as follows: 1, 601–800; 2, 501–600; 3, 401–500; 4, 301–400; 5, 201–300; 6, 101–200; 7, < 100; 8, no data.

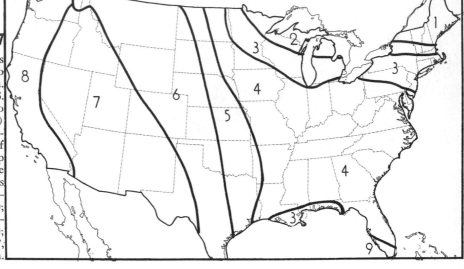

968

Evaporation regions: 1, evaporation much in excess of precipitation; 2, evaporation considerably in excess of precipitation; 3, evaporation usually in excess of precipitation; 4, evaporation in excess of precipitation in warm months; 5, precipitation in excess of evaporation in cooler months; 6, precipitation generally in excess of evaporation.

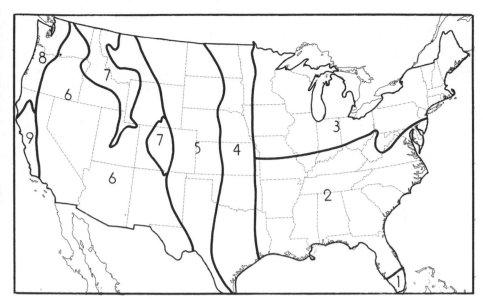

969

Climatic regions, after Van Valkenburg: 1, tropical; 2, humid, long hot summer, mild winter; 3, humid, cold winter; 4, occasionally dry; 5, occasionally wet; 6, regularly dry; 7, mountain climate; 8, humid, mild winter, cool summer; 9, mild wet winter, warm dry summer.

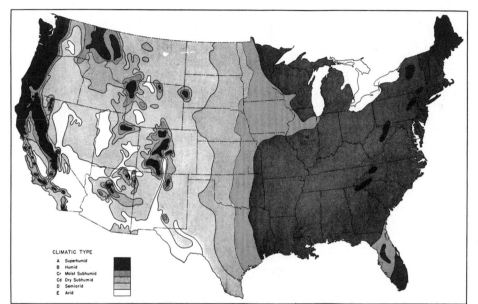

970

Generalized normal distribution of the principal climatic types.

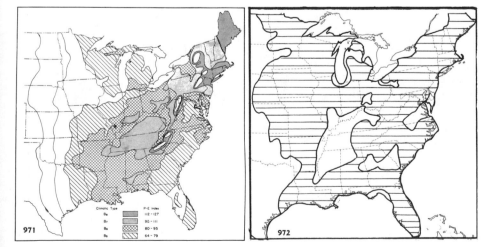

971

Subdivisions of the eastern humid climate.

972

The eastern region that normally is humid throughout the warmer season (May–September), shaded.

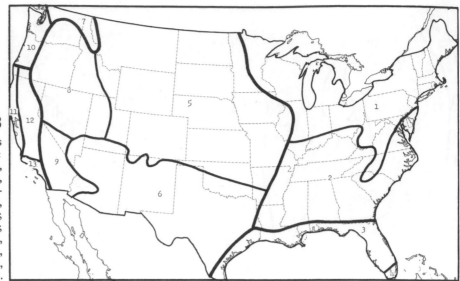

973

Climatic regions
(after Hult, 1893):
1, Canadian; 2,
southern states; 3,
Louisiana; 4, An-
tilles; 5, prairie; 6,
Mexican; 7, Fraser;
8, Utah; 9, Mohave;
10, Cascade; 11,
Coast Range; 12,
Sacramento; 13,
San Diego.

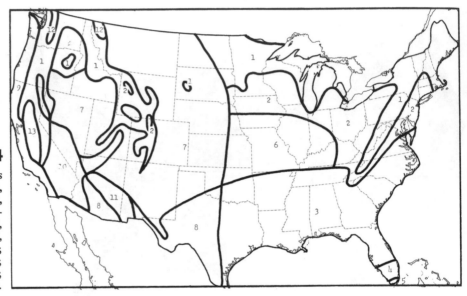

974

Climatic regions
(after Koeppen,
1900): 1, oak; 2,
hickory; 3, ca-
mellia; 4, liana; 5,
baobab; 6, corn; 7,
prairie; 8, mesquite;
9, heath; 10, simum;
11, high savanna;
12, birch; 13, olive.

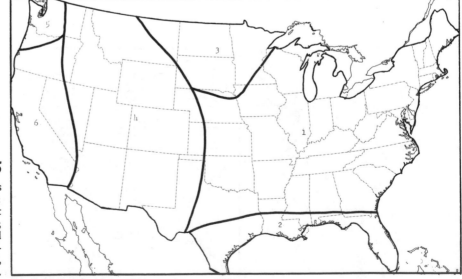

975

Climatic regions
(after Supan, 1903):
1, Atlantic; 2, West
Indian; 3, Hudson;
4, mountain and
plateau; 5, north-
west coastal; 6,
Californian.

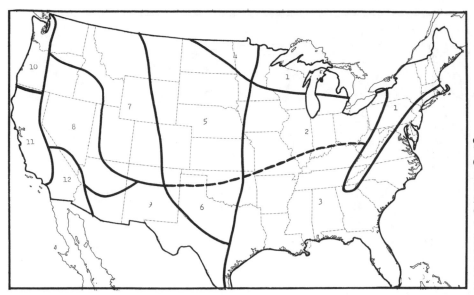

976

Climatic regions (after Herbertson, 1905): 1, St. Lawrence; 2, North China; 3, South China; 4, Siberia; 5, Turan; 6, South Turan; 7, Baikalia; 8, Mongolia; 9, Iran; 10, Western Europe; 11, Mediterranean; 12, Sahara.

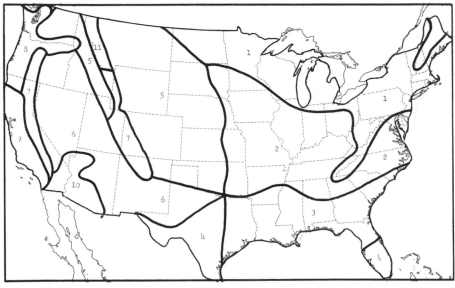

977

Climatic regions (after De Martonne, 1909): 1, Polish; 2, Danubian; 3, Chinese; 4, Senegal; 5, Ukraine; 6, Aral; 7, Norwegian; 8, Brittany; 9, Portuguese Mediterranean; 10, Saharan; 11, Arctic; 12, Siberian.

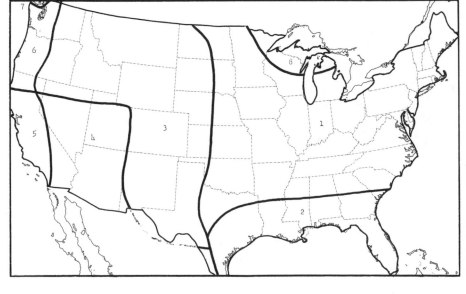

978

Climatic regions (after Dryer, 1912): 1, Mississippian; 2, Floridan; 3, interior; 4, Arizonan; 5, Californian; 6, Oregon; 7, Alaskan; 8, Canadian.

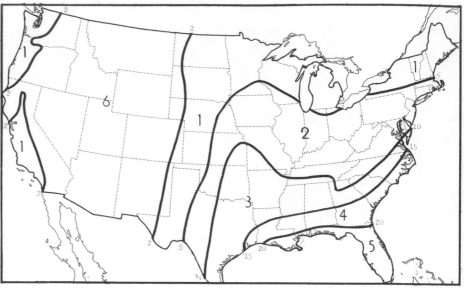

979

Climatic regions (after Livingston, 1916), in terms of the moisture-temperature index of plant growth $I_{mt} = I_t (I_p/I_e)$, where I_p is total rainfall, I_e is total evaporation, and I_t is a physiological temperature efficiency index, derived from measurements on growth of corn seedlings; numbers attached to the isopleths are values of I_{mt} divided by 1000.

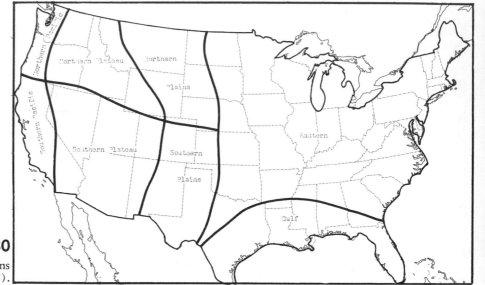

980

Climatic regions (after Ward, 1925).

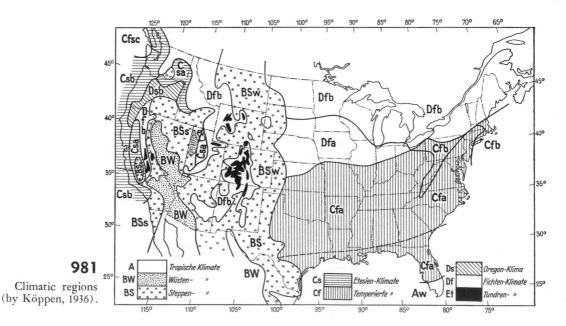

981

Climatic regions (by Köppen, 1936).

In Köppen's classification, only Florida has a tropical climate (A), temperature of coldest month over 64.4°F, and with a winter dry season (w). The desert (BW) and steppe (BS) climates that mark west coasts in subtropical latitudes the world over end in the southwestern United States where North Pacific storms bring ample rai s along the coast, but extend well to the north in the rain-shadowed interior. They have a summer dry season (s) west of the Rocky Mountains, when Pacific storms are weak, and a winter dry season (w) east of the Rockies, where winter cold prevents appreciable precipitation. Small areas of steppe climate occur west of the Sierras in the hot southern portion of the Great Valley of California and in Washington.

The true desert (BW) is found only in the immediate lee of the high Sierras and in the hot southwestern interior. On the higher, more exposed, and therefore moister areas, warm (C) or cool (D) temperate climates make promontories or islands in the dry ones of the West. Practically all have a summer dry season (s), except in the high Sierras and the Rockies ("Dfb"), which have numerous summer thunderstorms. These high lands, though marked "Dfb," include both the oak (Dfb) and the birch (Dfc) climates, which, however, are here characterized principally by conifers. The highest summits of the Rockies and Sierras, in general over 9850 ft, have no month over 50°, and therefore have a tundra climate (Et).

The Cs or Etesian (often called "Mediterranean") climate, a warm, maritime or semimaritime type with dry summers, is narrowly confined E to W by mountain barriers. It is greatly elongated S to N along the coast, however, by the mildness of the Pacific and the mountain ramparts to the east. The Sierras cut off Cs not far from the coast because they reduce the rainfall to steppe or desert levels in the lee. Farther east, however, on the piedmont of the high Wasatch Mountains in Utah, Cs reappears with the increased rainfall, and it extends across the plateau in the north, where the lower Cascade Range lets more moisture pass and the rain-provoking Rocky Mountain system bends farther westward. This climate appears in three forms. Csa, the olive type characteristic of Italy, is a rather dry type found in the rain-shadows of the western mountains — in the Great Valley of California, in Utah, and in the Columbia and Snake River valleys. The higher plateaus of Oregon, however, become so cold in winter, below 26.6° in January (D), and also cool in summer (b), that they are set off as a separate type (Dsb), called the Oregon climate, for it is found nowhere else in the world. Csb, evergreen heath, has its most pronounced development at Eureka, California, where the summers are so cool that the annual range is under 41°. Cfsc, with appreciable rainfall in summer, even though this season is markedly drier than the extraordinarily wet cold season, extends from Washington to Alaska.

In the eastern half of the country, broad areas, being without important mountains or hills, have much the same climates. The warm temperate, with all months over 26.6° (C) and with rains at all seasons (f), covers two-thirds of this great region. Its western boundary is practically the limit of the tall grass. Throughout, there is no marked dry or wet season, that is, no month has less than one-tenth as much as the wettest (f). In the South, marked off by the dashed line, the coldest month is over 50°, and the pine barrens and cypress swamps are characteristic vegetation. Practically all of this area has warm summers, July over 71.6° (a). It constitutes the most extensive Cfa climatic region in the world. In the northeast, a portion of the warm temperate climate, owing to altitude or cool coastal waters, has cooler summers, with the warmest month below 71.6° (b). This is the beech climate (Cfb).

Immediately to the north of Cfa on the plains is a cool temperate climate which has colder winters, below 26.6° in January (D), though, like Cfa, it has no pronounced dry season (f), and is nearly as hot in summer, July over 71.6° (a). This Dfa climate is named the Sioux climate. Cfa and Dfa together include the great cotton, corn, and winter-wheat belts.

To the north, stretching from Maine to the Dakotas, is Dfb, the Canadian climate, with snowy winters and moderately warm summers. It is the oak climate, with needle-leaved trees in the north and broad-leaved trees in the south.

982

Climatic regions (after Renner, 1934): 1, monsoonal tropical; 2, humid subtropical; 3, warmer humid continental; 4, cooler humid continental; 5, dry continental; 6, dry subtropical; 7, arid tropical; 8, Mediterranean subtropical; 9, marine; M, mountain.

983

Climatic regions (after Köppen, modified by Bengtson and Van Royen, 1940): 1, tropical rainy; 2, tropical steppe; 3, warm desert; 4, dry subtropical; 5, humid subtropical; 6, short, cold winter and long, hot summer; 7, long, cold winter and short, hot summer; 8, modified humid continental; 9, west coast marine; 10, middle-latitude steppe; 11, middle-latitude desert; 12, mountain.

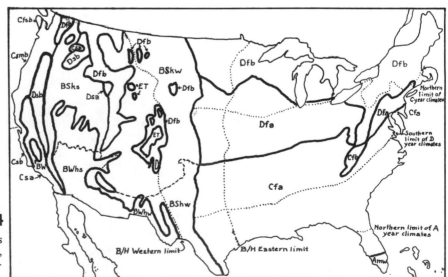

984

Climatic regions (after Köppen, modified by Ackermann, 1941).

The modified classification is as follows: — *Amw:* temperature of coolest month above 18°C (64.4°F); short dry season, but ground remains wet all year because of heavy precipitation during the rainy period; at least one month with less than 6 cm (2.4 in.) of precipitation. *BShs:* excess of evaporation over precipitation; precipitation (cm) numerically greater than temperature (°C) but less than twice the temperature; average January temperature above 0°C. *BShw:* excess of evaporation over precipitation; precipitation (cm) numerically greater than 14 plus the temperature (°C) but less than 14 plus twice the temperature. *BSks:* excess of evaporation over precipitation; precipitation (cm) numerically greater than temperature (°C) but less than twice the temperature; average January temperature below 0°C. *BSks* and *BSkw:* same as *BShs* and *BShw*, except that average January temperature is below 0°C. *BWhs, BWhw, BWks, BWkw:* same as *BShs, BShw, BSks, BSkw*, except that in *BWhs* and *BWks* precipitation (cm) is numerically less than the temperature (°C), and in *BWhw* and *BWkw* it is numerically less than 14 plus the temperature. *Cfa:* average January temperature below 18°C but above 0°C; no dry season; driest month of summer receives more than 3 cm (1.2 in.) of rain; average temperature of warmest month above 22°C (71.6°F). *Cfb:* same as *Cfa* except that average temperature of warmest month is under 22°C. *Cfsb:* same as *Cfb*, except that summer is relatively dry; not more than a third as much rain in the driest month of summer as in the wettest month of winter. *Csa:* average January temperature below 18°C but above 0°C; summer dry; not more than a third as much rain in the driest month of summer as in the wettest month of winter; driest month of summer receives less than 3 cm; average temperature of warmest month above 22°C. *Csb:* same as *Csa*, except that warmest month is under 22°C. *Csmb:* same as *Csb*, except that precipitation of rainy season is sufficient to compensate for short dry season; no serious drought. *Dfa, Dfb, Dsa, Dsb:* same as *Cfa, Cfb, Csa, Csb*, except that average January temperature is below 0°C, and average of the warmest month is above 10°C (50°F). *ET:* warmest month below 10°, but above 0°C.

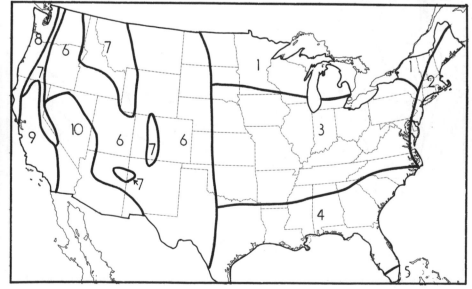

985

Climatic regions (after Köppen, modified by Blair, 1942): 1, colder humid continental; 2, colder humid continental, modified by ocean; 3, warmer humid continental; 4, humid subtropical; 5, trade wind rainy; 6, steppe; 7, mountain; 8, marine; 9, Mediterranean; 10, desert.

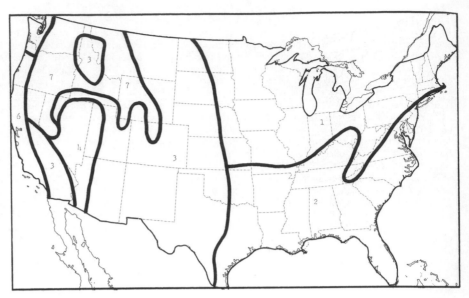

986

Climatic regions (after D. H. Davis, 1942): 1, humid continental; 2, humid subtropical; 3, steppe; 4, desert; 5, marine west coast; 6, Mediterranean; 7, subpolar.

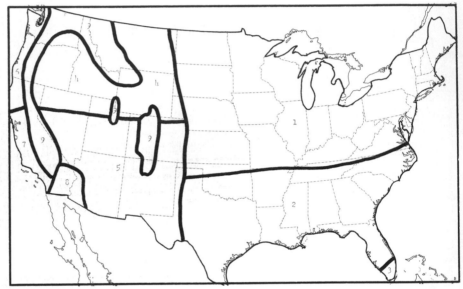

987

Climatic regions (after White and Renner, 1936): 1, humid continental; 2, humid subtropical; 3, monsoonal tropical; 4, dry continental; 5, dry subtropical; 6, temperate marine; 7, Mediterranean subtropical; 8, arid tropical; 9, mountain.

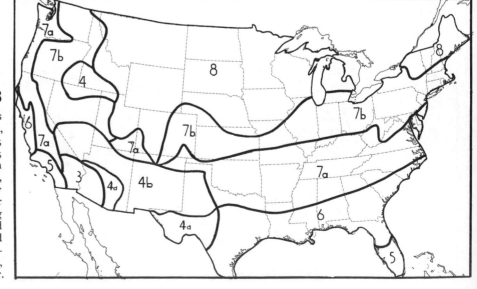

988

Climatic regions after Gorczyński, 1945): 3, desert; 4a, steppe, colder; 4b, steppe with mild winter; 5, mild and sunny winter; 6, milder moderate, long summer; 7a, mild moderate: 7b, cold moderate; 8, extreme climate, cloudy in cold winter.

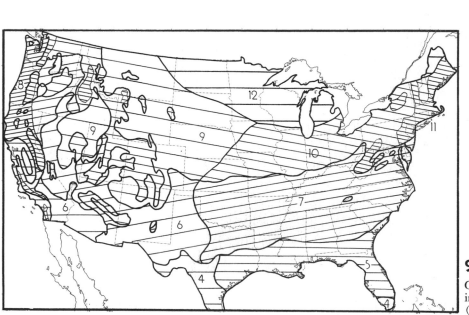

989

Climatic zones in January (Army classification of 1943): 1, very hot, dry (temperature over 86°F, precipitation less than 4 in.); 2, hot, dry (68°–86°, less than 3 in.); 3, hot, humid (68°–86°, over 3 in.); 4, warm, dry (50°–68°, less than 2 in.); 5, warm, humid (50°–68°, 2–8 in.); 6, mild, dry (32°–50°, less than 1 in.); 7, mild, humid (32°–50°, 1–5 in.); 8, mild, wet (32°–50°, over 5 in.); 9, cold, dry (14°–32°, less than 1 in.); 10, cold, humid (14°–32°, 1–3 in.); 11, cold, wet (14°–32°, over 3 in.); 12, very cold (below 14°).

990

Climatic zones in February (Army classification).

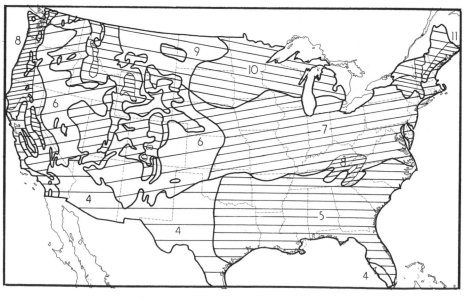

991

Climatic zones in March (Army classification).

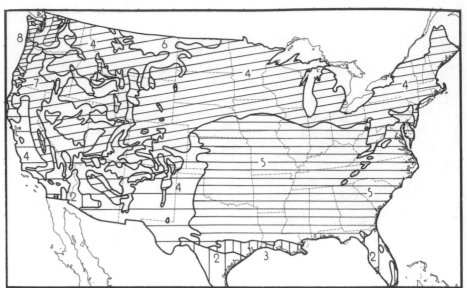

992

Climatic zones
in April
(Army classification).

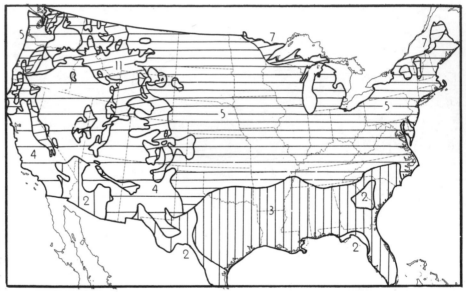

993

Climatic zones
in May
(Army classification).

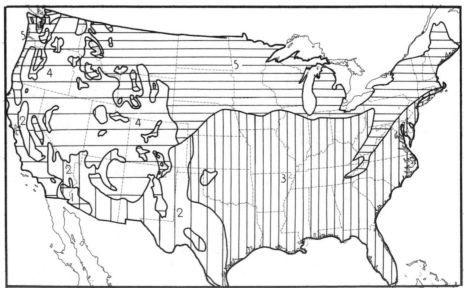

994

Climatic zones
in June
(Army classification).

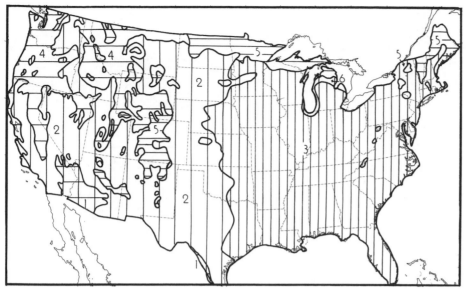

995

Climatic zones
in July
(Army classification).

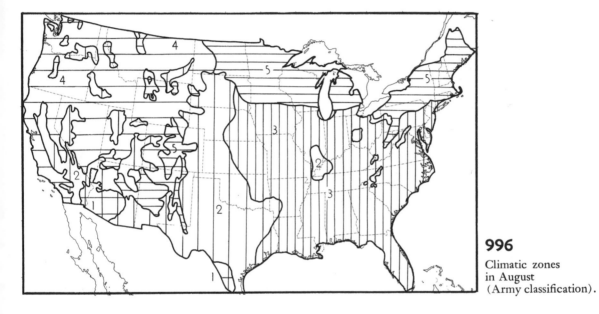

996

Climatic zones
in August
(Army classification).

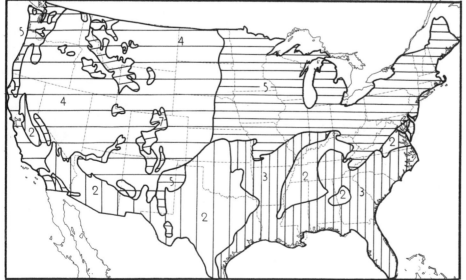

997

Climatic zones
in September
(Army classification).

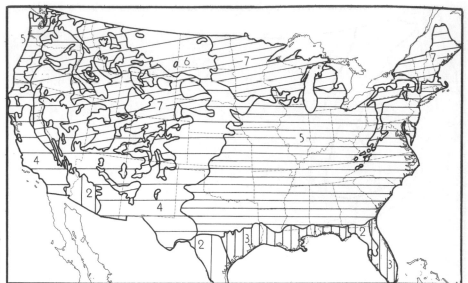

998

Climatic zones
in October
(Army classification).

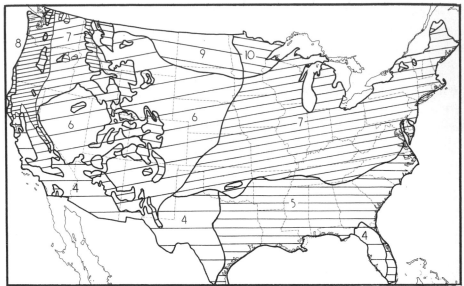

999

Climatic zones
in November
(Army classification).

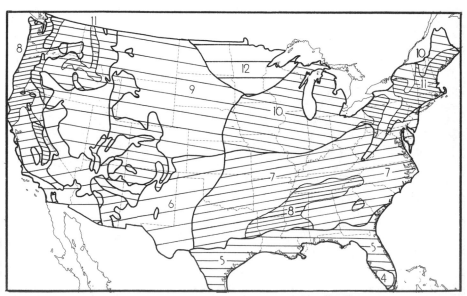

1000

Climatic zones
in December
(Army classification).

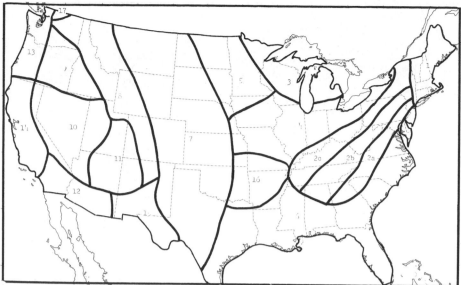

1001
Natural regions
(after Joerg, 1914).

The regions are as follows: 1, northern Appalachian highland; 2, southern Appalachian highland, (*a*) piedmont, (*b*) mountains, (*c*) plateau; 3, Great Lakes; 4, prairie with milder winters; 5, prairie with severe winters; 6, Gulf and Atlantic coastal plane; 7, Great Plains; 8, Rocky Mountain system; 9, Columbia plateau; 10, Great Basin; 11, Colorado plateau; 12, Sonoran desert; 13, cool coastal; 14, warm coastal; 15, Chihuahua desert; 16, Ozark highlands.

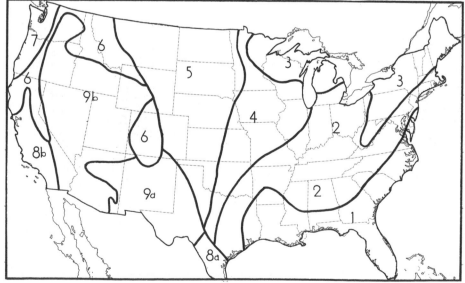

1002
Generalized vegetation map (after Livingston and Shreve, 1921): 1, southeastern forest; 2, deciduous forest; 3, northern evergreen forest; 4, prairie-forest transition; 5, grassland; 6, western conifer forest; 7, northwestern conifer forest; 8*a*, desert shrubs; 8*b*, semi-desert shrubs; 9*a*, semidesert; 9*b*, desert.

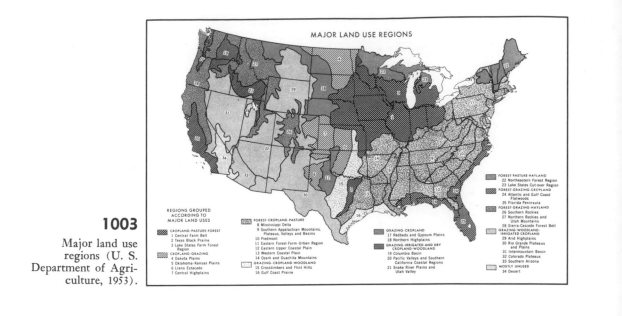

1003

Major land use regions (U. S. Department of Agriculture, 1953).

MAJOR LAND USE REGIONS

REGIONS GROUPED
ACCORDING TO
MAJOR LAND USES

CROPLAND-PASTURE-FOREST
1 Central Farm Belt
2 Texas Black Prairie
3 Lake States Farm Forest
  Region
CROPLAND-GRAZING
4 Dakota Plains
5 Oklahoma-Kansas Plains
6 Llano Estacado
7 Central Highplains

FOREST-CROPLAND-PASTURE
8 Mississippi Delta
9 Southern Appalachian Mountains,
  Plateaus, Valleys and Basins
10 Piedmont
11 Eastern Forest-Farm-Urban Region
12 Eastern Upper Coastal Plain
13 Western Coastal Plain
14 Ozark and Ouachita Mountains
GRAZING-CROPLAND-WOODLAND
15 Crosstimbers and Flint Hills
16 Gulf Coast Prairie

GRAZING-CROPLAND
17 Redbeds and Gypsum Plains
18 Northern Highplains
GRAZING-IRRIGATED AND DRY
  CROPLAND-WOODLAND
19 Columbia Basin
20 Pacific Valleys and Southern
   California Coastal Regions
21 Snake River Plains and
   Utah Valley

FOREST-PASTURE-HAYLAND
22 Northeastern Forest Region
23 Lake States Cut-over Region
FOREST-GRAZING-CROPLAND
24 Atlantic and Gulf Coast
   Flatwoods
25 Florida Peninsula
FOREST-GRAZING-HAYLAND
26 Southern Rockies
27 Northern Rockies and
   Utah Mountains
28 Sierra-Cascade Forest Belt
GRAZING-WOODLAND-
  IRRIGATED CROPLAND
29 Arid Highplains
30 Rio Grande Plateaus
   and Plains
31 Intermountain Basin
32 Colorado Plateaus
33 Southern Arizona
MOSTLY UNUSED
34 Desert

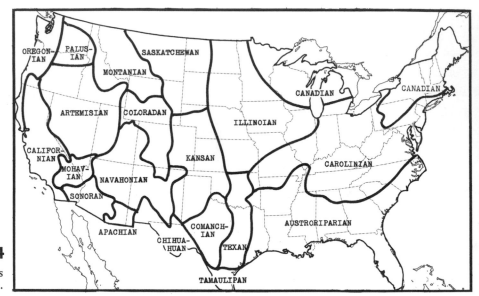

1004

Biotic provinces (after Dice, 1943).

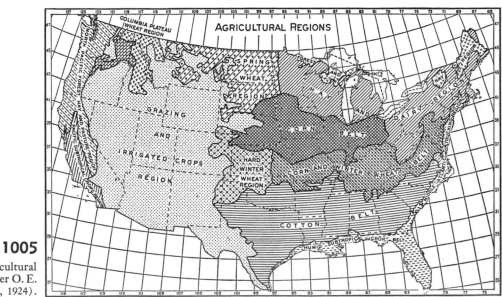

1005

Agricultural regions (after O. E. Baker, 1924).

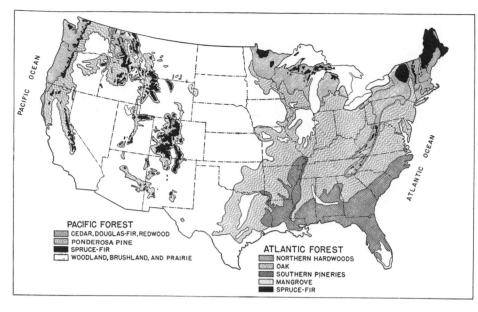

1006

Subdivisions of the forest belts (U. S. Department of Agriculture, 1941).

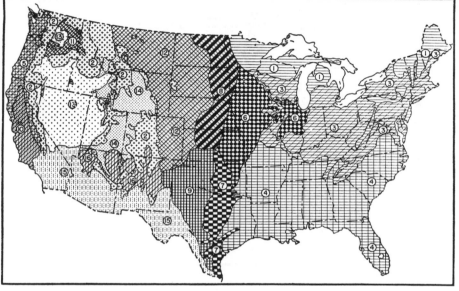

1007

Great soil groups.

The soil groups are as follows: 1, light-colored leached soils of the northern forested regions with included swamps and stony soils; 2, leached soils of the high mountains with thin soils on the slopes and areas of various soils in the adjacent valleys; 3, grayish-brown and brown leached soils of temperate forested regions, with some poorly drained soils and soils with claypans; 4, red and yellow leached soils of the warm-temperate forested regions with poorly drained soils of the Coastal Plains and alluvial soils of the lower Mississippi Valley; 5, red and grayish-brown leached soils of the northwest forested region with much hilly or stony soil and some alluvial soils; 6, dark-colored soils of relatively humid, temperate grasslands with some nearly black, poorly drained soils and some light-colored soils on steep slopes; 7, dark reddish-brown soils of relatively humid warm-temperate grasslands with nearly level black soils on marls and spots of light-colored leached soils; 8, dark-colored soils of subhumid temperate grasslands; 9, dark reddish-brown soils of subhumid warm-temperate grasslands with some hilly soils; 10, dark-colored to light-brown soils of the California valley and coastal mountains; 11, dark-colored to light-brown soils of the Northwest (Palouse) region; 12, brown to dark-brown soils of the semiarid grasslands with some hilly soils, sandy soils, and badlands; 13, grayish soils of the arid West (and Northwest) with soils of arid and semiarid mountains and mountain slopes; 14, grayish soils of the arid and semiarid intermountain plateaus and valleys; 15, reddish soils of the semiarid to arid Southwest; 16, brown to reddish-brown soils of semiarid southwestern high mountain plateaus and valleys.

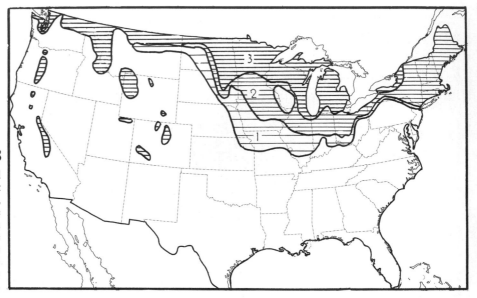

1008

Regions glaciated during the recent glacial period: 1, ice-covered at the greatest ice advance; 2, covered by the early Wisconsin ice sheet; 3, covered by the late Wisconsin sheet.

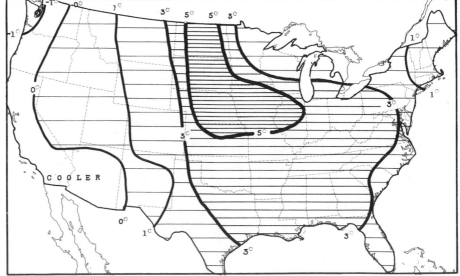

1009

February warming, 1895–1915 to 1916–1935 (near the Pacific, cooling occurred).

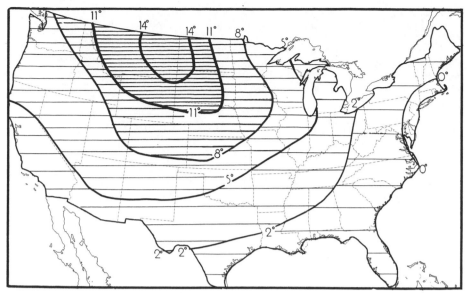

1010

February warming occurring in 35 years: difference in monthly mean temperatures, 1889–1891 and 1925–1927 (part of the Atlantic coast was cooler).

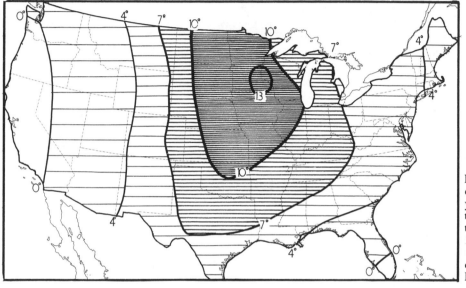

1011

December cooling occurring in 35 years: differences in the monthly mean temperatures, 1889–1891 and 1925–1927 (only the Pacific coast and southern Florida were warmer).

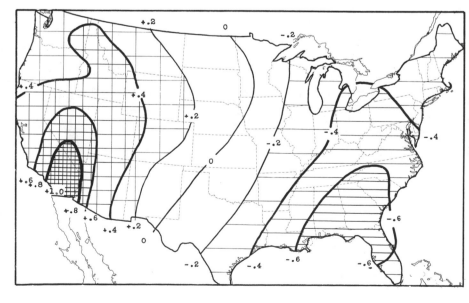

1012

Lines of equal correlation of mean January temperatures at San Diego with departures of January temperatures from normal over other parts of the United States (1880–1914); when the southwest is relatively warm in January, the southeast is relatively cool, and vice versa.

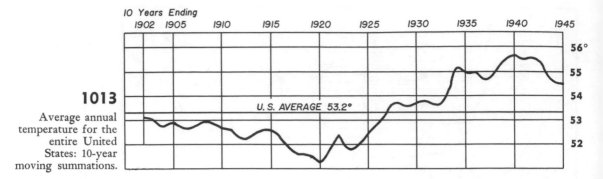

1013

Average annual
temperature for the
entire United
States: 10-year
moving summations.

U. S. AVERAGE 53.2°

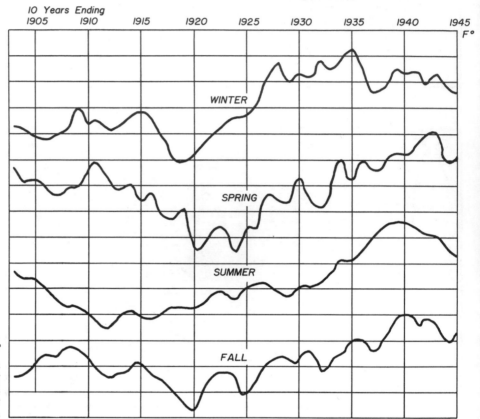

WINTER

SPRING

SUMMER

1014

Seasonal mean
temperatures for
the entire United
States: 10-year
moving summations.

FALL

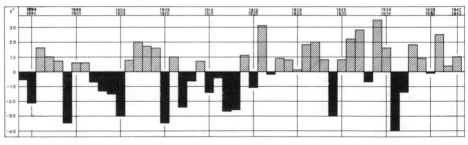

1015

Departures of
mean United States
winter temperature
from normal,
1894–1943; the
coldest winter was
1935–36, the
warmest was 1933–34.

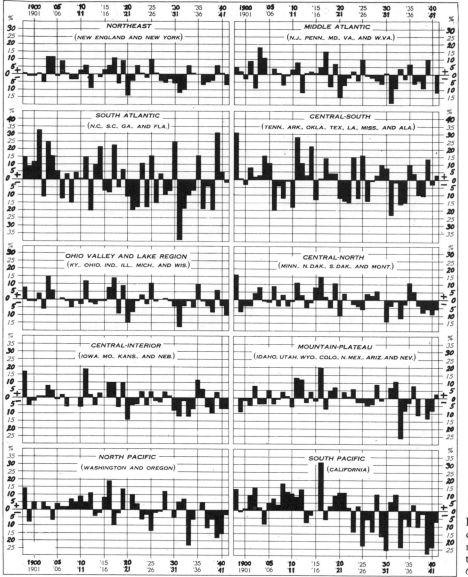

1016

Percentage departures from normal in daily temperatures below 65°, by regions.

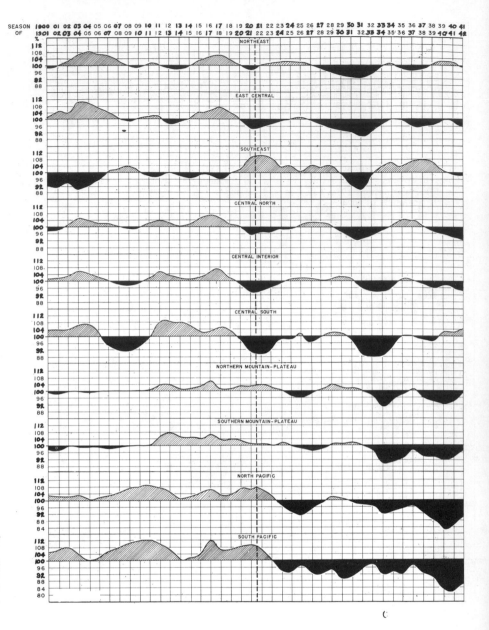

1017

Smoothed curves
of the regional
variation in
cool weather.

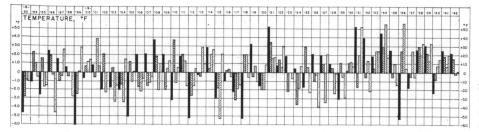

1018

Seasonal temperature departures from normal in a central region.

The region comprises Iowa, Nebraska, Kansas, and Missouri: winter, black; fall, dotted; spring, crossed; winter was warmest in 1921, coldest in 1899; summer was coolest in 1915, warmest in 1936; fall was warmest in 1931, coldest in 1896; spring was warmest in 1910, coolest in 1924.

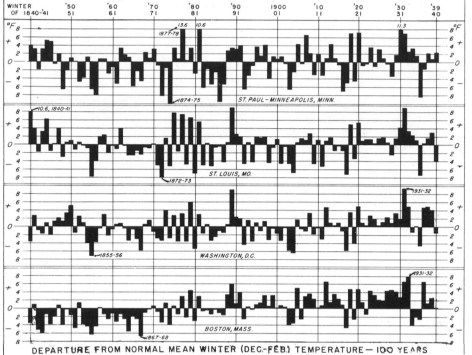

1019

Departure from normal of the mean winter temperature, 1841–1940.

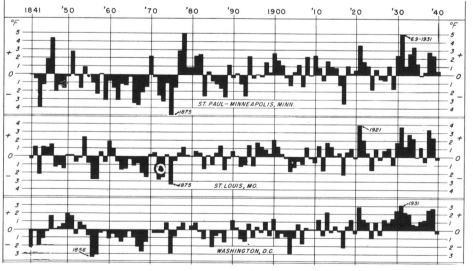

1020

Departure from normal of the mean annual temperature, 1841–1940.

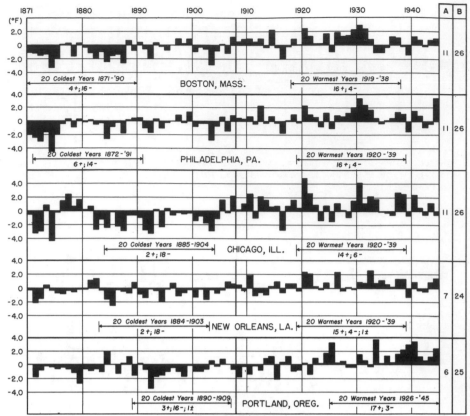

1021

Departure from normal of the mean annual temperature, 1871–1945.

A – No. of years above normal first-half of record
B – No. of years above normal last-half of record

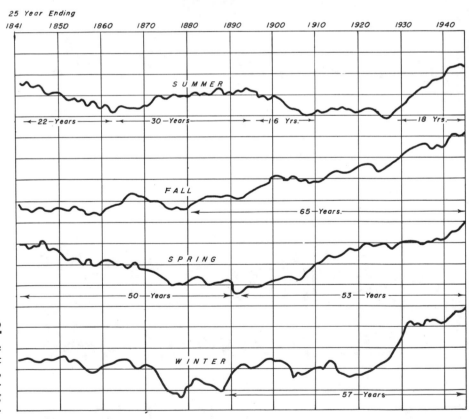

1022

Seasonal temperature changes at Washington, D. C., in 129 years (25-year moving summations).

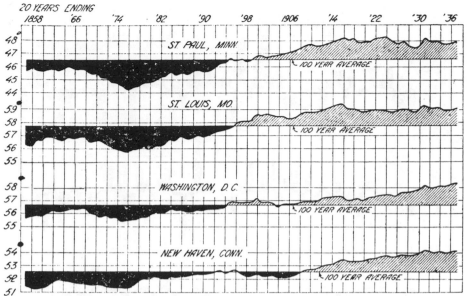

1023

Autumn temperatures, 1837–1937, at St. Paul, St. Louis, Washington, and New Haven.

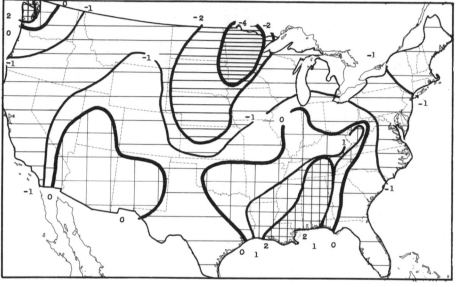

1024

Precipitation change (in.) between annual averages for 1896–1915 and 1916–1935, based on state averages (areas of increase are crossed).

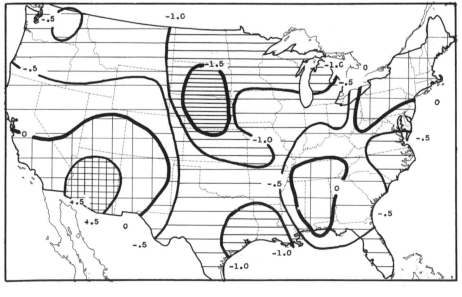

1025

Summer rainfall changes (in.) between averages for 1896–1915 and 1916–1935 (areas of increase are crossed).

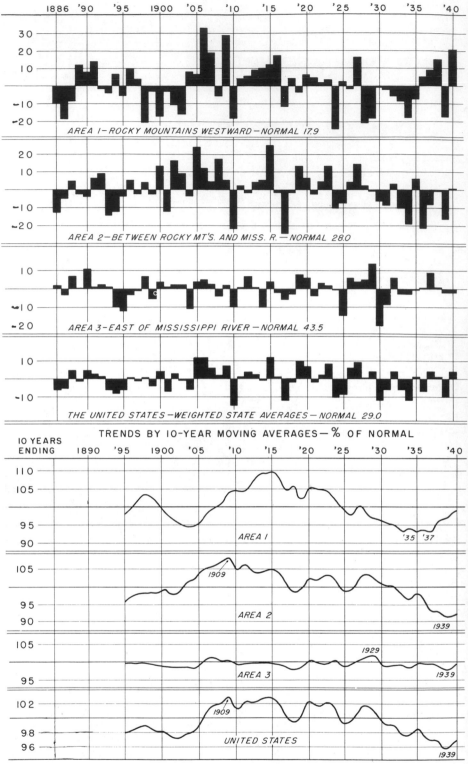

1026

Percentage departure of annual precipitation, 1886–1940, for the United States as a whole and for the western, central, and eastern thirds (approximately): bar graphs for each year; curves of trends by 10-year moving averages.

AREA 1—ROCKY MOUNTAINS WESTWARD—NORMAL 17.9

AREA 2—BETWEEN ROCKY MT'S. AND MISS. R.—NORMAL 28.0

AREA 3—EAST OF MISSISSIPPI RIVER—NORMAL 43.5

THE UNITED STATES—WEIGHTED STATE AVERAGES—NORMAL 29.0

TRENDS BY 10-YEAR MOVING AVERAGES—% OF NORMAL

10 YEARS ENDING

AREA 1

AREA 2

AREA 3

UNITED STATES

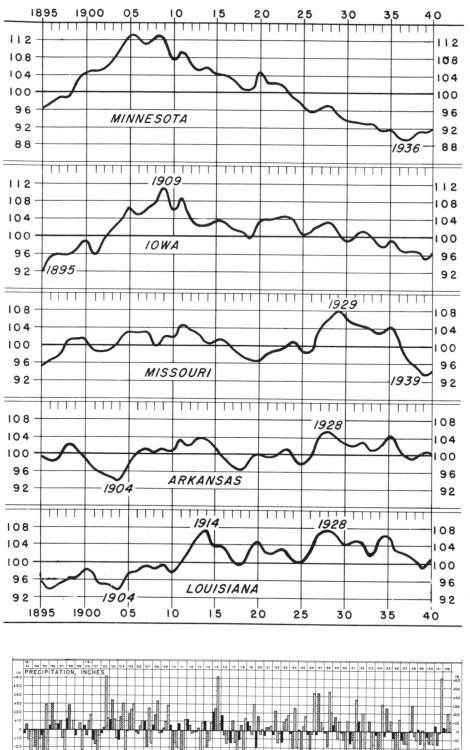

1027

Precipitation trends, Minnesota to Louisiana, 1896–1940, as shown by 10-year moving averages of annual percent of normal.

1028

Departures from normal of the average seasonal precipitation in a central region (Iowa, Nebraska, Kansas, and Missouri), 1893–1942.

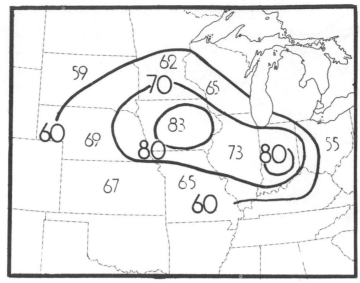

1029

Relatively dry Julies following relatively warm Junes (percent), based on state averages.

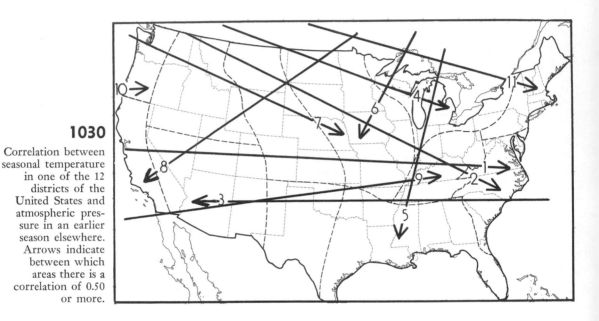

1030

Correlation between seasonal temperature in one of the 12 districts of the United States and atmospheric pressure in an earlier season elsewhere. Arrows indicate between which areas there is a correlation of 0.50 or more.

The departure from normal in the seasonal average temperatures in the district indicated correlates with the departure from normal in the average atmospheric pressure of some earlier season in the other district. A positive correlation indicates that relatively high pressures are followed by relatively high temperatures in the other area and that relatively low pressures are followed by relatively low temperatures in the other area. Conversely a negative correlation indicates the reverse relation: a high pressure results in a low temperature. Although none of the correlations here presented have strong forecast value, they are distinctly suggestive.

| Number | Temperature | | Correlation | Previous pressure | |
Fig. 1030	Season	District	Coefficient	Season	Place
1	winter	2	− 0.60	summer	Central Pacific
2	winter	2	− 0.50	fall	South Alaska
3	winter	10	− 0.50	fall	Bermuda
4	winter	3	− 0.50	fall	North Pacific
5	spring	6	− 0.50	summer	James Bay, Canada
6	spring	5	− 0.50	summer	James Bay, Canada
7	spring	4	+ 0.50	fall	Hawaii
8	spring	1	− 0.50	winter	South Alaska
9	fall	5	+ 0.50	summer	James Bay
10	fall	12	+ 0.50	summer	James Bay
11	fall	11	+ 0.50	spring	North Pacific

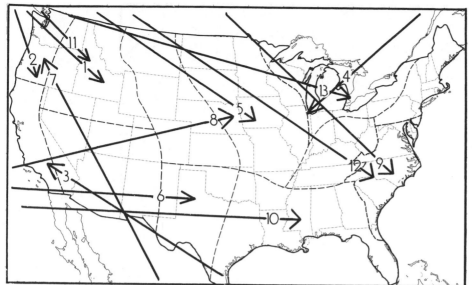

1031

Correlation between seasonal precipitation in one of the 12 districts of the United States and departures from average pressures during some earlier season elsewhere. Arrows indicate between which areas there is a correlation of 0.40 or more.

Number	Precipitation		Correlation	Previous pressure	
Fig. 1031	Season	District	Coefficient	Season	Place
1	spring	9	+ 0.50	fall	just south of Alaska
2	spring	11	+ 0.40	winter	near Bering Strait
3	spring	12	− 0.50	summer	northeastern South America
4	spring	3	+ 0.40	summer	South Greenland
5	spring	5	+ 0.40	summer	West Siberia
6	spring	8	+ 0.50	winter	Hawaii
7	summer	11	− 0.50	winter	New Mexico
8	summer	5	+ 0.50	winter	Hawaii
9	fall	2	− 0.40	summer	Manitoba
10	fall	6	− 0.50	summer	Hawaii
11	winter	9	+ 0.40	fall	near Bering Strait
12	winter	2	+ 0.40	spring	Unalaska
13	winter	3	− 0.40	fall	Unalaska

For most of the 48 states there are "climatological summaries" of the data accumulated by the Weather Bureau stations therein. These summaries are arranged by sections. Generally, they contain very few maps.

Climate and man, Yearbook of Agriculture, 1941 (U. S. Department of Agriculture, Washington, 1941; 1248 pp.), includes a summary of climatic data for each of the states with seven rather detailed maps: average January and July temperature, average date of the last killing frost in spring and first in fall, average number of days without killing frost, average warm season precipitation, and average annual precipitation. It contains also 44 page-size maps of the United States, presenting regional differences in 44 aspects of the climate, the differences being shown by isolines for most of the maps. These maps are about 50 percent larger than those of this *Atlas*, and are more detailed, but far less readily comprehensible.

Atlas of American agriculture (U. S. Department of Agriculture, Washington, 1936), presents in Part II, "Climate" regional contrasts in respect to some scores of aspects of the climate in rather detailed maps. The section on frost and the growing season, issued in 1918, deals with 1895–1914 data. *Section A, Precipitation and Humidity*, issued in 1922, also uses data for 1895–1914. It has seven double large page maps, thirty half large page maps, and fifty-six about the size of those in this Atlas. *Section B, Temperature, Sunshine and Wind*, issued in 1928, presents one double large-page map, 14 half large page maps, and 88 about the size here used. Most of the maps are based on 1895–1922 data. Sections A and B are by J. B. Kincer.

C. W. Thornthwaite, *Atlas of climatic types 1900–1939* (Miscellaneous Publication No. 421 of the Soil Conservation Service of the U. S. Department of Agriculture), presents eighty large half-page maps, one for each year, showing seven types of climate prevailing in the crop season of each year, and also for the year as a whole. The climatic types mapped are superhumid, humid, moist subhumid, dry subhumid, semiarid, and arid, each according to a complicated formula. Also given are a map of the normal climates, and one for the average growing season, and ten maps of the frequency of each of the seven climatic types for the crop season and for the year as a whole.

Maps of seasonal precipitation, percentage of normal by states for 53 years, 1886–1938, with tables of normals and ten wettest and ten driest seasons and years comprise Weather Bureau Publication No. 1353 (1942). The 212 maps of this bulletin are one-fourth page size but are detailed in showing the average precipitation percentages by states and seasons.

J. B. Kincer, *Normal weather for the United States* (Weather Bureau, 1943), presents for each of the months the average temperatures by states, average precipitation, lowest temperature of record, and average number of days with minimum temperature of zero or lower. The text, about two pages for each month, supplements the maps, especially in giving a table of the percentage of the years in which that month received less than 1 in. of precipitation for the state average, 1–2, 3–4, 4–5, and more than 5 in.

L. H. Bean, *Crop yields and weather* (Miscellaneous Publication No. 471, U. S. Department of Agriculture, 1942), presents 910 small maps of the percentage of normal precipitation by states for each of the months of each year from 1886 to 1941. The text gives the departure from normal of each state for each month of the period 1884–1939. Also given are the state average yield per acre for each year from 1866 to 1939 for wheat, corn, oats, and several lesser crops.

D. L. Yarnell, *Rainfall intensity-frequency data* (U. S. Department of Agriculture Miscellaneous Publication No. 204, 1935; 67 pp.), presents about 70 half-page maps showing the frequency of excessive rainfalls of various types by months during thirty years. The text gives mainly data upon which the maps are based.

A. J. Henry, *Climatology of the United States* (U. S. Weather Bureau, 1906), is a significant earlier work, the maps of which have been superseded by those in later publications.

Adolph F. Meyer, *Evaporation from lakes and reservoirs* (Minnesota Resources Commission, St. Paul, 1942; 111 pp., maps), presents 35 double page size maps of evaporation.

R. DeC. Ward, *The climates of the United States* (Ginn, Boston, 1925), is a fairly comprehensive college textbook on this subject. Most of the very few maps are redrawn from official Weather Bureau maps, chiefly from the *Atlas of American Agriculture*, but some are original. They are about the size of those in the present *Atlas*, and a little more detailed.

Several states have had somewhat extended climatological treatments, though for most of them the text consists chiefly of a reprinting of climatological data for the various Weather Bureau stations, and the maps chiefly or solely are comparable with the seven given for the individual states in *Climate and man*.

R. A. Mordoff, *The climate of New York State* (Agricultural Experiment Station Bulletin, Ithaca, 1925), has only a few maps.

S. S. Visher, *Climate of Kentucky* (Kentucky Geological Survey, 1928; 86 pp., 96 maps), is noteworthy as the first study of a state's climate having numerous maps.

A. J. Mitchell and M. R. Ensign, *Climate of Florida* (Florida Experiment Station, Gainsville, 1928, Bulletin No. 200).

W. H. Alexander and C. A. Patton, *Climate of Ohio* (Ohio Agricultural Experiment Station, Wooster, 1929, Bulletin No. 445).

R. DeC. Ward, C. F. Brooks, and A. J. Connor, *The climates of North America*, vol. 2, part J of W. Köppen and R. Geiger, *Handbuch der Klimatologie* (Borntraeger, Berlin, 1936).

C. F. Brooks, A. J. Connor and others, *Climatic maps of North America* (Harvard University Press, Cambridge, 1936).

J. M. Kirk, *The weather and climate of Connecticut* (State Geological and Natural History Survey, Bulletin No. 61, Hartford, 1939; 242 pp.), presents eight maps of the state and many tables of data.

S. S. Visher, *Climate of Indiana* (Indiana University, Bloomington, 1944; 511 pp.), is the most comprehensive of the state climatologies. It contains some hundreds of small maps.

S. D. Flora, *Climate of Kansas* (Kansas State Board of Agriculture Report No. 285, 1948; 320 pp.), is modeled after the foregoing, but contains relatively few maps of Kansas alone. The state is conspicuously indicated, however, on a score of official Weather Bureau maps of the United States. Most of the book presents the accumulated climatological data for the many stations in the state.

J. L. Page, *Climate of Illinois* (University of Illinois Agricultural Experimental Station Bulletin 532, 1949; 267 pp.), is predominantly a reprint of accumulated climatological data arranged by stations. Monthly maps of precipitation and temperature are given, and a map of the length of the frost-free period and of the annual snowfall.

J. B. Kincer, "Climate of the Great Plains," *Ann. Assoc. Am. Geographers 13*, 67 (1923).

R. J. Russell, "Climatic years," *Geogr. Rev. 24*, 92 (1934).

P. E. Church, "Temperatures of New England," *Monthly Weather Rev. 63*, 93 (1935).

SOURCES OF THE MAPS

Fig. 1, from U. S. Geological Survey.

Chapter 2. Normal Temperatures
Fig. 2, after U. S. Weather Bureau; Figs. 3, 6, 23, 26, after Kincer, *Climate and man;* Figs. 4, 5, 8, 9, 17–19, 21, 24, 25, 31–33, after Kincer, *Atlas of American agriculture;* Figs. 7, 13–15, 20, 22, 27–30, 34, 36, 38, 40, 41, original; Figs 10–12, 35, 37, 39, after Kincer, *Weekly Weather & Crop Bull.;* Figs. 16, 42, 43, after C. F. Brooks, A. J. Connor, and others, *Climatic maps of North America* (Harvard University Press, Cambridge, 1936).

Chapter 3. Normal Weekly Mean Temperatures
Prepared from 52 mimeographed official maps showing the precise average temperature for each of 123 climatic subsections, assembled under the direction of W. F. McDonald of the U. S. Weather Bureau (1944). The isotherms here shown were drawn through the 123 subsections in accord with the data.

Chapter 4. Normal Daily Maximum and Minimum Temperatures
Prepared from 52 mimeographed official maps showing the precise average maximum and minimum temperature for each of 123 climatic subsections, assembled under the direction of W. F. McDonald of the U. S. Weather Bureau (1944).

Chapter 5. Temperature Seasons
Figs. 148, 165, 170, 172–185, after Kincer, *Weekly Weather & Crop Bull.;* Figs. 149–163, 186–192, original; Figs. 164, 166–169, 171, after Kincer, *Atlas of American agriculture.*

Chapter 6. Killing Frosts; Growing Seasons
Figs. 193, 199, 206, after Kincer, *Climate and man;* Figs. 194, 196, 198, 201, 203, 205, 207, 209–211, original; Figs. 195, 202, 208, after *Atlas of American agriculture;* Figs. 197, 204, after U. S. Weather Bureau, separately issued sheet maps; Fig. 200, after Kincer, *Weekly Weather & Crop Bull.;* Fig. 212, after B. E. Livingston and F. Shreve, *The distribution of vegetation in the United States, as related to climatic conditions* (Carnegie Institution, Washington, 1921, Publication No. 284).

Chapter 7. House-Heating Requirement Contrasts
Figs. 213–218, 220–223, after Kincer, on back of weather map for February

23, 1945; Figs. 219, 224, 229–233, 238–244, original (Fig. 244 is based on *Monthly Weather Rev.*, Supplement 25, "Normal daily mean temperatures"); Figs. 225–228, 234–237, after Kincer, *Weekly Weather & Crop Bull.*

Chapter 8. Relatively High Temperatures

Figs. 245, 246, after Kincer, *Climate and man;* Figs. 247–261, 263–284, original; Fig. 262 after J. C. Hoyt; Figs. 273–284 are largely based on the state records to 1945 assembled by John R. Theaman, and the records to about 1945 at about 100 scattered relatively large cities; a few maps include data to 1952; Fig. 285, after Kincer, *Weekly Weather & Crop Bull.*

Chapter 9. Relatively Low Temperatures

Figs. 286, 287, 325, after Kincer, *Climate and man;* Figs. 288–293, 295–297, 303–323, original (Figs. 310–321 are based on the records at about 100 regular stations and on the state records to 1945 assembled by J. R. Theaman); Figs. 294, 299, 301, 302, after Kincer, *Weekly Weather & Crop Bull.;* Fig. 298, after Kincer, *Atlas of American agriculture;* Fig. 300 after Military Planning Division Office of the Quartermaster General, June 1947; Fig. 324 after R. J. Russell, *Trans. Am. Geophys. Union 24,* 125 (1943); Figs. 326, 327, after U. S. Weather Bureau.

Chapter 10. Temperature Ranges

Figs. 328–349, 354, 361–365, original; Figs. 350–353, after *U. S. Weather Bur. Bull. Q.;* Figs. 355–358, after Kincer, *Atlas of American agriculture;* Figs. 359–360, after Darkenwald, *Bull. Am. Meteorol. Soc.* (1933).

Chapter 11. Sudden Changes of Temperature

Figs. 366, 368, after U. S. Weather Bureau maps; Figs. 367, 369–371, original.

Chapter 12. Atmospheric Pressure

Figs. 372, 373, after C. F. Brooks, A. J. Connor, and others, *Climatic maps of North America* (Harvard University Press, Cambridge, 1936); Fig. 374, original, data after Bowie, *Monthly Weather Rev.* (1940).

Chapter 13. Winds

Figs. 375, 376, 385, 387, 388, 390, after Kincer, *Atlas of American agriculture;* Figs. 377–384, from Eric Miller, *Monthly Weather Rev.* (1927); Fig. 386, after Adolph Meyer, *Evaporation from lakes;* Figs. 389, 394, original; Figs. 391–393, from Gregg and Stevens, *Sigma Xi Quarterly* (1937); Fig. 395, from U. S. Weather Bureau.

Chapter 14. Storms

Fig. 396, after a daily weather map; Figs. 397, 412, 415, 416, 419, 420, 422, 423, original; Figs. 398, 417, after R. DeC. Ward, *Climates of the United States;* Figs. 399–404, after Weightman, *U. S. Weather Bur. Bull.* (1945); Figs. 405–407, 424–427, after Eric Miller, *Monthly Weather Rev.* (1932); Figs. 408–411, 413, 414, 421, after U. S. Hydrometeorology Report 5 (1947); Fig. 418, after Kincer, *Is our climate changing?* (Illinois Farmers' Institute, Springfield, 1937).

Chapter 15. Other Winds

Figs. 428, 429, original, in part after W. F. McDonald, *Atlas of climatic charts of the oceans* (U. S. Weather Bureau, Washington, 1938); Fig. 430, from T. R. Reed, *Monthly Weather Rev.* (1927).

Chapter 16. Sunshine, Cloudiness, Fog, Radiation

Figs. 431, 432, 434, 435, 440, original; Figs. 433, 442, after Kincer, *Weekly Weather & Crop Bull.*; Figs. 436, 437, 439, 453, after Kincer, *Monthly Weather Rev.* (1920); Figs. 438, 441, 443, 444, after Kincer, *Climate and man;* Figs. 445, 446, after Kincer, *Atlas of American agriculture;* Figs. 447–452, after H. H. Kimball, *Monthly Weather Rev.* (1919).

Chapter 17. Relative and Absolute Humidity

Figs. 454–459, 468, from Kincer, *Climate and man;* Fig. 460, original; Figs. 461–465, 469–473, after Kincer, *Atlas of American agriculture;* Figs. 466, 467, after G. R. Harrison, *Monthly Weather Rev.* (1931).

Chapter 18. Evaporation

Figs. 474–476, after R. E. Horton, *Trans. Am. Geophysical Union* (1943); Figs. 477–482, 489, 490, after Adolph Meyer, *Evaporation from lakes;* Fig. 483, original; Fig. 484, after Joseph Kittridge, *Am. J. Forestry* (1938); Figs. 485, 486, after C. W. Thornthwaite, *Trans. Am. Geophysical Union* (1944); Figs. 487, 488, after W. G. Hoyt, in O. E. Meinzer, ed., *Hydrology* (McGraw-Hill, New York, 1942); Fig. 491, after B. E. Livingston and F. Shreve, *The distribution of vegetation in the United States, as related to climatic conditions* (Carnegie Institution, Washington, 1921, Publication No. 284).

Chapter 19. Normal Amounts of Precipitation

Figs. 492–496, 501, 523, after Kincer, *Climate and man;* Figs. 497–500, 503–505, 509, 511, 519–522, 524–527, original; Figs. 502, 506, 512, 533–536, after Kincer, *Atlas of American agriculture;* Figs. 507, 508, 510, after C. F. Brooks, A. J. Connor, and others, *Climatic maps of North America;* Figs. 513–518, after B. C. Wallis, *Monthly Weather Rev.* (1915); Figs. 528–532, after Eric Miller, *Monthly Weather Rev.* (1933); Figs. 537, 538, after Kincer, *Monthly Weather Rev.* (1916).

Chapter 20. Normal Weekly Amount of Precipitation

These 26 maps are adapted from official maps prepared under the direction of W. F. McDonald of the U. S. Weather Bureau, 1944, based on the records at 1,749 stations for 1906–1935.

Chapter 21. Normal Shifts in Amount of Precipitation

Figs. 565–577, 582–589, original; Figs. 578–581, after Kincer, *Weekly Weather & Crop Bull.*; Fig. 590, after National Resources Board; Fig. 591, from Kincer, *Atlas of American agriculture.*

Chapter 22. Snowfall, Hail, "Excessive" Rains, Prospects of Early Rain

Figs. 592, 594, 604, after Kincer, *Climate and man;* Fig. 593, after C. F. Brooks and R. G. Stone, *Bull. Am. Meteorol. Soc.;* Figs. 595, 596, after Kincer, *Atlas of American agriculture;* Figs. 597–601, original; Figs. 602, 603, after Kincer, *Weekly Weather & Crop Bull.*; Figs. 605–609, after Hoyt Lemons, *Geographical Rev.* (1942); Figs. 610–613, after Yarnell, *Rainfall intensity-frequency data;* Figs. 614–625, after D. I. Blumenstock, *Weather Bureau Tech. Bull. 819* (1942).

Chapter 23. Normal Rainfall Intensity

Figs, 626–630, 633, 635, 637, 638, 641, original (633–641 deduced from

Yarnell's maps); Figs. 631, 636, 639, 642, after Yarnell, *Rainfall intensity-frequency data;* Figs. 632, 645, after D. H. Dyck and W. A. Mattice, *Monthly Weather Rev.* (1941); Fig. 634, after Kincer, *Climate and man;* Fig. 640, after Kincer, *Atlas of American agriculture;* Figs. 643, 644, original; Figs. 646–658, after W. F. McDonald, official, U. S. Weather Bureau (1944).

Chapter 24. Normal Runoff and Absorption
Fig. 659, after National Resources Board, 1934; Fig. 660, after Thornthwaite, 1944; Figs. 661–668, original (Figs. 666, 667 deduced from General Staff of the U. S. Army, monthly climatic maps, 1943); Fig. 669, after C. R. Williams, U. S. Geological Survey, Water Supply Paper 846 (1940), eastern U. S.

Chapter 25. Exceptionally Wet Years
Figs. 670, 671, 673, 675–692, 694–710, original; Fig. 672, after E. E. Lackey, *Monthly Weather Rev.* (1939); Figs. 674, 693, after Kincer, *Climate and man.*

Chapter 26. Exceptionally Dry Years
Figs. 711, 712, 729–761, original; Fig. 713, after E. E. Lackey, *Monthly Weather Rev.* (1939); Figs. 714, 727, deduced from Thornthwaite, *Atlas of climatic types;* Figs. 715–725, from J. C. Hoyt, U. S. Geological Survey Water Supply Paper 680 (1936); Figs. 726, 728, after Kincer, *Climate and man;* Fig. 762, after Kincer, *Monthly Weather Rev.* (1919).

Chapter 27. Frequencies of Dry Years
Figs. 763–766, 770–781, 790–809, original [the basic data partly from Kincer, "Tables of state average normals and of the ten wettest and ten driest seasons and years of 1886–1938," *U. S. Weather Bur. Bull.* No. 1353 (1942), and L. H. Bean, *Tables of precipitation departure for each month and year for many years* (Weather Bureau Miscellaneous Publication No. 471, 1942)]; Fig. 767, after Kincer, *Monthly Weather Rev.* (1919); Figs. 768, 769, after Thornthwaite, *Atlas of climatic types;* Figs. 782–789, after Kincer, *Atlas of American agriculture.*

Chapter 28. Frequencies of Wet Years
Figs. 810–812, 814–843, original (the data for the original maps were largely from the tables of state averages by Kincer and Bean mentioned in Chapter 27); Fig. 813, after Thornthwaite, *Atlas of climatic types* (1942).

Chapter 29. Precipitation Variability: Range and Ratios, Annual, Seasonal, and Monthly
Figs. 844–853, 858–875, original (data for many of these were deduced from L. H. Bean's tables mentioned in chapter 27); Fig. 854, after National Resources Board, 1934; Fig. 855, after W. Gorczyński, *Comparison of climate of the United States and Europe* (Polish Institute of Arts and Sciences in America, New York, 1945); Figs. 856, 857, after V. Conrad, *Monthly Weather Rev.* (1941).

Chapter 30. Precipitation Seasons
Figs. 876–883, original; Figs. 884–888, after Kincer, *Weekly Weather & Crop Bull.;* Figs. 889–893, original (deduced from Yarnell, *Rainfall intensity-frequency data*); Fig. 894, adapted from U. S. Hydrometeorological Report

No. 5 (1947); Figs. 895–899, original (deduced from Hoyt Lemons, Ph.D. thesis, University of Nebraska, 1941).

Chapter 31. Precipitation Regions

Fig. 900, after Kincer, *Climate and man;* Fig. 901, after Eric McDougal, *Geographical Rev.* (1927); Fig. 902, after Thornthwaite, *Atlas of climatic types;* Fig. 903, after Isaiah Bowman, *Geographical Rev.* (1935); Fig. 904, after National Resources Board, 1934; Figs. 905, 907, 908, original [a partly tabulated analysis of the precipitation data of the regions shown in Fig. 908 is given in *Ann. Assoc. Am. Geographers* (December 1942)]; Fig. 906, after Kincer, *Atlas of American agriculture.*

Chapter 32. Some Consequences of Climate and Weather on Agriculture and Health

Figs. 909, 927–929, after Kincer, *Weekly Weather & Crop Bull.;* Fig. 910, after J. W. Smith, *Agricultural meteorology* (Macmillan, New York, 1920); Figs. 911, 913, after O. E. Baker, "Agricultural regions of North America," in *Economic geography* (Worcester, Mass., 1926–1933); Figs. 912, 914, 930–939, original; Figs. 915–926, after O. E. Baker, C. F. Brooks, and R. G. Hainsworth, *Seasonal work on farm crops* (U. S. Department of Agriculture Yearbook, 1917, Washington, 1918); Figs. 940–944, after Ellsworth Huntington, *Civilization and climate* (Yale University Press, New Haven, 1924), or *Principles of economic geography* (Wiley, New York, 1940).

Chapter 33. Contrasts in Some Consequences of Climate Upon Land and Water

Figs. 945, 946, from Soil Conservation Service; Figs. 947–951, 953, original (Fig. 949 is after detailed maps by the U. S. Geological Survey); Fig. 952, from M. Bernard, *Climate and man;* Figs. 954, 955, after P. Church and E. Gueffroy, *Geographical Rev.* (1939).

Chapter 34. Climatic Regions

Figs. 956, 957, 960, 963, 968, 972, original; Fig. 958, after C. W. Thornthwaite, *Geographical Rev.* (1931); Fig. 959, after R. J. Russell, *Geographical Rev.* (1934); Fig. 961, after A. E. Parkins, *Ann. Assoc. Am. Geographers* (1926); Fig. 962, after R. Hartshorne, *Ann. Assoc. Am. Geographers* (1938); Figs. 964, 980, after R. DeC. Ward, *Climates of the United States;* Fig. 965, after B. C. Wallis, *Monthly Weather Rev.* (1915); Figs. 966, 967, after H. Jenny, *Missouri Agr. Exp. Sta. Res. Bull. No. 152* (1930); Fig. 969, after S. Van Valkenburg, *America at War, a geographical analysis* (Prentice-Hall, New York, 1942); Fig. 970, from *U. S. Weather Bureau Technical Bull. No. 808;* Fig. 971, from Thornthwaite, *Atlas of climatic types;* Figs. 973–978, 1001, after W. L. G. Joerg, *Ann. Assoc. Am. Geographers* (1914); Fig. 979, after B. E. Livingston, *Physiol. Res. 1,* 421 (1916); Fig. 981, from W. Köppen and R. Geiger, *Handbuch der Klimatologie,* vol. 2, part J (1936), p. 194; Fig. 982, after G. T. Renner, *Report of Land Planning Committee* (National Resources Board, Washington, 1934); Fig. 983, after N. A. Bengtson and W. Van Royen, *Economic geography* (Prentice-Hall, New York, 1940); Fig. 984, after E. A. Ackermann, *The Köppen classification of climates in North America* (Harvard University Press, Cambridge, 1941); Fig. 985, after T. A. Blair, *Climatology* (Prentice-Hall, New York, 1942); Fig. 986, after H. D. Davis, *The earth and man* (Macmillan, New York, 1942); Fig. 987, after C. L. White and G. T. Renner, *Human geography*

(Appleton-Century-Crofts, New York, 1936); Fig. 988, after W. Gorczyń-ski, *Comparison of climate of the United States and Europe* (Polish Institute of Arts and Sciences in America, New York, 1945); Figs. 989–1000, after U. S. General Staff Climatic Section, 1943; Fig. 1002, after B. E. Livingston and F. Shreve, *The distribution of vegetation in the United States, as related to climatic conditions* (Carnegie Institution, Washington, 1921, Publication No. 284); Fig. 1003, from Bureau of Agricultural Economics, U. S. Department of Agriculture, 1953; Fig. 1004, after L. R. Dice, *The biotic provinces of North America* (University of Michigan Press, Ann Arbor, 1943); Fig. 1005, after O. E. Baker, "Agricultural regions of North America," in *Economic geography* (Worcester, Mass., 1920); Figs. 1006, 1007, from *Climate and man.*

Chapter 35. Changes of Climate

Fig. 1008, after Geological Society of America, Glacial Map (1945); Figs. 1009, 1024, 1025, original [from data assembled by Larry Page, *Monthly Weather Rev.* (1937)]; Figs. 1010, 1011, after I. R. Tannehill, official U. S. Weather Bureau mimeographed report (1945); Fig. 1012, after T. A. Blair, *Monthly Weather Rev.* (1917); Figs. 1013, 1014, 1021, 1022, from Kincer, *Trans. Am. Geophysical Union* (1946); Figs. 1015–1020, 1026–1028, from Kincer, *Weekly Weather & Crop Bull.;* Fig. 1023, from Kincer, *Monthly Weather Rev.* (1940); Fig. 1029, after C. D. Reed, *Monthly Weather Rev.* (1925); Figs. 1030, 1031, original, deduced from R. H. Weightman, *Monthly Weather Rev., Supplement 45* (1941).

January precipitation, 202, 213, 272
  temperatures, 25–27, 36, 38, 39, 56, 57, 65, 96, 112, 118, 147, 149
Jenney, H., 393
Joerg, W. L. G., 377, 399
July precipitation, 203, 217, 274
  temperature, 30, 31, 37, 47, 48, 61, 69, 110, 113, 120, 141–143, 148, 149
June precipitation, 203, 217, 274
  temperatures, 29, 32, 45, 46, 60, 68, 69, 120

Kansas, Climate of, 394
Kansas crop yields, 350
Kentucky, Climate of, 394
Killing frosts, 82–93
Kimball, H. H., 396
Kincer, J. B., 393, 395–400
Kirk, J. M., 394
Kittridge, Jos., 397
Köppen, W., 366, 369–371, 399

Lackey, E. E., 262, 397, 398
Lakes, number of, 358
Land use regions, 378
Latitude effects, 8, 9
Lemons, Hoyt, 398
Lightning, 170, 171
Livingston, B. E., 368, 377, 395, 399
Longitude effects, 9
Lows, 163–167, 173

McDonald, W. F., 395–397
McDougal, Eric, 398
Maps of seasonal precipitation, 393
March precipitation, 202, 215
  temperature, 27, 41, 42, 58, 66, 150
Massachusetts crop yields, 352
Mattice, W. A., 397
Maximum rainfalls, 261–276
  annual, 261, 262
  monthly, 270–276
Maximum temperatures, annual, 107
  monthly, 112–122
  seasonal, 108
May precipitation, 202, 216, 273
  temperatures, 29, 44, 45, 59, 68, 98, 112, 119
Meinzer, O. E., 397
Meyer, Adolph F., 394
Miller, Eric, 396, 397
Minimum temperatures, 123–135
Minimum rainfalls, 277–308
Monsoonal winds, 175
Monthly Weather Review, 394–400
Mordoff, R. A., 394
Mountain effects, 18–22

New England climate, 5, 13
New York State, Climate of, 394
Normal Weather for the United States, 393
North-south contrasts, 8, 9
November precipitation, 220, 275
  temperatures, 35, 53, 63, 72, 99, 113, 121

October precipitation, 204, 220, 275
  temperatures, 33, 34, 52, 63, 71, 99, 101, 142, 144

Olympics, 11, 20, 148
Oregon type of climate, 5

Pacific Ocean effects, 10–13
Page, J. L., 394
Page, Larry, 399
Parkins, A. E., 362, 399
Precipitation, 197–335
  for alternate weeks, 213–221, 252–256
  average or normal, 197–260
  daily, 208–212
  14-day periods, 206, 207
  monthly, 202–206, 270–276
  seasonal, 197–201, 222, 228, 265–269, 281–299
  shifts in amount, 224
Precipitation range regions, 324–332
Precipitation ratios, 204–206
Precipitation regions, 340–343
Precipitation seasons, 332–334
Precipitation trends, 388–391
Precipitation types, 259, 260, 263, 295, 299, 310, 363
Precipitation variability, range and ratio, annual, 321–325
  monthly, 204–206, 299–306, 330–332
  seasonal, 295–299, 326–330
Pressure, atmospheric, 155

Radiation, solar, 182, 183
Rain, prospects of, 239–243
Rainfall, excessive, 244–252, 261, 262, 309–320, 335–337
  slight, 277–308
Rainfall intensity, 244–250
Rainfall intensity data, 394
Rainfall probabilities, 208, 239, 257
Rainfall records, 250, 262, 263, 270
Rainfall regions, 363
Rainfall types, 363
Reed, T. R., 396, 399
Renner, Geo. T., 370, 372, 399
Rivers and climate, 356
Rocky Mountains effects, 19
Runoff, 257, 258
Russell, R. J., 395, 396, 397

Sea-land breezes, 175
Seasons, beginning dates, 74–78
September precipitation, 219, 275
  temperatures, 32, 50, 62, 71, 113, 121, 150
Shreve, F., 377, 395, 399
Slope, average, 358
Smith, J. Warren, 398
Snowfall, 232–235, 335
Snow cover, 21, 235, 335
Soil Conservation Service, 399
Soil erosion, 356, 357
Soil moisture, 359
Soil regions, 379
Solar radiation, 182, 183
South Carolina crop yields, 352
South Dakota crop yields, 352
Spring commences, 87
Stone, R. G., 397
Storms, 163–174
  famous, 155, 174
Storm tracks, 163–166
Streams, permanent, 357

Summer begins, 90
  duration, 11, 115–117
Sunshine, duration, 177–183
  frequency, 180
Supan, Alex, 366

Tannehill, J. E., 399
Temperature, 23–154
  average, 23
    annual, 23
    monthly, 24
    seasonal, 24–35
    weekly, 38–55
  daily, maximum for alternate weeks, 56–64
    minimum for alternate weeks, 65–73
  high, 107–122
  low, 123–135, 383, 384
    average monthly, 130–135
    record, 129, 130–35
    seasonal, 124
  wet-bulb, 188, 184
Temperature drops, dates, 77, 80
Temperature efficiency, 95, 361
Temperature ranges, 138–144, 147–150
  daily, 147
  interdiurnal, 145, 146
  monthly, 141–144, 147–150
Temperature regions, 360–362
Temperature rises, dates, 75, 79, 87
  monthly, 27–35, 138
Temperature seasons, 74
Temperature trends, departures, 138, 381, 387, 390
Texas crop yields, 353
Theaman, J. R., 108, 250, 395
Thornthwaite, C. W., 393, 397–399
Thunderstorm frequencies, 4, 13, 15, 18, 167–170
Topography, some effects of, 7, 8
Tornado frequencies, 6, 171
Torrential rainfall, 9, 16
Tropical cyclones, 6, 172

United States Department of Agriculture, 393–400
United States Geological Survey, 395, 397
United States Weather Bureau, 393–400

Van Royen, W., 370, 399
Van Valkenburg, S., 365, 399
Vapor pressure, 187–190
Vegetable-garden zones, 349
Vegetation growth season, 344
Velocity of wind, 159, 160
Virginia crop yields, 353
Visher, S. S., 394

Wallis, B. C., 397, 399
Ward, Robert DeCourcy, 368, 394–396, 399
Warm weather duration, 112–122
Washington crop yields, 353
Weather consequences, 344
Weather map, 162
Weather, Normal, for the United States, 393
Weightman, R. H., 400
Wet-bulb temperature, 188, 189
Wet months, 261
Wet seasons, 261
Wet spells, 261
Wet years, 261
  frequencies, 293
White, G. Langdon, 399
Winds, 155, 175
Wind direction, 157–163
  and precipitation, 176
Wind velocity, 159, 160
Winds aloft, 161
Winter commences, 78

Yarnell, D. L., 394, 397, 398

Zero temperatures, 122, 125, 128
  frequencies, 84, 128
Zonal contrasts, 3–6, 151
Zones of seasonal temperatures, 79